# Worldly Desires

EDINBURGH STUDIES IN EAST ASIAN FILM
Series Editor: Margaret Hillenbrand

Available and forthcoming titles

*Independent Chinese Documentary*
Dan Edwards

*Tanaka Kinuyo*
Edited by Irene González-López and Michael Smith

*Worldly Desires*
Brian Hu

*The Cinema of Ozu Yasujiro*
Woojeong Joo

*Eclipsed Cinema*
Dong Hoon Kim

*Moving Figures*
Corey Kai Nelson Schultz

*Memory, Subjectivity and Independent Chinese Cinema*
Qi Wang

*Hong Kong Neo-Noir*
Edited by Esther C. M. Yau and Tony Williams

*"My" Self on Camera*
Kiki Tianqi Yu

edinburghuniversitypress.com/series/eseaf

# Worldly Desires

## Cosmopolitanism and Cinema in Hong Kong and Taiwan

Brian Hu

EDINBURGH
University Press

Edinburgh University Press is one of the leading university presses in the UK. We publish academic books and journals in our selected subject areas across the humanities and social sciences, combining cutting-edge scholarship with high editorial and production values to produce academic works of lasting importance. For more information visit our website: edinburghuniversitypress.com

© Brian Hu, 2018, 2020

Edinburgh University Press Ltd
The Tun—Holyrood Road
12 (2f) Jackson's Entry
Edinburgh EH8 8PJ

First published in hardback by Edinburgh University Press 2018

Typeset in 10/13 Chaparral Pro by
IDSUK (DataConnection) Ltd

A CIP record for this book is available from the British Library

ISBN 978 1 4744 2845 3 (hardback)
ISBN 978 1 4744 2846 0 (paperback)
ISBN 978 1 4744 2847 7 (webready PDF)
ISBN 978 1 4744 2848 4 (epub)

The right of Brian Hu to be identified as author of this work has been asserted in accordance with the Copyright, Designs and Patents Act 1988 and the Copyright and Related Rights Regulations 2003 (SI No. 2498).

# Contents

List of Figures and Tables vi
Acknowledgments viii
Notes on Romanization x

Introduction 1

1  Melodramas of Arrival and Departure: Jet-set Students in 1970s Taiwanese Romance 19

2  ABCs, Mixed-race Stars, and Other Monsters of Globalization 63

3  Setting the Stage: Hong Kong Musical Stars Take on the World 108

4  All the Right Moves: Mobile Heroes and the Shaolin Temple Film 143

5  The Cosmopolitan Brand: Film Policy as Cultural Work in the International Film Market 179

Conclusion 209

Works Cited 223
Index 243

# Figures and Tables

## Figures

| | | |
|---|---|---|
| I.1a | A waitress at a western-style evening ball . . . | 4 |
| I.1b | . . . is visually "rhymed" with a flight attendant for China Airlines | 4 |
| 1.1a, 1.1b | Rack focus from flowers to lovers (from *Moon River*, Liu Chia-chang, 1974) | 45 |
| 1.1c, 1.1d | Extreme zoom-in onto lovers in nature | 45 |
| 1.2 | Electric guitar opening to the *Moon River* title theme | 48 |
| 2.1 | Music video for L. A. Boyz, "Island Girl," 1995 | 78 |
| 2.2a | Daniel Wu's character showers in *Peony Pavilion* . . . | 79 |
| 2.2b | . . . as Joey Wong's character watches, clutching herself | 79 |
| 2.3 | A magazine spread fixates on Jenny Hu's signature face, eyes, and lips | 83 |
| 3.1 | "Lin Dai at Ballet" | 117 |
| 3.2a | A spinning wheel lands on a French dancer . . . | 120 |
| 3.2b | . . . which signals the dancers to launch into the can-can | 120 |
| 3.3 | Ting Hao takes the world | 123 |
| 3.4a–d | Spectacle of shopping in *Love Parade* | 126 |
| 3.5a | "Li Li-hua and Ting Ning take Cannes by storm" | 130 |
| 3.5b | "*TIME* photographer in action" | 131 |
| 3.6 | "Ivy Scores with U.S. Critics, Moviegoers" | 133 |
| 3.7 | "Americans Like Mandarin Movies" | 134 |
| 4.1a, 4.1b | Hu Dedi's final fight in *Five Shaolin Masters* | 162 |
| 5.1a | *Taipei Cinema Location Guide* (Taipei Film Commission, 2008) | 189 |
| 5.1b | *Taiwan's Innovativeness in Film* (Government Information Office, 2007) | 190 |
| 5.1c | Taipei Film Commission and Ile de France Film Commission advertisement | 191 |
| 5.1d | *Taiwan Cinema* (Government Information Office, 2006) | 192 |

| | | |
|---|---|---|
| 5.2a–d | Stills from "US$1,000,000 Subsidy for Filmmakers in Taipei City!" | 194–5 |
| 5.3 | The Hong Kong Film Development Council's "New Action" director's photo-spread | 202 |
| 5.4a | Salon Films advertisement, *The Hollywood Reporter* FILMART daily edition (2009) | 203 |
| 5.4b | Salon Films exhibition space, Hong Kong FILMART (2009) | 204 |
| C.1 | Crediting "China Taiwan" in *Tiny Times* | 219 |

## Tables

| | | |
|---|---|---|
| 5.1 | Pitching practices at film markets | 187 |
| 5.2 | Panelists for the "Hong Kong as Gateway to China" seminars | 199 |

# Acknowledgments

According to stray notes and scribblings, I've been working on material for this book since 2004, but I know that the seeds were planted a few years before that, when I took a trio of courses with Chris Berry during our felicitous overlap at University of California, Berkeley. My conversations with Chris and his ongoing support sent me on a lifelong, personal examination of Chinese cinemas, and I have never looked back.

Since then, I've been fortunate to continue that journey through conversations with countless scholars and friends, all of whom have made this book possible. For their inspiration and collegiality, I thank Aynne Kokas, June Yip, Chia-chi Wu, James Wicks, Robert Chi, Sangjoon Lee, Guo-juin Hong, David Desser, Rowena Aquino, Jason Gendler, Yulin Sun, Michael Berry, and Ping-hui Liao. Heartfelt thanks too to the committee that shaped this project in its dissertation stages at University of California, Los Angeles (UCLA): Nick Browne, Kathleen McHugh, Chon Noriega, and Purnima Mankekar. Although he didn't see the final product, so many of these pages are guided by the light of the late Teshome Gabriel.

Thanks to a Fulbright-Hays Award, I was able to conduct significant research while based at The University of Hong Kong. Esther Cheung, Gina Marchetti, and Esther Yau not only set me up with a home base for my research, but also offered precious insight into film studies in Hong Kong. I'm indebted to the staff at the Hong Kong Film Archive (including Sam Ho and Lesley Fung), the UCLA Film and Television Archive (especially Mark Quigley), the USC School of Cinematic Arts Library (the tireless Ned Comstock), the Taiwan Film Institute, the National Central Library of Taiwan, and the National Archive of Singapore. Sincere thanks go to Shaw Studios, Cathay-Keris, and the Central Motion Picture Corporation for permission to use archival images. For the remaining materials, I must shout out the ethnoburb video shops, the overseas eBay entrepreneurs, those hidden Mongkok DVD stores, the aunties at Guang Hua Digital Plaza, the nameless magicians that make up interlibrary loan, and the pair of trusty disc burners that accompanied me on every adventure.

So many of the ideas in this book are ripped from conversations with friends I first met at UCLA's Asia Institute. I am lucky to count as co-conspirators Chi Tung, Ada Tseng, Christine Chiao, and Angilee Shah. Thanks also to Clayton Dube, Winghei Kwok, Oliver Chien, Anne Lee, and Andrea Apuy for their camaraderie at the Institute and beyond. Together, we developed a critical framework for interrogating media industries as journalists, fans, and scholars. To that end, I also thank the media practitioners who lent their perspectives and provided me an indispensable context for the Hong Kong and Taiwan film industries: Patrick Lee, Eugenia Yuan, Carl Ng, Cheng Pei-pei, Arvin Chen, Bey Logan, Jennifer Jao, Eugene Suen, and Sharleen Liu.

Much love goes to my friends and colleagues in San Diego who gave this project a second wind: Vincent Pham, Yaejoon Kwon, Christina Ree, Glenn Heath, Jr., James Paguyo, Cynthia Kashiwagi, Lee Ann Kim, K. Wayne Yang, Todd Henry, and Michelle Chu. Special thanks to those who have encouraged me in ways that they may not realize; Mary Francis, Daniel Steinhart, Masami Kawai, and Kristof Van den Troost all kept this project alive with their support. I want to acknowledge my new colleagues at San Diego State University's School of Theatre, Television, and Film for their vote of confidence in my growth as a scholar.

It's been a joy to collaborate with the team at Edinburgh University Press (EUP). Thank you to Gillian Leslie and Margaret Hillenbrand for championing this project every step of the way, and thanks to Rebecca Mackenzie and Richard Strachan for their patience and terrific work in making this book a reality.

Most of all, thanks to all of my family in the US and Taiwan for their feedback and enthusiasm. The most joyous and unexpected by-product of this project was realizing that I was in fact writing the transnational story of my family and other families like ours. Finally, this book is dedicated to my mom and dad, whose love knows no borders.

# Notes on Romanization

This book acknowledges the fractured identities, uneven conventionalization, and individual idiosyncrasies that come to light when the Sinophone enters Euro-American academia. Every attempt has been made to use the most commonly encountered English sequencing and spelling of Chinese names. For instance, I use Ang Lee instead of Li An or Lee An, and Leslie Cheung instead of Zhang Guorong or Zoeng Gwok-wing. To minimize inconsistency and to acknowledge the palimpsestic peculiarities of cross-cultural distribution, I use the romanization of character names found in the English subtitles of the print or disc that I viewed. For Chinese names heard in films without English subtitles, I use the romanization system most commonly employed in English-language academia for the dialect spoken. Cantonese expressions, dialogue, and newspaper headlines are Romanized in the jyutping system, and Mandarin expressions, dialogue, and newspaper headlines are Romanized in the pinyin system.

# Introduction

When local, national, and racial identities seem confining, reductionist, hurtful, or even dangerous, when claiming these identities takes a toll on one's livelihood or sense of self-worth, there's a comfort in knowing that one can resort to universalist, seemingly undeniable and peace-seeking affiliations like "citizen of the world" or the "human race." Like the local, the universal is an imaginary shaped by political and historical forces, as well as an intense and imminently "real" feeling experienced through the body. Most cultures are equipped with the vocabulary and iconography for expressing local/national identities, for instance, through common languages, inherited and invented traditions, or cartological imaginaries. But beyond purely stating it, how does one prove to be a citizen of the world, which some have termed "cosmopolitanism"? And if the desire to seek comfort in cosmopolitanism is often a reaction to the difficulty of the local/national, must the process of cosmopolitanization itself be ambivalent, and must cosmopolitan discourse necessitate an interrogation of the instability of the local/national?

As small islands with thorny relationships with the national, Hong Kong and Taiwan provide useful examples for looking at the affective disjunctures between the cosmopolitan and the local. This book examines the important role that cinema played in imagining Hong Kong and Taiwan's place in the world during decades in which the idea of belonging and identity was under duress. Through colonial and post-colonial upheaval, riots and massacres, economic miracles and financial crises, Hong Kong and Taiwan felt the weight of the world both suppress and uplift its residents' senses of identity and standards of living. Meanwhile, the allure of transcending narrow strictures of national or provincial identity pervaded, with stories of globe-trotting Chinese businessmen and politicians, America-bound Little Leaguers, and jet-set tourists circulating in the zeitgeist. Neighbors and family members went to Japan, Australia, Europe, or North America for college, or to raise their children. Young people did ballet and the mambo, and those who excelled in these western arts went abroad to perform alongside the faces and bodies locals only saw on TV. With the concept of "the national" a source of much anxiety due to colonialism and crises of recognition, the promise of a cosmopolitan identity attached to cultural forms like music, fashion, dance, and style thrilled the rising middle classes, much to the benefit of the merchants who sold these sounds and images, and even of the government, which could harness cosmopolitan yearnings to promote patriotic initiatives.

The "world out there" wasn't an "other" space, lodged in a binary of us/them, East/West. Rather, it was a space where locals could imagine themselves traversing as active participants, even when economic realities and migration controls kept them physically in their respective islands. Cosmopolitanism, as Bronislaw Szerszynski and John Urry have noted, is not only characterized by physical travel, but also by virtual and mediated means of "inhabiting the world from afar."[1] Szerszynski and Urry cite the importance of visuality in this process, for recognizing our place in the world requires a new way of seeing it. Cinema, as one of the twentieth century's most wide-reaching means for proliferating "worldliness," not only brought the world to Hong Kong and Taiwan, but under the direction of local studios, producers, and policy makers, was a forceful and seductive way to imagine a cosmopolitan Chinese person and work through anxieties of belonging, nationalism, and the compression of time and space as a result of accelerating globalization. Cinema offered narratives of locals who had the skills and means to transcend borders, while still respecting older, more provincial, even national, identities. These films, produced in Taiwan and Hong Kong from the late 1950s to the early 2000s, were populated by cosmopolitan heroes and villains whose fates captured the ethics of borderless travel during a period in which the idea of mobility, hybrid identities, and non-national attachments were slowly, awkwardly transitioning from fantasy to reality. These popular entertainments featured colorful stock characters like musical performers adept in everything from can-can to hip-hop; fashion designers who transform Chinese qipao into Parisian haute couture; rich sons and daughters who make San Francisco and Rome their playgrounds; patriotic students who go abroad for study to return as national heroes; international spies who nab criminals alongside James Bond; hard-bodied martial artists who defend the honor of their compatriots in overseas Chinatowns; sex-addicts who know no borders when it comes to satisfying their thirst; gamblers and athletes who participate in international competitions; Chinese Americans who "return" to Hong Kong and Taiwan bringing international flavor; and mixed-race characters who carry the promise of a post-racial, post-national future on their bodies. While most locals in Hong Kong and Taiwan could not directly identify with the travels of these stock characters, they could see in them the immanent possibility of a future where the uncertainty of national and provincial identities can be resolved through the ideals of cosmopolitanism.

Local audiences often saw these stock characters with some suspicion for leaving and potentially betraying family and nation. But more often these characters were objects of envy and desire. Take, for instance, the female flight attendant, a profession deemed the "dream job" of many young women in Hong Kong and Taiwan, and a character central to popular films from *The Greatest Civil War on Earth* (Wang Tian-lin, 1961) to *20, 30, 40* (Sylvia Chang, 2004). Chinese-language cinema's most famous flight attendants are those in Evan Yang's 1959 classic *Air Hostess*, a Hong Kong-produced musical comedy that depicts the romantic tribulations of young women who travel the world, singing to the beats and scenery of lands beyond Hong Kong. Through strict training rituals (depicted in an amusing training sequence), their bodies become conditioned to serving passengers from all lands: they learn to speak with urban confidence and strut for the eyes of male travelers accustomed to a worldly femininity. They are, in other words, integral parts of the world system, bringing strangers together under the glamorous sign of the modern Chinese woman. As one publicity piece put it, "They help shorten the distance between people and facilitate the movement between nations."[2] Such a depiction captured the conditions for being a participant on the world stage (bodily training, playing to the male gaze) at a moment when integrating with capitalist modernity for most was a matter of hard work in gendered manufacturing spaces. *Air Hostess* was also the product of the studio MP&GI, which developed the figure of the hard-working musical starlet to brand itself as a grand and modern production, distribution, and exhibition company, as I will explore further in Chapter 3.

A comparison can be made to the depiction of the flight attendant in commercials for China Airlines starring Taiwan-born, Canada-educated supermodel Lin Chiling, who was a spokesperson for the airline in the early 2000s. In one such commercial, entitled "Service from the Heart, the New China Airlines," we begin at an evening ball, and the formal wear and faux-classical music suggest that we are in an ambiguous Western locale where rich white men intersect with doe-eyed Asian women. Lin Chiling's character ballroom dances with a white-haired, older white gentleman. They are serviced at the dining table by a smiling Asian waitress (Figure I.1a). This then cuts to a shot from inside an airplane, which then cuts to Lin Chiling getting off the plane and walking through the terminal. She makes eye contact with China Airlines' female flight attendants, who also happen to be leaving the plane. One flight attendant in particular smiles and nods to Lin, in a gesture reminiscent of the waitress's in the previous scene; in fact, both the waitress and the flight attendant appear to be played by the same actress (Figure I.1b). In a mere forty seconds, the commercial graphically and metaphorically connects China Airlines' in-flight service to the service of "international" standards, exemplified by the image of the waitress

**Figure I.1a**  A waitress at a western-style evening ball . . .

**Figure I.1b**  . . . is visually "rhymed" with a flight attendant for China Airlines gracefully serving Euro-American elites. Here, as in the *Air Hostess* example, Chinese service is made glamorous and inviting because it is depicted as up to the standards of the world. To identify with the female flight attendant is to be excited about servicing the world well. Except here, there is a second subject of identification: the worldly traveler herself. The appreciative nod by the cosmopolitan star Lin Chiling, envied for an elegance often attributed to her confident sexuality honed in North America,[3] affirms China Airlines' worldly credentials. The airline borrows Lin's transnational biography and style to legitimize their service, while also reminding viewers that cosmopolitanism can be achieved not simply through service, but also through consumption. That China Airlines is part-owned by the Taiwanese government adds an additional dimension; I will explore the relationship between propaganda, overseas study, and worldliness in Chapter 1. That the allure of the world is grafted on to the body of an overseas star is symptomatic of discourses of natural and alien bodies triggered by the "return" of the second-generation overseas Chinese, a phenomenon of the 1990s and 2000s I will explore in Chapter 2. In these examples, cosmopolitanism (here a kind of caring for and living among strangers) is evoked in conjunction with the desirable female body to celebrate Hong Kong and Taiwan's places in the world, as well as to suggest the conditions under which that participation is possible, conditions that are specific to each's historical contexts.

## Locating Cosmopolitanism

I use the term "cosmopolitanism" in both its classical and colloquial senses. From antiquity is Zeno's idea of the "cosmopolis," which combines the Greek words *kosmos* ("world") and *polis* ("city"), and Diogenes' idea of the "citizen of the world"—a worldliness that transcends local and city-state affiliations in favor of a universal identification. Kwame Anthony Appiah, proposing cosmopolitanism in debates on multiculturalism and globalization, reframes these classical ideals in terms of contemporary interactions with difference—what he calls "ethics in a world of strangers." Appiah sees in cosmopolitanism not the trappings of universalization, but the possible interactions we may have if we acknowledge shared obligations in ways that are respectful of cultural difference.[4] My analyses of Hong Kong and Taiwanese popular culture observe perspectives that reconcile the local within the universal, that proudly carve a distinct place in the world as opposed to simply disappearing into it. These are discourses of the local, the national, and the global that seek friendship and mutual understanding across borders, and in doing so, call out one's existence as Chinese, Hong Konger, or Taiwanese, satisfying yearnings for legitimacy and acceptance that are in short supply for "minor" cities and nations like Hong

Kong and Taiwan. This cosmopolitan yearning reflects governmental concerns (see Chapters 1 and 5) as well as industrial ones (see Chapters 2 and 3), and reveal the political and economic stakes of recognition, participation, and ownership on the world stage. In Taiwan, for instance, images of friendship across borders become a way to give Taiwan a "soft" but undeniable presence in an international system that doesn't recognize Taiwan as a nation, nor as much of an economic player with the rise of mainland China. Cosmopolitanism utilizes discourses of human rights, victimization, and intercultural appreciation to lobby that "Taiwan is part of the world," as one 2009 government billboard at the Taiwan Taoyuan International Airport proclaimed.[5]

From the colloquial sense of "cosmopolitanism" I borrow the connotations of a global urban culture usually identified with trend-setting cities like Paris, Tokyo, New York, and London. From these associations, cosmopolitanism gets its visual and sonic components: modern art and design, high fashion, global pop, English as a lingua franca, cityscapes, and urban soundscapes. There is also rhythm: the speed of the city, the calendar year of fashion, the sociology of time, the ideal of being "up to date." This cosmopolitanism is hierarchical and elitist, but inviting to participants from other locales to join in this cosmopolitan culture, which thrives due to the co-existence of and collaboration between cultures. Therefore, as an aesthetic, cosmopolitanism involves what Frederic Jameson would call both "gloss" and "color." Gloss refers to vertical application of style: a gleam, a smear. Color, on the other hand, is the equally striking, but horizontal separation of distinct visual patterns.[6] Cosmopolitanism as an aesthetic is visually exhilarating because it is a vertical application of glamor and modern pizzazz, as well a horizontal conglomeration of heterogeneous cultural elements that collectively produce a chromatic exuberance. The centralization of these aesthetic qualities within certain capitals gives cosmopolitanism in the Hong Kong and Taiwanese contexts a spatial orientation. Attempts at participation in this larger culture gesture toward Paris and Tokyo, and not toward other places (such as those in South America and Africa) that would otherwise be included according to the more universalistic, less hierarchical definition of cosmopolitanism provided by the Greeks. Colloquially, cosmopolitanism is above all a kind of city culture, and thus is attractive to locations like Hong Kong and Taiwan, which do not have easy access to the national and often only participate on the world stage as cities (Hong Kong as a city-state, Taiwan as "Chinese Taipei"). If Hong Kong and Taiwan cannot integrate internationally as nations, they can as aspiring "global cities." This is especially apparent in Hong Kong, where a 2001 state initiative promoted "Brand Hong Kong," a program developed to dub Hong Kong "Asia's

World City." As global cities, Hong Kong and Taiwan see themselves as producers and consumers of global commodities, including cinema, and they seek to attain cultural and political capital through these commodities. Assumption of the aesthetic of cosmopolitanism—attempts at that vertical varnish, positioning to add another color to the horizontal mix—viscerally and lavishly aim to prove Hong Kong and Taiwan's stature as global cities.

Focusing on the cosmopolitan city, and thus finding the global in the local, marks a significant rethinking of transnational Chinese cinema studies, as seen in the work of Yingjin Zhang and Michael Curtin.[7] Considering cosmopolitanism also allows us to rethink transnationalism by historicizing it. Chris Berry takes a step in this direction by distinguishing between the international and the transnational.[8] Berry surveys the literature of transnationalism in Chinese cinema studies and finds that the term has come to denote a wide variety of practices—so wide in fact that it risks losing currency as a critical category. He isolates two contradictory statements in Sheldon Lu's seminal book *Transnational Chinese Cinemas* that exemplify the danger of overusing the term. First is Lu's announcement that Chinese cinema studies must consider the transnational because of the recent globalization of Chinese cinemas in the international film market, and the second is Lu's observation that Chinese cinemas have, from their very beginnings in the late nineteenth century, always been transnational. According to Berry, these two claims—that Chinese cinemas have *always* been transnational, and that it is *now* transnational—in fact, speak to two different phenomena: an older international order in which national states still exercised sovereignty over trade and other interactions, and a newer order in which neoliberal conditions correspond to the diminished ability of nation-states to regulate cross-border encounters. These are, for Berry, different phenomena with different causes and implications, and therefore require different terminology; he terms the earlier era that of the international, and the more recent one that of the transnational.

Berry rightly does not provide a year or decade demarcating a shift from one epoch to the other, the reason being that the transnational arose out of the international, and not against it.[9] Berry is speaking of industrial contexts: the corporate and juridical systems that shape production in each era, and that gradually and unevenly changed to produce a new order. However, we can also think about the international and the transnational as driven by and producing different cultural and identity formations: local, national, dynastic, ethnic, and provincial affiliations in the earlier, and hybrid, flexible, and polyvalent identifications under the transnational. From the perspective of culture, it is even more difficult to conceive of a switch date. Regulatory systems and trade agreements can be instituted, in however staggered and drawn-out fashion. Culture, however, is a complex of multiple, overlapping negotiations and inconsistencies, a tension between what Raymond Williams has called dominant, residual, and emergent cultural practices.[10] How may we characterize this transitional period during which subjects reconcile older sentiments with exciting, utopic, frightening, and shapeless ones that can potentially undermine the categories they previously sought solace in believing in? In other words, how does one transition from thinking of the self as a citizen of a nation to being a citizen of the world? This book examines cultural production in this moment of transition: the ways that cinema imagines what one may look and sound like when stepping out into a global culture, under what conditions may this be acceptable, and what corporate and state institutions have a stake in making this transition more or less exciting, utopic, or frightening.

Sociologists of cosmopolitanism have theorized this transitional period before the ideals of cosmopolitanism are or will be realized. Ulrich Beck, in particular, has written about a process he calls cosmopolitanization, a period of "latent cosmopolitanism" and "banal cosmopolitanism" during which nationalistic flag-waving persists while subjects develop interests in consuming foreign pop music or foods from around the world.[11] While many scholars of cosmopolitanism focus on the utopic and ideological possibilities promised by cosmopolitanism, I am more interested in these "really existing cosmopolitanizations" and the cultural products that comprise and enliven them. In fact, in extending the period of my study into the early 2000s, I want to suggest that we have not completely entered the state of the transnational, with cosmopolitanism being one theoretical formation of it, nor do I necessarily believe in its inevitability. But my analyses of films produced in Hong Kong and Taiwan from the 1950s to the 2000s do reveal a grappling with the idea of a national past and present looking forward to a global future, and many of these works envision this transition occurring through the ideals of cosmopolitanism: cross-cultural friendship, mobility, worldly education and training, and global urban self-fashioning. Through bodies oriented outward—Chinese youth doing Western dance, Taiwanese students boarding planes, Hong Kong bodies miscegenating—these films confront a present on the verge of a future, and through their mere expressions of acknowledgment of this future, open up what Gilles Deleuze and Félix Guattari call a "possible world."[12] The audience's experience of these outwardly oriented bodies becomes that sensory "condition for our passing from one world to another," which allows us to imagine the depths of space beyond, and the transitions and inversions necessary to navigate it.[13] Cosmopolitanism as a conjured possible world is rooted in the "social reality of imminent possibilities,"[14] as a way for the national/local/provincial to confront the "normative challenges raised by difference, the reconfiguration of borders, and the many questions brought about by globalization."[15]

Specifically, these films face these challenges by presenting a hybridized cosmopolitanism: Chinese cosmopolitanism, Hong Kong cosmopolitanism, Taiwanese cosmopolitanism. There is a sense that, as Ulrich Beck puts it, "cosmopolitanism without provincialism is empty, [and] provincialism without cosmopolitanism is blind."[16] This insistence on holding on to a local identity, paradoxically seeing it as a precondition for larger, more universalistic affiliations, is shared by many scholars of cosmopolitanism who cannot seem to theorize the concept without attaching an adjectival modifier (rooted cosmopolitanism,[17] indigenous cosmopolitanism,[18] colored cosmopolitanism[19]) or having it modify a more "grounded" noun (cosmopolitan provincialism,[20] cosmopolitan patriotism,[21] cosmopolitan nationalism[22]). While reflecting on "the changing meaning of being Chinese," Leo Ou-fan Lee suggests the term "Chinese cosmopolitanism" to describe his identity and those of other marginal, exiled figures of Chinese descent. He combines these words because the pairing "embraces both a fundamental intellectual commitment to Chinese culture and a multicultural receptivity, which effectively cuts across all conventional national boundaries."[23] While Lee's intervention has been justly critiqued by Ien Ang for its commitment to a fundamentalist and "ontological Chineseness,"[24] it nevertheless rings true as a historical dilemma over a generation's international coming-out. A member of the first generation of overseas students (*liuxuesheng*) from Taiwan studying in the United States, Lee's perspectives, in many ways influenced by the "obsession with China" discourse of modern Chinese literature, were shaped by specific ideals of nation, world, self, and family, which I explore in Chapter 1. These were ideals motivated to contain the contradictory feelings incited by the promise of mobility and worldly encounter Lee felt growing up in a certain time in a certain national (and nationalist) context. For Lee, perhaps, to conceive of himself as cosmopolitan without "Chinese" is not possible. Thus, the impulse to hybridize the concept of cosmopolitanism speaks to the inherent discomfort in attempting to imagine a state of mind that cannot seem to "really exist." However, the paradox of provincializing cosmopolitanism, grounding it in familiar terms and identities that seem to contradict a truly global affiliation, is not merely a conceptual convenience intended to describe an almost-there or compromised ideal. The paradox gets to the nervousness over that ideal in the first place, the difficulty of conceptualizing our place in the world, and the creative ways in which we cope with, make sense of, and anticipate the possibility of being a global citizen. If we are studying the actual process of cosmopolitanization, we ought to, as Simon

Gikandi puts it, "read cosmopolitanism under the sign of its own anxieties, the fear of being one of the rootless crowd, and avoid the temptation to turn it into a free floating signifier."[25] The strategy taken by theorists to keep the term from floating away is to ground it with modifiers. The strategy of cinema to negotiate the anxieties of becoming global is the subject of this book.

Hyphenating cosmopolitanism risks indulging in the happy pleasures of hybridity as multiculturalism, and thus we need to consider not just what cosmopolitanization looks and sounds like, but what it does and how it pushes and pulls, threatens and liberates. It describes a historical process and has political dimensions. A way to think about this hyphenated cosmopolitanism is to engage the concept of the Sinophone, a critical approach that informs my intentional study of Hong Kong and Taiwan cinemas as parallel and intertwined yet separate from that in China, thus disrupting the usual pattern of studying each independently as local cultural and industrial formations, or the familiar "three Chinas" approach to transnational Chinese cinemas. As theorized by Shu-mei Shih, the Sinophone proposes a view on to places like Hong Kong and Taiwan that cannot be reduced to a China-centric diaspora and that considers them as localities with their own grounded, messy politics of ethnicity, race, and language shaped by European and Han Chinese colonialism.[26] Which isn't to say that "Chinese-ness" is dead; in fact, the threat of its proliferation is an important motivation for Shih's polemic. Rather, as I will show in this book, "Chinese-ness" gets affixed in culture as a response to trauma, as a marketing strategy—indeed, as functional rather than naturalized. What I find instead is that these films work through, in their distinct historical moments, matrices of local, national, regional, and global, and they do so under the seductive and equally functional sign of the cosmopolitan, a flexible and mobile identity primed to pivot to new economic possibilities, minoritization on a world stage, reverse migration, or diplomatic setbacks—circumstances unique to the peculiar politics of post-colonialism and positionality that island-states like Hong Kong and Taiwan played in the decades following 1949.

## Worldly Desires

This book seeks to intervene in the burgeoning field of Sinophone cinema studies by grounding the Sinophone in film pleasure and film culture, actively engaging cinema and media studies and its perspectives on genre, stardom, audience, and production. As Audrey Yue and Olivia Khoo acknowledge, early studies of the Sinophone were literary studies focusing on words and their creative usages.[27] And yet, many of the chapters in their pioneering volume on Sinophone cinemas focus primarily on film dialogue as a literary object of study. In this book, I am inspired by Shih's suggestion that the "phonic" of the Sinophone is not just verbal language but also visual language.[28] To that, I would add musical language as well, and also extend the object of study beyond film texts and toward all of the discursive production that makes up film culture. On screen and in film magazines, visual pleasure means costumes, muscles, dance, and racialized bodies; musical pleasure takes the form of global pop genres and non-diegetic score music. My study, too, considers the role of language—especially the proliferation of Englishes as varied as Hong Kong, American, Canadian, or African American—in the localization and cosmoplitanization of Hong Kong and Taiwan. But it reads words within the full embodied and intertextual field of the cinematic experience, as well as the larger formations of genre, stardom, and production culture that culminate in a multi-level spectacle of gloss and color.

Cinema, as a mass art exerting tremendous influence and incorporating a multitude of cultural and technological elements, is particularly suited to articulate a hyphenated cosmopolitanism. As an instrument and producer of the global, popular cinema, including that experienced in Hong Kong and Taiwan, is a spectacle of worldly pleasures, and a quintessential experience of what it means to be a global citizen. Caught up in the joy of the experience is a sense of an imagined community, to paraphrase Benedict Anderson: with ever-shrinking release windows, we can imagine strangers around the world watching the same film at the same time in an "extraordinary mass ceremony."[29] However, with its representational aesthetic and sense of wonderment for the profilmic event, cinema captures the specifics of a world that is not universal but particularized. Miriam Hansen's idea of the vernacular is useful here, for it captures cinema's fascination with discourse, idiom, dialect, and promiscuity as well as its susceptibility for circulation and translation.[30] Given these dual and intertwined proclivities, cinema may be an ideal vessel for what Homi Bhabha calls "vernacular cosmopolitanism," a vantage point that can "be on the border, *in between*, introducing the global-cosmopolitan 'action at a distance' into the very grounds—now displaced—of the domestic."[31] It is in this in-between space that we may best observe "banal cosmopolitanism" in all of its contradictory indulgences, torn allegiances, and polymorphous promiscuity. Grounded in the vernacular, cosmopolitanism becomes more than an ideology, moral stance, or mandate, and closer to what Appiah describes as a "sentiment": an emotion, a sense of responsibility, a poetry of belonging.[32] This book shows how in the second half of twentieth-century Hong Kong and Taiwan, cosmopolitan sentiments were embedded in cinematic practices, including narrative tropes such as generic elements and stock characters, and production practices such as the creation and maintenance of stars or the rituals of self-branding.

Studying the vernacular means tracking "poetic" discourses of cosmopolitanism in mass-produced and mass-consumed cinematic objects: genre films, fan magazines, advertising, ancillary publications, publicity photos and articles. Collectively, these materials attempt, with wildly varying levels of success, to make sense of Hong Kong and Taiwan's messy place in the world by fancifully jetting the consumer through flurries of romance, pathos, violence, comedy, excitement, musical pleasure, and the erotic.

This vernacular understanding of the transnational, and specifically the ways that the local, through mass culture, invests emotionally and morally in fleshing out its place within the transnational as cosmopolitans, is what I mean by the "worldly desires" of the book's title. Worldly desires are, for marginalized locales like Hong Kong and Taiwan, desires for the world and its consumable, philosophical, and touristic pleasures – but it is also that desire to see the world recognize and desire Hong Kong and Taiwan in return. "Worldly" also refers to the earthly, the secular, even the hedonistic. Thus, it points to bodily pleasures, so central to cinema and in fact most pop cultural pursuits: our desire to see/hear bodies on screen, as well as our own bodily reactions to the cinematic display. The term also then de-mythologizes the way we think about nationalism, Chineseness, diaspora, and even the cosmopolitan. Sonal Khullar borrows from Edward Said the notion that the "worldly" is a way to revive the "social and political horizons of cultural production," particularly those that typically bind culture to the state, thus unraveling reified bonds and seeking out their material and imaginative underpinnings.[33] Thus, this is a turn away from terms and affiliations endowed with an idealistic or "holy" stature and toward an understanding of affiliation, which Khullar argues is a historical process of decentering and imagination, as responsive and pragmatic.[34] There's money to be made and minds to be won by evoking such ideals, and cultural/social capital to be accumulated by playing along.[35] These pragmatics don't diminish the fervor or authenticity of the desire, and in fact challenge producers and consumers to yearn in altogether more imaginative, colorful, and vivid ways.

In acknowledgment of Chris Berry's argument about the difficulty of periodizing the transition from an international to a transnational order, this book focuses on several decades in the history of Hong Kong and Taiwanese cinema, from the late 1950s to the first years of the twenty-first century. Roughly speaking, I focus on two generations of Hong Kong and Taiwanese history: the first generation born in these locations after the drastic political and demographic changes from 1945 to 1949, and the generation of their children. This periodization not only corresponds to the mature decades of the Hong Kong and Taiwanese film industries, but also captures the kinds of films seen by future transnationals, specifically what Aihwa Ong has dubbed "flexible citizens," while growing up in Hong Kong and Taiwan.[36] Within these years are a number of historic events that help account for the prevalence of discourses of cosmopolitanism in Hong Kong and Taiwan: the US's Immigration Act of 1965 (and similar measures in Australia, Canada, and other Western countries) that created a new dream of mobility in Hong Kong and Taiwan; the development of national scholarships for study abroad in foreign universities; and the United Nations' expulsion of Taiwan in 1971 thus forcing the government to rethink strategies for global participation. Policy helped shape the kinds of films that were made. For instance, Taiwan's government-backed Healthy Realism movement of the 1960s and 1970s dictated that overseas studies characters in film be depicted as heroic when they are reintegrated into the Taiwanese economy, but villainous when they succumb to "Western" vices—especially sexual lasciviousness. I am interested in how these historical events and state policies helped produce new subjectivities and perspectives to be expressed in art and culture. For instance, Taiwanese writers and artists who traveled abroad returned with stories about life in North America and Europe, initiating the "overseas student literature" of the 1960s and 1970s. Children of Taiwanese and Hong Kong immigrants to the United States—dubbed American-born Chinese (or "ABCs")—became stock types in film, television, and popular music in the 1990s and 2000s. In recent years, much has been written about the cosmopolitan Chinese capitalist: that neoliberal entrepreneur who, through "flexible citizenship," transformed the Pacific Rim (and beyond) into the economic terrain of the diasporic Chinese. Scholars in sociology, anthropology, economics, and geography have shown that this phenomenon skyrocketed in the 1980s and continues today, as a result of shifting immigration patterns and trade policies in East Asia and North America. However, what hasn't been studied as systematically is the critical question of culture, except when reduced to essentialized "Asian values" or "Confucian Capitalism" discourse. I am interested in more proximate, historically specific cultural explanations, as well as how "flexible citizenship" is not simply a set of economic and political conditions, but also the story of two generations learning to be citizens of the world.

## Chapter Overview

In considering the pragmatic functions of cosmopolitan discourse, we must look at its articulation in specific historical, political, demographic, and economic contexts. How the cosmopolitan is evoked at any moment depends on Hong Kong and Taiwan's relationship to the idea of the world, its internal dynamics of multiculturalism, and its place within various international political, economic, and cultural networks, at a given time. Factors that come into play include cold war dynamics, in- and out-migration trends, diplomatic relations, and the signing of international trade agreements. Therefore, each chapter of this book looks at a different subperiod and focuses on a single notable cinematic trend within that subperiod. Collectively, the chapters build upon one another not just to cover vast historical ground, but also to more fully explore distinct articulations of cosmopolitanism such as through stardom, film genre, film culture, and industry practice, as well as the corresponding historiographic methodologies for studying those distinctive articulations.

Chapter 1 sets up several of the primary vectors through which I study the cosmopolitan in cinema: narrative, genre, policy. I look at the interplay of self, lover, family, and nation in the context of 1970s romantic melodramas in Taiwan, in particular through one of the stock characters of the genre: the overseas student, or *liuxuesheng*. I read these depictions alongside the government's propaganda projects (Healthy Realism and Healthy Variety), as well as local discourses of foreign travel and brain drain. These films, which range from government-backed productions like Pai Ching-jui's *Home Sweet Home* to Chiung Yao adaptations like Liu Chia-chang's *Moon River*, load emotional cues (such as music and visual excess) to reconcile the national and the cosmopolitan at the moment of disappearance: the disappearance of the nation (the Republic of China) from the international stage in the 1970s, and the disappearance of the son, daughter, lover, sister, or brother who, in the name of national and family honor, boards planes and vanishes into the sky. Chapter 2 imagines the anxious return of those overseas figures one generation later, when North American actors, musicians, and models like Maggie Q, Edison Chen, Nicholas Tse, Daniel Wu, Janet Hsieh, and the L. A. Boyz came to embody what locals in Hong Kong and Taiwan dubbed the "ABCs" (American-Born Chinese) of the 1990s and 2000s. I show how paradoxical notions of local and global are grafted on to the bodies of the "ABC star" and the mixed-race beauty: desire and repulsion, superhuman bodies and non-human ones. These uncanny star images activate discourses of the English language, racialization (especially through styles associated with African American genres), deformity, ghostliness, and sexuality to look forward to a "healthy" and more prosperous future for both society and the media industry.

The role of the media industry in developing these extraordinary cosmopolitan bodies cannot be understated. Beyond just defining the bodily difference of the cosmopolitan (a process I describe in Chapter 2), the industry can self-reflexively showcase the body's cosmopolitan coming-of-age and, in fact, make that process of cosmopolitanization itself be the spectacular event that imagines a glorious entrance onto the world stage. Chapter 3 looks at efforts by the two biggest Mandarin-dialect studios of the postwar years—Shaw Brothers and MP&GI—to brand themselves as cosmopolitan through the figure of the jet-set, fast-learning, and internationally beloved female star. The glamorous cosmopolitan bodies of actresses like Linda Lin Dai electrified the musical genre in particular (especially in the requisite "around-the-world" numbers of the 1950s and 60s), as well as graced the pages of house fan magazines *Southern Screen* and *International Screen*, which detailed their international travels. These moments set "cultural China's" cosmopolitanization to music, and choreographed and fashioned its seeming immanence to a Sinophone audience throughout the world.

Chapter 4 looks more closely at discourses of cosmopolitanism as they are allegorized vis-à-vis a diasporic imagination in the Shaolin Temple martial arts film, a subgenre that may not immediately be associated with cosmopolitanism. If the cosmopolitan women of the Shaw Bros. and MP&GI musicals reworked concepts of the "modern Chinese woman" of previous decades, the men of martial arts symbolically reworked tropes of masculinity to invent a foundational myth of mobility, adaptability, and competitiveness. In other words, films from *The 36th Chamber of Shaolin* to *Shaolin Soccer* invented a call-to-arms for a proto-cosmopolitanism that would make "Chineseness" more integrated with a world system in the 1970s and 1980s. These films, through the traumatic image of a burning Shaolin Temple and the dispersal of heroes who, through extraordinary training rituals, learn to cultivate secular powers of the martial arts, allegorize a particular Guangzhou-inflected cosmopolitanism to legitimize Hong Kong and Taiwan's places in the world.

The emergent cosmopolitanism I have been describing often begins when something vanishes (the loss of national status, the departure of loved ones, the fall of a cultural symbol). Chapter 5 looks at cosmopolitan discourse at the moment of disappearance for the film industry itself, and the role that cosmopolitan discourse plays in the state's attempts to resuscitate the Hong Kong and Taiwanese film industries. Specifically, I analyze the self-reflexive industrial texts produced by the Hong Kong Trade Development Council, the Hong Kong Film Development Council, the Taiwan Government Information Office, and the Taipei Film Commission during the first decade of the twenty-first century, when the market share for local films dwindled and cinema as a nationalizing discourse was reinvigorated from a position of scarcity. With fewer film texts to cite during this period, this chapter relies on ethnographic methods, analyzing the efforts by state representatives at some of the biggest international trade fairs: the American Film

Market (held in Santa Monica, California), the European Film Market (held in Berlin), the Asian Film Market (held in Busan, Korea), and Hong Kong's FILMART. At these film markets, Hong Kong and Taiwanese cinemas are branded as cosmopolitan through images of technological might, neoliberal advantage, cultural flexibility, and cross-cultural friendship. Finally, the conclusion raises questions pertaining to the elephant in the room looming behind and even triggering many of the phenomena in the book: mainland China.

# Notes

1. Bronislaw Szerszynski and John Urry, "Visuality, Mobility and the Cosmopolitan: Inhabiting the World from Afar," *The British Journal of Sociology* 57.1 (March 2006): 113–31.
2. Cited in Poshek Fu, "Modernity, Diasporic Capital, and 1950's Hong Kong Mandarin Cinema," *Jump Cut* 49 (Spring 2007) <http://www.ejumpcut.org/archive/jc49.2007/Poshek/2.html> (accessed March 25, 2011).
3. Liou Wei-gong, "Lin Zhiling shi chenggong de meixue jingji shangpin" *Liu xing li: Taiwan shishang wenhua ji*, Albert Chen, ed. (Taipei: Unitas Publishing, 2007) 31.
4. Kwame Anthony Appiah, *Cosmopolitanism: Ethics in a World of Strangers* (New York: Norton, 2006).
5. For a discussion of cosmopolitanism and legitimization for a "minor" nation, Taiwan, see Shu-mei Shih, "Cosmopolitanism among Empires," *Visuality and Identity: Sinophone Articulations across the Pacific* (Berkeley: University of California Press, 2007) 165–82.
6. Frederic Jameson, *Signatures of the Visible* (London: Routledge, 1990) 139.
7. Yingjin Zhang, *Cinema, Space, and Polylocality in a Globalizing China* (Honolulu: University of Hawaii Press, 2010); Michael Curtin, *Playing to the World's Biggest Audience: The Globalization of Chinese Film and TV* (Berkeley: University of California Press, 2007).
8. Chris Berry, "What is Transnational Cinema? Thinking from the Chinese Situation," *Transnational Cinemas* 1.2 (November 2010): 111–27.
9. Ibid. 120.
10. Raymond Williams, *Marxism and Literature* (Oxford: Oxford University Press, 1977) 121–8.
11. Ulrich Beck, *The Cosmopolitan Vision*, Ciaran Cronin, trans. (Cambridge: Polity, 2006) 18–20.
12. Gilles Deleuze and Félix Guattari, *What is Philosophy?*, Hugh Tomlinson and Graham Burchell, trans. (New York: Columbia University Press, 1994) 17–19.
13. Ibid. 18.
14. Gerard Delanty, *The Cosmopolitan Imagination: The Renewal of Critical Social Theory* (Cambridge: Cambridge University Press, 2009) 6.
15. Ibid. 9.

16. Beck 7.
17. Mitchell Cohen, "Rooted Cosmopolitanism," *Dissent* 39.4 (Fall 1992): 483–7.
18. Maximilian C. Forte, ed. *Indigenous Cosmopolitans: Transnational and Transcultural Indigeneity in the Twenty-First Century* (New York: Lang, 2010).
19. Nico Slate, *Colored Cosmopolitanism: The Shared Struggle for Freedom in the United States and India* (Cambridge, MA: Harvard University Press, 2012).
20. Dorota Kolodziejczyk, "Cosmopolitan Provincialism in a Comparative Perspective," *Rerouting the Postcolonial: New Directions for the New Millennium*, Janet Wilson, et al., eds. (London: Routledge, 2010) 151–62.
21. Kwame Anthony Appiah, "Against National Culture," *Text and Nation: Cross-Disciplinary Essays on Cultural and National Identities*, eds. Laura García-Moreno and Peter C. Pfeiffer (Columbia: Camden House, 1996) 175–90. See also Edwin Jurriëns and Jeroen de Kloet, *Cosmopatriots: On Distant Belongings and Close Encounters* (Amsterdam: Rodopi, 2007).
22. Peggy Levitt, *Artifacts and Allegiances: How Museums Put the Nation and the World on Display* (Berkeley: University of California Press, 2015) 3.
23. Leo Ou-fan Lee, "On the Margins of the Chinese Discourse: Some Personal thoughts on the Cultural Meaning of the Periphery," *The Living Tree: The Changing Meaning of Being Chinese Today*, Tu Wei-ming, ed. (Stanford: Stanford University Press, 1994) 229.
24. Ien Ang, *On Not Speaking Chinese: Living between Asia and the West* (London: Routledge, 2001) 46.
25. Simon Gikandi, "Between Roots and Routes: Cosmopolitanism and the Claims of Locality," *Rerouting the Postcolonial: New Directions for the New Millennium*, Janet Wilson, et al, eds. (London: Routledge, 2010) 22–35.
26. Shu-mei Shih, "Introduction: What Is Sinophone Studies?" *Sinophone Studies: A Critical Reader*, Shu-mei Shih, et al., eds. (New York: Columbia University Pess, 2013) 1–16.
27. Audrey Yue and Olivia Khoo, "Framing Sinophone Cinemas," *Sinophone Cinemas*, Audrey Yue and Olivia Khoo, eds. (London: Palgrave Macmillan, 2014) 3–4.
28. Shu-mei Shih, "Foreword: The Sinophone Redistribution of the Audible," *Sinophone Cinemas* x.
29. Benedict Anderson, *Imagined Communities: Reflections on the Origin and Spread of Nationalism*, rev. edn (London: Verso, 2006) 35.
30. Miriam Bratu Hansen, "The Mass Production of the Senses: Classical Cinema as Vernacular Modernism," *Modernism/Modernity* 6.2 (April 1999): 60.
31. Homi K. Bhabha, "Unsatisfied: Notes on Vernacular Cosmopolitanism," *Text and Nation: Cross-Disciplinary Essays on Cultural and National Identities*, Laura García-Moreno and Peter C. Pfeiffer, eds. (Columbia: Camden House, 1996) 202; emphasis in the original.
32. Appiah, "Against National Culture," 176–8.
33. Sonal Khullar, *Worldly Affiliations: Artistic Practice, National Identity, and Modernism in India, 1930–1990* (Berkeley: University of California Press, 2015) 14.

34. Ibid.
35. On the pragmatic functions of cosmopolitan discourse, see Aihwa Ong, *Neoliberalism as Exception: Mutations in Citizenship and Sovereignty* (Durham, NC: Duke University Press, 2006); and Inderpal Grewal, *Transnational America: Feminisms, Diasporas, Neoliberalisms* (Durham, NC: Duke University Press, 2005).
36. Aihwa Ong, *Flexible Citizenship: The Cultural Logics of Transnationality* (Durham, NC: Duke University Press, 1999).

# Chapter 1
# Melodramas of Arrival and Departure: Jet-set Students in 1970s Taiwanese Romance

Why do so many postwar Taiwanese and Hong Kong films begin and end in airports? The pattern is not unique to any single genre. To name only a few, there is the family melodrama *Her Tender Heart* (Tang Huang, 1959) about a mother living in Italy who returns to Hong Kong to visit her estranged daughter, the backstage musical *The Lark* (Hsieh Chun, 1964) about a chanteuse who travels Southeast Asia entertaining her fans, the spy film *Black Falcon* (Takami Furukawa, 1967) about an exotic globetrotter who gets mixed up in an international crime ring, and the comedy of ethics *Home Sweet Home* (Pai Ching-jui, 1970) about overseas students visiting family in Taipei. In many ways, beginning or ending a film with the arrival or departure of key figures exemplifies Tzvetan Todorov's "grammar of narrative," where a state of equilibrium is broken and various machinations are required to restore the disequilibrium back to a state of equilibrium.[1] In fact, there is an entire tradition of narratives of arrival and departure in literature (such as *Uncle Vanya*) and film (*On the Town*). In Chinese narrative, arrival and departure is often structured into the expectation of the *datuanyuan* (or "big reunion"), which implies a circular pattern of conflict and resolution, whereby stories end through a cosmologically driven return to an original state. Examples would include the revenge story and the story of family togetherness.[2] Daoist philosophy privileges this circular pattern of experience, whereby fulfillment is achieved not by adventuring into the outside world, but by self-reflexively turning back to the point of origin.[3] Not surprisingly then, the airport has become an especially dramatic setting for such narratives, from Hollywood to Hong Kong. With its impending boarding times and disappearance into the heavens, the airport departure connotes a finality that elicits tears, elation, and anticipation in the characters and the audience, as well as setting the scene for such clichés as the last-minute airport chase where men sprint past security guards and checkpoints to profess their love before it's too late. The return is a transcendence of that distressing finality with a harmonious one: reunion, resurrection, redemption.

That said, narratives of arrival and departure also have historically specific determinants, most obviously the availability of consumer air travel. Hong Kong-based Cathay Pacific began operations in 1946 and Hong Kong Airways a year later. The Hong Kong International Airport opened a passenger terminal in 1962. In Taiwan, commercial international air travel was serviced through Taipei's Songshan Airport beginning in 1950, and international service from the state-owned China Airlines began in 1966. The development of commercial air routes and airports satisfied the demand created by the rise of a new cosmopolitan class. Overseas tourism expanded beyond the reach of slow-moving ocean liners, allowing for greater and speedier integration into an international tourist culture. Meanwhile, air travel further facilitated international commerce, accelerating interactions along existing overseas Chinese business networks and creating new ties beyond Southeast Asia and into Europe, Latin America, and the United States, solidifying Hong Kong and Taiwan's stature as budding economic players on the world stage. The rise of commercial air travel also corresponded to a moment of liberalized immigration policy in the United States (1965), Canada (1967), and Australia (1973).[4] Soon it was not unusual for everyday residents in Hong Kong and Taiwan to have overseas family, friends, and neighbors who might occasionally return with stories (and commodities) of the West. Lastly, while there have always been Chinese students studying abroad, in 1962, the government in Taiwan reformed its education policy to make foreign study more accessible. With an empirical rise in what Iain Chambers has called "the planeur"[5] is a growing consciousness of and concern about the cosmopolitan figure, leading filmmakers to produce stories featuring planes, airports, and travelers.

However, while the empirical referent for such stories is necessary for their existence on film, it does not explain their emotional valence, or the narrative and stylistic strategies employed to represent the character of the cosmopolitan Chinese. Why, for instance, did so many films go as far as to begin and/or end with the arrival or departure of the overseas student (*liuxuesheng*), or hinge their primary conflict upon the disruption such an arrival or departure brings to his or her family and friends? I would hasten to call the *liuxuesheng* film a genre or movement in the sense that *liuxuesheng* literature is now acknowledged by scholars of Sinophone literature. Yet it is undeniable that in the postwar years, be it in Cantonese films like *Sweet Dreams* (aka *A Dream of Love*) (Tong Tik-sang, 1955) or Mandarin films like *Devotion* (Tang Huang, 1960), the character of the overseas student played a critical role in helping audiences in Hong Kong and

Taiwan come to terms with the emergent place of their citizenry within the circuit of global capital, knowledge, and diplomacy. While cold war propaganda may have depicted the West as liberated, beautiful, and technologically advanced, the films balanced such notions with the very real fear of the unknown and the suspicion that studying abroad, seeing the world, sojourning for the sake of the family and the nation—indeed globalization itself—could be very sad. Essential to this take on globalization, more specifically the desire for integration into the cosmopolitan, is my insistence that, while many theorists of cosmopolitanism see it as an end ideal—a proposition for equality—and indeed this idealism is what makes cosmopolitanism such a provocative notion today, I instead see cosmopolitanism as an anxiety-laden process that requires the mediation and sometimes compromise between competing affiliations of emotional importance. This process—of learning to travel, of acquiring "worldly" knowledge, of re-stylizing the self, of coping with absence—takes an emotional toll on the individual, at the same time that new (often glamorous) possibilities of the self are being forged.[6] The new cosmopolitans, such as overseas students, are subjects of fascination, envy, and attention, but also embodiments of loss and compromise. In postwar Hong Kong and Taiwan cinemas are countless melodramas that capture the contradictions inherent in the cosmopolitanizing of the self and of society. Their narratives of flight envision the beginnings of a world where, as Arjun Appadurai writes, "points of departure and points of arrival are in cultural flux, and thus the search for steady points of reference, as critical life choices are made, can be very difficult."[7]

Melodrama, of course, thrives on difficulty, and points of reference (such as nationalism, filial piety, and individualism) serve as tentative moral anchors that tighten the drama. In this chapter, I examine the moralizing, gendering, sexualizing, and nationalizing of overseas students in one specific period of Chinese-language cinema: 1970s Taiwan. I chose this period and this location because, as I will elaborate later, it is a moment during which the stakes placed on studying abroad escalated due to a string of diplomatic setbacks and due to the labor demands of a developing economy. These are also years when the state—through its own studio, the Central Motion Picture Corporation (CMPC), or through film policy—still wielded significant control over the content of films, and could thus motivate the sort of claims made on cosmopolitan characters like overseas students. However, I will argue for a more nuanced and historically contingent approach to film propaganda, one that seeks to break down what I see as misleading boundaries between policy and entertainment films, in order to show how all films employed a similar strategy for narrating the contradictions of the *liuxuesheng*, although they may ultimately take different moral and political positions. Specifically, these films invariably place the *liuxuesheng* within a matrix of family, lover, self, and nation. The melodrama does its best to satisfy all four pressures, and the ability to do so results in a happy ending, while the inability to do so results in a compromised one. Rey Chow's conception of the sentimental as a "mood of endurance" is useful in understanding how mixed feelings strike not as a dissipating of affect but as an intense, even oppressive, emotionality.[8] Indeed, what I am exploring here is the way that Taiwanese films of the 1970s made sense of the *liuxuesheng* through a fog of tears. Collectively, the films may not reveal any one ideological or even ethical position on the overseas student, and indeed single films may even be confused about what stance to take. Yet the films are united on the stance that the process by which this creature of globalization is (re-)integrated into the nation, the family, or a romantic coupling is muddled by sorrowful compromises and the melancholy of hesitant goodbyes.

## Beyond Propaganda/Entertainment: Sentimental Romanticism

Historical studies of mid-1960s to 1970s Mandarin cinema in Taiwan tend to split the industry into two main realms: the propagandistic cinema of the state-run CMPC, and the studio and independent costume films and romantic melodramas of companies such as Grand, Union, and First Films. The former type is seen as spreading the ideology of the dominant Kuomintang (KMT) Party, and is frequently considered synonymous with the "Healthy Realism" (*jiankang xieshi*) movement, while the latter is seen as entertainment cinema in competition and in co-production with Hong Kong cinema. From the perspective of financing, distribution, and publicity, there is indeed a difference between the two sectors, as propaganda films were heavily backed by state money and publicity. However, to overemphasize this difference, especially on the level of content, style, and film culture, elides the extent to which all narrative feature films existed within the same affective economy, pooled from the same creative resources, developed out of the same cultural and cinematic traditions, and responded to the same emergent social and cultural trends, such as patriotism, globalization, modernization, and liberalization. Emphasizing these differences also ignores the critical fact that though propaganda films by the CMPC had easier access to government support, they still competed in the film market with entertainment films from Taiwan and elsewhere, and thus were constantly appropriating styles and trends from other studios, as well as developing their own forms of entertainment to compete with the other players in the market. As former CMPC general manager Kung Hung recalls in his memoirs, "I've always felt that if CMPC had no box office, it would have no means to survive. And without a means to survive, it's useless to talk about propaganda, the [healthy realist] line, and state policy."[9]

In other words, if the state needed to propagate an urgent position, such as anti-Japan-ism as a result of the Diaoyutai Islands dispute in 1971,[10] it had to do so by evoking the same kinds of narrative, cinematic, generic, heroic, and emotional traditions, as well as by interfacing with the same set of social and moral concerns, that inspired entertainment films like the blissful teen romances adapted from the writer Chiung Yao. This realization draws attention away from propaganda as the art of persuasion and entertainment as the art of amusement, and toward a closer consideration of that creative well from which both drink. Mark Wollaeger has made a similar claim about the perceived antithesis of modernism and propaganda in the forty years before the Second World War. Wollaeger discusses the common perception of propaganda as political, persuasive, and populist, while modernism is shocking, unaligned, and "art for art's sake." He then argues that a more meaningful discussion of the two would emphasize that each is in their own way a response to the same crisis of information resulting from industrialization and modernity. Both served to provide "mechanisms for coping with information flows that had begun to outstrip the processing capacity of the mind; both fabricated new forms of coherence in response to new experiences of chaos."[11] Although there are political shocks such as World War I that may rally the need for propaganda, the works of film and literature that followed reflect a cultural inertia and resistant media ecology that is still preoccupied with the questions of living, knowing, and surviving the phenomenological and moral transformations brought forth by modernity. Works of propaganda simply rework formal and cultural tropes—many of which we may associate with modernism—for a more focused purpose.

Propaganda and modernism in Wollaeger's analysis are both responding to the disjunctures and inefficiencies of the new information flow of modernity, and likewise I would claim that Taiwan's popular culture—be it state-run or independent—provided for audiences a sensorial coherence to a nation on a brink. The rise of consumer culture resulting from US influence and protectionism, the "white terror" witch-hunting enforced by martial law, and the linguistic, political, and class conflicts between the *waishengren* and the *benshengren* were all everyday tensions that characterized life under the KMT administration in the postwar decades. Central to many of these anxieties was the shaky political-economic position of Taiwan in the world, with mainland China, the US, and to some extent Japan the major players that made Taiwan a potentially incoherent entity. Thus, the vexing question of Taiwan's international status—and metonymically the role of the individual Taiwanese person on the world stage—persisted as an inescapable foundation underlying so many aspects of social life and culture in Taiwan.

Of course, these concerns were not new. A fracturing sense of purpose and identity as a result of one's relationship to world trends was a preoccupation of semi-colonial Shanghai in the 1920s and 1930s, and colonial Taiwan in its fifty years under Japanese rule. And as in those earlier periods, a dominant sensibility that developed to cope with cultural incoherence, to conjure revolution or soften the blow, is a specific kind of romanticism with roots in Chinese literature and drama.[12] In its various incarnations across borders and history, this romanticism depicts political, social, and moral conflict in terms of an emotionally saturated, uncompromisingly sincere love story. In a developing Taiwan, this romanticism combines with the kind of sentimentality Rey Chow describes of a later period of Chinese cinema. According to Chow, this sentimentality, deriving from the Chinese term *wenqing zhuyi* ("warm sentiment-ism"), connotes an intense emotionality, but also moderation. Chow writes, "With this crucial sense of moderation in the foreground, the sentimental may thus be specified as *an inclination or a disposition toward making compromises and toward making-do with even—and especially—that which is oppressive and unbearable*."[13] As a variation on the romantic tradition of Chinese film and literature, this ethos of compromise and sacrifice—which Chow calls a "tone" and that I would, following Linda Williams on melodrama, call a "mode"[14]—thus takes as its topic the hard decisions to be made between lover, family, nation, and self. Does one sacrifice one's childhood romance in order to study abroad for the sake of family honor and national development? What makes these melodramas so compelling is that they could effectively convince audiences one way or the other. They could include us in the act of sacrifice and compel us to swallow our own tears just as the characters must.

This sentimental romanticism pervaded most genres in Taiwan, from family melodrama to *wuxia* to opera film, and was as prevalent in propaganda films as it was in entertainment films. The assumption that there is something unique about propaganda films is a result of the overemphasis on "healthy realism," a film movement celebrated by critics, state policy makers, and Chinese film historians perhaps because it gave a name to trends in Taiwanese cinema, allowing it to be discussed alongside socialist realism in mainland China and neorealism in Italy. Healthy realism was coined by the CMPC to describe its goal of producing films that reflected the "real" Taiwan, namely the everyday world of farmers and fishermen, but with a "healthy" outlook that would distinguish it from the uglier and more critical tendencies of Italian neorealism. As Emilie Yueh-yu Yeh and Darrell William Davis note, unlike neorealism, healthy realism is "a cinema of closure, of resolution, and of reassurance" that neatly tied indigenous life in Taiwan to civic initiatives.[15] Yet, as Guo-juin Hong has argued, while healthy realism films sought closure, they also revealed internal ideological tensions manifesting on the level of theme and style. Hong thus characterizes healthy realism through the self-contradictory concept of "stasis of change," in which modernization and its changes must reckon with the stasis of family values and national culture, all of which plays out paradoxically and dissonantly in narrative structure, sound, setting, and character.[16]

Perhaps this internal instability of healthy realism as policy, and the difficulty for sustaining ideological and aesthetic consistency across its films, led to a much-less remarked upon addendum to healthy realism a mere five years after the first healthy realist film *Oyster Girl* (Lee Chia and Lee Hsing). In September of 1968, the CMPC revised its terminology, replacing "healthy realism" with a broader and perhaps more accurate term "healthy variety" (*jiankang zongyi*). The purpose of this announcement was to acknowledge a shift that was already going on at CMPC: that propaganda should take the forms of all genres of entertainment, including musicals, action films, melodramas, war films, historical films, and comedies.[17] The term "healthy variety" better captures the breadth of films produced by CMPC as well as its determination to compete with other films in the marketplace. As Lee Tain-dow has noted, healthy realism was originally designed not only to propagate state ideology, but also to cater to the market demand opened up by the unprecedented success of the opera romance, *The Love Eterne* (Li Han-hsiang, 1963).[18] Healthy variety would continue that original impetus, only from more generic fronts. The term thus also describes how both propaganda and entertainment occupied the same affective register marked by the sentimental romanticism of which *The Love Eterne* is a classic.

Conversely, so-called entertainment films had "healthy" tendencies, in large part because they were produced by for-profit studios and independent companies eager to collaborate with the Taiwanese government to assure their financial and political safety. On the level of policy making, studios like Union actively worked with the KMT government, specifically with the Government Information Office and briefly with the Cultural Division of the Department of Education when it handled film affairs from 1967 to 1973, to lobby for sensible policy regarding such issues as protectionism, production and co-production assistance, award-giving, and even how the film profession should be officially defined.[19] And yet, as Huang Ren has noted, scholars tend to narrowly focus on an all-powerful Kuomintang government and its production arm (the CMPC) as monopolizing film discourse in Taiwan.[20] These studies of Taiwanese cinema analyze hegemonic processes, but focus overwhelmingly on coercion and less on concession and negotiation.[21] Meanwhile, on the level of film content, the entertainment films by Union, Grand, First Films, and others towed the official line (which they in some senses devised together) to avoid censorship and to attain awards, subsidies, and tax breaks. While perhaps not to the extremes of the CMPC, the other studios did not hesitate in extolling the virtues of patriotism in their formulation of sentimental romanticism.

Yet despite what Huang describes as an unbalanced attention placed on the films of the CMPC and the policies of the KMT government, no history of Taiwanese cinema has ignored the immense importance of the films adapted from the popular youth romances of novelist Chiung Yao. Lee Tain-dow calls the Chiung Yao film the most influential archetype and the backbone for romantic melodrama in Taiwanese film history.[22] And yet these historians primarily mention the Chiung Yao film to write it off as peripheral to the dominant narrative of state-sponsored propaganda films. The primary strategy for dealing with this wave of films is to dismiss it as a fad that provided an escape for young women coming of age in the late 1960s to the early 1980s. Indeed, escapism is the primary framework for most scholars with regard to the Chiung Yao phenomenon. For instance, James Udden calls the films "grotesquely escapist."[23] Similarly, Lee Tain-dow writes that given the diplomatic, political, economic, and social turbulence of Taiwan in the 1970s, the stories' insular male–female romances were a numbing retreat into the false stability of the private sphere.[24] Udden's and Lee's statements echo the positions held by most literary scholars on the Chiung Yao novels from which the films, and later television dramas, were based. In her pioneering study of Chiung Yao's fiction, Lin Fang-mei argues that love provides an escape from the era's social traumas: the white terror, the expulsion from the United Nations, the severing of ties with the United States. The tiny world of the three *"tings"* (the living room, the kitchen, and the coffee shop—or *ke ting, can ting,* and *kafei ting* in Mandarin) lets readers escape into safe, manageable domesticity far away from the immense uncertainty of the world stage.[25] Similarly, Chi Lung-zin argues that Chiung Yao's novels provided escape from the era's political and economic problems by spinning tales of unearthly emotions out of touch with reality.[26] These critics are, I believe, correct to tie the appeal of love in Chiung Yao's fiction to the socio-political traumas of Taiwan on the world stage. However, in referring to her films and novels as mere escape, the critics risk drawing an artificial line between Chiung Yao and non-Chiung Yao works, as if the latter was not also a palliative against social traumas, and as if Chiung Yao films did not also engage geo-politicized topics such as the overseas student, as I will explore later.[27] This effort to contain the Chiung Yao phenomenon results in depicting the films as merely a special topic in the history of Taiwanese cinema—a very popular and very influential fad—instead of showing how the phenomenon breathed fire into already bubbling social concerns and mobilized familiar tropes and character types to move the reader and the viewer into engaging ethically with concerns of self, love, family, and nation.

Much of the problem is the overblown focus on Chiung Yao herself, a symptom of the author-driven approach of much literary scholarship. The "Chiung Yao film" should not be understood simply as the corpus of films based on the novels of Chiung Yao. It is less an auteur category (in the traditional sense) than a generic one, with its own constellation of character types and semantic/syntactic configurations: generation gaps, love triangles, sibling affection. As Leo Ou-fan Lee has shown, the narrative elements of Chiung Yao's novels are in the tradition of May Fourth romanticism, especially the "Mandarin Duck and Butterfly" school, of the early Republican period.[28] Thus, Chiung Yao did not monopolize the narrative clichés that are now commonly attributed to her. Furthermore, as Chiung Yao became increasingly proactive about enforcing the copyright of her properties, many production companies who chose not to buy adaptation rights from her and her publisher, Crown Books, ended up producing countless Chiung Yao-type knockoffs, often picking from the same quartet of stars (Brigitte Lin, Joan Lin, Chin Han, and Charlie Chin), using the same composers, and including songs by the same pop stars (Fong Fei-fei, Jenny Tseng, and Kenny Bee). Certain images also became recycled in the knockoff films: slow-motion expressions of romantic bliss, musical montages of lovers running toward each other on a sandy beach, dynamic extreme zoom-ins on emotionally saturated faces (often repeated in succession for additional effect), the use of nature (especially birds, clouds, and flowers) as metaphors for personal anguish. In other words, Chiung Yao as a discourse transcended Chiung Yao the person, Chiung Yao the collection of novels, or Chiung Yao the film adaptation industry. The "Chiung Yao film," a category deployed as a marketing tool, a critical convenience, and a set of aesthetic conventions, came to denote an entire discourse of romantic sentimentalism in 1960s and 1970s Taiwan.[29]

As a result, the Chiung Yao film was also not mutually exclusive to the propaganda film—the "healthy" films most often studied by scholars of Taiwanese cinema in this period. Once again, there is a crossover in personnel. The state-owned Central Motion Picture Corporation was one of the first studios to capitalize on Chiung Yao adaptations, with films such as *Four Loves* (1965) and *The Silent Wife* (1965). The director of both of those films, Lee Hsing, was a specialist of both Chiung Yao-type melodrama and healthy variety-type propaganda. His colleague Pai Ching-jui also made both types of films for CMPC as well as for independent companies such as First Films and Ta Chung, the latter of which he co-founded with Lee Hsing. The same stars, too, appeared in both Chiung Yao melodramas and healthy variety. In addition to the four most famous stars (the "two Lins and two Chins") were Chen Chen, Kenny Bee, Tang Pao-yun, Ko Chun-hsiung, Judy Ongg, and others. In terms of music, the composer whose songs defined the decade, Liu Chia-chang, was equally adept at writing the famous patriotic anthem of *Victory* (Liu Chia-chang, 1976) as he was the title song to the Chiung Yao romance *Fantasies behind the Pearly Curtain* (Pai Ching-jui, 1974). Not surprisingly, both the Chiung Yao film and the healthy variety film invoked the same kind of affective register through similar images, musical cues, characters, and resolutions. The propaganda films may have communicated a clearer ideological position, and in fact many Chiung Yao films were ideologically confused on issues such as the nation and economic development. Yet both mobilized the same kinds of ethical considerations when it came to love, family, nation, and self, and did so emotionally through the sorrowful sacrifices of romantic sentimentalism.

## Struggles Of and Over the Overseas Student

As a figure that crosses borders and thus disrupts the equilibrium of the nation and the family, the overseas student plays a crucial role in the melodramatic working through of what counts emotionally as "home," in the sense that both nation (*guojia*) and family (*jiating*) are built upon the concept of home (*jia*). When the overseas student goes away to, say, a university in the United States, the home simultaneously feels the absence of the students' physical being, but also basks in the promise of a future moral/patriotic enrichment: the glorious return that brings honor to the family and human capital to the nation. But the overseas student brings back more than just knowledge and international experience. He or she brings back an entire cache of connotations associated with "the West." These associations manifest on the body of the overseas student: in dress, in movement, in sexuality. This excess is perceived as an impurity—a side effect of cosmopolitanism—that causes the anxiety that needs to be dealt with so that the overseas student can be reintegrated into the home. The fear of this excess is also what drives another common scenario: the decision to stay at home instead of pursuing a degree in a foreign country.

In Chinese communities throughout the twentieth century, studying abroad is limited to those who can pass qualifying examinations, those who can secure state and private scholarships, or those whose families can afford hefty tuition and living costs overseas. In other words, it is a rarity. Yet, the character of the overseas student in popular culture (especially literature and film) appears frequently and consistently throughout the century as a figure of great fascination —if only because many novelists and filmmakers themselves were overseas students.[30] David Der-wei Wang traces the phenomenon back to the late Qing era, arguing that before the so-called "overseas student literature" of postwar Taiwan, or even the Europe- and Japan-educated writers of the May Fourth movement, were turn-of-the-century writings fascinated with the exploits and miseries of Chinese students abroad, especially in Japan.[31] As the figure of the overseas student was historically motivated by state imperatives—learning "the West" to compete with Japan and Europe, becoming modern in science and technology—its appearance in literature combined the adventure of cross-cultural contact with the demands of the Chinese nation, especially following the Japanese invasion of Manchuria in 1931. As Ming-ju Fan puts it, in overseas Chinese literature, "evocations of the overseas student are not only expressions of individual freedom, but are discourses of the nation."[32] There is little consistency in how the overseas student becomes "typed" in Chinese literature and film. He or she can be depicted as a rich child from an elite family, or a struggling dishwasher slaving away in a foreign Chinatown; he or she can be an upholder of traditional Chinese values despite the seductions of the West, or a white-washed slave to Western fashion and habits; he or she can be prim and proper, or a clownish figure spouting out English phrases and dancing buffoon-like to Western rock and roll. In fact, to build the drama, to develop character motivation, and to picture the diversity of the overseas community, authors and filmmakers frequently chose to populate their stories with all of these oppositions, rather than settle for a single stereotype. However, as Fan notes in relation to overseas Chinese literature, across these various types there are consistent dynamics that guide the differential representation of women.[33] I will return to these differences when I present examples from Taiwanese cinema.

With respect to 1960s and 1970s Taiwanese society, the figure of the overseas student was depicted in popular culture within the same nexus of nation and romance as that of the May Fourth period. However, certain relationships were intensified as a result of state initiatives to promote overseas study, while curbing the brain-drain problem. The state remained a critical player in the story of the overseas student because it controlled the exit of citizens. As per the Republic of China guidelines for foreign study in 1954, any person choosing to study abroad must gain the approval of officials, although these guidelines were gradually relaxed in later revisions.[34]

Managing the flow of human capital was considered an integral strategy for science development in Taiwan, a project that initially focused on developing nuclear capabilities to combat mainland China, but that later shifted to the development of contractible or exportable technological skills attractive to multinational corporations.[35] Policy makers considered the local education system insufficient for building this infrastructure, so, through foreign study initiatives, the government encouraged overseas study for select individuals. However, due to the fact that most of this selected few were mainlanders (*waishengren*), overseas students did not feel deep ties to Taiwan, and, coupled with the prospect of higher salaries and better research facilities in North America, elected not to return to Taiwan following the completion of their graduate studies.[36] In 1960, a year before Qian Siliang, a member of the National Council for Scientific Development, announced in an address that brain drain was a serious issue, only

7.3 percent of students approved for overseas study returned to Taiwan. By 1965, this percentage was down to 5.1 percent.[37] The desire to keep foreign study a round-trip affair was made further urgent by Taiwan's increasingly insecure diplomatic status on the world stage, with most nations dropping official ties to the Republic of China in favor of the People's Republic of China on the mainland: France in 1964; Canada and Italy in 1970; Japan, West Germany, and Australia in 1972; and, most damagingly, the United States in December 1978. The United Nations also expelled the Republic of China in 1971. This domino effect was felt hard by local policy makers, who then saw "soft" politics like scholarly exchange as a way to maintain international relations when official diplomatic ones became impossible.[38] Strategies for curbing the brain-drain problem included building more state-of-the-art research facilities in Taiwan culminating with the Hsinchu Science Park in 1979, setting up returnee assistantships including job search advisement and complimentary return airfare, and producing guilt-inducing propaganda such as the Central Motion Picture Corporation's 1970 film *Home Sweet Home* about overseas students who rediscover the warmth of home on a visit back to Taipei. Bolstering the pull factors for return seemed to work. In the 1970s, the rate of return topped 20 percent, with 22.6 percent returning in 1973, 21.3 percent in 1974, and 24.7 percent in 1975.[39]

Overseas study became a fever, even a fetish, in the 1970s. An entire publishing industry developed around the figure of the overseas student. Popular guidebooks, with titles such as *The Road to Overseas Study* and *American Universities and Colleges*, gave advice on how to beat the Test of English as a Foreign Language (TOEFL), how to write cover letters, how to compose a successful statement of purpose, how to apply for scholarships, and how to survive in a foreign country like the US, the UK, Canada, or Australia.[40] In addition to the aforementioned overseas Chinese literature that saw a revival as early as the 1960s, there were also memoirs, such as *The Love of an Overseas Student*, about life and love while studying abroad,[41] and essay collections such as *Overseas Study and Chinese Society* and *Notes of a Student Studying Abroad* about nostalgia for home and the sense of patriotic duty.[42] Clearly, affect remained central, even in the works of non-fiction. Studying abroad is depicted as a heroic feat, with the weight of the nation and the economy resting on the scholar's shoulders, but also as a source of potential anxiety with regards to personal desire and social responsibility. Such works were produced not only for current and prospective overseas students, but also for their friends, families, and neighbors, all of whom were necessarily included in the ethical conundrum of foreign study. In this way, brain drain was never simply a political issue, but a popular form of moral panic experienced by all who strove to be a part of Taiwan's upwardly mobile class.

Nowhere was the collective dimension of the overseas student more apparent than in cinema, which, with a few exceptions, tended to focus on the events at home in Taiwan: what happens to the family and the nation as a result of overseas departure or return.[43] The films deploy many of the same stereotypes of the travel-abroad student and the overseas world depicted in overseas student literature and even some of the non-fiction books. The world abroad is sexualized, a place where, to cite a somewhat exaggerated scene in Joseph Kuo Nan-hung's *The Lost Romance* (1971), women lounge about in two-pieces and miniskirts around men's living quarters. Female overseas students are in danger of being pursued by slimy Americanized Chinese men like the fashion photographer Harry Oh in *Long Way from Home* (Liu Yi, 1974), who pulls out his camera and instructs the impressionable foreign student Shan-shan, "Don't be so rigid . . . come on, sexier!" And yet, the world out there can also be a space for personal or national rejuvenation. In *The Eternal Love* (Ting Shan-si, 1978), Fred Chen travels to the University of North Carolina (UNC) to study electrical engineering. He stands for hard work and patriotism (he is invigorated by the same spirit that motivates his anti-communist father), cultural flexibility (he tells his family at home that the educational system in the US is worth copying), and cosmopolitan harmony (he sings a song in English and Chinese to encourage hospital patients in North Carolina to treasure life). These varying, sometimes contradictory, depictions of overseas students led to conflicting messages about the role of overseas study in 1970s Taiwan. What is consistent is the emotional challenge such characters bring to the family, the romantic coupling, and the nation, as well as the sentimental romanticism that leads us to accept possible solutions to such challenges. In other words, we should examine not the representation or symbolism of such characters, but how they function within an aesthetic of compromise. I will focus on four important nodes of moral and emotional frenzy within this process: the dilemma of departure, the disruption of arrival, the fantasy of romantic space, and the specters of cosmopolitan casualties.

## *The dilemma of departure*

To go or not to go is the vexing question asked in so many films about overseas students. These are the films that most explicitly invoke the nation within an emotional economy competing with family, romance, and personal self-fulfillment. They pit national responsibility against family concerns and personal (especially romantic) interest. Although each film has a different melodramatic logic and therefore may end on different sides of the to-go or not-to-go dilemma, they all foreground the emotional stress of the possibility of cosmopolitanism.

Some films resolve this stress by demythologizing the association of going abroad as something heroic or enviable. They do so through the ethics of utilitarianism: there is nothing inherently good or bad about studying abroad, it is what studying abroad is good for that truly matters—good for the family, good for the economy, good for the nation. The emphasis on social purpose over personal self-fulfillment, on collective value over individual status or enrichment, is an example of a tendency Chris Berry describes of Chinese melodrama: the privileging of ethics (behavior within specific social and kinship roles) over morality (distinctions between good and bad psychological positions).[44] The drama *Shining Spring* (Yang Dao, 1977) thus begins with a recent graduate Huang Xinjie (played by Joan Lin) meeting her professor at a restaurant. She has received a scholarship to continue her studies abroad. However, the professor advises her not to go, and her cheerful smile disappears. He reminds her of a lesson from the theory of education that he presented in one of his courses: that one can learn while one teaches (*jiao xue xiang zhang*). The professor knows of a local home school where she can develop her teaching skills while helping out in a special-needs environment. Xinjie's smile returns and we are consoled into believing things will be okay if she stays. Through the professor's theory, coupled with Xinjie's enthusiasm, *Shining Spring* pedantically diminishes the value of overseas study (which is solely for learning) in contrast to contributing locally (which allows for learning *and* teaching). It is better to stay, the film suggests, if staying does more for society than leaving would. If 1970s Taiwan were a time when going abroad seemed the natural thing to do for those with the means, *Shining Spring* obliterates that assumption in its opening minute, effectively (through Joan Lin's smile and through the excitement of the forward-march pop song that follows the scene) making a case that given the right opportunities, staying can be more useful than studying abroad.

Such didactic speeches on the ethics of overseas study are not uncommon in this period. The Taiwan Film Company's *My Way* (Lei Chi-ming, 1977) begins on graduation day. Graduate Hu Chia-ling tells his classmates that one should only go abroad if one has a goal, and not merely for personal status. The film then contrasts the cases of three members of the graduating class in relation to the issue of going abroad: Chia-ling, his girlfriend Hsu Hui-shan, and their classmate Cheng-nan. Chia-ling feels the pressure to study abroad, but finally chooses to stay. He finds a job working on a highway construction project (a reference to the ambitious National Highway that was being built at the time) and, later, echoing the sentiments from *Shining Spring*, he says that he feels he's learned more working on the highway than he would have had he studied abroad. Meanwhile, Hui-shan wants nothing more than to go abroad and tells Chia-ling that she will leave him if that's what it takes. Having no means to leave, she marries a former overseas student who promises to show her the world. Her father chastises her, telling her that the world abroad is no paradise and that she should not marry somebody she doesn't love. The night before her departure, her parents cannot sleep, and her mother clutches a photo of the daughter she's about to lose. We get little news of Hui-shan after her departure, for she's replaced in the film and in Chia-ling's life by another woman: a tender, filial nurse who contributes to society rather than flies around the world for the sake of selfish pleasure.

However, *My Way* is not against overseas study despite its depiction of Chia-ling's and Hui-shan's attitudes, and in fact celebrates overseas study should we be assured that the student will return immediately to better Taiwan with the cosmopolitan experiences and skills acquired abroad. Cheng-nan is set for the US, although his family has anxieties over his departure. His sister half-jokingly fears having to one day speak in English to a white sister-in-law. His father commands him to return after his studies for the sake of the nation, and then buys for him a rice cooker, not only a symbol of "Chineseness," but also a concrete token of what Rey Chow has described as intimacy through the sharing of food.[45] Lastly, his grandfather tells Cheng-nan to return after his two years of study because he wants to be alive when he returns. This touching airport farewell is a moment of overwhelming pathos for it highlights the point that the entire family is frightened—that Cheng-nan will marry a white woman, that he will forget the nation and stop being Chinese, that he will never see his family again—and yet they persist in letting him go anyway, as they know he will bring back precious skills. Under these conditions, the family is willing to see Cheng-nan off to the edge of the world and, as an audience, we are so moved by this sentimental display of the family's self-sacrifice that we have no doubt that Cheng-nan will indeed return, unlike Hui-shan whose departure is marked not by pathos but by despair. The film ends as many propaganda films of the 1960s and 1970s do: with a song about national development, factories, rice paddies, bustling traffic, equality, and peace. This utopia of economic development is shared between Chia-ling who helped build the roads, and Cheng-nan who we believe will return to develop the nation further. Hui-shan, on the other hand, has been replaced by a woman who proves filial, as opposed to hedonistic.

In Yang Wen-kang's *Call of the Mountains* (1967), as with *My Way*, the banishing of the non-utilitarian overseas student is accomplished metaphorically through the banishing of the unsuitable mate. In much film romance, the unsuitable mate is the corner of a love triangle who, through various generic codes, is marked as undesirable and in the way of the "correct" romantic pairing. In *My Way*, Hui-shan is insincere (she will marry a man she doesn't care for), stubborn, and unpatriotic, while the nurse is loving and filial, and therefore the woman we hope ends up with Chia-ling. In *Call of the Mountains*, Ya-lan demands her boyfriend Chia-ming take her abroad with him, but upon returning to Taiwan after receiving an overseas master's degree in agriculture, Chia-ming discovers that he loves the land and knows he can help to develop it. Chia-ming looks at the destroyed lettuce and suggests that the farmers use pesticide and re-toil the soil. "The land is like a mother: you see it and you feel an intimacy with it," he says. However, Ya-lan will have none of Chia-ming's sense of duty; she's busy looking at fashion magazines and deciding what to wear when abroad—in other words, conflating cosmopolitan experience with cosmopolitan consumerism. Ideologically, Chia-ming and Ya-lan are opposites: the former being someone who travels abroad in order to return, and the latter being someone who travels abroad for selfish reasons of status. Ya-lan quickly becomes marked as the unsuitable mate, especially with the appearance of Hsiu-yu, the common girl from the land on which Chia-ming works. Hsiu-yu romantically anchors Chia-ming to the land (expressed in a musical montage during which the two run along a river and romance by a waterfall) and ensures that his overseas knowledge has a practical and patriotic outlet. Ya-lan is expelled from romance because she wants to leave for the wrong reasons, and through the character of Hsiu-yu, the film effectively convinces us that Ya-lan's fate is justified.

Ya-lan is not the only character in Taiwanese film to be more excited about what to wear while abroad than what skills to bring back to Taiwan. In the CMPC's *Long Way from Home*, we witness future overseas student Shan-shan go on an extended shopping spree, trying to decide which fashions would be most appropriate in California, where she plans to study. Her boyfriend Ming-cheng says she is wasteful, and she mocks him for being provincial. Ming-cheng does not understand why Shan-shan must study abroad if they are in love and he is staying in Taiwan to contribute to Premier Chiang Ching-kuo's "Ten Major Construction Projects," a national development initiative launched the same year as *Long Way from Home*. We know little about what Shan-shan will be studying, and we are expected to sympathize with Ming-cheng, who sees her plans as vain. Like Ya-lan in *Call of the Mountains*, Shan-shan must be punished for her selfish attitude toward overseas travel. The first, and more comical, punishment occurs when Shan-shan discovers that her new clothes are way too flowery for California, and that she indeed wasted her money. More serious is that, without a real goal for overseas study, she is easily swayed by the womanizing Henry Oh, becomes pregnant, and returns to Taiwan in shame. To salvage what bit of honor she has left, Shan-shan retreats to her loveless marriage, while Ming-cheng valiantly participates in the film's utopic final image of industrial development: the construction of the Taichung Port. That only women in these films are obsessed with the fashion (as opposed to the usefulness) of travel underscores the tendency with which the heroic, patriotic return to Taiwan is a position held by men, while women are easily swayed by non-utilitarian motivations. On overseas Chinese literature, Ming-ju Fan notes that the male overseas student is more likely to represent national concerns, whereas the female overseas student overwhelmingly represents personal, domestic dimensions.[46] Fan perhaps forces a dichotomy between the national and the personal; my film examples suggest that the national often involves sentimental self-sacrifice in the realm of the personal. Rather, I'd argue that, especially in the propagandistic films produced by CMPC and the Taiwan Film Company, men tend to occupy a heroic position not simply because they represent national concerns, but because they serve a utilitarian purpose that family members and lovers are willing to sacrifice for. The women, on the other hand, do not exhibit motivations worth sacrificing for, and thus are themselves sacrificed as unsuitable mates in the final romantic pairing.

Such machinations of melodrama may have long roots in literature and escalated into a dominant mode in 1960s and 1970s Taiwanese cinema, yet they were not immune to urgent political considerations. As tensions escalated after the U.N. crisis, Richard Nixon's visit to Beijing, and the continued diplomatic losses on the world stage, the CMPC and other studios produced a wave of patriotic films with anti-communist themes.[47] With respect to the character of the overseas student, the US's severing of diplomatic ties with Taiwan at the end of 1978 proved to be a watershed moment in determining how to ethically deal with Taiwanese cosmopolitans in America. Still, despite the new political shocks and the propaganda required to deal with them, films relied on the tradition of romantic sentimentalism, with its nexus of self, nation, family, and lover, to channel anti-US furor. *Land of the Brave* (Lee Hsing, 1981) follows the grown children of several Taiwanese families. Nearly all young people in the film have an opportunity to study abroad: Lin Chao-hsing to study agriculture in the US, Fan Ching-tao to study Western classical music in Italy, Chang Shu to study cosmetology in Japan. Once again, utilitarianism determines the film's ultimate attitude toward each (potential) overseas student. Chao-hsing is valorized for returning to Taiwan after the Carter administration's diplomatic break with the KMT government, and for vowing to commit his overseas education to helping build the agricultural industry in Taiwan. Ching-tao, the charismatic core of the film, celebrates Chao-hsing for his patriotism and remarks that "even though he studied abroad, he doesn't have the scent of a Westerner" (*mei you yang cong wei*), emphasizing that studying abroad does not necessarily connote impure motivations. Ching-tao himself is resolute about staying in Taiwan, adding that Bach and Beethoven provide nothing for the nation. Instead, he wants to develop a rock band in the mold of the popular campus folk movement, singing patriotic songs to lift the spirits of a demoralized nation.[48]

The central conflict of the film, however, regards the fate of Ching-tao's girlfriend Chang Shu, whose parents expect her to study in Japan. Ching-tao tells her not to, arguing that dwelling on beauty is a waste of time. Music, on the other hand, has a transformative social effect, so he invites her to join his band as they tour Taiwan. Chang Shu is thus torn between national imperatives and her lover's argument on the one hand, and her family's wishes on the other. The film resolves this tension through musical performance. Emilie Yueh-yu Yeh has shown how, through intertexual references and shot-reverse-shot structures, *Land of the Brave* uses popular song to rally the community under the name of the nation. As an "integrating force," the songs sung by Ching-tao's band bring together all sectors of the population regardless of age, race, class, and geographical location.[49] I would further emphasize that this communal spirit also borrows energy from the film's romantic momentum: the excitement of the musical numbers generates the audience's fervor in large part because we read it as the collaboration of lovers we want to see get together. This fervor, along with the intertextual excitement of spotting cameos by pop stars like Pao Mei-sheng and Chen Chien-fu and hearing the popular track "Descendents of the Dragon," convinces us to side with nation and romance against the non-patriotic, non-romantic, and non-utilitarian interests of Chang Shu's parents, who, upon discovering the infectious music, ultimately understand the power of love and the importance of sacrificing for the nation.

Even less overtly propagandistic films narrated the dilemma of going or staying as a question of romance at an especially isolationist and nationalistic historical moment. Galaxy Film's *Lovable You* (aka *Cute Girl*, 1980) and Ta Chung Pictures' *Spring in Autumn* (1980) depict the emotional confusion of women expected to follow their boyfriends abroad. In both cases, the boyfriend is an unattractive, snooty bore and, in both, the woman falls in love with another man: a fun-loving local engineer played by Kenny Bee. Directed by Hou Hsiao-hsien and shot by Chen Kun-hou, *Lovable You* ridicules the desire to go abroad as tedious and insincere, while staying in Taiwan is fun and a more authentic way to live life.

Directed by Chen Kun-hou and written by Hou Hsiao-hsien, *Spring in Autumn* concerns the anguish of the pregnant Annie (played by Joan Lin) whose boyfriend has left for the US and expects her to join him there. She chooses instead to stay in Taiwan with local engineer Cheng Wei. Unlike *Lovable You*, a comedy that can reject the foreign through ridicule, *Spring in Autumn* convinces us through moments of pathos that Annie makes the ethical choice in leaving her US boyfriend in favor of the rootsy Cheng Wei. Most powerful is a scene with an old neighbor whose grown son wants him to move to the US and live with him and his wife. The neighbor grudgingly accepts his fate, and we sympathize with his regret. He refuses to sell his house, a sign that he values only the local as his home. "What good is America anyway?" he asks. His words resonate with Annie's own predicament and we do not wish the same fate on her. Cheng Wei—along with his cute brother and sister and his charming dedication to family—stands for the local as home that Annie would lose should she move abroad with the father of her unborn child. The older generation's sacrifice is enough; the young adults must learn from past mistakes and forge a happier future—one based in Taiwan, not America.

Chen Kun-hou would go on to make the landmark film *Growing Up* (1983), often considered one of the first Taiwanese "New Cinema" films, and Hou Hsiao-hsien would be crowned the movement's figurehead with such films as *A Time to Live and a Time to Die* (1985) and *A City of Sadness* (1989). Many critics, both local and international, have celebrated the New Cinema movement for marking an ideological and aesthetic break from the past. However, as scholars begin to trace the movement's pre-history, it is becoming evident that the New Cinema forged something "new" by reworking long-standing cinematic traditions.[50] In 1985, before the Taiwan New Cinema was established as a major movement in world cinema, critic (and future *Crouching Tiger, Hidden Dragon* co-writer) Tsai Kuo-jung included Chen Kun-hou and Hou Hsiao-hsien in his seminal survey of melodrama in Chinese cinema. While Tsai notes Chen's and Hou's new directions into what he calls "realism," he also acknowledges that the directors do so by inverting the more fantastic elements of film romance (*langman wenqing pian*).[51]

## *The disruption of arrival*

In the previous section, I show that departure is rendered ethical through the promise of a utilitarian return. However, many films about overseas students further complicate this narrative by posing arrival back to Taiwan in terms of disruption: the arrival of the overseas student disrupts stable family values, and the arrival itself (which should be heroic) is disrupted by Taiwanese society's unexpected, selective rejection of the overseas student. These films frequently begin with the overseas student's arrival, but assumes him or her to be a poor romantic partner because of the associations of the overseas with sexual impropriety, with upper-class stuffiness, or with loss of "home" virtues. The films then proceed to reintegrate the overseas student by overcoming these assumptions (either by disproving them or by qualifying them), or to reject the overseas student outright as a potential romantic partner.

Three of director Pai Ching-jui's early films deal with the disequilibrium caused by the return of overseas students. *Accidental Trio* (aka *Not Coming Home Today*, 1968) follows the sexual misadventures of three characters in Taipei. Pai intersects the three mostly independent stories (they take place in the same apartment building) as they play out over one day and night, showing how each character is seduced away from the virtues of home, but ultimately stops short of transgressing filial duties and returns to their wives, children, or parents. Interestingly, two of the three stories are instigated by the sudden arrival of former overseas students who chose to continue living abroad following graduation. One of the three stories is of the innocent, sexually suppressed Chen Chen, who is the teenage daughter of a devout Christian father. On a rare day that Chen Chen is able to sneak away from her father's close eye, she meets a notorious womanizer who studied music in Europe and is now living in the US as a journalist. Appropriately nicknamed "Devil," the overseas student looks his name with his evil eyes and shadowy features. Devil exudes an exotic charm, throwing in occasional English phrases and smoothly getting Chen Chen drunk. Devil's status as a non-utilitarian overseas student translates in the comedy of a hedonistic playboy; his idea of smooth talk is proudly admitting to Chen Chen that he studied in four universities but graduated from none. The film's second story involves the reappearance of Anna into the life of Hua-cheng. When they were studying in the United States four years ago, Anna and Hua-cheng were briefly engaged. After their engagement ended, Anna decided to stay in the US and is now married to a man she doesn't love. Meanwhile, Hua-cheng returned to Taiwan and is now in an affectionate marriage. Anna arrives with the intention of seducing Hua-cheng and perhaps breaking up his marriage and winning him back. In Taiwan, they play golf (which the film dubs an "American" activity) and have sex (presumably also related to overseas impropriety). Both Chen Chen and Hua-cheng, as well as the protagonist of the third story, manage to find their way back home (to father in the first story, and wife in the second). All three stories come together and all sexual transgressors convincingly retreat home in large part due to the glue of the film's playful theme song ("Not Coming Home Today") that has since become a classic.[52] The song, sung by Yao Su-yung, shadows each story with its provocative declaration of unfiliality, as well as its warning: "Don't forget the sweetness of home." With its instantly singable melody and memorable lyrics, the theme song sutures the viewer into identifying with "home" as the film's ethical center. "Home" here refers to the domestic, Confucian home of parent–child and husband–wife. However, since two of the three stories concern the threat from non-utilitarian overseas students, and since the film begins by suggesting the generalizable nature of these stories (the credits and theme song play over images of anonymous apartment buildings throughout Taipei), we can expand "home" to also connote a larger local/national space that needs to be protected from the vices of the overseas world.

The national dimension of the arrival of the overseas student is more pronounced in Pai Ching-jui's most acclaimed film, *Home Sweet Home* (1970). As the classic example of a film that begins and ends at an airport, *Home Sweet Home* explores the emotional turbulence of six overseas student characters who visit Taiwan, only to decide to stay for good. All six arrive in Taipei on the same flight, and are scheduled to return to the states together several days later. In between arrival and departure, they all learn the values of home (represented by family, sexual propriety, and comfort), although some only come to this conclusion at the last minute just before departure. The multiple characters are organized into three narratives, each of which melodramatically resolves the quandary of individual and romantic will against the pressures of family and nation.[53] In the first, Chih-yun brings home his overseas Chinese wife Ju-yin. Chih-yun's mother fears that her son has married a woman with a "strange foreignness," and is relieved to discover that she is modestly dressed, pretty, and, most importantly, genteel. Ju-yin is quickly assimilated into Chih-yun's family. Meanwhile, Chih-yun is re-assimilated for having brought home an ideal Chinese wife. They decide to stay in Taiwan. The second story involves an overseas student named Len Lu, who is just the sort of woman Chih-yun's mother feared: trampy, prone to drunkenness, and impulsive—the classic unsuitable mate of Healthy Realism. Len Lu already has a sugar daddy in the US, but decides to try her luck back in Taiwan with an old flame named Wang Pu. However, Wang Pu is in a budding relationship with an innocent local artist named Hwei-min. Wang Pu scolds Len Lu: "These years you were abroad, you didn't pick up any good traits, only bad ones," referring to her un-ladylike moodiness and unruly sexuality. Len Lu's sexuality represents a threat to Wang Pu and Hwei-min's "decent" romance, and her re-assimilation requires her to denounce both men and start living with women for a change.

While the first two stories of *Home Sweet Home* have fairly obvious resolutions (bring home a good Chinese wife in the first, become a purified Chinese woman in the second), the final story is more torn, and, as a result, more poignant. That it can still find an "ethical" solution speaks to how convincing the ideology of Chinese nationalism was for viewers uneasy about the problem of the overseas student. After receiving his PhD in the United States, Wu Ta-jen stayed, and became involved with a white woman with whom he has a son. However, Ta-jen already had a wife and son in Taiwan who have faithfully been waiting for his return after ten years. Ta-jen is not depicted as evil or womanizing, as is the sleazy overseas student Ho Fan, a character from a subplot in the first story. Played by Ko Chun-hsiung, Ta-jen is classically handsome and decent in dress and demeanor. In silence, he strains to not offend his Taiwan wife with the truth of his adultery. Meanwhile, neither his US nor Taiwan sons blame him for not being an ideal father. In fact, it is their remarkable composure and forgiveness that makes Ta-jen so conflicted. Both sons deliver gut-wrenching lines that stir the audience in both directions, and confirm to Ta-jen that he is indeed stuck with an impossible dilemma. In a telegram, his US son pleads with him in English, "Dad, please get divorced as quickly as possible and come back to the states. I love you." Meanwhile, Ta-jen overhears his Taiwan son innocently ask his mother, "Dad really loves mother, doesn't he?" to which she can't bear to answer. Hearing the loyal words of innocent sons, we as viewers are left unable to choose one side over the other.

Or are we? The humanistic dilemma of betraying faultless sons is clearly impossible to resolve, so the film relies on gendered, class, ethnic, and national factors to ground the cosmopolitan back in Taiwan. *Home Sweet Home* contrasts the two women in Ta-jen's life. His Chinese wife Su-yuan is visually a character who begs for our sympathy: clearly once beautiful, Su-yuan (played by movie star Kuei Ya-lei in haggard makeup) is now sickly and disheveled because of the sacrifices she's been forced to make with her husband out of the country for ten years. Ta-jen's neighbor calls Su-yuan an ideal Chinese wife—a rarity even in classical Chinese stories, he says—for the hardships she's undergone for the sake of his family. Meanwhile, we know little about Ta-jen's American lover, not even her name. In a photo, we see that she is white, well-dressed, and has a modern hairstyle, implying that she is not working class. One of Ta-jen's old friends asks him, "With that foreign woman, can you really be happy?" This then dramatically cuts to an aching slow-motion shot of Su-yuan hard at work in the kitchen, requiring her son's help because she is too sick to tend to her duties alone. The friend's comment that a foreign woman cannot lead to happiness is not explained, nor is it challenged by Ta-jen. The film assumes that such an observation about foreign women should be self-evident, as is the fact that Ta-jen should want a poor but loyal Chinese woman rather than a rich but foreign American. As if the juxtaposition between the two women were not enough, Ta-jen is reminded of his duty to his country as an overseas student. Walking through a construction site, Ta-jen is treated as a celebrity because of a book he's written on water and soil. His old colleague pleads for him to stay and work on the nation's new construction projects—for even an adulterous foreign PhD is better than none at all. The ethnic and patriotic factors ultimately convince Ta-jen to stay, and we don't hear from his American lover and son again.[54]

The sexual impropriety of the overseas student has more tragic consequences in Pai Ching-jui's *Two Ugly Men* (1973). Xiuyun is an aspiring artist stuck in a loveless marriage to her boring husband Jincai. At a party, Xiuyun meets Yu Keyao, an artist who studied in Paris, where he learned not how to paint, but how to appreciate beauty, which he flirtatiously tells her. So desperate to make Xiuyun happy, yet so clueless about the dangers of the overseas student, Jincai allows his wife to keep seeing Keyao, who easily seduces Xiuyun and convinces her to run off with him. Jincai and Keyao represent two extremes: Jincai is obsessed with money, wants to have kids, and is loveless, while Keyao lives only for art, could not care less about children, and is teeming with passion. Their differences are underscored by Pai Ching-jui's signature use of over-the-top sound effects, as in a montage that alternates between Keyao's loud, angry Beatles and American soul music, with Jincai's tame classical. Their opposing traits map two extreme stereotypes about local men and overseas men, the former being overly polite and the latter being overly passionate. Given the expectations of the romance genre, both Jincai and Keyao are unsuitable mates because both are socially awkward and visually unattractive, as the film title reminds us. However, in the end, Xiuyun chooses the local, telling Keyao, "You're an overseas student and an artist. You call businessmen uncultured, you call the elites hypocrites. But at least they know how to treat women and love their wives." But it is too late, as Jincai has committed suicide because he feels he has lost Xiuyun. According to the film, the arrival of the overseas student brings sexual release, but also unnecessary complications that lead to a disruption of life and domestic order. In a classic scenario of melodrama, Xiuyun is too late in realizing Jincai's love for her and the sacrifices he has made for her happiness. Her suffering allows us to re-experience and re-appreciate the sentimental endurance of the local man under threat from the foreign.

Despite the extreme one-dimensional depiction of the overseas student in *Two Ugly Men*, these examples reveal that Taiwanese cinema had many, often conflicting, stereotypes for the overseas student. (There are "good traits" and "bad traits" as *Home Sweet Home*'s Wang Pu reminds us.) When the overseas student arrives in Taiwan, he may turn out to be the loyal, virtuous man ready to contribute to the local economy, as with Chih-yun in *Home Sweet Home*, or the brainy (and as it turns out, brawny) nuclear engineering masters Li Ping in the romantic comedy *Run Lover Run* (Richard Chen, 1975). Or he may be the philandering "Devil" of *Accidental Trio* or womanizing Ho Fan of *Home Sweet Home*. What matters is that they prove to their lovers, their families, and their neighbors that they can espouse local or national values, proof that must be spelled out sentimentally to contain the disruption of the overseas student's arrival. The revelation of their filiality to the family, their romance for the spouse, and their loyalty to the nation comes cinematically through the codes of melodrama: a moving theme song that grounds the characters in the family (as in *Accidental Trio* and to a lesser extent *Home Sweet Home*), or scenes where the overseas student pathetically discovers the pain he or she has caused those in Taiwan (as with the Len Lu and Ta-Jen stories in *Home Sweet Home*).

## *Fantasies of romantic space*

One of the most enduring misconceptions of the Chiung Yao film (in its generic sense) is that its drama is confined to the "three *tings*": the living room (*ke ting*), the kitchen (*can ting*), and the coffee shop (*kafei ting*). Meant as an insult, the "three *tings*" designation refers to the films' low-production values and cookie-cutter settings and scenarios. While the films are surely formulaic, and characters do frequently appear in these locations, the Chiung Yao film also imagines, and sometimes requires, the world beyond these domestic spaces.[55]

Perhaps because there is no convenient "*ting*" word to denote it, the "three *tings*" label overlooks one of the most important and prevalent locations of the Chiung Yao films: nature, especially the seashore (which includes beaches and cliffs). One of the most enduring clichés of the Chiung Yao film is the musical montage of lovers prancing on a beach or walking through a garden. In addition, so many Chiung Yao-type films evoke natural imagery through their titles: *Moon River, Gone with the Cloud, Cloud of Romance, The Clouds Know Your Name, The Wild Goose on the Wing, Where the Seagull Flies, A Love Seed, Love Comes from the Sea, Love under a Rozy Sky, The Marigolds, Orchid in the Rain, Rainbow in My Heart, The Valley of Butterfly, Rhythm of the Wave, The Forest of Forever, Evergreen Tree, Green Green Meadow, The Green Green Grass of Home*, and so forth. Lee Taindow, as many do, disparages this clichéd cornucopia of abundant vegetation and blissful landscapes, writing that these "images of wind, flowers, snow, and the moon" are "decadent" and "out of touch with reality."[56] On the other hand, I read such imagery as a poetic extension of the films' romantic, sentimental interrogation of a rapidly changing Taiwan coming to terms with its anxious place in the world. Nature in these films metaphorically serves as a utopic (and thus impossible) world—a space alone for lovers—away from the pressures of family, nation, and society.[57] Emilie Yeh Yueh-yu calls this utopia "an escape from obstructions."[58] Eva Illouz calls nature "the romantic décor par excellence" and a utopic "transgression" of capitalism whereby the absence of "references to social, family, or gender roles, enables the full expression of 'pure' feelings and thereby releases the authentic self."[59] In the overseas student narrative, nature may be an escape from the pressure of having to go abroad, or nature may be *in* the overseas world: a place away from Taiwan to escape to. On whichever nation or continent, nature in these films is a liminal space—a cosmos between home and other obligations. On the omnipresent beaches and seashores, it is the hazy boundary between home and not-home, a fantasy space of frozen time for lovers to dwell before the centripetal or centrifugal pressures of society pull them in or launch them away. Coming to terms with what counts as home and not-home, or negotiating the boundary between accommodation and exclusion, is the work of the sentimental, as Rey Chow argues.[60] These sublime scenes of nature thus capture the romantic spirit of defiance against the unyielding pressures of staying/going, inside/outside, and ethical/unethical. In these images of sandy frolics and forest adventures is a refusal to be a good or bad son or daughter. But this is a defiance that both the characters and the audience know is doomed, for the pain of the sentimental—the happy tears of self-sacrifice for the sake of duty—haunts every slow-motion embrace and deranged zoom-in to lovers' enraptured faces.

As Leo Braudy has written, films about nature "assert the need for a reconnection to what is vital in nature in order that we might escape the dilemmas history has forced upon us."[61] Indeed, vitality is what is sought by otherwise suppressed lovers when they inhabit their private playgrounds out in nature and away from the sweeping tides of globalization. Vitality is at the same time also what is in danger of being sacrificed in the emotional submission to the national/familial order in the films' sentimental finales. In *Love in a Cabin* (Pai Ching-jui, 1972), electrical engineering student Ying-shi (played by Alan Tang) romances journalist Cheng Ling (played by Chen Chen) in her cabin away from the city. There, they can escape to the beach, make love, and hold a private wedding ceremony for themselves. However, Ying-shi's father has other plans in store for his son. As a young man, his father gave up a Harvard scholarship to marry early and raise a family, and now he doesn't want his son to make the same mistake with Cheng Ling. However, Ying-shi refuses to study in the US, instead electing to stay with his lover in the cabin away from the world. Cheng Ling, on the other hand, comes to realize what an important opportunity overseas study is for Ying-shi, and sacrifices her own romantic satisfaction by leaving him so that he can go abroad. Her decision, based on the assumption that overseas study is more desirable than love, leads to a series of misunderstandings and conflicts, culminating in Ying-shi's death in a motorcycle accident. In *Love in a Cabin*, differing values regarding the overseas student (her belief that overseas study trumps love, versus his faith that love is more important) lead to tragedy for all. Ying-shi wants to uphold the fantasy of the cabin, but Cheng Ling sides with his family. Her sacrifice draws Ying-shi back into the influence of his father, and the fantasy of the romantic space away from the world shatters in violence.

In other cases, characters seek a private romantic space as a reprieve from the hardships of foreign study once they have arrived overseas. In *Long Way from Home*, Wei-yang, a full-time Berkeley civil engineering student and part-time Chinatown restaurant waiter, escapes the stress of study and work by spending time with his love interest Ai-hua by the rocky shores of San Francisco. As they run by the ocean in slow motion, a sentimental love theme, "Silver Waves," overtakes the soundtrack: "At our side are the pristine waves,/symbolizing our warm getaway./Let's soak in the silver waves and seagulls,/let's follow their lead without fear." The seashore scene takes place on the Pacific, on the border of San Francisco and Taiwan; the lyrics walk the character along that shimmery border. Later, the song (and flashbacks from the shore) will be reprised as reminders of their utopic romantic past when Ai-hua decides to give up her life in San Francisco and move with Wei-yang back to Taiwan, where he will work on the nation's Ten Construction Projects.

Similarly, in *Home Sweet Home*, four of the six overseas students visit Taiwan to escape something in the United States. For instance, newlyweds Chih-yun and Ju-yin flee their confining lives in New York by spending time on Chih-yun's parents' farm in Taiwan. They take a stroll through the hills and fields, and contrast Taiwan with their environment in the US. Chih-yun remarks, "In New York, I feel like a machine. Here, I feel like a real human being." Ju-yin adds that in the US, they never see the sun and are cramped in small spaces all day. Their romantic rejuvenation of vitality in Taiwan is further warmed by the violet magic-hour cinematography and the folksy acoustic guitar and whistle playing in the background. They bask in this utopic in-between space and time, but the heavenliness of nature is a suspension of reality, not an equilibrium point. They only reach a happy ending, as most of the overseas characters in *Home Sweet Home* do, by giving up their lucrative futures in the US and calling Taiwan their "home" again.

More cynical is Yang Dao's *Once More in the Evening* (aka *It's Sunset Again*, 1978) about an overseas student-turned-American engineer named Yu Meng-hu who sneaks away from his bratty and demanding wife Ya-ching to visit an old lover He Ling-na in Taiwan. Meng-hu and Ling-na re-kindle old flames, running through the grass and fishing by the water. They settle in a house in the mountains, away from both of their families. But his escape is cut short when Meng-hu is caught by his wife who comes to Taiwan to look for him. She drags him back to the United States and away from his mistress. Meng-hu and Ling-na's days in nature live on, but only in their memories. Ling-na is sometimes seen daydreaming, and we get melancholic flashbacks to their now-lost romantic utopia.

Ling-na's flashbacks to the romantic fantasy space in nature speak to how such scenes are perceived as uncontainable excesses that can't easily be forgotten. Following Christine Gledhill on melodrama, Pat Brereton has argued that sublime scenes of nature frequently surpass the confines of narrative and narrative closure, creating a utopia where human beings (including the viewers) become one with their natural surroundings. Brereton writes about moments of "unmediated" visual immersion in cinematic landscapes, in which the sheer image of nature needs no directorial manipulation to transport the viewer's imagination.[62] Taiwan's 1970s romances, on the other hand, are replete with mediation, and in fact exploit cinematic devices to embellish the scenes of nature with as much ornate excitement as possible in order to achieve sublimity. With the kind of sustained excess that has made them clichés, the scenes of nature inundate us with impressions of the characters' brimming pleasure, depicting through cinematic abstraction the lovers' oneness with nature and oneness with each other. Most obvious is the use of slow motion. Directors like Pai Ching-jui exploit slow motion's simultaneous elation and ghostliness, as in

*Love in a Cabin*, where Pai has his two lovers in the mountains joyously dancing and jumping up and down in slow motion for a full thirty seconds. The intense slow motion of the nature scene contrasts with the way that scenes of family obligation are edited through jarring jump cuts. Pai represents an escape from the visual discontinuities of social pressure as a sort of hyper-continuity (the excess of frames during slow motion) set to dream-like piano music. Liu Chia-chang's *Moon River* (1974), about an overseas woman on a romantic getaway before being married off, immerses us in the moment of romantic bliss through a combination of slow motion and freeze frames of lovers running on a beach. Other typical effects include the use of rack focus and extreme zoom-ins to extravagantly bring the characters in touch with nature, and to intoxicatingly borrow the picturesque world of nature to animate the characters' romance (Figures 1.1a, b, c, d).[63] These scenes often also feature characters making extreme, unnatural movements – jumping, prancing, gesticulating wildly – as if the widescreen fantasies require the characters to make bigger, overly articulate bodily movements. The uncanny other-worldiness of the scenes also comes from the fact that these locations are emptied of all other human beings, creating a utopic "time for us," to borrow the title of one of the most popular English songs in Taiwan during this era.[64]

We should also not overlook the importance of music and pop songs in enveloping such nature scenes with a mood of private romance. The mere

**Figures 1.1a and 1.1b**  Rack focus from flowers to lovers (from *Moon River*, Liu Chia-chang, 1974)

**Figures 1.1c and 1.1d**  Extreme zoom-in onto lovers in nature (from *The Wild Goose on the Wing*, Liu Li-li, 1979)

presence of non-diegetic music and vocals highlights such scenes as distinct—a space for lovers carved out of the film's ordinary audio-visual world. The songs thus correspond to the sudden appearance of cinematic devices well: jovial pop songs accompany the jarring and rapid edits of peppy running by the beach or the flirtatious pushing of one's partner into the ocean. Slow-motion scenes often accompany sentimental ballads bearing the title of the film—the *zhutiqu*. In such moments, the song tends to become the center of attraction, not only because it replaces all diegetic sound, but also because the songs circulated heavily in records and on the radio around the time of the films' release and thus were doubly familiar to audiences. Song lyrics frequently appear subtitled, literally replacing the space usually occupied by dialogue subtitles.[65] But aside from these verbal and intertextual attributes, there are thematic (in both senses of the word) functions of the songs in lifting the audience's emotions and giving life to the characters' private escapes. Building on Claudia Gorbman and Caryl Flinn, Emilie Yeh Yueh-yu astutely argues that the songs give form, however abstractly, to what otherwise can't be shown on film: sexual satisfaction, the transgression of patriarchy, a relief from bourgeois confines.[66] Like the utopia forged by nature's excess of narrative that Brereton describes, popular song's aura of romanticism threatens to escape the pressures of conformity (both to narrative as well as to family/nation structures), letting the characters and the audience take refuge in the fanciful lyrics and sentimental melodies.

The use of the *zhutiqu* in Liu Chia-chang's *Moon River* is worth examining more closely. The film's English title already intertextually suggests lyrical movie music, setting the mood for a film involving love, sacrifice, human trade, and nature. Meanwhile, the film's story brings to mind another Audrey Hepburn film, *Roman Holiday* (William Wyler, 1953). One night, a journalist, Ku, stumbles upon Rona, a beautiful, although drunk and disheveled, woman on his doorstep. Ku reluctantly takes her into his home and lets her stay the night, which causes him to miss an important press conference the next morning. However, it turns out that Rona is the rich overseas Chinese from New York that Ku was supposed to interview at the press conference. Soon, Ku and Rona fall in love. However, Rona is to be married to a Thai prince, and is only in Taiwan temporarily so that her family can announce her marriage to the press there.[67] Ku discovers her identity, as well as her nuptial fate, and has the option of pursuing her anyway, in hopes that she will refuse her arranged marriage. However, Ku's father advises him not to, for Rona's marriage to a Thai prince would help strengthen the nation's relationship with other countries.[68] Ku acquiesces, and in a meet-and-greet between Rona and journalists during a press conference that mirrors a similar one in *Roman Holiday*, Ku holds back his tears and acquiesces to his father and his country.

The title song plays in the film, in either its vocal or instrumental versions, to accentuate Rona's sadness over being married off and, later, over having to leave Ku, the actual object of her affection. For instance, the song appears when Ku asks Rona to leave the morning after she arrives drunk, when Rona tells Ku her ideals about "pure love," or when Rona and Ku say goodbye on the same staircase on which they first met. During the final press conference, Rona and Ku say nothing to each other; all we hear is the instrumental version of the theme song. This mirrors an earlier moment, when Rona composes a letter to Ku; we don't know what she's writing, yet the song tells us everything we need to know.

But what exactly does it say? Lyrics, of course, are one means of denotation in popular music. Here, the lyrics describe a narrator who wants to be free of inhibitions, to find her true self by floating along with nature:

Cloud river, ah cloud river,
Cloud river, I find myself in you.
Gone with the wind,
I still haven't found my true self.

Distant pieces of the white vast cloud river,
Like a misty fog covering over me.
I hope the breeze blows me along the cloud river,
Freeing me to the uninhibited shores.[69]

Here, the cloud river and the wind stand for a natural refuge against the pressures that have kept the singer from finding her true self. These are also images of movement: a breeze that blows, a river that flows. Such movement is not anchored in any specific geographical location; it only points to a fantastical "out-there." In the context of *Moon River*, the motif of movement aptly describes Rona's desire to escape her past in New York and her future in Thailand, and perhaps even the press conferences and family obligations of her present in Taiwan. Nature is associated with her beach and garden strolls with Ku in their private romantic utopia.

However, an interpretation of the song's verbal aspects does not completely account for its power, especially because most of the song's appearances in the film are instrumental. Indeed, many of the song's melodic aspects also bathe the scene in dreams of an escape to nature. In its complete version, played when Rona writes the letter, the song begins with a pleasant high-pitched tremolo, conjuring images of birds chirping and flapping their wings. This is followed by an electric guitar opening that descends with the reverb-y sway of a 1950s prom

## 48 Worldly Desires

**Figure 1.2** Electric guitar opening to the *Moon River* title theme

ballad (Figure 1.2). The instrumental opening has a descending melody, but it descends in steps, alternating downward movements with smaller upward ones, creating a rocking fall, like a leaf descending to earth. The melody then ascends briefly as if blown up by a gust of wind. The image of wind is later concretized in the song's lyrics, and by the entire film's general focus on a character who travels around the world, and finds the most joy cavorting in a fantasy of nature.[70]

Following the instrumental introduction is a main melody with an ABAB structure. The "A" sections are primarily made up of several ascending–descending phrases, which pop music semiotician Philip Tagg has called a "tumbling structure" of melody.[71] In other words, the melodies go up only to come back down. In the first two phrases, we hear the melody go up from F# to G#, only to stumble down to D#. The second phrase starts from that D#, jumps up even higher than ever to a high B, before stumbling back to G#, and back to where we started at F#. The effect is of not being able to break free of gravity, which corresponds to the sense of suppression sung in the lyrics during this section ("I still haven't found my true self"). However, the song's "B" section comes with a gust of optimism. The percussion picks up the rhythm and the singer unleashes lyrics about blowing away with the wind and rushing away with the river. The notes accelerate and are more staccatoed, a contrast with the more lyrical "A" section, and that contributes to the utopic daze of the lyrics ("Freeing me to the uninhibited shores"). Instead of tumbling down, the melodies here ascend, higher and higher, ultimately hitting a high D#, which section "A" came nowhere close to achieving. And whereas the phrases in section "A" mostly ended on a downward interval, all of the phrases in section "B" end upward. That the song ends not on the restraint of section "A," but rather on the total freedom of section "B," makes it a song of romantic and personal utopia. However, that the song is then played over scenes of departure, loss, and resignation to fate adds a sense of bitter irony. In scenes without dialogue, the title theme sings the characters' unsaid desires, yet the more pessimistic proceedings in the scene confirm for us that these desires are impossible. We return once more to Rey Chow's "mood of endurance." Despite the freedom expressed through the music, Rona must leave for the sake of her family, and

Ku must let her for the sake of the nation. The euphoria of romance that the film sings so compellingly must be sacrificed.

The overflow of emotion in the face of inevitable containment is perhaps the guiding sentiment in the Chiung Yao melodramas, and time and again it is the music and the fantasy of escape that carries this sentiment most forcefully and memorably. Critic and historian Huang Ren writes of Pai Ching-jui's Chiung Yao adaptation *Fantasies behind the Pearly Curtain*: "[The film represents] the lowest rung of Pai Ching-jui's abilities.... Luckily the lonely fury of the music, the beauty of the sets, and the nice romantic atmosphere, through sound and image make up for the holes in the script."[72] Although Huang insists that it is a coherent script, and not the aforementioned audio-visual spectacles, that accounts for a film's quality, his suggestion that these elements can overcome other shortcomings speaks to why *Fantasies* was the year's second highest-grossing Chinese-language film in Taiwan and why it has remained a favorite. And, thus, it is precisely in terms of the music and settings that we should engage the film textually.

*Fantasies behind the Pearly Curtain* relies on its title theme song, composed by Liu Chia-chang with lyrics by Chiung Yao, to convey high-school graduate Chi-ping's desires to escape the high expectations of her parents and the perfection of her older sister, who has just received a scholarship to study abroad. Chi-ping did not make it into college, and thus her access to escape is limited to her own imagination while peering through the pearly curtains in her bedroom, and by marrying the divorcee (and possible womanizer) Yung-fan, a former overseas student and now cosmopolitan businessman. Yung-fan proves his love to Chi-ping (and to the audience) because he composes the song "Fantasies behind the Pearly Curtain" for her. Its lyrics and melody give musical form to her hidden yearning to find somebody who will take her away. Yung-fan does, flying her to his forest home in the snowy hills of Italy. He takes her to see her first opera and her first bullfight, and vacations with her in the Netherlands, Greece, and Egypt. Indeed, as Huang Ren may note, it is music and setting that sweep Chi-ping and the audience off their feet. Yet, while abroad, Chi-ping knows that her fantasy of escape must come to an end and that she must resolve the tensions with her family by returning to Taiwan. "We are overseas," she maintains to her cosmopolitan husband, for whom nothing is foreign. "Of course, this isn't our home." Her own fantasies of cosmopolitan romance are curbed by the pressures of home—which connotes both family and nation.

I would argue that this desire to leave and fantasize anyway despite having to eventually be roped back into the home is inscribed musically in the very first phrase of the title song's melody. The lyrics are simply "I have a pearly fantasy." The melody, on the other hand, unleashes an unexpected gush of affect. The first four notes of the song (A, B, C#, and E) ascend along a basic pentatonic scale on A. This four-note sequence has many precedents in popular song and typically continues along the pentatonic scale with an additional two half-steps interval (F#) as in pop standards like George Gershwin's "Someone to Watch Over Me," Duke Ellington's "In a Sentimental Mood," and even the title song of the later Chiung Yao adaptation *Cloud of Romance* (Chen Hong-lie, 1977). However, "Fantasies behind the Pearly Curtain" surprises the listener by foregoing the expected two half-steps in favor of rocketing up nine half-steps to a high C#. The high C# calls attention to itself because it uncommonly jumps several notes on the pentatonic scale and because the large interval makes it difficult to sing (always notable in a culture of karaoke and sheet music[73]). The high C#, not surprisingly, corresponds to the Chinese character *"you"* ("secret" or "private") in the lyrics. At this unexpectedly high pitch, the C# underscores a private fantasy in excess of the norm. As sung by Xiao Lizhu for the film, the character *"you"* is a melismatic combination of C# and B, and Xiao's melancholic delivery of the surprising C# and its subsequent fall to B conjures a number of emotional possibilities: a regretful over-reaching, a confidence in spite of resistance, a longing for a place that does not exist.

The film comes back to this musical theme repeatedly throughout, in either its instrumental or vocal versions, to remind us of this sentiment for an impossible transcendence. When it appears in the film—as when Chi-ping's suitors announce their love to her, when Chi-ping's sister loses her leg and therefore can no longer study abroad, when Chi-ping flashes back to rolling in the Italian snow with Yung-fan—the title song keeps this fantasy of transcendence alive, and it crushes us because the melodrama repeatedly informs us that such a transcendence is impossible without compromise: Chi-ping can have romance but must return home; Chi-ping's sister can go abroad but must sacrifice romance.

## *Ghostly return*

In many ways, the title theme of *Fantasies behind the Pearly Curtain* haunts the two sisters, reminding them of dreams of love and travel that can never be. Haunting is one of the more vivid tropes of the sentimental, evoking shadows of other possibilities of the self that we are conditioned to ignore, yet cannot. Haunting, especially by ghostly figures, also provides a glimpse at our counterparts "out there"—cosmopolitan versions of ourselves who we lost once they flew beyond the borders of the familiar. Not surprisingly then, haunting is a provocative strategy for depicting the anxieties inflicted by overseas students—children, siblings, lovers—floating abroad in an unknowable space. Two Taiwanese films during *liuxuesheng* fever, *Love Can Forgive and Forget* (Liao Hsiang-hsiong, 1971) and *My*

*Cape of Many Dreams* (Liu Li-li, 1981), imagine how families in Taiwan cope with the deaths of their daughters studying abroad by conjuring the daughters' ghosts through ventriloquist figures.

An entire field of critical inquiry has emerged surrounding ghosts and the trope of haunting. Inspired by Jacques Derrida's suggestion in *Specters of Marx* that ontology is actually a "hauntology" whereby living and dead, past and present (and indeed future), presence and non-presence, existence and non-existence co-exist through the figure of the ghost that straddles all such categories. For Derrida, the choice to acknowledge the spectral figures that surround us is an ethical one, for such a choice asks that we understand the ghosts that we have made (through war, violence, racism, colonialism, sexism, and so on), the ghosts we are making, and the ghosts yet to be. It matters not if such ghosts exist, for questioning the ontology of the specter is an elision of responsibility. Instead, Derrida directs us toward the hauntings that are everywhere but nowhere, reminding us that justice requires that we "speak *of the* ghost, indeed *to the* ghost and *with* it."[74]

But what exactly is the ghost Derrida refers to? In *Specters of Marx*, Derrida most directly refers to the ghost that is Marx (an especially contested conceit in the post-USSR, "end of history" period in which Derrida gave the lectures that resulted in the book), as well as the many ghosts present in Marx's writing (such as the specters of labor in the commodity and the specter of communism's haunting of Europe). From these ghosts, theorists have postulated more generalized ones rattling the many chains latched by global capitalism. These are the ghosts that comprise a shadow economy—undocumented immigrants, guest laborers, sponsored workers, non-immigrant international students—often women or people of color, all of whom remain on the peripheries of both their home and host nations, occupying a spectral position of a present non-presence where their status as citizens is precisely a non-status. As Vicente L. Rafael reminds us in his study of Filipino history, it is not only the underclass that is occluded from sight, but also the privileged sojourner and the immigrant who turn up as spectral presences that haunt the nation and the economy. Rafael acknowledges that there are differences between these variations of the overseas Filipinos—what Aihwa Ong has termed "splintering cosmopolitanism"[75]—but allows these different ghosts to talk to one another, and to us, in order to better elucidate globalization's often mysterious effects on identity and the nation.[76] Similarly, Taiwan is an island of haunting, where capital exploits aboriginal tribes and other oppressed groups, and attracts migrants (especially from Southeast Asia) and then ritualistically renders them invisible. And then there are those sent abroad in the name of the nation or the economy—workers, students—who are thus absent from society, but then conjured locally in everything from popular culture to political speeches to family remembrances. Why and how these conjurings happen, and what they have to do with the emotions surrounding the cosmopolitan, is the motivation behind my readings of *Love Can Forgive and Forget* and *My Cape of Many Dreams*.

Both films, strangely enough, are about the deaths of young women studying abroad overseas, and the trouble that follows when unrelated lookalikes are found on the streets of Taiwan and then hired to "play" the dead woman so as not to upset the victim's grandparents, who do not yet know of her death.[77] In both instances, the lookalike is a dummy ghost in a ventriloquist act meant to soften the blow of cosmopolitanism and its potential for tragedy (such as death in a foreign world, or death in a plane crash). Gray Kochhar-Lindgren argues that we should pay attention to the ways we ventriloquize the dead, for doing so allows us to better understand the terms on which we choose to live.[78]

In the CMPC film *Love Can Forgive and Forget*, the young Zhang Meihong (played by Judy Ongg) is trained to speak, sing, and dance as the American *xiao liuxuesheng*[79] Xiao Qi, who has gone missing in a plane crash. Meihong is given new clothes and lessons in behavior and posture by Xiao Qi's family in Taiwan, so as to please Xiao Qi's aging grandfather who has certain expectations and anxieties about his granddaughter who has been overseas for seven years. As in the training sequences of the MP&GI and Shaw musicals we will encounter in Chapter 3, the scenes of Zhang Meihong learning cosmopolitanism are energetic, sensational scenes of a woman's body molded into place. Meihong, to the family's disapproval, is fidgety, spontaneous, and naughty, dances to rock music, chews gum, and wears loudly colorful clothes. She has bad posture and manners, and wears ponytails. Furthermore, she speaks limited English. On the other hand, Xiao Qi is refined, quiet, high class, and likes classical music. Thus, Meihong is trained in what her teachers call "*yang weir*" (literally, the scent of the foreign). She is instructed by a male teacher to walk in a straight line with a book balanced on her head. The camera then cuts down to a close-up of Meihong's sashaying rear end. The instructor then uses his hand to slap her in the rear, disciplining and shaming her wayward sexuality.

When it comes down to performing the cosmopolitan (ventriloquizing the dead Xiao Qi), Meihong struggles, revealing the friction involved when a local girl inorganically embodies the returned overseas student. Meihong proves unable to use a fork and knife, to speak convincing English, or to convert US to New Taiwan Dollars, leading to much comedy. However, it turns out that these qualities of the foreign are unimportant to Xiao Qi's grandfather. Just as Derrida notes that the process of speaking to and through ghosts is one of deciding which specters to remember and inherit, Meihong's ghostly performance of Xiao Qi is ultimately not about mimicking her, but of performing the qualities that the living wish to imagine of those who have died. After several failed attempts at acting the refined cosmopolitan, Meihong tries song and dance. Instead of projecting the foreign on her body and her behavior, she tries to entertain the grandfather in cosmopolitan performance. As with the 1950s and 1960s Mandarin musicals, Meihong performs the song and dance of several Western cultures.[80] She does a flamenco, then puts on a bullfighting performance, and finally sings "Lemon Tree" in English. As much as she can, she integrates the grandfather into each performance—for instance, he, in his wheelchair, plays the bull. What is different about this musical evocation of the cosmopolitan (versus the behavioral one) is that it allows Meihong to actively prove filiality to the grandfather: she is entertaining him, taking care of him, and keeping him company. As it turns out, filiality through the cosmopolitan is what it ultimately takes to convince the grandfather that Meihong is surely Xiao Qi, for that is the specter of a long-lost granddaughter that he wants to imagine. When it is later revealed that Xiao Qi in fact did not die in the plane crash, the grandfather accepts Meihong anyway, for despite her bad habits and spontaneous demeanor (which contrasts directly to the refined Xiao Qi who we finally meet), Meihong demonstrates filial cosmopolitanism, a harmonious combination of two seemingly paradoxical values, a harmony reinforced by the film's culminating *datuanyuan* plus one: the grandfather, the living granddaughter, and her ghostly twin.

In *My Cape of Many Dreams*, the family undergoes a much more strained process of mourning, ghost-conjuring, and exorcism, especially compared to the more optimistic and ideologically transparent *Love Can Forgive and Forget*, which was made by the state-run CMPC. In *My Cape of Many Dreams*, based on a Chiung Yao novel and produced by Chiung Yao's production company Super Star, the dead woman's family is held accountable for pressuring her abroad and therefore leading to her death. Thus, the haunting of the ghost spooks the family into confronting their past actions and present assumptions. The presence of the dead girl's lookalike—the specter's medium or the ventriloquist dummy—provides the family a surrogate with whom to work past the trauma of death via love and forgiveness.

*My Cape of Many Dreams* concerns the Sang family, whose matriarch has already lost a son and daughter-in-law in a plane crash in New York. One of her grandsons, Erh-hsuan (played by Chiung Yao film regular Chin Han) has recently learned that his sister Sang Sang, who had been studying abroad in the United States, committed suicide there. Sang Sang was driven abroad because her family did not approve of her boyfriend Hao-jun (played by Kenny Bee), and having Sang Sang go to study in the US seemed a productive way to break up her romance while giving her a healthy environment. Instead of reporting Sang Sang's death to his dying grandmother, Erh-hsuan enlists a Sang Sang-lookalike named Lu Ya-ching (played by Shirley Lu Hsing-ling) to pretend to be Sang Sang coming back to Taiwan to make peace with the family before the grandmother passes away. When Ya-ching (as Sang Sang) first meets the grandmother, her performance exceeds everyone's expectations. Her mannerisms, her sweet-and-sassiness, and most of all her tearful filiality are spot-on and the grandmother calls their family reunion the best present she has ever received in her eighty years. Meanwhile, Erh-hsuan is so moved by Ya-ching's performance that he starts to fall in love with her—an indirectly incestuous way of assuaging the grief posed by his sister's suicide, a death that he is partly responsible for.

However, Ya-ching soon becomes possessed by Sang Sang's spirit, who arrives on the scene through song. In Sang Sang's old bedroom, Ya-ching discovers a photo of Sang Sang playing a guitar, as well as sheet music to a song called "Cloak of Dreams." Suddenly, we hear acoustic guitar notes play the instrumental opening of the song. The notes drift into the scene with the kind of ghostliness that Michel Chion would call *acousmetre*, the figure we can hear but not see on-screen.[81] The arrival of the song breaks down the usual distinction between diegetic and non-diegetic sound in that its opening guitar notes may be a non-diegetic musical cue in the score, or the pseudo-diegetic reflection of what Ya-ching is hearing in her head, as triggered by the sight of the photograph and the sheet music.[82] But other cues suggest that it is the acoustic presence of Sang Sang's ghost: we are in Sang Sang's old room, and we know of the unresolved circumstances surrounding her suicide. In much writing on spectral figures in literature and film—for instance, Thu-huong Nguyen-vo's study of Vietnamese refugees[83] or Esther M. K. Cheung's work on haunted spaces in Hong Kong[84]—the ghost is evoked through the excess of realism: magical realism in the former and urban realism in the latter. *My Cloak of Many Dreams*, too, conjures Sang Sang's spirit through a ghostly *acousmetre* that overlaps non-diegetic on diegetic, non-presence on presence, the unreal on the real. Our suspicion of the ghost is confirmed when the film then cuts to flashbacks of Sang Sang and her old boyfriend Hao-jun out in nature—on rocks, on grass, by the water, in a garden, smiling at each other, and running on the beach during sunset. When we cut back to Yi-ching, she seems to have absorbed all of those images as if they were her own memories. She should not know what Hao-jun looks like, yet we (and she) see him in the flashbacks. She is becoming Sang Sang in ways that neither she nor Erh-hsuan expected or perhaps even desired when they concocted the conjuring. Yi-ching starts to become fascinated by Sang Sang's old boyfriend Hao-jun, and he with her. The two start to see each other, in nightclubs and out in nature. Hao-jun, who until meeting Yi-ching did not know of Sang Sang's death, starts to play "Cloak of Dreams" on his guitar. Thinking his relationship with Sang Sang also contributed to her death, Hao-jun is haunted by Sang Sang's ghost as well. The song reoccurs throughout the film, in moments of anguish, nostalgia, and regret. It sometimes conveys the innocent joy of returning to an old equilibrium point: when the family was together and Sang Sang and Hao-jun were in love. However, through singer Lee Pi-hua's airy, ambiguous performance of Chiung Yao's ghostly lyrics (about mending a cloak and the mysterious lover who wears it), the song also conveys the impossibility of such a return, since Sang Sang is dead, as her musical ghost reminds us. While the song's usage in the film may not always refer directly to Sang Sang's death, the song captures a mood of responsibility, anguish, and reconciliation, which we may note as having been sparked by the spectral return of Sang Sang.

The love triangle (or rectangle, if we include the dead Sang Sang) feels unresolvable due to a number of factors: there is no easily identifiable unsuitable mate, Hao-jun loves Yi-ching because she reminds him of his dead lover, Yi-ching loves Hao-jun only through the lost memories of a dead woman, Erh-hsuan loves a woman who resembles his dead sister. Despite these complications, each pairing makes sense to us because of the musical score—typically an instrumental variation of "Cloak of Dreams"—which envelops the scenes like a magnetic field that draws the characters together. Each pairing forces on the characters and the viewer a dilemma of how to resolve the love triangle.

Meanwhile, Yi-ching impresses Sang Sang and Erh-hsuan's grandmother, even after the grandmother discovers that Yi-ching is in fact not Sang Sang. As in *Love Can Forgive and Forget*, the imposter's compelling performance of filiality (in both cases confirmed by the presence of her tears, which the films suggest is not fakeable) allows her to be integrated into the family, even after the truth of her identity is revealed. In the sentimental moment of inclusion, the grandmother suggests that Yi-ching should marry Erh-hsuan, thus setting into motion a number of melodramatic machinations that result in their marriage. The film therefore ends with the exorcism of Sang Sang's spirit from Yi-ching's body. The grandmother finds out the truth, thus ending Yi-ching's need to keep channeling Sang Sang. More importantly, the song "Cloak of Dreams" is divorced from Yi-ching's uncanny arrival when it becomes a positive force in everyone's life rather than a haunting presence brought upon by Yi-ching's appearance. At the end of the film, Hao-jun has opted to become farmer, silhouetted dramatically in the final shot at the edge of a cliff at sunset. But he's also a folk singer in the mold of late-1970s Taiwanese rustic campus folk star Yeh Chia-hsiu. In a TV appearance publicizing his debut record, Hao-jun performs "Cloak of Dreams"—except now the song does not connote the haunting of Sang Sang, but rather becomes his inspiration on his road to material and spiritual success. In other words, the specter of Sang Sang lives on, not to create anguish, but to inspire Hao-jun's career and, in a jump of logic that only music can accomplish, also inspires the marriage between Yi-ching and Erh-hsuan, who we see together in love as the song plays in the background. The living have chosen to maintain a dialogue with the ghost so that they can go on living. They need to make peace with Sang Sang, who both Erh-hsuan and Hao-jun in their own ways drove away to the United States and therefore to her death, and they do so by mobilizing her memory into the realm of national/cultural stability (the development of agriculture through the sublime depiction of nature, the reconstitution of filial relations through romance).

Recent evocations of the cosmopolitan in critical theory and in popular culture have been quick to acknowledge that cosmopolitanism is always interrelated with the local and, in linguistic terms, it modifies the local, as in such neologisms as "cosmopolitan patriotism" (Kwame Anthony Appiah[85]) and "cosmopolitan nationalism" (Ulrich Beck[86]). In the melodramas of 1970s Taiwan, nationalism was indeed made cosmopolitan, and the process of modification (that is, the rhetoric of demonstrating how one informs the other) made sense to audiences through the intensification of the romantic impulse from Sinophone literary and cinematic traditions, tempered through the agony and pathos of sacrifice that Rey Chow describes as the sentimental.

But what exactly was the "cosmopolitan" to be added to nationalism? Cosmopolitanism could be found in certain images and locations: high fashion, overseas colleges, airports that begin and end films. These are concrete things and spaces with clear empirical referents. However, the mere presence of things and locations was not sufficient to modify—and, in fact, fuel—nationalism. Cosmopolitanism needed to be embodied. But if the bodies are overseas, and their brains drained from the nation, the empirical body is not so easy to access and represent. Indeed, the body could only return as a specter, and popular culture could only access it through a process of ventriloquism. Speaking as the ghost and taking on its various identities (gendered, sexualized, ethnicized, nationalized) became a way of making sense of the overseas student within the discourses of nation, family, romance, and self. This process ensured that the shadowy figure of the overseas student could be recognizable, containable, and even utilitarian. But what would happen if the cosmopolitan returned and was compromised, deformed, even monstrous? Could they still be contained? To what extent would society and the culture industry even want to contain them? I explore these questions with regards to the mixed-race star and the ABC "returnee" in the next chapter.

# Notes

1. Tzvetan Todorov, *The Poetics of Prose* (Ithaca: Cornell University Press, 1977) 108–12.
2. For a discussion of *datuanyuan* with regards to early cinema in Shanghai, see Zhang Zhen, *An Amorous History of the Silver Screen: Shanghai Cinema, 1896–1937* (Chicago: University of Chicago Press, 2005) 182–7.
3. Zhang Longxi observes that the Daoist dialectic of departure and return is similar to concepts in Buddhism and Confucianism, as well as in Christianity, nineteenth-century American philosophy, and Neoplatonic thought. As such, we should not be surprised that the narrative of departure and arrival is common in world film and literature. Zhang Longxi, "'A Paradise within Thee, Happier Far': The Dialectic of Return and Reversal," *Unexpected Affinities: Reading across Cultures* (Toronto: University of Toronto Press, 2007) 95–125.
4. Bernard P. Wong adds that in addition to the Immigration and Nationality Act of 1965, prospective immigrants were attracted to the United States because of the progress made by the Civil Rights Movement and the opportunities provided by the Equal Opportunity and Affirmative Action programs of the period. Wong, "Hong Kong Immigrants in San Francisco," *Reluctant Exiles? Migration from Hong Kong and the Overseas Chinese*, ed. Ronald Skeldon (Hong Kong: Hong Kong University Press, 1994) 239.
5. Iain Chambers, *Border Dialogues: Journeys in Postmodernity* (London: Routledge, 1990) 58.
6. Anthony Elliott and Charles Lemert, *The New Individualism: The Emotional Costs of Globalization* (London: Routledge, 2006) 3–13.
7. Arjun Appadurai, *Modernity at Large: Cultural Dimensions of Globalization* (Minneapolis: University of Minnesota Press, 2006) 44.
8. Rey Chow, *Sentimental Fabulations, Contemporary Chinese Films* (New York: Columbia University Press, 2007) 17–19.
9. Kung Hung, *Ying chen hui yi lu* (Taipei: Crown, 2005) 147.
10. On cinema's response to the Diaoyutai dispute, see Lu Fei-I, *Taiwan dianying: zhengzhi, jingji, meixue (1949–1994)* (Taipei: Yuanliu, 1998) 180–3.
11. Mark Wollaeger, *Modernism, Media, and Propaganda: British Narrative from 1900 to 1945* (Princeton: Princeton University Press, 2006) xiii.
12. See, for instance, Leo Ou-fan Lee, *The Romantic Generation of Modern Chinese Writers* (Cambridge, MA: Harvard University Press, 1973). Lee also makes the connection between May Fourth fiction and the 1960s and 1970s romantic novels of Chiung Yao, although he does so primarily to critique the latter as bourgeoisie and unsophisticated. Leo Ou-fan Lee, "'Modernism' and 'Romanticism' in Taiwan Literature," *Chinese Fiction from Taiwan: Critical Perspectives*, ed. Jeannette L. Faurot (Bloomington: Indiana University Press, 1980) 21–7.
13. Chow 18; italics are in the original.
14. Linda Williams, "Melodrama Revised," *Refiguring American Film Genres: History and Theory*, ed. Nick Browne (Berkeley: University of California Press, 1998) 42–88.

15. Emilie Yueh-yu Yeh and Darrell William Davis, *Taiwan Film Directors: A Treasure Island* (New York: Columbia University Press, 2005) 30.
16. Guo-juin Hong, *Taiwan Cinema: A Contested Nation on Screen* (New York: Palgrave Macmillan, 2011) 81.
17. Huang Jian-ye, ed. *Kua shiji Taiwan dianying shilu: 1898–2000 (zhong)* (Taipei: Council for Cultural Affairs, 2005) 569. The term was publicized in mainstream movie magazines as well. For instance, see "Huigui Zhongying yi nian lai," *Milky Way Pictorial* 142 (January 1970): 6.
18. Lee Tain-dow, *Taiwan dianying, shehui yu lishi* (Taipei: Yatai, 1997) 122.
19. Huang Ren, "Lianbang tuidong zhengfu dianying zhengce," *Lianbang dianying shidai*, ed. Huang Ren (Taipei: Chinese Taipei Film Archive, 2001) 34–41.
20. Ibid. 35.
21. One example is Liu Hsien-cheng, *Taiwan dianying, shehui yu guojia* (Taipei: Yatai, 1997).
22. Lee Tain-dow 150.
23. James Udden, *No Man is an Island: The Cinema of Hou Hsiao-hsien* (Hong Kong: Hong Kong University Press, 2009) 37.
24. Lee Tain-dow 154.
25. Lin Fang-mei, *Jie du Qiongyao aiqing wangguo* (Taipei: Commercial Press, 2006) ii.
26. Chi Lung-zin, "Qiong Yao xiaoshuo (1963–1979) zhong de xingbie yu lishi," *Liuxing Tianxia: dangdai Taiwan tongsu wenxue lun*, eds Yao-Te Lin and Meng Fang (Taipei: Times Publishing, 1992) 62.
27. In a short essay, Wenchi Lin asks that scholars read the Chiung Yao film in terms of the ethos of "hard work" and other values of Healthy Realism. "More than Escapist Romantic Fantasies: Revisiting Qiong Yao Films of the 1970s," *Journal of Chinese Cinemas* 4.1 (March 2010): 45–50.
28. Leo Ou-fan Lee, "'Modernism' and 'Romanticism' in Taiwan Literature," 22–5.
29. On authorship as a functional discourse, see Michel Foucault, "What is an Author?" *Language, Counter-Memory, Practice: Selected Essays and Interviews*, ed. Donald F. Bouchard (Ithaca: Cornell University Press, 1977) 113–38.
30. Among the more notable writers who studied abroad are Lu Xun, Qian Zhongshu, and Xu Zhimo in the pre-1949 period, and Pai Hsien-yung, Wang Wen-hsing, and San Mao in postwar Taiwan. Among filmmakers, the first director frequently cited for employing his foreign experience to strengthen the Taiwanese film industry is Pai Ching-jui, who studied at the Centro Sperimentale di Cinematografia (Experimental Film Centre) in Rome. See Kung Hung 134–5.
31. David Der-wei Wang, "Jia Baoyu ye shi liuxuesheng: wan qing de liuxuesheng xiaoshuo," *Xiaoshuo Zhongguo: wan qing dao dangdai de zhongwen xiaoshuo* (Taipei: Rye Field, 1993) 229–36.
32. Ming-ju Fan, *Zhong li xun ta: Taiwan nüxing xiaoshuo zonglun* (Taipei: Rye Field, 2008) 111.
33. Ibid. 111–50.
34. Chen Tzong-hsien, "Wo guo fudao liuxuesheng huiguo fuwu zhi yanjiu," MA Thesis, National Chengchi University, 1977, 57–69.

35. J. Megan Greene, *The Origins of the Developmental State in Taiwan: Science Policy and the Quest for Modernization* (Cambridge, MA: Harvard University Press, 2008) 72–3.
36. Ibid. 65.
37. Sun Chen, "Investment in Education and Human Resource Development in Postwar Taiwan," *Cultural Change in Postwar Taiwan*, eds Stevan Harrell and Huang Chün-chieh (Taipei: SMC Publishing, 1994) 103.
38. Greene 119.
39. Chi-ming Hou and Ching-hsi Chang, "Education and Economic Growth in Taiwan: The Mechanism of Adjustment," *Experiences and Lessons of Economic Development in Taiwan*, eds Kwoh-ting Li and Tzong-shian Yu (Taipei: Academia Sinica, 1982) 483.
40. *Liuxue zhi lu* (Taipei: Zhongxi Liuxue, 1973); Wellington Chang, *Meiguo ge daxue ji xueyuan yu liumei jiangxuejin shenqing shuxin* (Taipei: Meidao Meiyu, 1971); see also Shu Cheng Guang, *Au, Niu, Jia, Nanfei liuxue shenqing* (Taipei: Xiaoyuan, 1978); Kan Chu-cheng, *Meijian liuxue shenqing yu shuxin* (Taipei: Zhongxi Liuxue, 1982).
41. Chang Tao-fan, *Liu xuesheng zhi lian* (Taipei: Tao-fan Wenyi, 1978). See also Ma Hsing-yeh, *Wo de liuxue shenghuo* (Taipei: China Daily News, 1981).
42. Tao Longsheng, *Liuxuesheng yu zhongguo shehui* (Taiwan Student Bookstore, 1978); Liu Chi, *Liuxue sanji* (Taipei: Water Buffalo, 1967).
43. Given the diminishing demand for local films in Taiwan in the 1970s, the overproduction by independent producers, and the high cost of filming abroad, Taiwanese films in the 1970s tended to be shot locally. There were also special factors that encouraged films to be about Taiwanese people in Taiwan, rather than Taiwanese abroad, such as the CMPC's decision to end US film shoots following the severing of diplomatic ties in 1979. See Lu Feii-yi 220.
44. Chris Berry, "*Wedding Banquet*: A Family (Melodrama) Affair," *Chinese Films in Focus: 25 New Takes*, ed. Chris Berry (London: BFI Publishing, 2003) 186.
45. Chow 20.
46. Fan 112.
47. Lu Feii-yi 222–3.
48. Campus folk songs (*xiaoyuan mingge*) were simplistic, palatable songs with images of love and innocence. Sonically similar to songs by American performers like Lobo, Simon and Garfunkel, and Peter, Paul, and Mary, the campus folk song performed Chinese youth identity with the backing of the recording industry and the national government. For a discussion, see Tzeng Huoy-jia, *Cong liuxing gequ kan Taiwan shehui* (Taipei: Laureate, 1998) 136–76.
49. Emilie Yueh-yu Yeh, "College Folk and National Identity: *Land of the Brave* (1981)," "A National Score: Popular Music and Taiwanese Cinema," Diss. University of Southern California, 1995, 110.
50. Examples include Hong 87–103 and Udden 28–48.
51. Tsai Kuo-jung, *Zhongguo jindai wenyi dianying yanjiu* (Taipei: Taipei Film Archive, 1985) 277–82.
52. Critic Huang Ren attributes the film's success in part to what he calls a "bizarre" (*guaiyi*) song. The strangeness of its emotional a cappella opening, followed by its fun, bouncy verse, and then a restrained bridge, lends to the awkward feeling of

alternating licentiousness and morality – an ambiguity that matches the film's tone well. Huang Ren, *Dianying alang: Bai Jingrui* (Taipei: Asia-Pacific Press, 2001) 105.

53. As James Wicks eloquently writes, "The situation that the characters experience in the film is precisely the predicament of the populace in Taiwan in general: how can total freedom be achieved when that existence is managed, controlled, and manipulated by the state?" James Wicks, "Projecting a State That Does Not Exist: Bai Jingrui's *Jia zai Taibei/Home Sweet Home*," *Journal of Chinese Cinemas* 4.1 (March 2010): 24.

54. Pai Ching-jui himself reinforces the nationalist fervor of the film: "Overseas students all love the nation," he's quoted as saying in a magazine article on *Home Sweet Home*. "An Interview with Prof. Pai Ching Jui," *Milky Way Pictorial* 142 (January 1960): 18.

55. In the afterword to her 1976 novel *Ren Zai Tian Ya*, Chiung Yao writes that traveling abroad reinvigorated her sense of home and nation, and that the stories she heard of overseas students (*liuxuesheng*) and overseas Chinese (*huaqiao*) were the inspiration for the present book. Chiung Yao, *Ren zai tianya* (Hong Kong: Crown, 1992) 235–6.

56. Lee Tain-dow 167.

57. The potential trangressiveness of the space of nature was well noted at the time, for instance, in the controversy over the song "Olive Tree," sung by Chyi Yu and featured in the film *Your Smiling Face* (Tu Chung-hsung, 1979). The song was banned from radio and television broadcast. Some have suspected that its lyrics (by popular travel novelist San Mao) may encourage young people to leave home and seek solace in the olive trees, flying birds, mountains, and vast grass fields of the lyrics. For a brief description of the controversy, see Ma Shih-fang, "Olive Tree," *Taiwan liuxing yinyue 200 zui jia zhuanji*, eds Cora Tao, Ma Shih-fang, and Yeh Yun-ping (Taipei: China Times Publishing) 124–5.

58. Yeh 68.

59. Eva Illouz, *Consuming the Romantic Utopia: Love and the Cultural Contradictions of Capitalism* (Berkeley: University of California Press, 1997) 92. On romance as a "utopia of transgression," see pages 6–11.

60. Chow 19.

61. Leo Braudy, "The Genre of Nature," *Refiguring American Film Genres: History and Theory*, ed. Nick Browne (Berkeley: University of California Press, 1998) 304.

62. Pat Brereton, *Hollywood Utopia: Ecology in Contemporary American Cinema* (Bristol: Intellect Books, 2005) 13.

63. Udden argues that the use of excessive zoom-ins in 1970s Taiwanese cinema was a way to disguise visual deficiencies resulting from meager resources such as film stock and time restrictions. Udden 40–1. See also David Bordwell, *Figures Traced in Light: On Cinematic Staging* (Berkeley: University of California Press, 2005) 192–4. For a breakdown of the genre's "excessive" stylistic features, see Emilie Yueh-yu Yeh, "The Road Home: Stylistic Renovations of Chinese Mandarin Classics," *Cinema Taiwan: Politics, Popularity and State of the Arts*, eds Darrell William Davis and Ru-shou Robert Chen (London: Routledge, 2007) 203–16.

64. "A Time for Us" is the pop vocal version of Nino Rota's love theme from *Romeo and Juliet* (Franco Zeffirelli, 1968).

65. For a discussion of film songs' intertexuality and film–music symbiosis, see Brian Hu, "The KTV Aesthetic: Popular Music Culture and Contemporary Hong Kong Cinema," *Screen* 47.4 (Winter 2006) 407–24.
66. Yeh 68.
67. Fan Ming-ju observes that overseas women in overseas student literature are frequently depicted as having added exchange value for their ultimate transaction in marriage. Fan 117.
68. By 1974, Thai–ROC relations were already on the brink. Thailand would officially sever ties in favor of the PRC one year later.
69. The various covers of the song have slightly different wordings. My translations are based on the lyrics as sung in the film.
70. Here I interpret the musical structures as what Philip Tagg terms "kinetic anaphones," musical onomatopoeia that mirrors real-world perceptions like drifting or falling. Tagg, "Method and Procedure," *Ten Little Title Tunes*, Philip Tagg and Bob Clarida (New York: Mass Media Music Scholar's Press, 2003) 99–101.
71. Philip Tagg, *Everyday Tonality: Towards a Tonal Theory of What Most People Hear* (New York: Mass Media Music Scholar's Press, 2009) 61.
72. Huang Ren, *Dianying Alang: Bai Jingrui* 146.
73. In fact, the numbered notation (or *"jianpu"*) for the popular title song of *Fantasies behind the Pearly Curtain* was published for fans and potential singers in the pages of the fan magazine *Cinemart*. "Bai Jingrui, Huang Zhuohan song le yi kou qi: Qin Xianglin tongyi yanchu Yi Lian You Meng," *Cinemart* 60 (December 1974): 61.
74. Jacques Derrida, *Specters of Marx: The State of the Debt, the Work of Mourning, & the New International*, trans. Peggy Kamuf (New York: Routledge, 1994) xix; emphasis in the original.
75. Aihwa Ong, "Splintering Cosmopolitanism: Asian Immigrants and Zones of Autonomy in the American West," *Sovereign Bodies: Citizens, Migrants, and the State*, eds Thomas Blom Hansen and Finn Stepputat (Princeton: Princeton University Press, 2005) 257–75.
76. Vicente L. Rafael, "'Your Grief is Our Gossip': Overseas Filipinos and Other Spectral Presences," *White Love and Other Events in Filipino History* (Durham, NC: Duke University Press, 2000) 204–27.
77. A similar scenario occurs in Bu Wancang's *Dreams Come True* (1960), in which a poor flower girl disguises as a rich girl from San Francisco, whose boat arrives late to Hong Kong.
78. Gray Kochhar-Lindgren, "Static: Ghostwriting, Hong Kong, and Globalization," University of Hong Kong, 10 November 2009, lecture.
79. *Xiao liuxuesheng* refers to those who went abroad for foreign study while in primary or secondary school, and thus are assumed to be more assimilated in the host culture than a college- or postgraduate-aged *liuxuesheng*.
80. Meihong is played by Judy Ongg, who was well known at the time for having recently returned to Taiwan after a decade as a teen singing and acting star in Japan. For the audience, knowledge of Ongg's backstory contributes to the authenticity of Meihong's cosmopolitan musical ability and consequently the believability

of her ability to win the grandfather's heart through song. In case the audience did not make the connection between character and acator, the film begins with a friendly reminder: an opening scene shows Meihong at a talent show, where she is noted for her resemblance to one Judy Ongg.

81. Michel Chion, *The Voice in Cinema*, trans. Claudia Gorbman (New York: Columbia University Press, 1999) 17–29.
82. For more on the ghostly effects of film music – the supernatural presence of non-diegetic music, as well as non-diegetic music *as* a manifestation of the supernatural – see K. J. Donnelly, *The Spectre of Sound: Music in Film and Television* (London: BFI Publishing, 2005), especially pages 8–9, 22–4.
83. Thu-huong Nguyen-vo, "History Interrupted: Life and Material Death in South Vietnamese and Diasporic Works of Fiction," *Journal of Vietnamese Studies* 3.1 (Winter 2008): 1–35.
84. Esther M. K. Cheung, *Fruit Chan's Made in Hong Kong* (Hong Kong: Hong Kong University Press, 2009). See also Esther M. K. Cheung, "*Durian Durian*: Defamiliarisation of the 'Real,'" *Chinese Films in Focus II*, ed. Chris Berry (London: BFI Publishing, 2008), 90–7.
85. Kwame Anthony Appiah, "Against National Culture," *Text and Nation: Cross-Disciplinary Essays on National and Cultural Identities*, Peter C. Pfeiffer and Laura García-Moreno, eds. (Columbia: Camden House, 1996) 175.
86. Ulrich Beck, *Cosmopolitan Vision*, Ciaran Cronin, trans. (Cambridge: Polity, 2006) 49.

# Chapter 2

# ABCs, Mixed-race Stars, and Other Monsters of Globalization

In my conversations with individuals who grew up in Hong Kong and Taiwan during the 1990s and early 2000s, I noticed a startling trend about the perceptions of Chinese Americans—the so-called "ABCs" ("American Born Chinese"). I expected the old complaint about cultural loss or even ethnic disloyalty, the claim that Chinese Americans are too Westernized or not Chinese enough. But that, as I eventually realized, is the perspective of an older generation, the generation of romantic overseas patriots that I discussed in the previous chapter. That was the perspective sensitive to the sojourner's national disloyalty and abandoning of one's home that L. Ling-chi Wang describes in his formulation of the "structure of dual domination."[1]

However, the younger Taiwanese and Hong Kongers didn't speak of loss, which implies a desire to protect a pure state, but of difference, which implies hybridity or even mutation. "They're just different," was a frequent answer to my questions about perceptions of "ABCs." My interviewees' inability to articulate that difference is testament to the fact that this difference presented no major moral cause for worry, as had been the case with the foreign students in Taiwan during the brain-drain 1970s. Furthermore, my interviewees could not articulate that difference because those differences were usually on the level of the visual and the aural, not on the level of loyalty with its familiar propaganda slogans and other religious/nationalistic sermonizing. When pressed to describe those perceptual differences in detail, the responses tended to be "they just look different" or "they just sound different," as if they *felt* those differences and even thought it unnecessary to articulate those differences because they should be self-evident. Pressed further, respondents may mention acquired environmental differences (American accents, tanner skin, pierced ears, tattoos, more muscular build for men, chubbier face and body for women) and, strangely enough, phenotypic ones as well (higher-bridged noses, narrower and more angular faces, taller frames). That Chinese Americans may not be genetically very different from their cousins in Hong Kong and Taiwan seemed beside the point to my respondents, as was the fact that the respondents were making these points to a Chinese American researcher who may find it strange to be othered in such a way. After all, "they're just different"—the proof of which is on their bodies, in their experiences, and in their voices.

This discourse of naturalness, be it biologically or socially determined, pervades beyond the testimonies of my interviewees. Popular writing also reveals perspectives of the "natural" that I, having grown up in the United States, find somewhat unexpected. A glowing review of the self-titled 1997 album by San Francisco-raised pop balladeer Shunza reads, "because she grew up in America, she's deeply influenced by black music," as if being Chinese American implies a natural internalization of African American musical tradition.[2] In another review, this time of the California-raised pop trio L. A. Boyz, a Taiwanese writer explains that the basic difference between an American singer and a Taiwanese singer lies in the former's "added muscles and healthier bodies."[3] As many of the differences articulated by my respondents and in the mass media are bodily differences (from the quality of vocal cords to the development of muscles), the difference that ABCs represent are similar to those represented by mixed-race people. In both cases, bodily differences are deemed natural and predictable, and, in both cases, those differences are frequently posed in "best-of-both-worlds" discourse. (For example, an ABC can have the musculature of the Westerner, plus the youthful face of the Chinese; a mixed-race person can have the large eyes of the Caucasian and the sleek hair of the Asian.)

From the examples given by my respondents, there is no doubt that these stereotypes of overseas Chinese, and of mixed-race Asians, are shaped by images in the media, in particular film, television, and popular music. In this chapter, I look at the period of the early 1990s to the early 2000s, when 1.5- and second-generation Chinese from the US, Canada, Britain, and Australia were recruited by production companies, TV networks, and record labels to bring a cosmopolitan flair to the Hong Kong and Taiwanese pop culture industries. This is a decade of rapid media saturation of programming from the West, especially with the proliferation of home video, cable television, and the Internet.[4] Globalization scholars have observed that the appearance of Western styles and genres in the non-West has not led to a homogenization of media images, but rather has sparked efforts to localize foreign content and has inspired local artists to appropriate foreign styles in creative and even empowering ways. However, there is frequently a credibility problem, as Asian consumers find local artists unconvincing in their attempts to rap, to sport American fashions, or to act as multilingual, globe-trotting heroes in action films. At a moment in which popular media sought coevality with Hollywood, Madison Avenue,

Paris, Tokyo, and London by producing local content up to a world standard, the "natural" difference of "ABCs" and mixed-race actors, models, singers, dancers, and DJs provided what I call "world cred." Here, cosmopolitanism with (hybridized) Chinese faces and bodies provides convincing visual proof of local competitiveness. Unlike the cosmopolitanism of the Shaolin Temple heroes (Chapter 4) or the overseas students (Chapter 1), where worldly abilities are acquired in the body and in the mind as the result of training, the cosmopolitanism represented by exotified ABCs and mixed-race stars are represented as naturally embodied. This cosmopolitanism arrives viscerally with the shock of the superficial: the shape of a nose, the shade of skin, the size of muscles, the incongruous sound of a "Chinese" person with an overseas accent. This is the force of what some have called "the strangeness of cosmopolitanism."[5] It elicits sensations of beauty, ugliness, the sublime, repulsion, and fascination much before it invites moral or nationalistic judgments. Given the importance of physical appearance and other "superficial" qualities in this construction of the cosmopolitan, it makes sense to look at star images and employ the tools of star studies (cross-media constructions of celebrity, the fluidity between image and reality, the work of acting, the star as capital) to explore the ways cosmopolitanism seduces local consumers.[6]

The periodization of this phenomenon is largely a result of generational change. The 1990s and 2000s were the coming-of-age of the generation of Hong Kongers and Taiwanese born to parents who grew up in Hong Kong and Taiwan after 1949, decades that began in poverty and then developed into "Asian tigers" economic success. In Taiwanese parlance, this younger generation is made up of the "7th graders"—referring to the Taiwanese born in the "70s" by the Republic of China calendar, or from 1981 to 1990 by the Gregorian calendar. The "7th graders" are known as a privileged generation born during or after the economic boom and therefore didn't experience the economic, cultural, and political turbulence of their parents and grandparents. Simultaneously, in North America, Europe, and Australia, a generation was born to Hong Kong and Taiwan immigrants who went abroad for study or business as a result of relaxed immigration policy in the 1960s and 1970s. These are relatively wealthy immigrant families residing outside of the old Chinatowns and in the new "ethnoburbs" like Monterey Park, California, where young Chinese Americans (who were born in the US or moved when young) grew up in an environment that was exposed to the popular culture of Hong Kong and Taiwan.[7] At the same time, these immigrant families accumulated cosmopolitan cultural capital to secure a place in an otherwise white society, for instance, by sending their children to learn dance or classical music.[8] These immigrant children thus became the "front line" of the process of migration, and were "the focus for parents' fears and aspirations for the future and for the tension between cultural continuity and change," as Liesbeth de Block and David Buckingham write of "global children" more generally. They add that these children are media savvy and soak up a range of local, national, and transnational media in their new environments.[9]

This young generation was not the first generation of Chinese American youth to "return" to the land of their ancestors.[10] Gloria Heyung Chun has written of young Chinese Americans who traveled to China in the 1930s and 1940s to help strengthen China's reputation on the world stage and thus make conditions better for Chinese Americans in the United States.[11] But the appearance of American-born men and women of Chinese ancestry in Hong Kong and Taiwan (and even less so in post-revolution China) did not attain pop cultural visibility until the 1990s. Prior to this, Chinese Americans were conjectural figures, theorized through melodrama, science fiction, and comedy as Westernized and deviant versions of the "real" thing. For instance, in the 1984 TVB serial *The Clones*, Tony Leung Chiu-wai (a distinctively local actor) plays a Hong Konger who grew up in America and therefore has become a troublemaker with fancy hair and a bad attitude. His scientist father makes a well-tempered, filial clone of the son to bring back to Hong Kong, thus fantastically positing a "good" Chinese American against a "bad" one in moral terms similar to that of the melodramas of arrival and departure of Taiwan in the 1970s.

However, Chinese Americans arrived to a very different media ecology in the 1990s, a time in which Taiwan and Hong Kong youth were watching MTV, renting VHS tapes of Hollywood films, and surfing the Internet, eager to consume the latest in world fashions, music, and dance, and more than that, to imagine their own people as actively in-step with the rest of the world. On the similar and simultaneous case of Japan, Bruce White writes that local youth have "a need for social and imaginative mobility," and that the consumption of global commodities creates imaginative interconnections that satiate that desire to be on the move.[12] In the case of Hong Kong and Taiwan, Chinese Americans embodied those imaginative interconnections in a way that spectacularly announced that mobility was possible. Upon encountering this Hong Kong and Taiwanese cultural environment, Chinese Americans found that there was in fact a term for people like them: "American Born Chinese," or "ABC."[13] The term playfully, and somewhat pejoratively, associates Chinese Americans with elementary English, mocking Chinese Americans' proclivity to speak in English by reducing them to a phonics rhyme that even Hong Kongers and Taiwanese know. More importantly, the term "ABC" alternates the grammatical structure of "Chinese American," in which the noun is "American," a strategic (and at one time much-debated) placement to proclaim the Americanness of a community frequently banished as "perpetual foreigners" by the American mainstream media. The term "ABC" claims the Chinese American as a Chinese who happens to be born in America, thus inscribing his or her membership in cultural China. The term illustrates Sau-ling C. Wong's observation that Asian Americans and Asian American culture undergo a process of "Asian nationalist recuperation," whereby American-ness is downplayed to foreground Asian Americans' role in a master narrative of an Asian nation.[14] However, the case of the "ABC" complicates Wong's model because, as I will show later, while media representations of "ABCs" in Hong Kong and Taiwan do subjectize Chinese Americans as Chinese, they don't completely downplay Americanness, instead uncovering the cosmopolitan negotiations within cultural nationalism itself.

Within this environment, whereby producers, agencies, and record labels sought cosmopolitan talent to cater to a demand to see Chinese performing the world, a good number of Chinese Americans, Chinese Canadians, and Chinese Brits became ABCs, CBCs, and BBCs stereotyped by their "natural" differences from local Chinese. Hong Kong and Taiwan had assimilated a number of foreign-born or foreign-raised stars in the 1970s and 1980s (such as Bruce Lee, Jenny Hu, Sally Yeh, Maggie Cheung, Michael Wong, David Wu, David Huang, and Christy Chung), but they did not recruit aggressively until the mid-1990s.[15] Some of the more successful bicultural stars of that later generation included: Jeff Huang, Stanley Huang, CoCo Lee, Karen Mok, Alex To, Eason Chan, Faith Yang, Shunza, David Tao, Leehom Wang, Flora Chan, Kelly Chan, Kelly Lin, Karena Lam, Nicholas Tse, Stephen Fung, Daniel Wu, Terence Yin, Edison Chen, Lawrence Chou, Maggie Q, Elva Hsiao, Jeffrey Kung, Evonne Hsu, Wilber Pan, Christine Fan, Denise Ho, Marsha Yuan, Eugenia Yuan, Angela Chow, Jaycee Chan, Charlene Choi, Vanness Wu, Khalil Fong, Justin Lo, Lisa S., Lara Veronin, Janet Hsieh, Godfrey Gao, and Jin Au-yeung. Many of these stars went on to develop their craft as actors, singers, directors, and entrepreneurs in ways that allowed them to shed their "ABC" status, but all started off in the industry by navigating the "ABC" label that gave them work while pigeonholing them into stereotypical parts.[16]

## Monsters and New Humans

In Cantonese, a common word denoting the foreign is *gwai*, meaning "ghost." Most famously, white people in Hong Kong are pejoratively called *gwailo*, sometimes translated as "foreign devil," but more accurately translated as "ghostly one," which gets to the way in which the phrase subhumanizes the foreign. Other common phrases for foreign figures include *gwaimui* (ghost girl), *gwaizai* (ghost boy), and *hakgwai* (black ghost). In many Chinese traditions, ghosts are considered objectionable and hostile beings; there are holidays for keeping ghosts at bay and, under most circumstances, to even speak of ghosts is considered unlucky. The word *gwai* has therefore also taken on other associations such as deceit (as in *gaau gwai*, or *gau gui* in Mandarin, which refers to playing tricks), disbelief (as in *mat gwai*, or *gui dongxi* in Mandarin, which is equivalent to the English "What the hell?"), and sickness (as in *zaugwai*, or *jiugui* in Mandarin, which is an informal term for an alcoholic). That Chinese born or raised overseas are sometimes referred to as *gwaizai* and *gwaimui* in Hong Kong speaks to how flexible and reliable the ghost is in possessing uncanny subjects that society doesn't quite know where to place or how to classify. As not-quite-humans, ghosts and other human-like monsters are what Noël Carroll calls "category errors," deformations of nature that are ugly (and sometimes beautiful) in form and spirit.[17] Ugliness and monstrosity is a discourse through which a community can contain the chaos of social change. It allows society to map in- and out-groups via "natural" discourses of science and beauty.

The evocation of ghosts and other kinds of not-quite-human monsters has a long history in Chinese culture. Specific to the issue of monstratizing the unknown is the history of birth defects and eugenics discourse in imperial and Republican China. In these eras, the monstering of human beings could come about through external contact. For instance, in imperial China, pregnant women were advised not to look at "ghostly or monstrous images" (*guiguai xingxiang*) for fear that her fetus would take the shape of the monster the mother sees.[18] Although doctors and commentators would later be influenced by Darwinian and Mendelian evolutionary theory in the late Qing and Republican era, the belief persisted that contact with the unknown, even merely having the fear of monsters and ghosts, could lead to "strange fetuses" (*guaitai*).[19] This included the fear elicited by violent films, which could "hit the eye and stir the heart" (*chumu jingxin*), and thus have adverse effects on the shape and spirit of the child.[20] During the Republican period, concern about hybrid creatures and freaks of nature took on nationalistic undertones. As Frank Dikötter writes, "monsters became the ominous signs of racial degeneration, the portents of national decline, the embodiment of a failure to harness the natural forces of progress."[21] Protecting the national body from exposure to monstrosity was a means to elevate China's place as the "sick man of Asia," to compete with Western forces and economies, and develop into a just and cosmopolitan nation.

At the same time, however, other philosophers, commentators, and eugenicists, influenced by both Medelism and Lamarckism (with its emphasis on environmental, as opposed to genetic, factors) as well as folk and scientific warnings against in-breeding, found that contact with the biologically different could lead to the development of a stronger race. For Lu Xun and Chen Duxiu, eugenics meant searching "among beastly barbarians for new blood."[22] Republican-era historian Gu Jiegang argued that China had to search its barbarian neighbors for "infusions of fresh blood."²³ Late-Qing reformist Kang Youwei imagined a utopia where Asian/white discord could be transcended through the development of a harmonious Eurasian super-race. Kang celebrated racial intermarriage as one way toward the creation of this new race. But Kang felt that Lamarckian ideas of "soft inheritance" could as well. He noticed that Chinese children born abroad could take on the physical characteristics of other races (such as skin color and body shape), and so migration and physical contact was a means through which this super-race could emerge.²⁴ The idea of a "new race" based on Chinese–Western hybridity reappears in many turn-of-the-millennium Hong Kong science-fiction films and techno-thrillers, as I will show later.

Contemporary anthropologists Jean and John Comaroff have also borrowed the metaphor of the monster to describe an emergent youth culture as a result of global flows of people and media. In describing adults' ambiguous responses to "our nightmare adolescent, wearing absurdly expensive sports shoes, headphones blaring gangsta rap, beeper tied to a global underground economy,"²⁵ the Comaroffs find that the figure of the adolescent, a turbulent product of global capital, comes to stand for "the terrors of the present, the errors of the past, the prospect of a future." These bizarrely dressed, suspiciously connected global citizens are thus "idealizations and monstrosities, pathologies and panaceas."²⁶ Foreign-born Chinese can be seen as similarly monstrous. The progeny of Hong Kong and Taiwan's brightest and most promising academics and entrepreneurs who had the means and the ambition to go global, these youth are deformations of Chineseness, mutants exposed to the rays of Western culture, Western values, and Western air, whose parents most certainly let the sensations of the foreign "hit the eye and stir the heart." These would-be wonder-kids "return" to Hong Kong and Taiwan with dyed-hair, baggy pants, and Ivy League degrees. In Hong Kong, they are spatially associated with the upscale Central district, where they spend their days interning in Asia's most menacing skyscrapers and their nights cavorting with rich Europeans in Lan Kwai Fong clubs or Soho bars. In Taiwan, ABCs are commonly associated with the glitzy new nightclubs in Taipei's Eastern District, in the night markets by the Mandarin Training Center of National Taiwan Normal University, in the bars with Taipei American School alums around the upscale Tianmu neighborhood, or on any basketball court in Taipei, screaming obscenities in English. In the heyday of the ABC star in Hong Kong, gossip columns would frequently report on the night-life shenanigans of stars like Maggie Q, Richard Sun, Daniel Wu, and Edison Chen, with one Taiwanese report going as far as explaining the phenomenon by saying that "perhaps all those steak hamburgers have given them better physical endurance, because those ABC stars sure love hanging out at nightclubs."²⁷

If Republican China was a time in which monstrosity was seen as a racial defect or, for others, a possibility of racial reinvigoration, hamburger-fueled monstrosity in Hong Kong and Taiwan of the 1990s and early 2000s was an object of fascination, adoration, and, ultimately, rejection. The trope of the sexualized monster (such as vampires) in world literature and media aptly captures forbidden desire, a desire taken to the limits of the human, only to be roped back under the guise of an unbreachable morality or mortality. Not surprisingly then, ABC stars, frequently called *guaizai* and *guaimui* in the Hong Kong press, sometimes start their careers playing beasts and ghosts in film. Then-supermodel Maggie Q's first film role was in *Model from Hell* (Chiu Chun Keung, 2000), in which she played a sexy model possessed by a demon to seduce innocent and not-too-innocent men. An early David Wu role in *A Tale from the East* (Manfred Wong, 1990) finds him mistaken as a ghost because he speaks with a different dialect and has anachronistic hair and clothes. Eugenia Yuan's two starring roles to date in Hong Kong have been as ghosts: first in Peter Chan's entry, *Going Home*, to the omnibus film *Three* (2002), and second in the Pang Brothers' *The Eye 2* (2004). In *The Twins Effect* (Dante Lam, 2003), vampires are played by black and white actors, as well as a mixed-race star (Anthony Wong) and a Chinese Canadian (Edison Chen). Most representative perhaps is Edison Chen's role in the teen romantic comedy *Nine Girls and a Ghost* (Chung Shu-kai, 2002), which playfully blurs the line between character and celebrity. The title is a reference to the film's story of nine girls who meet a handsome young ghost, as well as an intertextual reference to the films' stars: the nine-girl pop group Cookies and the *guaizai* teen idol Edison Chen. In the film, Chen plays a handsome ghost who fantastically floats back to earth wearing an oversized suit and surrounded by pink bubbles. His boyish good looks and exotic cool win the heart of Stephy (played by Stephy Tang). However, as is the case with all ghosts in Chinese film, Edison has major emotional baggage (he was once a bully who died in a car crash in which he also killed an innocent girl). Even though Edison atones for his sins, Stephy still cannot have him for he is, by nature of being subhuman (in both senses of the "ghost"), inaccessible. In the film's melodramatic final scene, Edison is forced to say goodbye as Stephy professes her love. By his "natural" differences, a ghost is always a ghost; he may be the object of much adoration, he may even have helped the girls defeat their rivals in high-school basketball, but he is ultimately from another world and therefore unattainable. This cycle of adoration and rejection also captures the Hong Kong media and public's perceptions of Edison Chen preceding and following a number of public relations debacles culminating in a much-publicized sex scandal in 2008 that led to his forced exile from the mainstream entertainment industry.

The prodigal monster is not only associated with specific spaces, but also with a temporality distinct from that of locals. In the minds of the Republican eugenicists, the hybridized Chinese was a creature of the future, a human ideal that would ensure the survival of the race. In more recent discourse, portents and hybrid beings, especially mixed-race populations, often stand for the hope (and often confusion) of a post-racial, and even post-national world with cosmopolitan ideals of equality for all. Cynthia L. Nakashima has traced the history of mixed-race discourse in the United States, and observes that mixed-race Asian Americans have become the "functional representatives" of a future-looking color-blind America seeking alliances in an increasingly globalized world.[28]

In Hollywood, race is also temporalized, with mixed-race characters frequently populating the not-too-distant future of science fiction. Jane Park argues that multi-racial actors like Keanu Reeves and Vin Diesel have been imagined as the faces of a post-racial world, although admittedly without dismantling existing hierarchies of white and non-white.[29] Leilani Nishime and Mary C. Beltrán argue further that Reeves and Vin Diesel represent heroism in a utopic future in which mixed-race individuals thrive as humankind's savior at "the end of time" in the case of *The Matrix*, and the lone survivors in the case of *Fast and the Furious*, set in a multicultural Los Angeles that Beltrán calls a "millennial city."[30] These scholars stop short of describing these multi-racial stars as a new species, which makes less sense in the American context than it does in the Hong Kong one, where mixed-race and even mixed-culture individuals are regularly compared to ghosts and other portentous beings. In another article, Nishime does argue that the sci-fi cyborg can allegorize contemporary idealizations of multiculturalism.[31] Turn-of-the-millennium science-fiction films in Hong Kong concretize that allegory further by casting "ghostly" ABC stars in the role of robotized human beings. In *Avenging Fist* (Andrew Lau and Corey Yuen, 2001), Chinese American pop star Leehom Wang plays a genetic experiment in combat, whose powers, although envied by his peers and by the audience, turn out to be evil. Wang's genetic advantage makes him cocky, and the film plays out by alternating between an admiration of his superior fighting and a reservation about the advances brought by futuristic technology. A similar ambiguity exists in *Purple Storm* (Teddy Chan, 1999), in which Daniel Wu plays a Chinese Cambodian adopted by an American family and who eventually studies science at the Massachusetts Institute of Techology (MIT). Soon, he is recruited and trained by a transnational terrorist organization and, after he loses his memory, is brainwashed and retrained by the Hong Kong police force. While Wu's character never becomes a cyborg in the strict sense, we witness his spectacularly muscled body groomed, reprogrammed, and utilized like a man-robot's. Again, the audience is caught between cheering on the swiftness of this killing machine, and being disgusted by the dehumanizing way in which murder has been programmed into him by all sides. In these examples, the ambiguity over the cyborg figure is mutually enforced by society's ambiguity over the deformed ABC.

*Gen-X Cops* (Benny Chan, 1999) and *Gen-Y Cops* (Benny Chan, 2000) skip hybrid cyborgs altogether, directly comparing ABCs to aliens and mutations of humankind by nature of their foreign styles, Western demeanors, and unusual skills. The *Gen-X Cops* and *Gen-Y Cops* franchise, and to a lesser extent *Bishonen* (Yonfan, 1998) and *Young & Dangerous: The Prequel* (Andrew Lau, 1998), single-handedly introduced Hong Kong to a new crop of overseas Chinese and multi-racial film stars like Daniel Wu, Nicholas Tse, Terence Yin, Stephen Fung, Jaymee Ong, Edison Chen, Maggie Q, Rachel Ngan, and Richard Sun. Emilie Yueh-yu Yeh and Darrell William Davis call the franchise, along with *Purple Storm* and others of the period, a "strange cosmopolitan fantasy," with its unusually bilingual stars, overseas villains, and high-tech styles.[32] The films carry an intriguing Chinese title: *Te Jing Xin Renlei*, which can be translated as "Special Cops, New Humans." (Kwai-Cheung Lo prefers "new species."[33]) What makes the cops, played by Nicholas Tse, Stephen Fung, Sam Lee, and Edison Chen across the two films, paradigmatic of a "new human" is not some literal cyborg or multi-racial nature, but (with the exception of Lee) their "ABC" status, represented by their lack of discipline, their penchant for risk-taking, their laid-back attitudes, their punk haircuts, and their trendy clothes.[34] The characters they play may even be local Hong Kongers, yet the connection between the actors' biographies and the characters' style and demeanor was inescapable to audiences of the time, and it was reinforced by intertexual materials like one newspaper article aghast at bad-boy Nicholas Tse's preference to perform his own stunts even without accident insurance.[35] The article made sure to mention Tse's North American ties as well, further connecting the film (and thus the "new human") with ABCs. *Gen-Y Cops* takes the ABC stylings further, using English in about half of the film's dialogue. (One reviewer called the film a "Hong Kong-styled foreign language film" starring actors with "yellow faces and white minds."[36]) The film envisions the new human as distinctly multicultural in its casting of bicultural and multi-racial young stars, and cosmopolitan in its narrative of multilingual young professionals who can flexibly interact with both the Hong Kong and the American police. Throughout Hong Kong pop culture, the sound and image of the ABC became shorthand for an authentic cosmopolitanism; the hybrid aesthetic represented by their bodies was sufficient to demonstrating worldliness. A December 26, 2000 RHK TV special about Hong Kong cinema's place on the world stage of computer graphics and cinematic digital effects cast Edison Chen, with his spiked hair, oversized sweater, single earring, and Canadian-accented

Cantonese, as narrator, as if the mere presence of an ABC and his monstrous demeanor could help authenticate a documentary about Hong Kong's high stature producing Hollywood-style special effects.[37]

In Hong Kong and Taiwan popular culture, ABC stars are commonly discussed in terms of "next generation" and "evolution" discourse. Los Angeles-educated pop star David Tao is celebrated and canonized as having revolutionized Taiwanese pop music by importing elements of R&B, rap, and soul. Pop trio L. A. Boyz's dance moves were dubbed "ahead of the times" by the Taiwanese media.[38] In the liner notes of their debut album, the three Chinese American teens who composed 1990s pop group Babes were called "super new humans" (*chao xin ren lei*) who would "let [Taiwanese] pop music and dance compete with the world" and "revolutionize the Taiwan music world" with their denim overalls, braided hair, beanies, and Bobby Brown-inspired pop R&B.[39] The English title of *Gen-X Cops* was chosen precisely for studio Media Asia to celebrate its young overseas stars as the next incarnation of action heroes.[40] The 1998 film *Young & Dangerous: The Prequel*, which introduced mainstream film fans to Nicholas Tse and Daniel Wu, pitched these new stars as the next generation of Hong Kong bad boys. The film is almost an exact re-tread of the earlier *Young & Dangerous* films, with scenes that are seemingly recreated shot-for-shot. However, in this prequel, we see the street thug characters as they were when they were younger. By casting new stars in old parts, the producers could mark Tse and Wu as familiar, but younger, badder, and more fashionable—in other words, the stars of the future. The prequel form also allows Tse and Wu to become uncanny look-alikes of the original actors. The uncanny, of course, only heightens the sense of the strange and the unfamiliar, drawing attention to differences like face shape and muscle size—the cosmopolitan difference lent by their ABC personas. The effect of the uncanny—familiar but exotic, local but worldly—is also visually and aurally produced by the fact that so many of these "ABC" stars are descended from famous celebrities. The face may look familiar, but we're thrown off by the tough-guy hair and earrings; the voice may have a familiar tenor, but now has an American accent. The effect of this monstratization of a beloved celebrity is both terrifying and mesmerizing. Examples of famous progeny include: Nicholas Tse (son of Tse Yin and Deborah Dik), Jaycee Chan (son of Jackie Chan and Joan Lin), Terence Yin (son of Jenny Hu), Stephen Fung (son of Julie Shih Yin), Brandon Lee (son of Bruce Lee), Marsha and Eugenia Yuan (daughters of Cheng Pei-pei), Leehom Wang (nephew of Lee Chien-fu), Joyce Cheng (daughter of Lydia Sum and Adam Cheng), and Carl Ng (son of Richard Ng). As children of the famous, they're also "rich kids" in the public eye thanks to an aggressive paparazzi culture, which reports them getting into car accidents in the streets of Central when few in

Hong Kong even have cars, or jetting back and forth between famous parents and friends in Asia and North America. Thus, they represent "spoiled" in two senses: they grew up with advantages that others don't have, and they "spoil" the literal and symbolic images of their iconic and beloved parents.

There is nothing new about heralding a "new generation" of stars, as that tactic has long been an effective means for attracting young consumers, differentiating product, and rebranding. The 1960s, for instance, saw the rise of teen idols like Josephine Siao, Connie Chan Po-chu, and other go-go girls and cover bands. The idea of cover bands, however, connotes a kind of playacting. They were singers and stars mimicking Hollywood, London, and Tokyo, localizing foreign songs through translation and remaking foreign melodramas and action films. As Chris Berry has shown of the Chinese and South Korean blockbuster, mimicry invites an acknowledgment of difference. At times, that difference can lead to an empowering sense of local identity and tradition. At other times, however, difference sparks feelings of inferiority and a lack of coevality.[41] The new generation of foreign-raised stars in the 1990s and 2000s mediated those differences, compromising the calls for local identity (so strong in the pop culture of the 1980s) but bringing authenticity to the performance of worldliness. These stars did so not as locals playacting the role of the foreign, but by being something physically, even genetically, different altogether. They are not just kids acting, but a new variant—a cosmopolitan species mutated out of foreign environments.

The metaphors used to describe the overseas Chinese—monsters, ghosts, new humans, aliens—bring that difference to the level of the body. Bodies are perceived as especially provocative because they appear to have a kind of concreteness and indestructibility that ethnicity, culture, and textual performance lack. They can be shocking when they are different, because the differences don't seem performed, but rather natural, ingrained, permanent. When the cosmopolitan is on the skin, in the bone structure, and in the grain of the voice, it is no longer playacting. Not surprisingly, it is on the body that many "ABC" stars evoke their cosmopolitanism. Not all ABC stars have the same bodily attributes, and in fact many of the stereotypical attributes contradict one another.[42] But some attributes have become so associated with certain performers and their overseas star personas, that they have become representative of general perceptions that local Hong Kong and Taiwanese fans have of overseas Chinese communities. It is then worth examining individual cases of how these alien bodily differences were concocted vis-à-vis pleasure and repulsion, how they became generalizable to all overseas Chinese, and how they became emblematic of, and in some cases redefined, the industry of stardom, gossip, and casting in Taiwan and Hong Kong in the 1990s and early 2000s.

## L. A. Boyz's muscles

During an impersonation contest on the popular Taiwanese cable show *I Love Hei Se Hui*, three young women lovingly mocked 1990s pop trio L. A. Boyz with a performance of their 1992 hit "Jump."[43] In addition to the 1990s oversized flannel, the performers chose one additional accessory to accentuate the distinctiveness—and strangeness—of L. A. Boyz: a muscle suit. Indeed, in their heyday, L. A. Boyz were considered hyper-muscular in a Taiwan that was not obsessed with bodybuilding. Their muscles were objects of fascination, and the trio was not averse to going sleeveless or shirtless in TV appearances, album art, or music videos to satiate that fascination. In the promotional materials for their 1994 release *Fantasy*—album art, music video—they are almost exclusively shirtless, hanging out on piers and beaches. Exaggerated by the gleam of the sun, their muscles flare with a gratuitousness rarely seen on singers and actors of Chinese descent.

This isn't to say that Hong Kong and Taiwanese media have had a shortage of muscled men, as evidenced by the massive (MP&GI's resident beefcake Roy Chiao, 1970s kung fu icon Bolo Leung) to the chiseled lean (martial arts heroes Jimmy Wang Yu and Jackie Chan), to the massive *and* chiseled (Bruce Lee). With the exception of Chiao, whose juxtaposition with slender male co-stars Peter Chan Ho and Kelly Lai Chen always made him a freak of nature, the earlier muscled stars belonged to the martial arts world of intense training and exceptional feats. One understood why they were so muscular: their bodies are a consequence of living by the code of the *jiang hu*, where *wu* masculinity was expected to overpower the more graceful, more literary *wen* masculinity.

L. A. Boyz's muscles can similarly be explained by an association with a specific "world." This is the world abroad, of Venice Beaches and *Men's Fitness* magazines. It is also the world of white action stars and black athletes, all popular in Hong Kong and Taiwan. Somehow, an association—even a causation—has been made in the minds of the Hong Kong and Taiwan media that living overseas naturally inflates Chinese muscles. As one of my interviewees jokingly puts it, "You can tell how long a Chinese person has been in the US by the size of their muscles." This is not an isolated sentiment. In the Taiwanese music review quoted earlier, we see how there was a popular understanding that the basic difference between local and American singers are the latter's muscles, which, for the reviewer, explained the beefy look of L. A. Boyz. The L. A. Boyz were not alone in this association. Further demonstrating the correlation were muscled (and frequently shirtless) ABC male stars like Michael Wong, David Wu, Nicholas Tse, and Daniel Wu.[44] Even slender pretty-boy Leehom Wang appeared with shirt unbuttoned on the cover of his second album, *If You Heard My Song*. Wang seemed to have to fit a certain ABC type, whether he had the exaggerated body to do so or not. The video for his Prince-inspired 1996 song "Call for Me a Thousand Times" features him shirtless with jeans. The hard sidelighting in the video is clearly designed to strategically cast shadows to accentuate Wang's pecs and abs. Similarly, California-raised David Tao, not known for his physical strength (although being a cop in LA County is part of his legend), is shown working out in the opening scene of the Hong Kong concert film *Love Can World Tour* (2006).

The size and shape of these overseas stars is more peculiar if we consider how, at the time, gym culture was not mainstream. A study conducted in 2001–2 found that in Taiwanese women's magazine advertising, Western male models were undressed 43 percent of the time, while Asian male models only 5 percent of the time.[45] The same study found that college-aged heterosexual Taiwanese men do not inflate their ideals of how muscular they should be compared to how muscular they actually are, nor do they overshoot how muscular they believe women expect them to be, which contrasts with the more muscle-obsessed results found in similar studies of American men.[46] That gym culture is associated with the foreign is further pronounced by the fact that perhaps the biggest gym chain in Hong Kong and Taiwan then was called California Fitness, which opened its first Hong Kong branch in 1996. The gym's spokesperson was Jackie Chan, who by 2005 (when his partnership began) was very much seen as an overseas star.

Muscles are thus a foreign import, and muscled Chinese men an uncanny mutation of global interactions. Kwai-Cheung Lo calls Chinese muscles a "sublime" sight that represents "the inadequacy of form to content"—that is, the sight of the globally feminized Chinese as a muscular male.[47] The sublime "alien" muscles of Bruce Lee thus represent Hong Kong at home and abroad as a negative relation: he is Hong Kong by possessing what Hong Kong (and Chineseness more generally) should not have.[48] The later ABC stars like L. A. Boyz and Daniel Wu don't "represent" Taiwan, Hong Kong, or Chineseness in quite the same obligatory way, and thus cannot be a negative to a positive conception of national/local identity. The sublimity of their muscles does, however, conjure the sensation of "inadequacy of form to content," not to "represent" either at home or abroad, but to announce the arrival of a new human: the cosmopolitan Chinese. The advertisements, TV appearances, and films proclaim the new possibilities of the Chinese body once it is mobile, flexible, and engaged with the outside world.

That muscles are both foreign and physically powerful make them potentially threatening. The imposing image of sharply defined bulges and sinewy mass is not just one of racial difference, but seeming racial superiority. When muscles are the province of martial arts heroes, they are the pride of a nation, often standing up against foreign invaders. However, when they are associated with the foreign world, even on the bodies of stars of Chinese descent, they stand for a physical threat from the outside. But, as I claimed earlier, the ABC stars of the 1990s and early 2000s were not perceived as un-Chinese or disloyal, but simply "new humans." How can the threat of muscles be curbed without resorting to the familiar recourse of insisting that these muscles be loyal to a "Chinese" cause?

When the L. A. Boyz arrived in Taiwan in 1992, they became poster-boys for a popular "healthiness" movement. Their muscles were read not as physical threat, but as signs of healthy attitudes and physical fitness associated with American culture. The agile and energetic dancing bodies of L. A. Boyz copycats Babes were called "healthy and beautiful" by the Taiwanese press,[49] and David Wu was deemed representative of the "healthy 1990s."[50] L. A. Boyz's muscles were assimilated into this fitness craze. Although the muscularity of their dance-filled videos—their emphasis, often through slow motion, on power moves and acrobatic feats—could potentially incite fear due to the dancers' superhuman excess, their muscles were made less threatening through the discourse of healthiness. For instance, in early 1993, the *United Daily News* ran weekly instructional features on how to perform the L. A. Boyz's signature dance moves. While there was often a tongue-in-cheek suggestion that no reader could possibly mimic their superhuman moves, the instructional mode of such pieces seemed to even the playing field of physical fitness, while still mythologizing the L. A. Boyz's bodies. Their muscles were also softened by the fact that many of their shirtless images in album covers and videos were of them out in the sun (as if at play) or in the bedroom (as when they appeared in nothing except pajama pants on their 1993 album *Ya!*), as opposed to on the streets or other spaces associated with violence or rebellion (Figure 2.1).[51] The L. A. Boyz also promoted healthiness when they (and their dance moves) appeared in a series of anti-smoking public service announcements produced by the Taiwan Department of Health. L. A. Boyz, and other ABC stars in Taiwanese pop, not only were celebrated for their healthy bodies, but their healthy minds as well. L. A. Boyz were seen as "being able to both study and sing," thanks to frequent reports about their progress in high school and then college in the United States.[52] Their lyrics reflected a healthy prospective on life and upper-middle-class suburban aspirations. Over a sample from MC Breed & DFC's "Ain't No Future in Yo' Frontin'," Steven Lin boasts about being a "superman" on "Jump":

Super cool, super fit, super fast, super slick,
Super in tennis ball, super in basketball,
Super in management, super intelligent![53]

**Figure 2.1** Shirtless and out under the sun: music video for L. A. Boyz, "Island Girl," 1995

Similarly, in the liner notes of their first records, U.S-based artists Leehom Wang and Shawn Sung were depicted as young prodigies, thus drawing attention away from any rebellion their lyrics and musical genres may suggest (especially in the case of the rapper Sung), and toward their academic accomplishments and creative genius.[54]

L. A. Boyz's muscles never oozed sexual deviance, as that would be inconsistent with the healthy image they were expected to project. However, especially in Hong Kong, ABC muscles were associated with a voracious sexual appetite and also became an object of the heterosexual female and homosexual male gaze. For instance, in *Wonder Women* (Gan Kwok-leung, 1987), Michael Wong plays a foreigner who is frequently shirtless and the object of sexual desire. Wong also starred as sexual predators in risqué Category III films like *Fatal Love* (Lo Kin, 1993) and *Midnight Caller* (Chang Kuo-ming, 1995). David Wu played a philandering husband with a scruffy face and buff body in *Finale of Blood* (Fruit Chan, 1991).

Perhaps no ABC movie star was as shirtless (and sometimes pantsless) as Daniel Wu, and no director revealed more of Wu than Yonfan. Often credited for discovering Wu, Yonfan cast him in his 1998 film *Bishonen*, opposite other overseas Chinese stars like Stephen Fung and Terence Yin. In the film, Wu plays a sexually ambiguous policeman we sometimes see only wearing briefs while pillow-fighting or caressing his lover. In one sex scene, he is shown in the shower, as his lover, played by Terence Yin, lathers his chiseled pecs and abs. In Yonfan's 2001 film *Peony Pavilion*, Wu plays a teacher who catches the eye of a fellow teacher played by Joey Wong. In an early encounter, Wang's character spies on her young co-worker as he showers naked outside, his muscles sculpted by the hard top light and glistening from the water poured on his chest (Figures 2.2a, b). Yonfan depicts Wu as a beautiful innocent, too young and naïve to realize how seductive his strapping body is to the men

**Figure 2.2a**   Daniel Wu's character showers in *Peony Pavilion* . . .

**Figure 2.2b**   . . . as Joey Wong's character watches, clutching herself

and women around him. That innocence diminishes the physical threat of the muscles, transforming them into inanimate objects of beauty. The same goes for the shirtless poses that Wu makes on skin-care billboards, ads that emphasize the perfection of his skin and tone, rather than the ferocity of his muscles.

In other instances, however, Wu's muscles do become a threat. In *Cop on a Mission* (Marco Mak, 2001), Wu's chest, buttocks, and legs are bared in multiple slow-motion shots of him showering naked and walking out in a towel. We also see him shirtless in a swimming pool and several times in a sauna. In this film, his muscles correspond to his virility, which contrast him directly to a heavy-set, impotent gang boss played by Eric Tsang. The gangster's wife is immediately drawn to Wu's beautiful body, and she secretly strays from her husband to make love to the younger, more muscular Wu. The threat that he and his body pose to the gangster are eventually placed in check after the secret relationship is revealed, Wu is captured, and then buried alive. The ABC's muscles may be seductive, and may even satisfy otherwise unsatisfiable yearnings, but the threat they pose to an existing order must be contained—the monstrous body can be enjoyed as object of beauty or vessel of sexual satisfaction, but it must ultimately be kept outside, often by death. After they thrill with the shock of the sublime, the possibilities of the Chinese body imagined by the ABC's muscles are then surveilled through the local gaze, and then classified accordingly (by healthiness, beauty, threat, and so forth).

## *Maggie Q's face*

Like the sublime sight of Chinese muscles, the ambiguous faces of mixed-race stars in film and modeling represented new—and profitable—possibilities for popular culture and the popular culture industry. One of several mixed-race models to appear on the Hong Kong entertainment scene at the turn of the millennium, Maggie Q was the first to attain local, regional, and international success. Like many of those female models, Maggie Q immediately transitioned to film, and her mixed-race face—with its long shape, sharp nose, and wide lips—became a cross-media sensation: an object of fascination among fans and in gossip rags, and a fleshy logo for fashion and media companies seeking international status. It mattered little that she was not actually part Chinese (Maggie Q's mother is Vietnamese); in public discourse she was a *wan hyut ji* (mixed race) like Nancy Kwan, Jenny Hu, or any of the other daughters born to Chinese and white parents. It also mattered little whether she represented her non-white side well as a proper Chinese woman. What mattered was the added value—the racial mixing that made her appear the cosmopolitan par excellence—embodied by her face.

The economic value of mixed-racial features was not unknown in the Hong Kong film industry. In 1959, Hollywood producer Ray Stark contacted MP&GI head Lok Wan Tho about casting one of his actresses for the female lead in Stark's forthcoming adaptation of *The World of Suzie Wong*. Lok recommended house actress Ting Hao. Stark rejected Ting Hao, whose looks he could only call "interesting," adding that he was looking for an actress with "aquiline features."[55] By "aquiline," Stark referred to a taller, more eagle-like nose, as opposed to what Sander L. Gilman has called the "Oriental nose"—the flatter, rounder nose of Ting Hao common to many Asian men and women.[56] Stark ultimately cast mixed race (and aquiline) actress Nancy Kwan for the role, a part that would go on to shape the representations of Asian women in Hollywood for decades. In not having a mixed-race face on his roster, Lok Wan Tho lost an opportunity to internationalize one of his actresses and, perhaps, his studio.

The appeal of mixed-race features as specially marketable beauty was not lost to other studios in Hong Kong. In the press, 1950s Great Wall star Angel Chan Si-si's large eyes were the subject of much fascination and envy, leading many to speculate whether "she is of alien blood." But Chan was never monstratized, despite descriptors like "alien." For all of the speculation, there was always the added biographical detail confirming her purity—"in fact, she is a Chinese," read one article—consoling fans that her mixed-race features were merely stylistic, and that at heart Chan was 100 percent Chinese.[57] Actress Chu Fang faced similar scrutiny, and capitalized from the obsession fans had with her large eyes and high nose.[58] In both cases, the insistence that they are actually Chinese, in spite of their mixed-race features, speaks to the anxiety over racial mixing in a fairly conservative colonial Hong Kong. As Vicky Lee puts it, Eurasians during this era were "the living embodiment of colonial encounters" and especially of the "protected woman" living with a white man.[59] In this Hong Kong, Eurasians had to "take a side" in order to fit into a highly segregated community, and the discourse around actors and actresses with mixed-race features certainly attempted to categorize the stars as one or the other.[60]

Such was the case with Jenny Hu, born to a Chinese father and German mother, and raised in Taiwan and Germany. Hu would become one of the biggest box office draws of Mandarin cinema in the late 1960s and early 1970s. Passed over by Loke Wan Tho and MP&GI,[61] Hu signed with Shaw Brothers and was introduced to fans in 1965 in the pages of *Southern Screen*. Before she even appeared on-screen, Hu was touted as the head of Shaws' incoming class of young actresses in the studio's fan magazine. Every introductory article addressed her mixed-race features. *Southern Screen*'s first article on Hu read: "The nose's high bridge, the wide lips, the square shoulders, and those beautiful eyes—isn't that the girl eating ice cream on the streets in *Roman Holiday*?" But when asked about her resemblance to Audrey Hepburn, Hu is quoted as responding, "I don't think I'm like anybody. I am just Jenny Hu, a regular Chinese girl."[62] In other words, Hu needed to publicly insist on her Chineseness, which takes the form here of feminine modesty. And yet, despite Hu's insistence, Shaw Brothers felt inclined to include both quotes: one to highlight Hu's external hybridity, and another to remind readers of her internal purity/loyalty. Hong Kong of the 1960s craved worldly feminine looks while insisting on racial segregation. Into the 1970s, as Hu became a veteran of Mandarin cinema, married, and bore a son, countless publicity articles appeared about her domestic life. Many read like one in *Cinemart*, which celebrated her filiality to her working (Chinese) husband and her sacrifice for her young son, and depicted her cooking and washing clothes. "Just because she's half foreign doesn't mean she lives like a foreigner," it added, reminding readers of her mixed race while suggesting that her domestic behavior is 100 percent Confucian.[63] In films, we often only see one, if any, of Hu's character's parents, to account for the ambiguity insinuated by her mixed race without doting on it. *The Eternal Obsession* (Kenneth Tsang, 1976) is the rare film that addressed her foreignness directly, and in a moment with shades of the "tragic mulatto" character of American literature and film, Hu's character is denied food for being a "foreigner," to which she angrily declares, "I'm a Chinese." And yet, despite the fact that Hu's "foreignness" was made negative in film and journalistic narratives about her, it was precisely her Caucasian features that the press obsessively fetishized and celebrated throughout her career. "Your wide lips—only one possess[es] them, and they are your trademark," read one magazine's letter to the actress. "But not just your lips, but those eyes, that nose."[64] Photo spread after photo spread lingered over those parts in particular, with one 1974 collage featuring cutouts of her eyes and lips (Figure 2.3). As if confirming the importance of mixed-race features on the Chinese woman for Western consumption, Jenny Hu was chosen to represent all of Shaw Brothers in a much-discussed *Life Magazine* feature of the powerhouse studio introducing Shaws to a Western readership. The magazine's cover image was a close-up of Hu's large eyes, sharp nose, and flat lips. If Hu was a Hong Kong "tragic mulatto," it was precisely because of the awe the public held for her Western features—wonderment that made her a star but consequently led to her being typecast as sex kitten (through mixed-race's association with promiscuity and prostitution) and kept her from acting in costume pictures (which was especially critical in the 1970s with the rise of the martial arts film). Try as she might, Hu ultimately could not pass as "Chinese."

"I'm a Chinese" also paraphrases the first lines ever spoken on-screen by Eurasian actor Michael Wong. In an early scene of the adventure film *City Hero* (Dennis Yu, 1985), Wong's character, nicknamed Gwailo (ghostly one), introduces himself to fellow soldiers by insisting that he is Chinese and that he is

**Figure 2.3** A magazine spread fixates on Jenny Hu's signature face, eyes, and lips (*Cinemart*, August 1974)

"of the same voice and breath" (*tung seng tung hei*) as anyone else in his platoon. And yet in film after film into the 1990s, Wong's characters are called "*gwailo*." Wong's mixed-race features lent him an exotic sexiness and provided seeming verisimilitude to the Cantonese his characters invariably spoke, especially in the

1980s and early 1990s. Yet the film scripts only allowed him to pass as ghostly foreigner, and very rarely as Chinese. As *City Hero* suggests, there may be a period of uncertainty during which a new actor can experiment passing as one race before getting lumped into another. Such was also the case with Eurasian actor Anthony Wong, who played white in his debut film *My Name Ain't Suzie* (Angie Chan, 1985), but has passed as Chinese ever since, even acting in period films. For actors of this generation, Eurasians could exploit mixed-race appeal, but ultimately had to take a side. Jenny Hu, Michael Wong, Anthony Wong, and others were racial monsters who could only be integrated into a community of entertainers the same way they would in Hong Kong society: by passing.

But the mixed-race "monster" took on different meanings under the intensified globalization—especially inter-racial marriage and migration—of the turn of the millennium. Mixed-race stars, like their muscular brothers, were still contained as non-threats within an entertainment industry that could therefore safely exploit their "new human" appeal. However, the threat they posed was no longer that of "How Chinese?" or "How Western?" The question turned away from the binary of loyalty versus assimilation in L. Ling-chi Wang's formulation of "dual domination," and toward the possibilities of racial transcendence. The appeal of these stars was no longer in how they managed to beautifully balance Chinese ways with Audrey Hepburn looks, but rather how a certain cosmopolitan look—an amalgamation of worldly urban beauty—could suggest new frontiers of experience for Hong Kong and Chinese culture and industry. Often, as in the case of Maggie Q, that look was centered on the face.

As Richard Rushton argues, in his elaboration of Gilles Deleuze's work, the face doesn't merely reveal the thoughts or emotions of the person beneath it, but conceives possible social relations and possible worlds.[65] Or as Deleuze, in collaboration with Félix Guattari, puts it, "It is not the individuality of the face that counts but the efficacy of the ciphering it makes possible, and in what cases it makes it possible."[66] Rushton notes that faces are typically conceived of as signs that express internal states, as when a smile betrays happiness. He traces this tendency to Darwin's *The Expression of the Emotions* and similar studies that attempt to categorize facial expression in either universalistic or culturally specific systems of signification. We certainly see this strategy for reading faces at play in earlier encounters with Eurasian faces in Hong Kong. As in phrenology, there is an attempt to "feel out" the faces of Chan Si-si, Jenny Hu, and Michael Wong, seeking patterns of "too Chinese" or "too Western" to make judgments about everything from filial piety to sexual impropriety. But the turn-of-the-millennium Eurasians did not inspire readings for meaning, but rather spawned discourses of possibility, and it is this function of the face—what it "does" as opposed to what it "means"—that interests Rushton and Deleuze. The constellation of seemingly incongruous signs on the faces of Eurasian-looking stars do not merely point inward toward the individual's inner subjectivities, but point outward unto possible configurations of racial encounters, hybrid states, and global ambitions. The Eurasian face announces "now this is possible": surely new possibilities in Chinese physicality, but also, through the thrill of beauty, new possibilities for global partnerships and Chinese ambitions on the world stage. Thus, the face is not simply a collection of stable signs and meanings, but a vector with an anchor and a direction that points to possible fields of experience and social encounters.

Four quotes about model/actress Maggie Q illustrate such possible frontiers suggested by the Eurasian face in turn-of-the-millennium Hong Kong. The first is from Hong Kong film industry writer/producer Bey Logan, who worked with Maggie Q on *Gen-Y Cops* and *Dragon Squad* (Daniel Lee, 2005). Both are action films, largely in English, explicitly directed toward international markets. In a *Time Asia* cover story about Eurasians in Asian entertainment, Logan is quoted as saying, "Who better to personify the diversification of Hong Kong movies than a Eurasian actor . . . It's a face that everyone can identify with and accept." With regards to Maggie Q in particular, he adds, "When you look at Maggie, you see the whole world in her face."[67] Maggie Q's face thus suggests a mass identification that, to the producer, transcends racial boundaries, a topic of special interest to a film industry anxious about racial difference, cultural translatability, and audience racism, all of which were fixations in the post-Jackie Chan, post *Crouching Tiger* period of co-production and global sales. For the industry, Maggie Q was a mediating figure between Hong Kong (and perhaps greater China) and the elusive international market. As with the case of Nancy Kwan and Suzie Wong's nose, a Eurasian face is pitched as a neutralized form of Chineseness, one that the rest of the world could see itself in, and therefore identify with on-screen and consume. If Western identification with Chinese actors was seen as an impossibility, Maggie Q's Eurasian face suggested otherwise.

A similar sentiment is expressed by Michael Ying, then the chief executive of Esprit Holdings, which runs the Esprit fashion line. Asked why he replaced Taiwanese model/actress Shu Qi with Maggie Q to represent the Esprit brand, he responded that a mixed-race face is better for introducing new products in overseas markets.[68] Esprit had just acquired Australia's Red Earth cosmetics line and needed a face to expand the line in Esprit's branches in Asia and around the world. Maggie Q, fresh off the "new humans" blockbuster *Gen-Y Cops* and on the doorstep of Hollywood with *Manhattan Midnight* (Alfred Cheung, 2001) and *Rush Hour 2* (Brett Ratner, 2001), seemed a logical choice. As Red Earth products focused on the face, the company sought a model whose features could stand for the faces of as many potential consumers as possible. Makeup—especially of the eyes, cheeks, and lips—is a detail-intensive process and, with the face being the center of so much racial discourse, therefore requires a model whose details are not alienating to certain populations. The Eurasian face, as Joanne Rondilla puts it, is a "relatable ideal" of beauty.[69] To paraphrase Logan, the more of the world that can see itself in Maggie Q's eye shape, skin tone, and lip size, the wider the potential reach of the makeup line. Maggie Q's Eurasian face thus virtualizes a company's transnational reach; it graphically maps out the possibility of the world consuming Red Earth products.

Maggie Q's arrival in the Hong Kong entertainment scene coincided with the moment many local studios and conglomerates sought international markets, as was the case in the fashion and cosmetics world with Esprit. Maggie Q was one of several "ABC" and mixed-race stars signed by power agent Willie Chan (who famously made Jackie Chan a star) at a moment when he, in conjunction with Jackie Chan's JCE Movies and Emperor Multimedia Group, tried his hand at English-language production. *Manhattan Midnight*, starring mixed-race actors Maggie Q and Michael Wong, was one such production. Maggie Q also found work with regionally and globally ambitious Media Asia Films, which produced the aforementioned *Purple Storm*, *Gen-X Cops*, and *Gen-Y Cops*, the third a US–Hong Kong co-production that featured Maggie Q. With Jing's Production, Media Asia also produced the English-language sexploitation thriller *Naked Weapon* (Ching Siu-tung, 2002) starring Maggie Q and other Asian Americans such as Daniel Wu, Anya, and Andrew Lin. In the lead-up to the release of *Naked Weapon*, much of the gossip surrounding the film centered on whether Maggie Q and co-star (and former boyfriend) Daniel Wu would have a sex scene together. When asked whether audiences could expect such a scene, producer Wong Jing, ever the showman, responded, "Well you know Maggie Q is a ghost girl [*gwai mui zai*], so perhaps."[70] In many ways, Wong's comment follows the phrenological tradition of feeling out physical characteristics to make assumptions about moral character, in this case, noting that her half-whiteness equates with a casualness regarding sexuality. But aside from judging Maggie Q and stereotyping foreigners, Wong's quote uses Maggie Q's mixed-race look as a way to entice viewers with uncertainty. "Perhaps" (*waa m maai*), he says, hitching the ambiguity of Maggie Q's race to the anything-goes soft-core circus that is Wong Jing's specialty. If the Bey Logan and Michael Ying quotes suggest the ways in which Maggie Q's face virtualizes the global reach of Hong Kong, Wong Jing's suggests the sexual possibilities that may emerge when the global reaches Hong Kong.

That Maggie Q's character in *Naked Weapon* is mixed race never surfaces as a problem in the narrative. Her "foreign" features are easily co-opted into the logic of the film based on their association with sexual possibility that Wong sells so unabashedly in his quote to the media. However, Maggie Q's Western look did arise as a potential issue when she appeared in the period film *Three Kingdoms: Resurrection of the Dragon* (Daniel Lee, 2008). Because they represent a globalized future, mixed-race stars have historically found it difficult to appear in costume pictures; Jenny Hu never did and, after twenty years in the industry, Michael Wong finally appeared in a *wuxia* film with *Seven Swords* (Tsui Hark, 2005).[71] However, given her local, regional, and international appeal, Maggie Q is a box office draw, and thus was cast opposite superstars Andy Lau and Sammo Hung in the China-Hong Kong-South Korea co-production *Three Kingdoms: Resurrection of the Dragon*, based on stories from the famous historical novel *Romance of the Three Kingdoms*. In the special features of the *Three Kingdoms* DVD, director Daniel Lee defended his casting of the Eurasian actress, first by citing historical accuracy. According to Lee, because Han Chinese interacted with "barbarians" (*hu ren*) during the Three Kingdoms era, it would not be unlikely that a Chinese general like Cao Cao would have descendants with the "flavor of a barbarian" (*hu ren de wei dao*), and therefore casting a mixed-race star would be accurate. However, aside from historical authenticity, Lee claims also to have cast Maggie Q because she suggested new possibilities of Chinese femininity. In the same DVD featurette, Lee says that he wanted to depict a woman who was both beautiful and fierce. "What we needed was unlike what we are used to when we think of [Chinese] women, and so I thought of the more western Maggie Q."[72] Here, Maggie Q's mixed-race features—her "barbarian flavor"—is evoked to imagine possibilities of Chinese femininity (beauty *and* fighting spirit) that is allegedly unlike what audiences normally get with "pure" Chinese actresses. There is also the implication that it takes a Westernized actress to embody those sentiments, and therefore a Hawaii-raised, biracial, and bicultural actress like Maggie Q would be most appropriate. In other words, Lee wants viewers to see that a racially and culturally Westernized actress helps realize new possibilities for Chinese characters and Chinese filmmaking. This final quote shows how filmmakers rationalized their attraction to mixed race in terms of creative liberation from Chinese gender types and from perceived restrictions posed by local casting.[73]

## *Janet Hsieh's tan*

Maggie Q's Eurasian features overshadow another aspect of her look commonly associated with the overseas star: tan skin. If overseas Chinese men may be stereotyped for muscles, overseas Chinese women are thought to be immediately identifiable by their figures and their skin tone. Many Chinese American women I've spoken with testify to having faced scrutiny over their "American-sized bodies" and their darker skin. These traits have been naturalized through various discourses of diet and recreation that mark overseas Chinese as having inherently different kinds of bodies as a result of their exposure to the rest of the world. Incidentally, body shape and skin tone are precisely the two dominant parameters for defining feminine beauty in Taiwan and Hong Kong, and the local entertainment industries (everything from print advertising to TV to film) are populated with actresses and models with rail-thin figures and glowing white skin. How does desire for thin and white reconcile with fascination with the "new human" Chinese, who may be heavy and dark? "Mutated" overseas celebrities like Janet Hsieh have challenged local expectations of beauty and obsessions with pale skin, simultaneously showcasing new worldly possibilities of the Chinese body while fitting within dominant discourses of skin color by remaining marginalized as inherently different.

There is a belief, especially among Euro-American critics, that the skin-whitening craze in Asia is based on an adherence to colonial and post-colonial standards of beauty. This position is often voiced in efforts to discredit the expansion of transnational media (and their ideals of beauty) into developing nations, especially the extent to which their global penetration has imposed definitions of femininity that are based on racial hierarchies.[74] However, this is only part of the story. I have already shown how multinational cosmetics and entertainment companies rely on racial ambiguity, and not just whiteness, to attract consumers of all shades. Scholars have also pointed to traditional idealizations of whiteness in Asia that predate contact with the West. In ancient China, for instance, those with dark skin—the "black-headed people"—were associated with the laboring classes and those bearing fair skin with the aristocracy who could afford not to spend time under the sun.[75] Hegemonic standards of beauty deriving from the West do of course inform the aesthetics of "white" in China, but so do longstanding palettes of beauty within China, as well as regional, intra-racial discourses of femininity, especially those from Japan.

Emma Jinhua Teng has observed that "whiteness" often becomes a "floating signifier" in critical discourse, slipping between a racial category and a chromatic one.[76] This slippage often masks the ways in which white skin is racialized locally, where it may not simply refer to Caucasian features. For instance, a study of Hong Kong consumers' reactions to skin whitening advertisements reveals that locals differentiate between Chinese and Caucasian forms of white skin, with special attention paid to differences in skin texture and clarity.[77] Meanwhile, a billboard featured prominently in Taipei subway stations in mid-2000 features two models: a Chinese woman with pearl-white skin and a Caucasian woman with a dark tan; the advertisement's pitch is that beauty products can help Chinese women achieve an ideal of whiteness quite distinct from the bronze look favored in the United States.[78] It is clear from this evidence that the desire for fair skin does not merely express a desire to attain a Western standard of beauty but, rather, it is a way to attain a specific Asian feminine ideal informed by class consciousness and reinforced by intra-racial standards of beauty from Japan and Korea. It is no surprise then that overseas Chinese—typically associated with an elite, jet-set class with the means to immigrate—are considered racial freaks when they "return" to Taiwan and Hong Kong as dark as outdoor laborers. Tan, non-laboring women are seen as oddities of Chineseness, kissed by the Western sun and seemingly oblivious to the standards of beauty of their own people.

So, what happens when an "ABC" woman with seemingly perfect specifications—a MIT double major in biology and Spanish, who speaks five languages, was a youth violin prodigy who played at the White House and throughout Europe, has a black belt in taekwondo, and is a fashion model—arrives in Taiwan darker than the rest of the crop? Under what terms can she be a local star? Armed with cosmopolitan credentials, Janet Hsieh has become a sex icon, a TV host, and a symbol of Taiwan on the world stage, especially because, like L. A. Boyz a decade earlier, she speaks the Taiwanese dialect more fluently than the Mandarin one. (Hsieh publically identifies as an "ABT": American-born Taiwanese, although that doesn't preclude her from being typecast as "ABC," the star persona explored in this chapter.) Hsieh is most famous as the host of *Fun Taiwan*, an English-language travel show about Taiwan produced by Discovery Travel & Living for broadcast around the world, as well as in Taiwan. Perhaps as a result of her travels, Hsieh is perceived to have darker skin than the pale white of most Taiwanese celebrities. Online and on the streets, locals have commented on Hsieh's dark skin. One journalist recalls that when spending a day with Hsieh in public in Taiwan, one frequently hears passersby tell the TV host, "Whoah, you're so dark! . . . You're even darker in person."[79] On *Fun Taiwan* and in print, Hsieh is indeed tanner than the local ideal, sometimes even flaunting her tan lines. Some fans online have joked about the need for photographers to customize lighting setups to reduce Hsieh's tan. In many fashion spreads and publicity photos, Hsieh's tan is sometimes blown out by a strong key light to make her more acceptable to local tastes, as in a June 2010 spread in *FHM International Chinese Edition*. In this sense, Hsieh is a "lighting problem" for an entertainment and modeling industry expecting fair skin.[80] In fact, when Hsieh first entered the industry as a model, she was told that she'd need to be lighter (and lose weight) to succeed. But, ultimately, Hsieh found a way to be herself and sell her distinctiveness. Meanwhile, the industry and the Taiwanese media found a way to assimilate Hsieh's look vis-à-vis her "ABC" persona.

The most obvious way that Hsieh could take advantage of her "foreign" tan was by selling it as a mark of cosmopolitan authenticity. As the host of a travel show, Hsieh's tan was bodily proof of her experience and commitment to exploring the outdoors. Her show *Fun Taiwan* depicts Hsieh as constantly on the move under the sun, hopping in and out of a Jeep wearing a tank-top, crawling through alleyways, exploring fishing villages, and interviewing street vendors. Hsieh's tan is a palimpsest of her international travels, which she documents, through text and photos, in her book *Traveling with 100 Toothbrushes*.[81] One of the longest chapters of her book is entitled "Beauty on the Go," and through her personal beauty secrets while on transpacific flights or strategies for packing cosmetics, Hsieh links her physical appearance with her experiences as a jet-set cosmopolitan. Hsieh looks the way she does *because* she travels, not in spite of it, the chapter seems to suggest. Janet Hsieh's personal look is also tied to cosmopolitan authenticity in an *FHM* magazine spread, with a headline that reads (in its original English), "The Real Woman in the Real World." Accompanying revealing photos of Hsieh, including one where her arm is clearly more naturally tanned than her (typically unexposed) thighs, is an introduction to Hsieh's appeal. When she's out in the real world (referring to her international travels), "there's no pretending to be beautiful," the article reads, attributing her looks to her natural state while on the road. "Only now can we deeply understand how 'not faked' can be sexy," it adds.[82] The authenticity of Hsieh's beauty is analogous to the authenticity of Hsieh in her travels and her persona as "a real woman in the real world." The tone of the article suggests that it takes a world-traveled woman like Hsieh to teach local Taiwanese what authenticity in beauty really is.

There is a similarly pedantic tone in other instances of advertisers, critics, and even government representatives' attempts to assimilate Hsieh's worldly skin tone into the Taiwanese mainstream. As with the case of L. A. Boyz's muscles, Janet Hsieh's tan is celebrated in various discourses of physical and spiritual health. Some locals were surprised that a model as dark as Hsieh could be a spokesperson for sunscreen, as skincare products in Taiwan are typically sold for their aesthetic, rather than protective, functions.[83] But when asked about her use of sunscreen, Hsieh responds, "I'm not afraid of being tan, I'm only afraid of burning," turning the conversation away from white beauty and toward dark health.[84] Her tan also represents active, outdoor lifestyles typically associated with the United States. Her look is "passable in the United States," but will lead her to being called "black chick" in Taiwan, as one article put it.[85] And yet it is ideal for companies seeking an authentic spokesperson for outdoor fashions and sporting goods, such as specialized brand bicycles. Meanwhile, a *Harper's Bazaar* story ties her dark skin to not being afraid to get dirty while on risky outdoors adventures.[86] That spirit of adventure is combined with her skin tone in phrases commonly used to describe Hsieh's healthy lifestyle: *jian kang shai hei* (healthy tan), *jian kang fu se* (healthy skin color), *jian kang mei* (healthy beauty). In these profiles, Hsieh's willingness to be dark is thus not only a testament to her healthy body, but a healthy outlook on life. An article celebrating acts of courage by Taiwanese celebrities includes a profile of Janet Hsieh, who, at the beginning of her modeling career, fended off criticisms of being overweight and too dark, and discovered a way to be both happy about herself and still have professional success.[87] Even the government military magazine *Youth Daily*

*News*, published by the General Political Warfare Bureau, celebrated the courage and tenacity represented by Hsieh's "healthy look": "Janet gets darker and darker, but as long as she can be on the move, up mountains and into the seas, she doesn't care."[88] In these examples, Hsieh's look is moralized as outgoing, healthy, and bold. These moralizing references to Hsieh's dark skin are reminiscent of longstanding practices in Chinese culture of reading feminine virtue in skin color. In Confucian texts, the term *nü se* (woman color) refers to the beauty that emerges on the face as a result of stirrings of the heart.[89] It thus also evokes sexual and romantic energy, in addition to physical capability and feminine demeanor. Today, the phrase *lian se* (face color) refers to complexion, as well as emotional equilibrium. Efforts to "read" Janet Hsieh's "foreign" skin color for physical and inner beauty thus correspond to efforts to understand the moral and spiritual implications of being a worldly Chinese/Taiwanese woman.

If Janet Hsieh's tan envisions new physical, emotional, and even moral possibilities associated with the world beyond Taiwan, it also allows her, and other dark-skinned actors and actresses, to play characters beyond the usual Han Chinese. If beautiful tanned skin is associated with the foreign, it makes sense then that actresses with that look can more easily play characters of other races. Janet Hsieh was once slated to star in a TV serial *Ni wa wa* (Clay Doll) about aboriginals because, as one gossip rag put it, "Janet wouldn't need special darkening makeup, she already looks like an aboriginal."[90] Similarly, the natural-toned Maggie Q played a character with "barbarian" blood in *Three Kingdoms: Resurrection of the Dragon*. Chinese Canadian actress Christy Chung, a Hong Kong industry veteran who is also not afraid of baring her somewhat darker skin, has played Himalayan in *Samsara* (Pan Nalin, 2001) and Thai in the Hong Kong co-production *Jan Dara* (Nonzee Nimibutr, 2001). According to American-raised actress Eugenia Yuan, who has played ghosts in her two starring Hong Kong roles to date, a foreign look has provided her opportunities to play more challenging, unusual roles. However, just as she is often mistaken for Filipino, Malaysian, or Singaporean on the streets of Hong Kong, the tan Yuan is not offered many "normal" Hong Kong roles where she can play an ordinary, ethnically Chinese person.[91] The darker-skinned overseas actress is therefore every shade of the world except white—that is, except the Chinese ideal. She is praised for her healthiness, sense of freedom and individuality, and racial flexibility, but in practice "she can play anybody" easily slips into "she can play anybody except us," as actresses like Yuan, who won awards for playing non-local ghosts but has yet to be cast as anything else, quickly discovered. Dark skin is expressed in positive terms, often to prove a point about health versus beauty, or individuality versus conformity, but its bearers remain special cases; the press, the industry, and the public may recognize the progressive message that tanned skin represents, even the fact that one day we should all be as tan as Janet Hsieh, but nobody wants to actually have it, or accept this "new human" look as their own just yet.

## *Edison Chen's English*

A similar case can be made for the American-accented Cantonese or Mandarin of the "ABC" star. Fans in Hong Kong and Taiwan often fawn over the "cuteness" of the accents, and yet, as I'm told, no local would want to be caught speaking so improperly. The exoticism of the North American, or in some cases British or Australian, accent allows locals to infantilize the overseas Chinese, containing the sublime awkwardness posed by the muscles, the hybrid features, the dark skin, and the fluent English. The accent also maintains the perception of an inherent bodily difference—observed here on the level of vocal inflection—of the overseas Chinese. The foreign accent goes hand-in-hand with the ABC's frequent use of overseas English on-screen and in interviews, a language choice perceived as an aberration in Chinese-language media, as well as a source of much anxiety in societies with a shaky relationship to English more generally.

As Tan Chee-Beng has argued, although language is no criteria for Chinese identity (because ethnic identification is not the same as cultural identification), language continues to be a battleground on which Chinese identity and authenticity is debated across communities, nations, and regions.[92] In Hong Kong, the persistence of English, as the language of the (ex-)colonizer but also a necessary skill for international trade, continues to trigger debates about local identity, national integration, and international advantage. Spreading English beyond the missionary schools, the compulsory education reforms in the late 1960s and 1970s made English nominally required for Hong Kong youth. Incidentally, the same years also saw the widespread recognition and formalization of Chinese as an official language of Hong Kong. Thus, English and Chinese (Cantonese, when spoken) emerged in those decades as dialectical; anxieties about the "rise of Chinese" couldn't escape lamentations about the "falling standards of English," and vice versa. The debate intensified as the 1997 handover neared, and with the development of the "trilingual, biliterate" language policy after 1997. What Kingsley Bolton calls the "Hong Kong complaint tradition" raged, with academics, critics, politicians, and the everyday person offering their two cents about the alleged decline in the city's English ability and what (if anything) should be done about it.[93] Most incendiary, and certainly provocative, was the analysis offered by one local linguist, Benjamin T'sou, who claimed that local Hong Kong people, despite years of English education, were "cultural eunuchs" because they know "what things could or might be in cultural terms but [are] not able to participate."⁹⁴ The sexual and gendered implications of the eunuch metaphor reveals the degree of this anxiety over language, as well as the extent to which language proficiency is deemed to be necessary for Hong Kong's vitality. The metaphor also makes more understandable the consequent sexualization of English through figures like Edison Chen, who in a single body fuses wise-cracking, care-free English with libidinal appetite.

In Taiwan, English is also widespread thanks to the prevalence of Anglo-American (and undubbed) media such as film, television, and popular music. It is also taught in compulsory education at all levels, as well as in cram schools and through multimedia instructional materials such as *Studio Classroom* and *Let's Talk in English*, found on newsstands, on the radio, on TV, and online. The nervous, and often resented, drive to learn English is institutionalized through the notorious national examination system, which determines admission into public secondary schools and universities. However, in Taiwan, and to some extent in Hong Kong, English-language education is segregated between regular, Chinese-based education and that found in American, international, or bilingual schools such as the Taipei American School or the National Experimental High School in Hsinchu's Industrial Park. The segregation in education also reveals itself in social terms, with those who learn English in American or international schools, and who therefore speak English as Americans or British do, self-segregating themselves in their own social spaces, and being considered by non-fluent locals to be outsiders of class privilege and dubious morality. Thus, in Taiwan, a (however forced) desire to acquire English to gain social standing runs parallel with a recognition and resentment of true fluency in the expensive and exclusive American schools and among the "ABCs" who are thought to occupy similar class backgrounds.

Film was able to sidestep many of these anxieties over language through the longstanding tradition of relying on post-synchronous sound. In the name of realism and quality, Taiwanese cinema famously turned away from dubbing with the landmark *A City of Sadness* (Hou Hsiao-hsien, 1989), for which sound designer Tu Duu-chih imported portable digital audio tapes (DATs) for use during filming. For similar reasons, mainstream Hong Kong cinema went sync-sound in the mid-1990s. With exceptions like *Heart to Hearts* (Stephen Shin, 1988), Hong Kong films in the 1980s were post-synchronized in both Cantonese and Mandarin dialects, often with voice performers different from the actors who played the parts during filming. Therefore, North America-raised stars like Sally Yeh and Michael Wong, neither of whom spoke fluent Chinese when they arrived in Hong Kong in the 1980s, were dubbed in fluent Cantonese and Mandarin for those respective markets. Although they were known for being overseas Chinese, their accents and use of English were washed over in the post-synchronization process, thereby smoothening over any awkwardness over having foreign sounds come out of Chinese faces. One of the first Hong Kong films to employ sync-sound in the 1990s was the action film *Final Option* (1994). Director Gordon Chan has claimed that he chose to go sync-sound to create a documentary-like action experience different from the more embellished John Woo tradition. The film was also a breakthrough for Eurasian actor Michael Wong, who could not speak fluent Cantonese. Chan argued his case against resistant producers, claiming that special police forces in Hong Kong (like the one played by Wong in the film) were usually English-speakers, and therefore the film needed Wong to speak in his native English to give the film greater realism.[95] The result, as with Wong's reprisals in the many *Option* sequels, is a film that combines English and Cantonese through code-switching and code-mixing—similar to the ways the languages are combined in everyday professional life in Hong Kong.

However, because *Final Option* was shot in sync-sound, Michael Wong's Cantonese dialogue was delivered with a strong American accent that would come to define Wong—and other "ABCs"—for the rest of his career. The accent became so ingrained in his star persona that even post-1994 films that are post-synchronized are dubbed with an American accent, as on the Cantonese audio for *XIMP* (Kenneth Lau, 1999).[96] Michel Chion has written about the ways characters may be dubbed inappropriately, as with a demon voice for a little girl in *The Exorcist* (William Friedkin, 1973), thereby "creating a monster."[97] In the case of Michael Wong, dubbing a "ghostly" sound on the "*guaizai*" is both inappropriate (in that it monstratizes the character) and appropriate (in that it puts the foreign monster in his proper place). Wong's fluent English is thus always complemented by his imperfect Cantonese, leading him to be ridiculed as an actor even when he is one of the few major actors in Hong Kong who can convincingly portray colonial authority figures like police squadron leaders. The potency of his worldly fluency—a fluency deemed impossible in Hong Kong or perpetually under par by the "complaint tradition"—is contained by handicapping his Chinese.

The infantalization of ABCs and their language challenges has become a significant part of their public appeal. Public mocking of their accents and Chinese illiteracy is a kind of welcome ritual for overseas Chinese breaking into the Hong Kong and Taiwan entertainment industries. The L. A. Boyz were "celebrated" for their "funny westernized Taiwanese,"[98] and picking on their elementary Chinese was a popular game on variety shows.[99] Daniel Wu took a drubbing for his Cantonese pronunciation in *City of Glass* (Mabel Cheung, 1998), and subsequent films *Cop on a Mission*, *Love Undercover* (Joe Ma, 2002) and *House of Fury* (Stephen Fung, 2005) contain self-reflexive scenes in which his character is lampooned for his poor Cantonese. Chinese audiences laughed at Leehom Wang's "ABC-accented

Mandarin" in *Lust, Caution* (2007), directed by Ang Lee, a notorious stickler for sync-sound even for non-native actors.[100] Maggie Q was compared to an elementary school student by a reporter who watched her write a basic Sinitic character.[101] Canada-raised actor-singer-songwriter Nicholas Tse has felt compelled to admit his inability to confidently write lyrics in Cantonese or Mandarin.[102] The inability to read and write characters, even if speaking and listening are competent, is common to many 1.5- and second-generation overseas Chinese, and this illiteracy has become a source of amusement in "infotainment" specials like behind-the-scenes DVD featurettes. In the special features for films like Daniel Wu's *Enter the Phoenix* (Stephen Fung, 2004) and Edison Chen's *Dummy Mommy without a Baby* (Joe Ma, 2001), we witness the ABC stars struggling with their dialogue or hear from co-stars who mock the overseas actors' Cantonese. In featurette after featurette, there is a fetishization of Wu's and Chen's shooting scripts, in which their Cantonese dialogue is completely re-transcribed phonetically. The spectacle of their struggle is here inscribed in the monstratizatization of the Chinese language, converted into Romanized gibberish, a kind of illegible mutation similar to the strange Chinese muscles, aquiline noses, and foreign tans that locals have learned to find both fascinating and repulsive.

For Edison Chen in particular, the "bad" Cantonese accent has played an integral part in his reputation as a "bad" boy movie star, the North American accent holding on as evidence of his defiance with regard to integrating in Hong Kong. His use of English, too, becomes a sign of attitude. The regional MTV program *Whatever Things*, an Asian combination of MTV's stunt and prank shows *Jackass* and *Punk'd*, features Chen as English-speaking host. In two of his Hong Kong films, Edison Chen uses predominantly English in bad-boy roles. In *Gen Y-Cops* and *Trivial Matters* (Pang Ho-cheung, 2007), Chen speaks in a style adapted from what linguists have termed African American Vernacular English (AAVE), thus borrowing local stereotypes of African American deviance for his characters' (and perhaps his star) personas. For instance, Chen's speech includes monophthongizations of diphthongs, copula drops, and alveolar nasals for velar nasals in double-syllable words, as in his memorable retort in *Trivial Matters*: "naw, you trippin' girl!"[103]

Local interpretation of Chen's English as defiant and arrogant came to a startling climax in early 2008. Three weeks after hundreds of nude photos involving Chen and his sexual partners (many of whom were famous actresses in the Hong Kong entertainment industry) leaked onto the Internet, Chen held a press conference publically apologizing to the women whose images were inadvertently distributed, and to the people of Hong Kong for the disturbance the incident caused. In his profession of guilt and involvement in the collapse of several high-profile careers, Chen decided to use his native English in arguably his most famous English-language "performance" to date. Instead of tying Chen's language choice to his vulnerability or sincerity, the Hong Kong media chose to interpret his use of English in the same way Hong Kong scriptwriters and audiences had been understanding his English since his film debut eight years earlier: as a playful, hyper-stylized invocation of an incorrigible bad boy. On his talk show, famed entrepreneur Wilfred Wong acknowledged the performative and rhetorical nature of Chen's decision to use English. Wong called Chen's performance "just about perfect" (*gan fu jyun mei*), arguing that the use of English would remind Chen's audience of his overseas upbringing and his "ghostly" (*guai zai*) background, and therefore compel listeners to be more understanding of his indiscretions.[104] In this case, the press not only noted the performativity of Chen's bad-boy "ABC" English, it also, by acknowledging and then deconstructing the connotative power of Chen's English, sought control over it. By identifying the ABC's rhetorical move, the local media could call him out on it: trying to attribute your actions to your overseas background is clever, but it isn't fooling anybody, Wong seems to be saying of Chen's decision. Once again, language choice is evoked, by Chen and the local media, to draw distinctions between cultural insider and outsider. The decision for an overseas person to "not speak Chinese" in places like Hong Kong, Taiwan, and China can never merely be a neutral one; due to the "haunting of Chineseness" characteristic of the diasporic condition, using English is necessarily a political act, as Ien Ang has powerfully argued.[105] In the fallout from his apology, Chen's use of English gets reinscribed by pundits as strategy on a linguistic battleground where the power to speak in English is a subject of cultural, political, economic, and as the "eunuch" metaphor suggests, sexual anxiety. Chen can't simply speak in English as a Canadian national; his English will always be "ABC English," fraught with irony, mockable immaturity, moral ambiguity, and class privilege.

## "World Cred"

Edison Chen's association with AAVE recalls one of the claims of naturalness with which I began this chapter: that because singer Shunza "grew up in America, she's deeply influenced by black music." Why overseas Chinese are associated with African American vernaculars and styles is worth considering further, for it brings us back to the question of the role that the cosmopolitan "ABC" plays in imagining Hong Kong, Taiwan, or cultural China on the world stage.

Shunza is not the only overseas Chinese musician who performs African American genres. L. A. Boyz were among the first to bring hip-hop and breakdancing to Taiwan, David Tao is often dubbed the first to popularize new jack soul and R&B, and Shawn Sung is considered the first to perfect rap in Mandarin. Countless other Chinese Americans and Chinese Canadians have broken into the Chinese pop world through hip-hop or R&B. CoCo Lee, Leehom Wang, Elva Hsiao, Wilber Pan, Vanness Wu, Khalil Fong, and Jin Au-yeung have all, through music, dance, and fashion, flaunted contemporary African American styles. Edison Chen not only raps (in English, Cantonese, and Mandarin), but is also a fashion entrepreneur in the mold of Jay-Z and Scott Combs. Many of these artists are known for inserting English into their music. Beyond the occasional English word or phrase common in Asian pop for decades, these artists have entire verses (either sung or rapped) in their native English. The association of the overseas Chinese with hip-hop is so ingrained in the local consciousness that Daniel Wu spoofed the ABC rapper in his fake boy band Alive, as depicted in the hybrid documentary *Heavenly Kings* (Daniel Wu, 2006). That nobody seemed to realize the characters were spoofs further proves how "natural" the association has become.

But why hip-hop? We can think about national and transnational factors that bring Chinese American artists to the genre. Within American hip-hop are qualities that may appeal to Chinese American artists, and Asian American musicians more broadly. For one, hip-hop in the United States has long held an affinity for Asian culture, as with the New York scene's fascination with martial arts imagery, language, and characters, with the music of the Wu-Tang Clan being the most famous and visible example.[106] It is not surprising then that Asian Americans have sought a home within the genre. Hip-hop and other African American cultural forms also afford Asian Americans opportunities to negotiate their own social and class positions in the United States. In her study of language use among Southeast Asian Americans, Angela Reyes found that the appropriation of AAVE gives non-African American minorities an ability to identify with subcultural formations in the United States, to shape their own generational affiliations, and to define their own class identities vis-à-vis blackness.[107] Hip-hop culture has proven open to marginalized groups seeking accreditation through blackness; because of the persistent black–white binary in hip-hop, Latinos, Asian Americans, and multi-racial people in the United States often choose blackness to demonstrate their musical authenticity through racial performance.[108] In a society where it is sometimes more "authentic" to be black than to be white, it shouldn't be surprising that some Asian Americans (as well as other non-blacks) have paradoxically sought in hip-hop an arena through which to exert their own identities.

If we think of Chinese American hip-hop as transnational, and not simply based on national racial dynamics, we discover other reasons Chinese American artists turn to the genre. Mainstream hip-hop, with its obsession with wealth and consumerism, confirms the class stereotypes of overseas Chinese within Hong Kong and Taiwan, and therefore invites overseas Chinese to participate in an un-problematized, even exciting, way. Equally important is the fact that, of the popular music genres marketable in Hong Kong and Taiwan, hip-hop is one that acknowledges origin—"where one's from"—and thus can be self-conscious about the presence of unusual bodies (muscled, tanned, accented) clearly from somewhere else. Chinese American stars in Hong Kong and Taiwan hip-hop don't have to hide their international backgrounds, but can even flaunt and exploit them. Thus, Jin Au-yeung can release a Cantonese album called *A.B.C.* about his experiences as an overseas Chinese, and Leehom Wang can rap about the different Chinese accents within the diaspora on tracks like "Cockney Girl." More specifically, however, "ABC" rappers typically don't rhyme about their locatedness in the United States or Canada, nor do they rep' hometowns as American rappers often do, but rather they flaunt their cosmopolitanness as jet-set Chinese, as Jin raps in a guest appearance on Leehom Wang's "Heroes of Earth": "I keeps it blazing/from Shanghai to Beijing/stop in Taiwan back to Hong Kong where they stay doing they thing."[109] Leehom Wang in particular has explored the possibilities of hip-hop in imagining a cosmopolitan Chinese identity. Beyond the passport imagery sprinkling cosmopolitan flavor to the album art of his 2002 greatest hits disc *Evolution* (a motif also found in the liner notes to CoCo Lee's 1994 debut *Love from Now On*, dubbed a "Music Passport"), Wang incorporates the cosmopolitan into his self-theorization about Chineseness as he sees it. Inspired by African Americans' repossession of the "n-word," Wang has developed what he calls "chinked-out music," a "sound that is international, and at the same time, Chinese."[110] Chinked-out, as observed through Wang's music and videos, is hip-hop fashioned out of high-brow "Chinese" elements (kun opera and ethnic minority music) and given the slick and sexy gleam of a jet-set lifestyle.[111] (The video for "At that Faraway Place" features Wang, like a Western anthropologist going into the Orient or a Maoist songwriter seeking rural sounds, collecting songs in small Chinese towns, as he raps about traveling the world and living between hotels; the aforementioned song "Cockney Girl" includes a roll-call of all the Chinese accents he's heard around the world.) Other "ABC" hip-hop artists are less articulate about their cosmopolitan motivations, but frequently embody that lifestyle through their designer street fashions and muscular dance moves.

Therefore, what we have is a genre that accommodates, even celebrates, extraordinary, monstrous Chinese bodies that can perform the world—"extraordinary" referring to bodies stylized by fashion, muscles, and accent, and "the world" referring to both local cultural traditions (such as kun opera or Chinese pop) and the cultural forms of even the most distant communities, with black culture considered the ultimate, most exotic culture of all. This hyphenated identity—the Chinese-cosmopolitan—reworks one of the foundational characteristics of hip-hop: to rep' a 'hood. In *The 'Hood Comes First*, Murray Forman argues that evocations of space and place in hip-hop are expressions of what is taken to be authorial truth: the ghettos of rap narratives are what Lefebvre calls "spaces of experience" that bear witness to actual events. These are localities believed to be inhabited by real people, and hip-hop artists, through the discourse of "the real," co-opt these spaces in culturally meaningful ways.[112] When a rapper rhymes about what happened "here," he or she is understood to be testifying to a certain reality and, in doing so, claiming ownership of that space. But when an "ABC" star like Leehom Wang sings or directs videos about hopping from New York to London to Shanghai to Taipei, he is not narrating a "here" but a "there, there, and there." Like the rapper representing the corners of the Bronx or the streets of South Central Los Angeles, the overseas stars rep' the "out there," a glamorous space they claim as within their locus of experience. The genre, through its conventions of space and truth, lends credence to the stars' foreign street gear, their "black" dance moves, and their Western musical ability, because through the music there is the connotation that they have been abroad, consumed the foreign world, and let it indexically change their bodies and behaviors in ways no local has. That world is embedded in the voice as well, the accent tracing the peculiar contours of the foreign and the "perfect" English an authentication of the cosmopolitan. If hip-hop in the US is obsessed with the ideals of "street cred," "ABC" acts in Taiwan and Hong Kong represent the appeal of "world cred"—bodily, linguistic, and consumerist proof that they are tapped into larger transnational networks, be that an affiliation with a certain Chinese cosmopolitan class, or a belonging to what H. Samy Alim calls the "global hip hop nation."[113]

For those in Hong Kong and Taiwan seeking worldly status—political, economic, cultural—there is often a credibility problem. Cultural scholars frequently overstate the agency of local appropriation of dominant, hegemonic culture emanating from the West. In hip-hop, for instance, so much has been written about the political rap produced in post-colonial societies, celebrating the creativity, translation, and appropriation of active listeners thousands of miles away from the Bronx.[114] But what kind of resonances do these political rappers have outside of Western academia? In Hong Kong and Taiwan, for instance, politically "conscious" rap groups like LMF and Blacklist Workshop are celebrated among academics and critics for their adaptations of Western styles to proclaim their own local identities.[115] But these marginal acts have mostly subcultural appeal, and their popularity and ability to win hearts and initiate public debate pales in comparison to those of Leehom Wang, Edison Chen, or L. A. Boyz. These foreign-raised stars are hyped as worldly wonders who don't sound forced singing in English and apparently don't look strange posing in the studio with African American collaborators (as Wilber Pan did when he rapped alongside R&B star Akon). If hip-hop culture is characterized by its "discursive bricolage," an accumulation of imagery, sounds, and attitudes from the "space of experience,"[116] then "ABC" stars prove their accumulated world cred through the genre's rhetoric of authenticity. Their versions of the world aren't merely the imaginary worlds concocted by locals, but a bricolage of cosmopolitan culture suggested by experience and guaranteed by their bodies. And at that moment of guarantee—the sublime appearance of muscles, the grotesquerie of the tan, the uncanniness of mixed race, the cacophony of the accent—the overseas Chinese star becomes a cosmopolitan type (the "ABC") who exudes authenticity but must then be a perpetual outsider, a cultural and biological mutation, a monstrous child of globalization.

# Notes

1. L. Ling-chi Wang, "The Structure of Dual Domination: Toward a Paradigm for the Study of the Chinese Diaspora in the United States," *Amerasia Journal* 21.1–2 (1995): 149–69.
2. "*Shunzi*," *Taiwan liuxing yinyue 200 zuijia zhuanji* [Taiwan Popular Music: 200 Best Albums], eds Cora Tao, et al. (Taipei: China Times Publishing, 2009) 25.
3. Liu Youpan, "94 nian yi yue ding qi sai," *The Box Office* 195 (February 1994): 33.
4. By the 2000s, Taiwan had one of the highest cable penetration rates in the world, with rates frequently above 80 percent. Many cable networks imported programming from the West, or were Taiwanese ventures of American networks like HBO.
5. Stephanie Hemelryk Donald, Eleonore Kofman, and Catherine Kevin, "Introduction: Processes of Cosmopolitanism and Parochialism," *Branding Cities: Cosmopolitanism, Parochialism, and Social Change*, Stephanie Hemelryk Donald, et al., eds. (London: Routledge, 2009) 3–4.
6. On the dimensions of film stardom and what they suggest for star studies, see Christine Geraghty, "Re-examining Stardom: Questions of Texts, Bodies and Performance," *Reinventing Film Studies*, eds. Christine Gledhill and Linda Williams (London: Arnold, 2000) 183–201.
7. Min Zhou, "Coming of Age at the Turn of the Twenty-First Century: A Demographic Profile of Asian American Youth," *Asian American Youth: Culture, Identity, and Ethnicity*, eds. Jennifer Lee and Min Zhou (London: Routledge, 2004) 48.
8. Aihwa Ong, *Flexible Citizenship: The Cultural Logics of Transnationality* (Durham, NC: Duke University Press, 1999) 88–92.
9. Liesbeth de Block and David Buckingham, *Global Children, Global Media: Migration, Media and Childhood* (New York: Palgrave, 2007) viii.
10. I have "return" in parentheses to highlight the common misconception by those in Taiwan and Hong Kong that ethnic Chinese born abroad can "return" to places they may have never been. Many Chinese Americans can attest to their confusion over phrases like *hui Taiwan* (return to Taiwan) and *fan Hoeng Gong* (return to Hong Kong) when they visit Taiwan or Hong Kong for the first time.

11. Gloria Heyung Chun, "Shifting Ethnic Identity and Consciousness: U.S.-born Chinese American Youth in the 1930s and 1950s," *Asian American Youth: Culture, Identity, and Ethnicity*, eds Jennifer Lee and Min Zhou, (London: Routledge, 2004) 119.
12. Bruce White, "The Local Roots of Global Citizenship: Generational Change in a Kyushu Hamlet," *Japan's Changing Generations: Are Young People Creating a New Society?*, Gordon Mathews and Bruce White, eds. (London: Routledge, 2004) 53–4.
13. Variants that also pun foreign broadcasting networks include "British Born Chinese" (BBC) and "Canadian Born Chinese" (CBC). Interestingly, there was little initial attempt to clarify their identities as "American born Hong Konger" or "American born Taiwanese," indicating the incomprehensibility of Taiwanese and Hong Kong diasporas in the 1990s and early 2000s. There has, however, been some attempt to claim a Taiwanese diaspora with self-professed "ABTs" like Janet Hsieh.
14. Sau-ling C. Wong, "When Asian American Literature Leaves 'Home': On Internationalizing Asian American Literary Studies," *Crossing Oceans: Reconfiguring American Literary Studies in the Pacific Rim*, Noelle Brada-Williams and Karen Chow, eds. (Hong Kong: Hong Kong University Press, 2004) 32–5.
15. In Hong Kong in the early 2000s, talent manager Willie Chan was most active in discovering and promoting overseas Chinese actors like Maggie Q, Edison Chen, and Daniel Wu. In Taiwan in the mid-1990s, record labels, struggling to find fresh talent locally, held music competitions in major US cities to recruit young Chinese Americans. Eva Tsai, "Boyz, Babes &. . .: American Chinese Climb the Taiwan Pop Chart," *Sinorama* 218 (August 1996): 55.
16. Lisa Funnell, "Repatriation of Overseas Chinese Stars in Post-1997 Hong Kong Cinema: Daniel Wu, a Case Study," *Transnational Cinemas* 2.2 (2012): 163–78.
17. Noël Carroll, "Ethnicity, Race, and Monstrosity: The Rhetorics of Horror and Humor," *Beauty Matters*, Peg Zeglin Brand, ed. (Bloomington: Indiana University Press, 2000) 40.
18. Frank Dikötter, *Imperfect Conceptions: Medical Knowledge, Birth Defects and Eugenics in China* (London: Hurst, 1998) 52–4.
19. In fact, such beliefs continue to circulate in the present, albeit in a more reflexive fashion, as with the dog-man offspring in the Pang Brothers' *The Child's Eye 3D* (2010).
20. Dikötter 100.
21. Ibid. 72.
22. Yuehtsen Juliette Chung, *Struggle for National Survival: Eugenics in Sino-Japanese Contexts, 1896–1945* (New York: Routledge, 2002) 69.
23. Laurence Schneider, *Ku Chieh-kang and China's New History* (Berkeley: University of California Press, 1971) 264.
24. Emma Jinhua Teng, "Eurasian Hybridity in Chinese Utopian Visions: From 'One World' to 'A Society Based on Beauty' and Beyond," *Positions* 14.1 (Spring 2006): 138–9.
25. Jean Comaroff and John Comaroff, "Reflections on Youth, from the Past to the Postcolony," *Frontiers of Capital: Ethnographic Reflections on the New Economy*, Melissa S. Fisher and Greg Downey, eds. (Durham, NC: Duke University Press, 2006) 278.

26. Ibid. 268.
27. Lin Guihong, "Huo gun chi duo le niupai hambao, tili tebie," *Commons Daily* (March 9, 2003), *WiseNews* database, February 1, 2010.
28. Cynthia L. Nakashima, "Servants of Culture: The Symbolic Role of Mixed-Race Asians in American Discourse," *The Sum of Our Parts: Mixed Heritage Asian Americans*, Teresa Williams-León and Cynthia L. Nakashima, eds. (Philadelphia: Temple University Press, 2001) 42.
29. Jane Park, "Virtual Race: The Racially Ambiguous Action Hero in *The Matrix* and *Pitch Black*," *Mixed Race Hollywood*, eds Mary Beltrán and Camilla Fojas (New York: NYU Press, 2008) 182–202.
30. Leilani Nishime, "*The Matrix* Trilogy, Keanu Reeves, and Multiraciality at the End of Time," *Mixed Race Hollywood*, eds Mary Beltrán and Camilla Fojas (New York: NYU Press, 2008) 290–312. Mary C. Beltrán, "The New Hollywood Racelessness: Only the Fast, Furious, (and Multiracial) Will Survive," *Cinema Journal* 44.2 (Winter 2005): 59.
31. Leilani Nishime, "The Mulatto Cyborg: Imagining a Multiracial Future," *Cinema Journal* 44. 2 (Winter 2005): 34–49.
32. Emilie Yueh-yu Yeh and Darrell William Davis, "Japan Hongscreen: Pan-Asian Cinemas and Flexible Accumulation," *Historical Journal of Film, Radio and Television* 22.1 (2002): 64–5.
33. Kwai-Cheung Lo, *Chinese Face/Off: The Transnational Popular Culture of Hong Kong* (Urbana: University of Illinois Press, 2005) 108.
34. All of these characteristics are listed in a newspaper article attempting to define what makes these young characters "new humans" and "gen-x." "'X shidai' nianqingren te zheng," *Wen Wei Po* (June 21, 1999): Entertainment section.
35. Chen Jiaxin, "Xie Tingfeng tiaojiang san wu mai bao xian" *Sing Tao Daily* (January 6, 1999): Entertainment A27.
36. Gu Liyang, "Gen-X Cops" (review), *Next Magazine* (December 21, 2000): 242.
37. "Teji xin ji yuan," *IT dangan II*, narr. Edison Chen, RHK, 26 Dec. 2000, Television.
38. Zhu Liqun, "L.A. Boyz *xia yue quan sheng xunhui yanchang*," *Min Sheng Bao* (January 20, 1994): Film/TV 11.
39. Liner notes, Babes, *Babes*, Golden Point, 1995.
40. Bey Logan, personal interview, February 18, 2010.
41. Chris Berry, "'What's Big about the Big Film?' 'De-Westernizing' the Blockbuster in Korea and China," *Movie Blockbusters*, Julian Stringer, ed. (London: Routledge, 2003) 225–6.
42. Stuart Hall has written of the ways stereotypes of communities often come in contradictory pairs. "The Spectacle of the 'Other,'" *Representation: Cultural Representations and Signifying Practices*, Stuart Hall, ed. (London: Sage, 1997) 226–9.
43. *Wo ai hei se hui*, Channel [V] Taiwan, July 9, 2007.
44. In a 2012 article, Lisa Funnell observes that Daniel Wu is shirtless in at least one scene of every film he is in. Funnell 170.
45. Chi-Fu Jeffrey Yang, et al., "Male Body Image in Taiwan Versus the West: *Yanggang Zhiqi* Meets the Adonis Complex," *American Journal of Psychiatry* 162 (2005): 266.

46. Ibid. 264–5.
47. Lo 82.
48. Ibid. 87–8.
49. "Babes – nüsheng ai nansheng" (review), *The Box Office* 260 (August 28, 1996): 55.
50. Chen Qiumei, "You yi ke fangren de haizi xin: Wu Dawei," *Nong Nong* 100 (November 1992): 88.
51. The members of L. A. Boyz would appropriate the streets when they shed their pop-star glean and reconvened in 2003 as the hip-hop mega-group Machi.
52. Tsai 57.
53. A US-based reporter professes her confusion upon hearing these "goofy" lyrics. In response, L. A. Boyz member Jeffrey Huang notes, "We're like role models. . . . We go to school, we're good kids that know how to dance and rap, and we speak Taiwanese." Ashley Dunn, "Rapping to a Bicultural Beat: Dancing Trio from Irvine—the L.A. Boyz—Scores a Hit in Taiwan," *Los Angeles Times* (April 5, 1993) <http://articles.latimes.com/1993-04-05/entertainment/ca-19527_1_dancing-trio> (accessed January 26, 2011).
54. On ABC achievement as a fantasy of Chinese global success, see Grace Wang, *Soundtracks of Asian America: Navigating Race Through Musical Performance* (Durham: Duke University Press, 2015) 152–64.
55. Correspondence with Paramount Pictures Corp., Loke Wan Tho Collection, National Archives of Singapore, Singapore.
56. Sander L. Gilman, *Making the Body Beautiful: A Cultural History of Aesthetic Surgery* (Princeton: Princeton University Press, 1999) 98–111.
57. "Chan Si-si: A Veteran Starlet of the Great Wall," *Union Pictorial* 51 (February 1960): 11–13. The use of the word "alien" is from the article's original English.
58. "Puyu yi ban de xin xing Zhu Fang," *Milky Way Pictorial* 91 (October 1965): 42–3.
59. Vicky Lee, *Being Eurasian: Memories across Racial Divides* (Hong Kong: Hong Kong University Press, 2004) 8, 19–20.
60. On racial segregation and passing in Hong Kong, see Steven Frederick Fisher, "Eurasians in Hong Kong: A Sociological Study of a Marginal Group," M.Phil. Thesis, University of Hong Kong, 1975.
61. Loke Wan Tho's papers indicate that Jenny Hu (called by the Cantonese "Jenny Woo" in correspondence) was suggested to the studio in September 1962. However, Hu never appeared in an MP&GI film. Correspondence with Hech Hock Meng, September 1962, Loke Wan Tho Collection, National Archives of Singapore, Singapore.
62. "Shaoshi xin xing: Hu Yanni," *Southern Screen* (August 1965): 30.
63. "Jenny Hu to Produce Her Own Films," *Cinemart* 1 (January 1970): 42–3.
64. "Hu Yanni: mei zai qizhi li," *Cinemart* 5 (May 1970): 35.
65. Richard Rushton, "What Can a Face Do? On Deleuze and Faces," *Cultural Critique* 51 (Spring 2002): 219–37.
66. Gilles Deleuze and Félix Guattari, *A Thousand Plateaus: Capitalism and Schizophrenia*, trans. Brian Massumi (London: Athlone Press, 1988) 175.

67. Hannah Beech, "Eurasian Invasion," *Time.com*, April 23, 2001 <http://www.time.com/time/magazine/article/0,9171,106427,00.html> (accessed December 13, 2010).
68. Several news outlets paraphrased Ying's comments, although he is never quoted directly. "Lin Qingxia wei laogong zuo sheng zhao pai," *Hong Kong Commercial Daily* (March 16, 1999): C08; Bao Bao, "Q nü lian jie zhong zhi Xing Liyuan yao pai guanggao," *Hong Kong Daily News* (March 16, 1999): C01; "Lin Qingxia li wai he yi: di ku dou zhe Esprit," *Tin Tin Daily News* (March 16, 1999): B02.
69. Joanne L. Rondilla, "Making a Better Me? Pure. White. Flawless," *Is Lighter Better? Skin-tone Discrimination among Asian Americans*, Joanne L. Bondilla and Paul Spickard, eds. (Lanham: Rowman & Littlefield, 2007) 90.
70. Chen Meixiang, "Maggie Q *Wu Yanzu fu jiu qing*," *Apple Daily* (June 4, 2002): C04.
71. Even some Chinese Americans like Daniel Wu are considered too "ghostly" (*gwai gwai dei*) to be in costume pictures. Jan Tung, "M zi zou gaan zai gim jiu lou pei gu, Ng Jin Zou gam wai ngai seot hei sang," *Hong Kong Daily News* (February 26, 2001): C04.
72. "Interviews: Daniel Lee—Director," *Three Kingdoms: Resurrection of the Dragon*, dir. Daniel Lee, 2008, Lionsgate, 2010, DVD.
73. On industrial self-rationalization and behind-the-scenes interviews as reflexive discourse, see John Thornton Caldwell, *Production Culture: Industrial Reflexivity and Critical Practice in Film and Television* (Durham, NC: Duke University Press, 2008).
74. See, for example, Susanna George, "Media and Globalisation: A View from the Margins," *Feminist Media Studies* 4.1 (March 2004): 86–7.
75. Perry Johansson, "White Skin, Large Breasts: Chinese Beauty Product Advertising as Cultural Discourse," *China Information* 8.2–3 (Autumn–Winter 1998): 60–1.
76. Teng 141.
77. Solomon Leong, "Who's the Fairest of them All? Television Ads for Skin-Whitening Cosmetics in Hong Kong," *Asian Ethnicity* 7.2 (June 2006): 173–4.
78. In fact, a comparative study of cosmetics advertising in Taiwan and US fashion magazines in 2001 and 2002 reveals that advertisements in Taiwanese magazines are significantly more likely to include fair-skinned models than those in the United States. Yu-Rong Pu, "Comparisons of Cosmetic Advertisements: Strategies for Cultural Adaptations in Women's Magazines in Taiwan," MA Thesis, University of Florida, 2003.
79. Wu Chongjia, "Hei pi sheng shou bai," *China Times Weekly* 1579 (May, 27 2008), republished in *Janet Hsieh's Website* <http://janethsieh.site88.net/index.php?load=read&id=18> (accessed December 21, 2010).
80. On the way ideologies of skin color are embedded in technology, see Richard Dyer, "The Light of the World," *White: Essays of Race and Culture* (London: Routledge 1997) 82–144. On skin tone and technology in the East Asian context, see "Photo Opportunity: Kodak, Fuji Face Off in Neutral Territory, China's Vast Market," *Wall Street Journal Europe* (May 29, 1996): 1, 7.
81. Janet Hsieh, *Dai 100 zhi yashua qu lüxing* [Traveling with 100 Toothbrushes] (Taipei: Gao Bao, 2010).

82. He Peiru, "The Real Woman in the Real World," *FHM International Chinese Edition* 120 (June 2010): 95.
83. Zhu Meifang, "Janet qiao fangshai, hei liang daiyan gua baozheng," *China Times Showbiz* (May 25, 2009) <http://showbiz.chinatimes.com/2009Cti/Channel/Showbiz/showbiz-news-cnt/0,5020,110511+112009052500013,00.html> (accessed December 22, 2010).
84. Lin Wanyin, "Janet baobei mei ji zhuchiren, kang yan yang jiu kao zhe 3 ping," *United Daily News Happy Life Weekly* <http://mag.udn.com/mag/happylife/printpage.jsp?f_ART_ID=202459> (accessed December 22, 2010).
85. Feng Yixian, "Janet bingtai jianfei 22 gongjin, baoshi de youyuzheng," *Next Magazine* 499, republished in <http://85st.5dforum.com/viewthread.php?action=printable&tid=2348> (accessed December 22, 2010).
86. Cai Yuchun, "Janet, dai zhe haoqi qu lüxing," *Harper's Bazaar Taiwan*, republished in *Yahoo! Fashion Taiwan* (June 14, 2008) <http://tw.fashion.yahoo.com/article/url/d/a/080714/23/dk4.html> (accessed December 22, 2010).
87. Jabbar, "Kuaile shi shenme? Cong Tsai Kangyong chu gui tan qi," *United Daily News Blog* (December 6, 2008) <http://blog.udn.com/cooljabbar/2449731> (accessed December 22, 2010).
88. Zhou Yuxun, "Janet bu 'Zhuang' shishang ye hen mei," *Youth Daily News* (December 15, 2007) <http://news.gpwb.gov.tw/newsgpwb_2009/news.php?css=3&nid=32356&rtype=8> (accessed December 22, 2010).
89. Eva Kit Wah Man, "Female Bodily Aesthetics, Politics, and Feminine Ideals of Beauty in China," *Beauty Matters*, Peg Zeglin Brand, ed. (Bloomington: Indiana University Press, 2000) 170.
90. "Jie xi qiang Jin Zhong, Janet bi tui Gao Huijun, Tian Li," *Next Magazine* 359, republished in *Otaru Blog* (May 3, 2008) <http://hi.baidu.com/otaru/blog/item/520b22faf65e3b8c9e5146c0.html> (accessed December 22, 2010).
91. Eugenia Yuan, personal interview, February 12, 2010.
92. Tan Chee-Beng, "Ethnic Chinese: Language, Nationality and Identity," *Chinese Overseas: Comparative Cultural Issues* (Hong Kong: Hong Kong University Press, 2004) 111–34.
93. Kingsley Bolton, "Hong Kong English: Autonomy and Creativity," *Hong Kong English: Autonomy and Creativity*, Kingsley Bolton, ed. (Hong Kong: Hong Kong University Press, 2002) 14–18.
94. R. Lord and B. K. T'sou, "Chinese and the Cultural Eunuch Syndrome," *The Language Bomb* (Hong Kong: Longman, 1985) 15–19, quote on page 17.
95. Gordon Chan, cited in Thomas Podvin and David Vivier, "Interview with Gordon Chan, from the Beat Heat to A-1," *Hong Kong Cinemagic* (1 January 13, 2005) <http://www.hkcinemagic.com/en/page.asp?aid=319&page=6> (accessed December 25, 2010).
96. Mixed-race, British-raised Hong Kong actor Carl Ng has similarly been dubbed in Cantonese with a foreign accent. Carl Ng, personal interview, February 25, 2010.
97. Michel Chion, *The Voice in Cinema*, trans. Claudia Gorbman (New York: Columbia University Press, 1999) 132.

98. Zhu Liqun, Film/TV: 11.
99. Wang Lanfen, "L.A. Boyz laopo L hao," *Min Sheng Bao* (August 19, 1995): Film/TV: 11.
100. "Wang Lihong 'chu chang' bei xiao ABC kouyin de Putonghua jiang taici," *Sina News* (November 1, 2007) <http//news.sina.com.tw/ents/sinacn/cn/2007-11-01/111835181559> (accessed December 4, 2007).
101. "Guai mui zai se fai ceon," *Sing Tao Daily* (February 3, 2003): Z2.
102. Xiang Jiang Yan Ren, *Shi da mingxing qing ai shengya* (Hong Kong: Huan Qiu, 2007) 339.
103. In this particular instance, Chen's smirking character is at a bar hitting on an English-speaking Asian woman. When she calls him out for being disgusting (his pick-up line involves urine in public restrooms), his retort is meant to defend his vulgarity as good citizenship. In a parallel scene in *Gen-Y Cops*, Chen's character explodes in AAVE slang and phonology in an English-language scene opposite fellow overseas Chinese actor Richard Sun. In both scenes, Chen can be seen as "playing himself." With *Trivial Matters*, he appears in a cameo playing an unnamed, English-speaking character; meanwhile, the *Gen-Y Cops* scene was largely improvised. Edison Chen, personal interview, October 20, 2011. See also, Bey Logan, cited in Arnaud Lanuque, "Interview Bey Logan," *Hong Kong Cinemagic* (December 18, 2004) <http://www.hkcinemagic.com/en/page.asp?aid=71&page=1> (accessed December 27, 2010).
104. "Zing cing: Wong Jingwai tai lou jau san jyun," *Oriental Daily News* (February 23, 2008): A8. "Wong Jingwai: dou hip faat jin 'gan fu jyun mei,'" *Wen Wei Po* (February 23, 2008) <http://paper.wenweipo.com/2008/02/23/HK0802230035.htm> (accessed December 27, 2010).
105. Ien Ang, *On Not Speaking Chinese: Living between Asia and the West* (London: Routledge, 2001).
106. On the influence of kung fu on African American popular culture, see Amy Abugo Ongiri, "'He Wanted to be Just Like Bruce Lee': African Americans, Kung Fu Theater and Cultural Exchange at the Margins," *Journal of Asian American Studies* 5.1 (February 2002): 31–40; Fanon Che Wilkins, "Shaw Brothers Cinema and the Hip-Hop Imagination," *China Forever: The Shaw Brothers and Diasporic Cinema*, Poshek Fu, ed. (Urbana: University of Illinois Press, 2008) 224–45; Frances Gateward, "Wong Fei-Hung in Da House: Hong Kong Martial-Arts Films and Hip-Hop Culture," *Chinese Connections: Critical Perspectives on Film, Identity, and Diaspora*, Tan See-Kam, Peter X Feng, and Gina Marchetti, eds. (Philadelphia: Temple University Press, 2009) 51–67.
107. Angela Reyes, "Appropriation of African American Slang by Asian American Youth," *Journal of Sociolingustics* 9.4 (November 2005): 509–32.
108. On the black–white dichotomy in hip-hop, see Anthony Kwame Harrison, "Multiracial Youth Scenes and the Dynamics of Power: New Approaches to Racialization within the Bay Area Hip Hop Underground," *Twentieth-century Color Lines: Multiracial Change in Contemporary America*, Andrew Grant Thomas and Gary Orfield, eds. (Philadelphia: Temple University Press, 2009) 202–3.

109. Leehom Wang and Jin, perf. "Heroes of Earth," *Heroes of Earth*, Sony Music Taiwan, 2005.
110. Leehom Wang, *Shangri-La*, liner notes, CD, Sony Music Taiwan, 2004. On the controversy over the term "chinked-out" among Chinese Americans, see Brian Hu, "Column: Pop Goes the C-Words," *Asia Pacific Arts*, UCLA Asia Institute (April 13, 2006) <http://www.asiaarts.ucla.edu/article.asp?parentid=42893> (accessed December 27, 2010).
111. For an astute discussion of the mediating factors of minoritization, Han nationalism, and a transcultural Mandopop on the music of Leehom Wang, see Grace Wang, 169–78.
112. Murray Forman, *The 'Hood Comes First: Race, Space, and Place in Rap and Hip-Hop* (Middletown: Wesleyan University Press, 2002) 22–3.
113. Alim defines the Global Hip Hop Nation (GHHN) as "a multilingual, multiethnic 'nation' with an international reach, a fluid capacity to cross borders, and a reluctance to adhere to the geopolitical givens of the present." H. Samy Alim, "Straight Outta Compton, Straight *aus München*: Global Linguistic Flows, Identities, and the Politics of Language in a Global Hip Hop Nation," *Global Linguistic Flows: Hip Hop Cultures, Youth Identities, and the Politics of Language*, H. Samy Alim, Awad Ibrahim, and Alastair Pennycook, eds. (London: Routledge, 2009) 3.
114. See, for instance, the essays in Dipannita Basu and Sidney J. Lemelle, *The Vinyl Ain't Final: Hip Hop and the Globalization of Black Popular Culture* (London: Pluto Press, 2006).
115. On LMF, see Angel Lin, "'Respect for Da Chopstick Hip Hop': The Politics, Poetics, and Pedagogy of Cantonese Verbal Art in Hong Kong," *Global Linguistic Flows: Hip Hop Cultures, Youth Identities, and the Politics of Language*, H. Samy Alim, Awad Ibrahim, and Alastair Pennycook, eds. (London: Routledge, 2009) 159–78.
116. Forman 11.

# Chapter 3

# Setting the Stage: Hong Kong Musical Stars Take on the World

While the great majority of Hong Kong residents in the 1960s did not have the financial or political means to directly experience the rest of the world, most had no problems conceptualizing what the rest of the world was like, and what one's relationship to that "out there" was. Popular culture—magazines, cinema, fashion, fiction—played a critical role in making the world in the popular imagination and, more importantly, positioning audiences before the world as active, integrated, and desiring participants. Precisely because the world is distant, it requires orientation in order for it to be conceptualized rather than merely flashed before our eyes in an array of exotic colors, faces, landscapes, and landmarks. In their classic text *Metaphors We Live By*, George Lakoff and Mark Johnson argue that conceptualization is structured by metaphor, and that metaphors allow us to make sense of concepts in terms of "direct physical experience" within specific cultural contexts.[1] In other words, concepts make sense to us through relationships we understand in everyday life. For instance, take the amusement park attraction as metaphor for "the world." The famous Disneyland ride "It's a Small World" conceptualizes the world in terms of youth, diversity, and small-ness; riders thus come out with a sense of the world as quaint, harmonious, and melodic. Or take Beijing's World Park, immortalized by Jia Zhang-ke's 2004 film *The World*, in which visitors can stroll the park grounds, touring miniatures of famous landmarks from around the world—the Pyramids, the Eiffel Tower, New York's World Trade Center. The effect is not one of awe, but of mastery; we can walk these grounds and "see the world without leaving Beijing," as the park's slogan proudly (and ironically) declares. The effect is partly based on our directional, experiential relationship to the exhibits: we are made to feel large in comparison to the miniaturized wonders of the world. This embodied, directional experience of the world in metaphorical terms requires interaction and orientation to be understood.

With its own spatial logics, and other audiovisual dynamics, film can present concepts through metaphor as well.[2] If we look broadly to film culture, we can see how the consumer is positioned within metaphoric systems of desire. In this chapter, I will explore how this interaction is possible in the case of 1960s Hong Kong, when the two dominant studios Shaw Brothers and MP&GI conceptualized "the world" via the metaphor "the world stage" (*shijie wutai*) and its related concepts "the international stage" (*guoji wutai*) and "the international film stage" (*guoji yingtan*). These are common metaphors used in Chinese then and now.[3] As used in studio discourse, the term is actually two metaphors in one: the stage before the world (in that the whole world is watching), and the staging of the world (as when one performs "worldliness"). In my analysis, I will show how these two metaphors enforce each other through star discourse.

Looking simply at the films produced by the two studios, it is easy to claim (as many have) that the studios are opposites: MP&GI emphasized urban modernity, Shaws celebrated Chinese tradition. However, considering the film culture that both studios manufactured—through their house magazines, through advertising—it's clear that both branded themselves rather as cosmopolitan, and both did so via the body of the Chinese actress standing on the world stage, a metaphor that borrowed gendered star discourses from 1930s Shanghai cinema to provide much visual splendor and exotic appeal at a moment when the Mandarin film industry in Hong Kong sought to develop more internationally and regionally competitive modes of production, distribution, and exhibition.

Cosmopolitanism implies certain relationships between people around the world. The classical idea of the cosmopolitan as a "citizen of the world" takes everyone as equals at the altar of the ballot box. This concept of the world is assumed to be universal across history and space, although upon closer scrutiny "the world" and its citizens have been defined by and mapped according to political and ideological interests. Even in the context of ancient Greece, and until relatively recently in the West, citizenship was gendered as male. In the film culture of Shaws and MP&GI, the "citizen" is gendered and ethnicized (the Chinese woman), as is "the world" (the male gaze of urban, first world capitals like New York, Los Angeles, Paris, and Tokyo). There is also a third player: the global Sinophone audience, which is made to feel part of this cosmopolitan encounter through consumption. This triangular relationship is held together through the metaphor of the world stage.

To use Lakoff and Turner's terms, a metaphor exists when the properties of a source domain (in this case, the stage) are mapped onto the properties of a target domain (the world). In other words, properties of the stage help us conceptualize our relationship to the world. These properties are never given, but rather are chosen carefully to create a desired effect, which in the case of

MP&GI and Shaw Brothers can reflect an aesthetic principle and/or a marketing strategy. Properties of "the stage" include:

1) A performance. What does one perform when one is being watched by the rest of the world? What does one perform to appear "worldly"? What styles does one assume? What genres are appropriate? What narratives are compelling? In what language will the performance be verbalized?
2) A performer. How old? What gender? What body shape? What fashions? What training is required?
3) An audience. Domestic or international? What gender? What can we assume in terms of cultural capital, taste, and prejudice?

The answers to these questions are culturally and economically motivated, and determine the choices made by the studios to illustrate the "world stage" metaphor. Interestingly, in the mid-1950s to the mid-1960s, both studios settled on one genre in particular to perform the world for the overseas and domestic audience: the musical. The musical is especially appropriate because it systematizes performance (singing, dancing) and performer (the musical star), and it can make assumptions about the audience (a "worldly" audience that appreciates international musical styles). It is a genre in which the ethnicized, gendered body is prominently displayed in a showcase of flesh, fashion, and talent. And since the Shaws and MP&GI musicals are typically a combination of the Shanghai nightclub film and what Rick Altman categorizes as the "backstage musical,"[4] the films also contain within them an actual stage on which performers sing and dance before a diegetic audience, which serves as a surrogate for the film audience. The musical genre in these years thus functions as a system of styles and stars with a pragmatic function: to brand the studios as cosmopolitan to the domestic and international consumer.

## Musical Stars: Continuities and Discontinuities

Like much of the Mandarin-dialect cinema, the Hong Kong musical of the 1950s and 1960s has its roots in 1930s Shanghai, an industry that found popularity in part by developing a star system in tandem with the young recording industry. The creation of the genre arose from pragmatic considerations: a desire to attract new audiences from existing ones, and a strategy to cross-promote singers, songs, magazines, and films. The development of the star system in Shanghai during the 1930s came out of the possibility of profitably bringing the established stars of the recording industry on to movie screens. By far the most popular composer of the time was Li Jinhui, and his dance troupe, the Bright

Moon Song and Dance Troupe, dazzled audiences from Shanghai to Hong Kong. Originally a composer of patriotic children's songs, Li found a lucrative outlet for jazzy love tunes in the sheet music and gramophone markets. Aided by these new mass media, Li's songs became staples of Shanghai's nightclub scene. And with the introduction of sound in film, Li discovered an outlet that would define the rest of his career. The film industry thrived under a "no song, no movie" formula, and the symbiosis between record companies like RCA-Victor and Pathé and the film studios fueled the song-hungry movie industry. In 1931, Li's Bright Moon Song and Dance Troupe was bought out by the Lianhua Film Studio and as it transformed into the Lianhua Song and Dance Team, Li's team of musical performers, including Li Lili and Zhou Xuan, popular singers of the time, became queens of the Shanghai film industry by the end of the decade.[5] As most of the films of this era were musical in nature and the stars were extracted from existing popular song and dance troupes, the star system in Shanghai had a close symbiotic relationship with the record and performance industries, and the studios and dance hall directors exploited this connection.

The most important way that filmmakers took advantage of stars' double duty as singer/dancers and screen actresses was by making films about sing-song girls. Therefore, cinema would benefit because audiences would easily "buy" into the fantasy of the films since the actresses are essentially playing themselves, while record companies would profit since the films were essentially audio/visual commercials for current songs and popular singers. As Sam Ho notes, many of these films depicted hardships faced by sing-song girls who were often prostitutes in addition to singers: "Giving the songstress a tough life and depicting [her] entrance into the profession because of special circumstances gave the audience a go-ahead to identify with the person behind the mike."[6] The songs from these popular films would then become published as sheet music, which in turn would profitably become the popular songs in dance clubs. Andrew Jones calls this process a "media loop," which he writes, "was fundamental to the emergence of a star system in Shanghai's commercial media culture. The growth of the broadcasting industry, the availability of gramophone records, and the popularity of sound films all ensured that Li's music could move out of schools and theaters and into public and private social spaces."[7] Therefore, both the movie studios and the record/dance hall industries encouraged the exchange of talent between media.

However, this would not be possible if audiences didn't bring their experiences and knowledge of one media into their reception of the other. For example, in order for audiences to bring the biography of actress Zhou Xuan into a film like *Street Angel* (Yuan Muzhi, 1937), they would have to have knowledge of her background before watching the film. The primary way that audiences were made aware of stars and their backgrounds in music was through film magazines. In his study of Republican-era Shanghai culture, Leo Ou-fan Lee writes that from 1921 to 1949, there were 206 such magazines; some were trade journals (such as *Dianying yuebao*) and some were popular photo magazines devoted to tracking the latest news and gossip on film stars (such as *Qingqing dianying* and the best-seller *Liangyou*).[8] Jones adds, "part of the business of these publications was to manufacture, organize, and channel consumer desires through the creation of stars."[9] Therefore, the presence of these tabloids and magazines shaped the way audiences perceived stars, especially when the stars were playing characters similar to the images depicted by the gossip papers. In this way, print culture was able to reinforce the symbiosis between film and record industries while profiting from the biographies of screen actresses.[10]

When émigrés from Shanghai cinema arrived in Hong Kong following the Second World War and the Communist Revolution in 1949, many of these industrial conventions—a star system featuring female singers, movie magazines detailing the lives of stars—arrived as well. Singer-actress Zhou Xuan continued to be popular for émigré Li Zuyong's new studio Yonghua. Other major actresses of the Shanghai world—Bai Guang, Chen Yanyan, Li Lihua—became cornerstones of the postwar Hong Kong cinema. Yonghua, as well as other studios like Hsin Hwa and Shaw Brothers, continued to make musical films in the Shanghai style, often utilizing the old songwriters (Yao Min, especially) and taking place in unnamed cities resembling pre-Revolution Shanghai. And, continuing the Shanghai tradition, it was the female star who represented the pep of modernity, flaunting a healthy body able to perform the tasks of a new world.[11] However, by the mid-1950s, a Hong Kong consciousness developed within the genre, resulting in what Stephen Teo has called the "made-in-Hong Kong musical."[12] These are films, like *Songs of the Peach Blossom River* (Wang Tian-lin and Zhang Shankun, 1956), which announced their settings as being Hong Kong, not a generic city or rural town in the mainland. Yet, formally, the musicals were still in the Shanghai mold: compositions still had the flavor of folk ballads, while dance was fairly nonexistent, with actresses singing while seated, walking along the countryside, or crooning on a stage. And as Jean Ma has compellingly argued, the "alignment of femininity with musical spectacle" persisted into the postwar years and it was cinema's singing woman that best possessed "an irresistible appeal to the senses as an embodied display of the new, the fashionable, and the allures of modern mass culture."[13]

The musical stage took on new energies when the Cathay Organisation, run by Loke Wan Tho from family business funds, revolutionized the Mandarin film production business in 1956 by leasing the old Yonghua set and setting up the production studio Motion Picture & General Investment Limited (MP&GI). The Loke family's background was not 1930s Shanghai, but Malaysian and Singaporean real estate (including theaters), factories, and mines.[14] Loke himself was not from Shanghai, but Kuala Lumpur. As a teen, Loke was sent to school in Montreux, Switzerland, and later studied English Literature and History at King's College of the University of Cambridge. As he would later confess in speeches to residents in Singapore and Malaya, Loke never learned Chinese well enough to confidently speak it in public, and indeed all of his personal correspondence was in highly literate English. He staffed his studio with executives who shared his bicultural background. Loke hired the bilingual white film distributor Arthur Odell to run International Film, the Cantonese-dialect predecessor to MP&GI, and hired former Fox intern Robert Chung to be the general manager of MP&GI. Chung's hiring was part of a larger strategy to import Western management techniques to MP&GI.[15] On the musical front, MP&GI enlisted Filipino instrumentalists who had taken much of Asia by storm.[16] While MP&GI continued to utilize the musical genre and the strategy of singer-actresses from Shanghai cinema, it did so in a way that emphasized the studio's cosmopolitanism, an attribute it felt could differentiate MP&GI from other Mandarin studios in a fairly competitive market. Unlike the Shanghai-influenced musicals of other studios, MP&GI's musicals began to aggressively showcase dance and musical styles from around the world: Yi Wen's 1957 film *Mambo Girl*, starring Grace Chang, being the most famous early example,[17] and Yi Wen and Wang Tian-lin's 1963 *Because of Her* being the most extravagant.[18] MP&GI's musicals staged the world's music, and MP&GI's actresses embodied the confident, flexible assimilation of whatever happened to be fashionable in the world music scene.

Never to be outdone, Shaw Brothers too adopted MP&GI's strategy of imbuing its product with an aura of cosmopolitanism—that is, a worldliness on par with Hollywood, Japan, and Western Europe—that smaller studios could not afford to maintain.[19] And it was indeed a major financial investment. From 1957 to 1961, Shaws built a world-class studio lot in Clearwater Bay, which it frequently touted in its house fan magazine, *Southern Screen*. The studio similarly reminded audiences that it sends young stars and technicians abroad, especially to Japan, to study filmmaking,[20] or that it is in talks with American and European companies for prospective co-productions that could help raise the studio to world filmmaking standards. As MP&GI did with their *International Screen* fan magazine, Shaw Brothers used *Southern Screen* to promote its studio and its products. These magazines served a number of functions. First, it notified audiences about upcoming studio releases, typically by giving audiences a peek at films still in production. Second, the magazine created a community of viewers out of disparate audiences scattered throughout the Chinese diaspora.[21] For instance, *Southern Screen* had mail-in guessing games that would encourage viewers from around the world to interact with the magazine, and thus feel like participants in a regional film culture. MP&GI distributed the aptly named *International Screen* in twenty-seven locations, from India to San Francisco,[22] and even gave the magazine away for free on airplanes, signaling their commitment to catering to a dispersed, cosmopolitan audience.[23] Third, they promoted the studio brand by projecting a certain image of their stars and creators. Studio branding is critical to achieving product differentiation in a competitive market. It speaks directly to Shaw Brothers' chosen strategy for branding that the first article published in the very first issue of *Southern Screen* is a chronicle of actress Linda Lin Dai's trip to Japan, with photos of her at the airport. In fact, the second article in that same inaugural issue is called "Li Lihua flies abroad, flies back," and details Li's travels in the United States, complete with photographs of her in Hollywood. Indeed, the entire first issue, like those that followed, was full of news on foreign co-productions, various travels by actresses (and very occasionally men), and stars' cosmopolitan skills (on Lam Fung's latest dance style they wrote: "she creates the dance which is in fact a combination of the dancing postures of China, Malay, Thailand, Indonesia and India accompanied with the strongly oriental music").[24] As I will later show, this emphasis on actresses' foreign travel and worldly skills re-enforced their multi-cultural song-and-dance performances on-screen by giving them off-screen validity.

But first I want to emphasize the fact that the studios saw their stars as not merely symbols of cultural change (for example, the "modern woman"), but as instruments in a competitive film industry in colonial Hong Kong. Stars like Grace Chang are often celebrated by critics and scholars alike for embodying a certain Hong Kong modernity by dancing the mambo, the cha-cha, and the habanera, and I wouldn't necessarily argue otherwise.[25] Less remarked upon is the way Chang and others were produced discursively, not simply to symbolize modern femininity, but to serve a social and economic function for the studios who owned their images.[26] As Paul McDonald argues, stars are not merely embodiments of cultural meanings, as Richard Dyer has famously shown, but are also a form of capital: an investment in personality, physicality, and beauty to achieve product differentiation.[27] In the Hollywood studio system (which MP&GI and Shaw Bros. both strove to replicate in the 1950s and 1960s), studios own the rights to stars and therefore can exclusively exploit them for promotional purposes. In fact, in the Hong Kong case, the signing of a new or established star to an exclusive contract was enough to warrant an article in the pages of *Southern Screen* and *International Screen*. Therefore, understanding the function of stars means understanding their roles in projecting the studio's economic agenda, be it on-screen, in print, or in person as ambassadors of the studio to domestic, regional, and international audiences. Thinking back to the "world stage" metaphor, this means that the performer of worldliness to a world audience is directed by a ringleader backstage who needs her to perform a certain kind of cosmopolitanism to keep audiences in theaters. Cosmopolitanism as a style not only took advantage of Shaws' and MP&GI's economic and cultural resources, but also served to excite Southeast Asian audiences about dreams of the world beyond the confines of the nation, already a tenuous concept to those living in places with anxious relationships with "the national," such as Hong Kong, Singapore, and Taiwan.

In the following, I will focus on one star in particular—Linda Lin Dai—not only because she starred in musicals for both MP&GI and Shaw Brothers, but also because she was the biggest Mandarin film star of her day, celebrated by critics and audiences alike. For instance, in Taipei, the biggest market for Mandarin films, Lin Dai's films were the annual box office champion among all Chinese-language films in 1957, 1958, 1959, 1960, and 1966.[28] However, my analysis of the studios' branding of Lin as the ideal cosmopolitan can be extended to other contracted stars (Grace Chang in particular), especially in terms of training, travel, fashion, and dance.

## Preparing Cosmopolitan Bodies

Sociologist Jennie Germann Molz has argued that debates on cosmopolitanism focus exceedingly on cosmopolitanism as a philosophical and moral outlook on society.[29] What she sees as lacking is a consideration of the materiality of cosmopolitanism, which may include such features as consumption and fashion. These are everyday experiences that Dick Hebdige calls "mundane cosmopolitanism"[30] and what Ulrich Beck calls "banal cosmopolitanism."[31] Molz is interested, in particular, in the ways in which cosmopolitanism becomes embodied. Scholars frequently discuss cosmopolitan activities like tourism as abstract concepts, but Molz is interested in, for instance, how people's bodies become cosmopolitan when they travel: what vaccinations to take before you go abroad, what to wear when you explore other countries, and so forth.

Molz examines the issue of embodied cosmopolitanism from two angles, both related to the idea of "fitness." First, she looks at the ways in which bodies become "fit to travel": that is, how to make your body more flexible to different locations. For instance, tourists exercise and train their cardiovascular and muscular strength prior to certain kinds of travel. They also receive vaccinations to make their bodies more adaptable to foreign locations. Second, Molz looks at the ways in which bodies "travel to fit." In other words, once you have arrived, what part do you perform in order to fit in. This does not mean "going native" and trying to pass as a local, but rather trying to look like a cosmopolitan traveler who belongs in the foreign country without necessarily being from there. This may include manipulating one's racial features (for instance, through racial passing or self-exoticism) or choosing the right language to speak. So Molz analyzes online travel guides that give suggestions for fashion as well as for mediating racial and linguistic differences. Her two-pronged framework (preparing cosmopolitanism, performing cosmopolitanism) is useful for analyzing the construction of mobile female bodies in the Lin Dai's films. How is Lin Dai depicted as "fit to travel" and how does she appear to "travel to fit" in with the rest of the world?[32]

First, how is Lin Dai depicted as "fit to travel"? In the Shaw Brothers 1961 film *Les Belles* (Doe Ching), Lin Dai's character is able to travel to Japan and don the clothes and performance styles of any world culture because the film first shows us that her dancing ability is sufficiently accomplished and cosmopolitan that she can convincingly participate on the world stage. Early in the film, we see spectacles of her undergoing training rituals that condition her body for cosmopolitan performance.[33] As in many of these films, Lin Dai is presented as one of many (mostly female) performers, moving in unison to the beat of a male director, in this case played by Chen Hou. This scene begins with a long shot of bodies on the stage, followed by an exchange of gazes in medium-length shot-reverse-shots. In the medium shots, we see the director's anger when he notices that some women are conversing with male dancers during rehearsal. The exchange of gazes between the Lin Dai and Chen Hou characters communicates to the viewer two points: first, that there is a mutual disdain between the two that must be overcome and will likely result in romance; and, second, that the male director is in charge, not in the Mulvey-an sense of domination by controlling the gaze, but in the Foucauldian sense of bio-power in that his gaze ensures that her training benefits the cosmopolitan performance, rather than her petty self-interest. Through the training regiment, we witness the heroism of bodily sacrifice, a prototype for the motif of training that Shaw Brothers would develop more extravagantly in the 1970s with the Shaolin Temple films, as I will show in the next chapter. As in those later films, the training sequence in *Les Belles* proves to us the worthiness of the characters' bodily skill, so that they can utilize it later when it matters most. In the case of *Les Belles*, that moment is the moment of performance in cosmopolitan Japan.

In addition to these examples from the films, Lin Dai's fitness for travel is also depicted through Shaw Brothers' house magazine *Southern Screen*. For instance, throughout the late 1950s and early 1960s, we find articles about Lin Dai accumulating human and cultural capital that enables her to participate on the world stage as a performer. In one article, we discover that she is learning ballet (Figure 3.1).[34] Here, the photo layout as well as the article text emphasizes the fact that Lin Dai's instructor is a white woman from Britain. The pages comprise of large images of Lin Dai's body on display in a leotard, in poses that highlight qualities of her body conditioned for performance: flexibility, balance, posture. In another article, Lin Dai is shown perfecting the hula-hoop, which, as the article informs us, is sweeping the major countries of the world, and that Lin

**Figure 3.1** "Lin Dai at Ballet"

Dai will show off in the forthcoming film *Spring Frolic* (Yueh Feng, 1959).[35] Most revealing of all is the text of a film program for *Les Belles* published by Shaw Brothers and distributed in movie theaters. Among its articles is a description of the strenuous training Lin Dai underwent while shooting the film in Japan:

> This film's many difficult dances were filmed in Japan, with the dancers from Japan's best dance troupe. Everyone knows that [Japanese dancers] undergo strenuous training from the time they are kids. If the main dancer (as Lin Dai is in this film) can't even compare with the dancing of the background dancers, she will be a laughingstock. But with Lin Dai as the lead, you can be sure she'll be as talented and well-rounded a star as any experienced dancer.[36]

The naturalness to which the program can proclaim "everyone knows" about Japanese talent points to the high esteem that Shaw Brothers and the local audience put on the Japanese entertainment industry. That one "can be sure" about Lin Dai's performance in relation to Japan points to the naturalness by which the Shaw Brothers audience can be assured of her ability to train.

Shaw Brothers' task of billing Lin Dai as a consummate cosmopolitan in terms of cultural and bodily flexibility was made easier by the fact that the studio was simply continuing the star discourse already set in place by MP&GI when Lin was one of its top stars. MP&GI's 1956 film *Merry-Go-Round* was also shot in Japan and even then, Lin was being praised for her learning ability. According to a studio program/song-book, Lin Dai went to Japan to study with the "renowned Shochiku Revue" for the role, and her instructors there called her a "cinematic genius, but what was most surprising [to them] was her desire to learn more."[37] So when Shaw Brothers signed Lin Dai away from MP&GI, they were investing in MP&GI's investment in her as a cosmopolitan performer.

It was also well known at the time that Lin Dai studied acting at Columbia University (announced, of course, in *Southern Screen*[38]), ensuring fans that her command over her body and emotions is up to the standard of the world elite.[39] Audiences were constantly reminded of Lin Dai's world-class acting ability in publicity materials. Few trailers and articles failed to describe Lin Dai as the "movie queen of Asia" (*Yazhou yinghou*) for her unprecedented multiple victories at the Asian Film Awards. Her publicity moniker not only proved that her acting ability made her the best in Asia, it also made her the symbolic representative of Asia on the world stage.

In fact, this fitness to represent the local on an international scale was a position Shaw Bros. and MP&GI envisioned for all of their female stars, even those without the credentials that Lin Dai had. It was not simply that Shaw and MP&GI actresses had the human and cultural capital to be "fit to travel"; they were also at the forefront of helping to mobilize all of Hong Kong's entry into the cosmopolitan world through bodily conditioning. Shaw Brothers, in particular, aggressively made this facet of their studio well known. For instance, in 1965, *Southern Screen* included two articles featuring actress Cheng Pei-pei. In the first, Cheng Pei-pei teaches traditional Chinese dance to a flight attendant so that the flight attendant can promote Hong Kong tourism in a trip to the United States.[40] In the second article, we see Cheng Pei-pei training Hong Kong's Miss Universe contestant the basics of Chinese dance, which she can utilize in the international competition.[41] Thus, Shaw actresses were depicted as not only fit to travel, but also able to use their fitness to condition the bodies of other aspiring cosmopolitans like flight attendants and beauty queens. Indeed, actresses, flight attendants, and beauty queens were ideal female cosmopolitans in Hong Kong in the 1960s, and Shaw Brothers had its hands in bringing all three professions within its sphere of influence. Most notably, Shaw Brothers took an active role in sponsoring local beauty pageants, including the Miss Hong Kong pageant, whose winners go on to represent Hong Kong in the Miss Universe competition. Shaw Brothers also routinely offered acting contracts to pageant winners, most notably, 1959 Miss Hong Kong second runner-up Lily Mo Chou, who had bit parts in a number of Shaw films, including *Les Belles* and *Love Parade* (Doe Ching, 1963).[42] Thus, Shaw Brothers presented its actresses as properly selected and conditioned on the levels of acting, performance, and beauty, such that the studio could appear convincingly world class.

## Staging Cosmopolitan Bodies

Following Molz's model, I am also interested in how the female body is presented as "traveling to fit" in the rest of the world. I see "traveling to fit" occurring in both spatial and temporal spheres. Spatially, there is actual physical travel to other lands in these films. For instance, in the MP&GI film *Hong Kong-Tokyo Honeymoon* (Yoshitaro Nomura, 1957), Lin Dai plays a singer who travels to Japan, where she is invited to perform in a filmed music show. In *Les Belles*, we see Lin Dai again travel to Japan, where her dance performances are applauded by the Japanese, who, like the French, are considered in Hong Kong society to be ideal cosmopolitans. However, aside from actual travel, there is also symbolic travel through musical numbers. In countless Shaws and MP&GI musicals of this period, there is an extended musical sequence in which we see and hear the actors perform cultural dances from around the world.[43] For instance, in *Les Belles*, the dance troupe performs an extended stage show in which the dancers take on the cultural dances of France, Thailand, Malaysia, Spain, Japan, and China. Each dance is announced by a spinning wheel with toy figures corresponding to each culture: wherever the wheel lands, the dancers will perform the dance of that culture (Figures 3.2a, b). The spectacle is both musical (each contains some sort of "ethnic" musical accompaniment) and bodily (which includes dance moves as well as the fashions and hairstyles that adorn them[44]). However, it is also a spectacle of spontaneity; with breathless speed, the dancers demonstrate their ability to take on seemingly any culture they are called upon to perform.

**Figure 3.2a**   A spinning wheel lands on a French dancer . . .

**Figure 3.2b**   . . . which signals the dancers to launch into the can-can

MP&GI's *Cinderella and Her Little Angels* (Tang Huang, 1959) has two similar sequences. In this film, Lin Dai plays Danning, an orphan all grown up, but still holding on to the traditional ways of her warden, played by MP&GI's stock mother Wang Lai. At the orphanage, Danning sings songs to teach the younger girls to sew in an environment that is little more than a glorified sweatshop. Danning is proficient in fashion, but only the everyday, practical sort; when asked to produce "Brigitte Bardot fashions" (in Chinese: "*BB zhuang*"), she rebels in indignation. However, soon the handsome tailor (played by Chen Hou) turns her via an extended makeover scene (haircut, posture, costumes, and so forth) from simple orphan girl to cosmopolitan beauty fit for the runway. In a stunning moment of transformation, we find Danning having shed her peasant clothes and now sashaying in high fashion to the sounds of a pop song. The first of the musical numbers is a fashion show exhibiting the modern cosmopolitan woman, parading international fashions (Parisian, Japanese, American, Chinese, 1930s Shanghainese) while enjoying the lifestyles of luxurious urban culture (partying, traveling, skiing).[45] The thrill is in the multicultural fashions, as well as in Lin Dai's ability to strike fierce runway poses, an ability the film proved to us via the makeover sequence that Lin Dai had mastered. The ultimate display of her mastery on the runway thus completes a transformation from fashion as utility to fashion as cosmopolitan spectacle.[46] The second such scene comes late in the film. Titled the "June Bride" sequence, the scene depicts Danning wowing the fashion world, showcasing wedding gowns from throughout Asia: Malaysia, India, Japan, Thailand, China. As in *Les Belles*, the musical number moves at breakneck speed, a short, superimposed title signaling the move to the next location. In each segment of the musical number, we see Danning acting demure in the styles of many countries, performing their wedding rituals alongside Chen Hou's character. Her cosmopolitan femininity (universalized via the image of a white wedding dress) makes her budding relationship with the tailor ever more charming and thrilling to the audience.

*Love Parade* ends with a very similar musical number: a fashion show that takes the performers and the viewers from Paris to Japan to Indonesia and the Philippines, and finally to China. As with *Cinderella and Her Little Angels*, the emphasis is less on dance and more on female bodies fashioned ethnically. Again, the effect is the sensation of seeing the female body (presumably Chinese) proving that it is fashionable in any costume, be it kimono, sarong, or qipao. The string of ethnic costumes displays the ability for fashion to denote mobility across cultures. Roland Barthes writes that "travel is the great locus of Fashion"[47]; the musical sequence in *Love Parade* literalizes Barthes' claim via stage performance. The effect of this travelogue-like sequence—made spectacular through editing, glamorous lighting, and Lin Dai's confident poses—isn't simply the representation of the Chinese woman's mobility. Rather, it serves to, as Tom Gunning writes of the travelogue, "supply essential tools in the creation of a modern worldview"—in this case, to provide evidence of the Chinese cosmopolitan's shared ownership of the world's cultures. (Gunning quotes travel film pioneer Burton Holmes's idealistic, although revealing, claim that "to travel is to possess the world," which in the *Love Parade* context could describe the character's, the actress's, the studio's, as well as the film audience's travels.)[48] Finally, after the women in the sequence demonstrate their cosmopolitanism through multicultural fashion, they end by showing off their ability to wear the clothes of the "global woman"—literally marked as global by the presence of a large replica of the planet Earth. These are clothes deemed "universally" fashionable for women (the wedding dress, the nightgown, workwear, shopping clothes), and, more specifically, the uniform of the cosmopolitan first-world female consumer. In this final sequence, Lin Dai's fashioned body is literally multiplied spatially through optical effects, and temporally through editing trickery. Through these effects, she's transformed into a hyper-ideal cosmopolitan woman—so ideal, in fact, that it convinces her embittered husband played by Chen Hou to fall in love with her once again.

What wins him—and the audience—over is the utopia of cosmopolitan fashion presented for the diegetic fashion-show audience, as well as for the film audience. Specifically, the utopic sensation in these films is the characters' —and thus the actresses' —adaptability and worldliness: in *Les Belles*, we see the characters take on any culture, literally at the spin of a wheel. In *Love Parade*, they take on any culture at the turn of a page in a fashion yearbook. As true cosmopolitans, they can fit in anywhere because their performances are deemed strong enough, and because their fashions are cosmopolitan enough. These scenes depict utopias of cosmopolitan belonging in the worlds of performance and fashion, both set to music. In a classic essay, Richard Dyer argues that musical utopias in film imagine fantastical solutions to social tensions, inadequacies, and absences.[49] If 1950s and 1960s Hong Kong were years of cultural crisis marked by migration and exile, then films like *Les Belles*, *Cinderella and Her Little Angels*, and *Love Parade* transform spatial dislocation into spatial hyper-mobility, from loss of home to being at home anywhere in the world. Furthermore, if these were years of cramped spaces and housing crises, the films' musical numbers depict Hong Kong characters in wide open spaces—literally as wide as the globe itself.

We also see this utopic vision of cosmopolitan mobility in the studio discourse presented in *Southern Screen*, *International Screen*, and other promotional materials. And once again, that mobility is embodied by the figure of the female star. As stated previously, the first issue of *Southern Screen* dedicated much space to celebrating the mobile Shaws actress, but this tendency extended well beyond the first issue, and was also prevalent in *International Screen*. Other movie magazines—including those of other studios as well as independent magazines—also picked up on the stories of cosmopolitan stars, but none of them published these stories as frequently, nor did they have access to the personal photographs and anecdotes that made *Southern Screen* and *International Screen* so exciting to fans. Studio newsreels also capitalized on their privileged access. For instance, Shaw Brothers' *Linda Lin Dai's Wedding*, originally shown with Lin's *Les Belles*, gives fans an inside look at her marriage ceremony and banquet, and ends with images of her boarding a Pan-Am flight for her honeymoon abroad.[50] Very often, the magazines also read like travelogues. Many articles are of actresses writing back to magazine readers about their travels overseas: Lin Tsui writes to readers from her honeymoon in Rome,[51] Ivy Ling Po reports from Japan,[52] Lin Dai sends a postcard from Niagara Falls.[53] Some show actresses at work, shooting on location abroad: You Min on set in Hawaii,[54] Li Ching in Seoul.[55] Most show actresses at play, posing in front of world landmarks and schmoozing with foreign celebrities: You Min having tea at Toshiro Mifune's house,[56] Ting Ning at the Eiffel Tower,[57] Lin Dai posing with Kirk Douglas in Hollywood.[58] Collectively, these articles highlight the spectrum of faces, poses, and fashions of Hong Kong actresses who fit in the world stage as trendy tourists and celebrities. Perhaps the most representative depiction of the studios' idealization of cosmopolitan femininity is a graphic of MP&GI actress Ting Hao in the pages of *International Screen*. The accompanying text tells of the amiable world community that has embraced Ting Hao: "people everywhere around the world were so charitable, treating her with modesty and respect.... But let's be get to the point: she's young and beautiful—of course she'll be loved everywhere. A woman with beauty, a nice smile, and etiquette can easily travel the world."[59] The graphic is of Ting Hao holding a globe and stepping from continent to continent as onlookers of various ethnicities smile at her (Figure 3.3). Stylish,

**Figure 3.3** Graphic from *International Screen*: Ting Hao takes the world (image courtesy Cathay-Keris Films Pte. Ltd.)

pleasant, and with a song in her heart, Ting Hao is welcomed anywhere in the world, proclaims *International Screen*.

But it wasn't enough for Shaw and MP&GI actresses to travel, although they certainly seemed to do so quite frequently. The greatest source of pride for the studios was that their actresses were hired by Japanese, European, or American studios to appear in roles overseas. No matter how small the part, these instances were guaranteed to make the pages of the studio magazines. When MP&GI star Lin Tsui was hired to star in the United Artists' adaptation of James Michener's *Hawaii*, the announcement became fodder for articles across several issues of *International Screen*. "How did Lin Tsui manage to catch Hollywood's attention?" ran one headline, followed by a celebration of Lin's cosmopolitan skills: "They gave Lin Tsui an English test, and immediately found Lin Tsui to be the best choice."[60] Lin's character was ultimately cut from the script, but by then Lin was already heralded as a local hero on the world stage.[61] MP&GI's biggest moment was when top star Grace Chang was invited to dance and sing in Mandarin and English on the *Dinah Shore Chevy Show* in the US, representing Hong Kong in the episode's tour of Asian Pacific musical cultures. *International Screen* readers were given a play-by-play account of Chang's every move in Los Angeles. The article also emphasized the program's high ratings ("60 million American TV audiences!" it proclaimed) to show just how riveting was Chang's multi-cultural performance before the world stage.[62] Shaw Brothers was especially proud of its actress Angela Yu Chien, who had a supporting role as a Chinese woman in the Swiss-German thriller *Coffin from Hong Kong*. The April 1964 issue of *Southern Screen* dedicated an entire four-page spread to celebrating Yu Chien's integration into the global film community.[63] The studio showed equal fanfare for Essie Lin Chia's role in British thriller *Sumuru*. Shaws' biggest moment was an aborted one. In 1958, Otto Preminger visited Hong Kong to scout locations and talent for his adaptation of Pierre Boulle's *The Other Side of the Coin*. While there, he "hand-selected" young Shaw actress Pearl Au to come to the US with him to study English and acting, so that she can star in a future production of his. Au became an instant celebrity in the pages of *Southern Screen*. Readers received updates on her Hollywood travels (pictures in front of the Capitol Records building, dining with Cary Grant, and so on) and learned of Au's grueling training regiment at "America's most famous pronunciation school."[64] Unfortunately for Au, the film was never made, and she returned to obscurity. However, regardless of the final result, via those articles, Shaw Brothers was able to bolster its cosmopolitan credentials to its Southeast Asian audiences.

In this period, few Shaw actresses were depicted as more mobile than Lin Dai, without a doubt the biggest Shaw star of her time. Articles on Lin Dai's travels were timed to coincide with the release of her film *Love Parade*, as if to meld the distinctions between Lin Dai's cosmopolitan role and Lin Dai's cosmopolitan star persona. The spectacle of fitting in the world of high fashion in *Love Parade* is reinforced by the spectacle of Lin Dai fitting in the world of cosmopolitan leisure. In the July 1962 issue, we get a long article about *Love Parade*, this time showcasing the film's "Around-the-World" fashion musical number, in particular the Japanese and Parisian sets.[65] In the September 1962 issue of *Southern Screen*, the graphic layout confirms that the primary spectacle of the film is precisely its multiculturalism and global perspective: the kimonos, the qipao, a replica of the planet Earth.[66] In the following issue, that perspective is transferred onto Lin Dai the star, who is seen traveling throughout Europe in an extended report.[67] In the January 1963 issue, we get another long article, this time detailing Lin Dai's life at home after returning from a vacation in Europe and the United States.[68] The film was then released a few weeks later, on January 23. *Love Parade* remained in the public consciousness—or at least in the pages of *Southern Screen*—for several months longer. In the April 1963 issue, we also read about Lin Dai's latest trip to the United States, as well as her trip to South Korea, where she is filming the Hong Kong/Korea co-production, *The Last Woman of Shang*.[69] Through travel around the world, be it imagined cinematically in films like *Les Belles* and *Love Parade* or celebrated textually and pictorially in the pages of *Southern Screen*, Shaw Brothers' main female stars were depicted as thoroughly fitting in a cosmopolitan world of leisure and commerce.

However, "traveling to fit" as a textual motif is not only spatial, but also has a temporal dimension. As Shu-mei Shih has shown in relation to 1930s Shanghai literature[70] and 1990s Taiwanese film and television,[71] cosmopolitanism (even if imagined) is frequently evoked to assert one's coevality with the rest of the world. So, the fact that the Lin Dai character is applauded by Japanese audiences in *Les Belles* asserts that she, and by extension Hong Kong, is as hip as Japan, the cosmopolitan capital of Asia. Likewise, in *Love Parade*, we see the Chen Hou character selling his avant-garde fashions to white costumers, a demographic the film suggests is an authority on cutting-edge fashion. One of the most popular and enduring theories of fashion is the so-called "trickle-down theory," which argues that fashion trends begin in fashion capitals like Paris, London, and Tokyo, and then trickle down to other locales around the world. The "trickle-down theory" has in recent years been criticized for various reasons.[72] Peter Braham, for instance, has argued that the trickle-down theory is a top-down model that denies the existence of what he calls "multiple fashion systems."[73] Nevertheless, the "trickle-down" myth persists, especially among the everyday public, whether or not the theory itself is correct. If there is a common belief that fashion emanates from Paris and Tokyo and spreads around the world, how do taste-makers in other fashion systems like those in Hong Kong assert their inclusion in the world fashion elite, not as consumers a few seasons behind, but as fellow producers coeval with the cutting edge? One way is by capturing the spectacle of speed in the depiction of the local fashion scene. The lyrics at the beginning of the *Love Parade* number begin by proclaiming that the movements of clouds in the sky are no match for the speed by which women's fashions transform year by year. Indeed, what we see on-screen is a giant fashion yearbook for 1963, which opens and takes us on a tour of the world's newest outfits, many adorned by Chinese bodies. In the final portion of the musical number, in the aforementioned moment in which Lin Dai, through editing trickery, magically changes clothes in rapid succession, we get the latest fashions, worn by the most fashionable of actresses, presented before us as a spectacle of not just style, but speed (Figure 3.4). The quick edits and discontinuity jar the viewer with a frenzy that Linda Williams has called "maximum visibility": that vantage point from which we can best be aroused by visual spectacle.[74] Through the magical temporal discontinuities in this moment of *Love Parade*, we see before us a maximum of fashioned bodies in a minimum of time—in other words, not just the appearance of fashion, but the *velocity* of fashion. Parading one's designs at the speed of high fashion and passing through the giant on-screen numbers "1963," marks Shaw Brothers as synchronous, contemporaneous,[75] and at the same velocity with the world in an "empty, homogenous time" that is not simply the temporal basis of the nation (as Benedict Anderson has famously argued[76]), but also that of

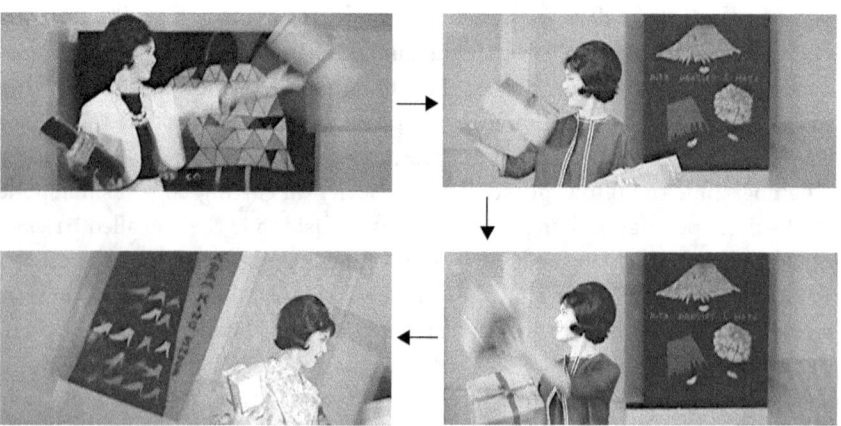

**Figures 3.4a, 3.4b, 3.4c, and 3.4d**  Spectacle of shopping in *Love Parade*

networked cosmopolitan communities around the world (the fashion scene, for instance). And as Partha Chatterjee adds, "People can only imagine themselves in empty homogenous time; they do not live in it. Empty homogenous time is the utopian time of capital."[77] The musical spectacle of coevality, constructed by the capital-seeking Shaw Brothers to appear in step with the world fashion market, provides the imagination possible for audiences to experience their integration into the world system.

A second way in which *Love Parade* displays a cosmopolitan attitude toward fashion in order to prove its coevality is by integrating Chinese fashion—namely the qipao—into French and Japanese fashion culture in the utopic fashion show. The implication is that *Love Parade*'s Chinese-coded qipao is as hot—even as avant-garde—as the latest from Paris or Tokyo. As the characters move onto the world stage and are marked as coeval with the fashion vanguard, they become coded as Chinese through the qipao. We see this not only in the films, but in *Southern Screen* as well. For instance, at the Asian Pacific Film Festival in 1964, there was a special night in which each national representative shows off its own national dress. Here, Shaw Brothers participates in the international fashion show by having its female models strut onstage in fashionable qipao as representatives of Hong Kong.[78] This image of the Hong Kong actress in qipao surrounded by foreign women in their own national costumes became a common motif that recurs in the pages of *Southern Screen* until the qipao went out of fashion in the mid- to late 1960s.[79] Fashion scholar Hazel Clark has observed that the qipao has become the "national dress" for Hong Kong when it participates in international competitions like the Miss Universe pageant.[80] *Love Parade*'s depiction of the qipao is consistent with the deployment of the qipao at Miss Universe and elsewhere: it's depicted as beautiful, feminine, and in step and in time with the ethnic or national costumes of any other cosmopolitan culture. Cosmopolitanism in this sense is not simply a bland flattening out of distinct cultures, but a process of tying national identity to discourses of gender, beauty, and mobility. Thus "traveling to fit" means manipulating the national, not by negating it, but by deploying it as the key to accessing the world stage, as well as a source of ethnic pride.[81]

## Gazing at the World

So why would Shaw Brothers and MP&GI invest so much effort and so many resources in depicting women as fit to travel and traveling to fit? Perhaps it has something to do with their own expansionist desires during this period. MP&GI's Loke Wan Tho was constantly on the lookout for potential co-productions with some of the biggest players in Asia and abroad. He frequently used his actresses as leverage in negotiating agreements. Thus, branding his actresses as cosmopolitan not only pleased his domestic fans, but also raised their worth in the world film economy. For instance, Shin Toho Studio requested Lin Dai by name when casting Chinese actors for a Japanese production.[82] Loke Wan Tho offered Lin Dai to Leon Britton of Milbrit International Associates who had lined up a Hollywood co-producer and was now seeking a Hong Kong partner for a Hong Kong-based film. Loke also brought up Lin Dai's name in co-production negotiations with prolific Manila-based studio L. V. T. Pictures, which was making a musical. Loke's other major cosmopolitan star, Grace Chang, was one of several actresses mentioned when Hollywood's Allied Artists International inquired about borrowing a Chinese star to play Suzie Wong in the forthcoming motion picture adaptation of *The World of Suzie Wong*. To convince Allied Artists of his star's suitability for the role, Loke pointed to Chang's English-speaking ability and world-class musical skill. When *Suzie Wong* producer Ray Stark and Paramount representative George Weltner passed on Chang, Loke proposed Ting Hao. His justification was that Ting Hao "attracted the most attention" at the region's biggest multi-cultural event, the Asia-Pacific Film Festival, and because she could easily "brush up" on her English.[83] She, too, was ultimately rejected, as detailed in Chapter 2.[84] Although none of these co-production and foreign role opportunities amounted to the international breakthrough Loke desired for MP&GI, they did help MP&GI develop relationships with the major film players of the world. After all, Loke's Cathay Organisation was not only a producer of Mandarin, Cantonese, and Malay films, it was also a distributor and exhibitor of films from around the world.[85] In fact, many of the companies with which Loke (unsuccessfully) negotiated co-production deals with were ones he successfully kept as distribution partners. By showing off his cosmopolitan actresses, he was showing off the cosmopolitanism of the company as a whole, which invested in much more than just film production.

None of these specific co-production aspirations ever made it to the pages of *International Screen*. However, readers heard plenty about MP&GI's collaboration with the Toho Company over a series of co-productions starring MP&GI actress You Min, and with Shochiku for the "historic" Lin Dai co-production *Hong Kong-Tokyo Honeymoon*, which *International Screen* lauded in terms of its promotion of cosmopolitan harmony:

> It is said that the cooperation of art and culture means the forerunner of world's peace. It indicates the blending together of higher human aspirations, thus bringing all races and nationalities together. We are happy to witness that such an ideology of utopianism is now maturing into reality, as evidenced by what happened recently in the motion picture world.[86]

Then there were the rumors planted by MP&GI. Although many of the studio's cooperative agreements with foreign producers fell through, this did not stop MP&GI from using the possibility of cooperation to boost its stars' international credentials. Lin Dai, again, was a recipient of much international blessing, real or fictional. An MP&GI film program read: "One hears that Lin Dai is soon off to Italy to film. One also hears that she's off to Hollywood to work with a major American studio. These happy rumors show off Lin Dai's artistic life to come and her future glory. She will shine a light on the unlimited brilliance of the Chinese film world."[87] Readers were also privy to MP&GI stars' many collaborations with non-film international companies, especially airlines—the ultimate symbol of cosmopolitanism in the 1960s, and to which MP&GI dedicated an entire musical film, *Air Hostess* (Yi Wen, 1959), to celebrating. You Min, for instance, was invited by Alitalia Airlines to fly to Rome for their inaugural Hong Kong flight.[88] Loke Wan Tho and his staff were also seen traveling the world, which paralleled his fame as the chairman of Malayan Airways.[89] Such depictions ended when Loke and much of the MP&GI's management died in a tragic plane crash in 1964, sending the studio into disarray, and, ultimately, its demise.

Shaw Brothers, too, made no secret their desire to co-produce with Europe and Hollywood, and to enter foreign markets outside of the Chinatown circuit. Textually, that amounted to articles reporting on Shaws' negotiations in Hollywood and rumors about co-production proposals. Pictorially, that amounted to images of Shaw executives Run Run Shaw and Raymond Chow, the only men who received frequent coverage in *Southern Screen* in this period, standing beside their glamorous actresses as they traveled throughout the world to film festivals and other events.[90] Together, the male executives and the female stars were the face of Shaw Brothers, and their collective travels showcased the studio's cosmopolitanism. A study of embodied cosmopolitanism then goes beyond the question "What does the actress wear to travel?" to a question more like "What does the actress wear when representing Shaw Brothers overseas?" An example is the July 1963 issue, in which Shaw Brothers is depicted as having a major presence at the Cannes Film Festival. The studio participates in the festival by having a film (*Empress Wu*) in competition. But it also participates in international festival culture through ethnic female dress, paraded for the gaze of the Western world (Figure 3.5a). In this layout, we are presented with photos of Li Li-hua and Ting Ning wearing Tang Dynasty costumes from the film, posing before white photographers. "Li Li-hua & Ting Ning take Cannes by storm," the caption reads, signaling Shaws' global coming-of-age.[91] The image of Shaw actresses being photographed by foreign photographers in fact was not uncommon throughout the pages of *Southern Screen*, culminating most extravagantly with an article about *LIFE Magazine*'s arrival at the Shaw studio to photograph Shaw actresses at work, at rest, and at the beach (Figure 3.5b).[92]

130　Worldly Desires

**Figure 3.5a**　"Li Li-hua and Ting Ning take Cannes by storm"

# Hong Kong Musical Stars Take on the World   131

**Figure 3.5b**   "*TIME* photographer in action"

Another article in the magazine has the headline "Ivy Scores with U.S. Critics"—referring to Ivy Ling Po—for her performance in *The Love Eterne*, a costume opera film (Figure 3.6).[93] The article's layout includes a clipping from a *The New York Times* review of the film. The English text surrounding the clipping writes that the *Times* film critic, Bosley Crowther, found Ivy Ling Po's acting "fascinating" and "vastly entertaining." He also found the traditional Chinese set designs and costumes quite superior. In addition, in the Chinese text of the *Southern Screen* article, there is a Chinese translation of an excerpt from Crowther's review, in which he says of Ling Po's cross-dressing performance, "I'm simply astonished that this character was played by a girl, and even more astonished that it's played by an actress without formal acting training. Her performance is by no means inferior to our most outstanding actors, and she has a vast future ahead of her." The *Southern Screen* article then goes on to suggest that New York critics predict an Oscar in Ling Po's future. However, when checked against the original *The New York Times* review of *The Love Eterne*, we find that the only portion of the *Southern Screen* article that is consistent with Crowther's original review is the part about Crowther liking the exotic costumes and sets. In fact, Crowther actually found *The Love Eterne* "tedious" and likely to leave "even a fascinated viewer. . . thoroughly wearied before the end."[94] In one sense, we can simply criticize the Shaw studio for deceiving its readers with false news about its up-and-coming star. But more insightful is to notice *how* Shaws decided to fabricate Ling Po's international acclaim. That the only thing *Southern Screen* faithfully translated from the original was Crowther's acclaim for the exotic set designs and costumes speaks to Shaw Brothers' pride in their ability to produce "Chineseness," a skill that presumably no other studio in the world could do as well. And of all topics they could have fabricated, they chose to emphasize Ling Po's fitness to compete as an actress on the world stage: her fitness to travel, if you will. *Southern Screen*'s infidelity to the original review should not simply be dismissed as deception, but should be understood as a performance of desires—in this case, Shaw Brothers' desires for cosmopolitan belonging.[95]

And this cosmopolitan belonging—embodied once again through the mobile Hong Kong woman—is double-sided. It not only suggests that Hong Kong can participate on the world stage, it also suggests that the world stage can participate with and consume Hong Kong cinema, which fits into Shaw Brothers' goals of transnational expansion. In a *Southern Screen* article entitled "Americans Like Mandarin Movies," we see Shaw Brothers' exhibits under the gaze of Americans at the US World Fair held in San Francisco (Figure 3.7).[96] In the article, there are photographs of white Americans touring the exhibits of "Shaw's Galaxy of Stars" and gazing at a giant poster of *The Kingdom and the Beauty*, starring none other than Lin Dai. That same month, Shaw Brothers

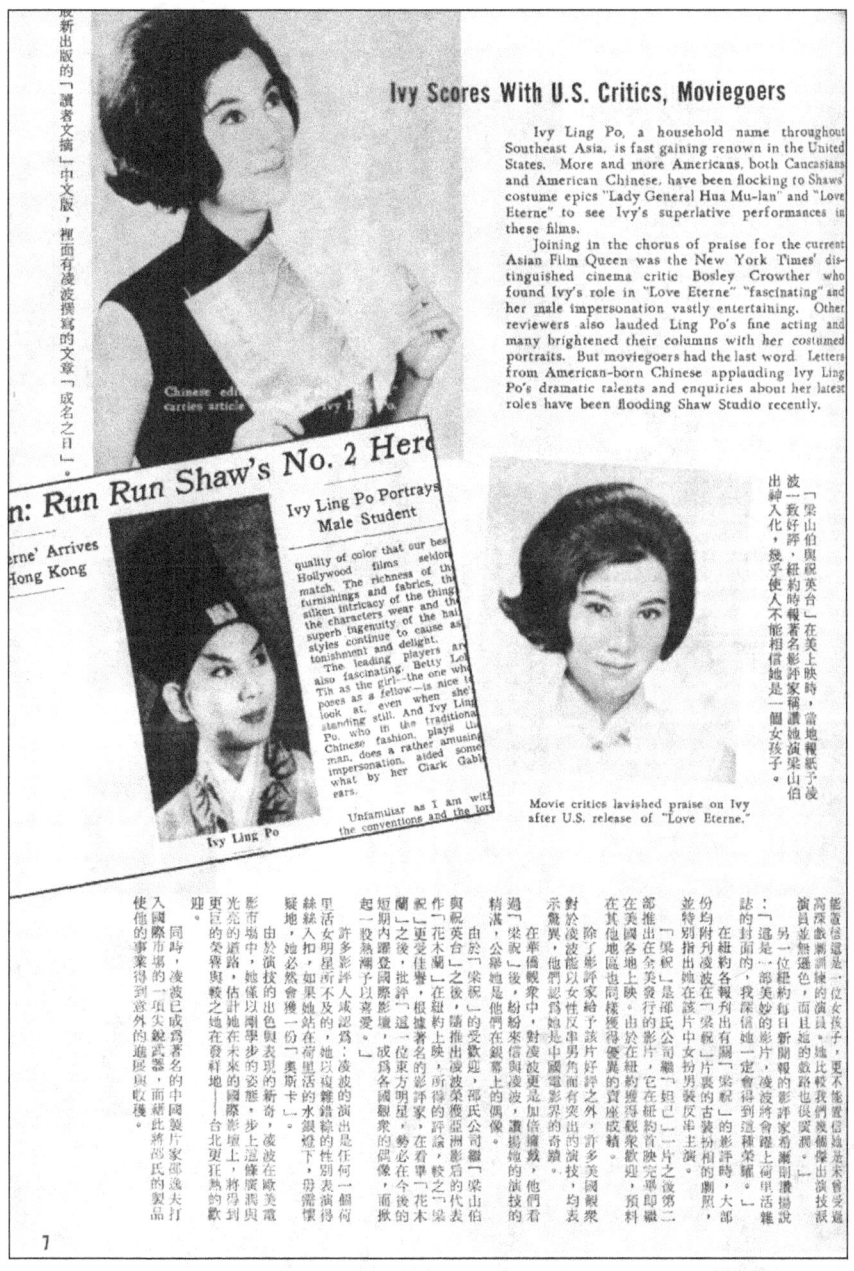

**Figure 3.6** "Ivy Scores with U.S. Critics, Moviegoers": top third, Ivy Ling Po photo, English headline, English text; second third: original *The New York Times* review, with portions erased and cropped; bottom third, Chinese "translation" of original *The New York Times* review

• At the 7th U.S. World Fair, San Francisco may be found portraits of the Shaw brothers, Runme and Run Run, presidents of the Shaw Organisation.

A billboard for "The Kingdom and the Beauty" and pictures of Shaw's Movie Town.

• Photos of Shaw stars are hung at the U.S. Fair.

## Americans Like Mandarin Movies

You're wrong if you think Hong Kong's Mandarin films are screened only in Southeast Asia. Mado-in-Hong Kong Chinese movies are currently gaining wide popularity among Caucasian and American-born Chinese audiences in the United States.

Frank Lee, well-known film distributor and owner of San Francisco's Union Theatre, who made a business visit to Hong Kong in October, said increasing numbers of Americans are enjoying quality Mandarin pictures there. He added that Mandarin films are now comparable with Hollywood productions in all respects, including acting and technique.

When the Union Theatre opened last May, the first picture shown was "Diau Charn," starring award-winning Ivy Ling Po. This picture played to packed houses and drew rave reviews, Mr. Lee said.

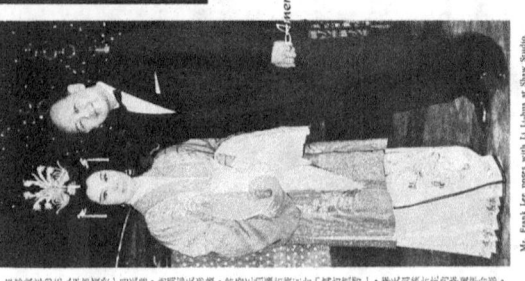
Mr. Frank Lee poses with Li Li-hua at Shaw Studio

**Figure 3.7** "Americans Like Mandarin Movies"

released their first film in non-Chinatown theaters in the United States; that film was *The Last Woman of Shang*, another Lin Dai vehicle. Thus, it is not simply that Shaw actresses fit in the world community as tourists and movie stars, but also that Shaw Bros. as an organization fits in the world film market as an object of envy and consumption.

But what is this article and dozens like it doing in *Southern Screen*, a movie magazine produced not for Western audiences interested in Shaw Brothers, but for Sinophone viewers throughout Southeast Asia, audiences that presumably already adore and consume Shaw films? What the articles show is that it's not enough for Shaw Brothers to want to be under the Western gaze, as Rey Chow has sophisticatedly shown in relation to Fifth Generation filmmakers;[97] it's that readers throughout Southeast Asia can gaze at the West gazing at Shaw Brothers. If Chow argues that Chinese filmmakers achieve recognition by flaunting their "to-be-looked-at-ness" in the international film festival circuit, the *Southern Screen* articles suggest that there is scopophilic pleasure—even pride—in knowing that one is looked-at, because being looked at signals participation in the cosmopolitan film community, of which Cannes is the capital.[98] It's not simply that Shaw Brothers can compete on the world stage; in fact, we know from the fabrication of the *The New York Times* review that this is not completely true. What is important is that Shaws is able to unify and win over a heterogeneous, transnational Southeast Asian audience via the utopic image of the mobile Chinese woman fit to travel and traveling to fit in global cosmopolitan culture. Sek Kei argues that Shaw Bros. united the diasporic Chinese audience via a nostalgic image of a "China dream."[99] Sek Kei is not alone in this view of the overseas Chinese audience; Ian Jarvie,[100] Peggy Chiao Hsiung-ping,[101] and David Bordwell[102] have made similar claims. However, through a close reading of films like *Love Parade* and *Les Belles* (popular films with contemporary settings that Sek Kei neglected to consider in his formulation), in conjunction with a reading of the contextual material in *Southern Screen*, we gain a more nuanced view of the interactions between Shaw Brothers and its Southeast Asian audience. The "China dream" is in fact not simply a vision of old China, pitched to exiles longing for "home." Rather, it is a longing for "the world"—a vernacular dream of Chinese bodies untethered, mobile, modern, and on display, participating on the world stage as coeval cosmopolitans.

The world stage is thus a manufactured level playing field on which Shaw Brothers and MP&GI make a case for their equality as Chinese cosmopolitans; the women's bodies are the proof. The "world out there" is the audience in two senses: one, in that they were actual, paying patrons of these films at festivals and art houses, or they were actual foreign producers looking to co-produce with Hong Kong; two, in that they were a fictionalized overseas audience, narrated on film and in print to demonstrate Shaw and MP&GI's cosmopolitan legitimacy that competing studios never came close to demonstrating. The world out there watched as Chinese actresses did their best to dance at the international standard and sport fashions that could be the envy of runways anywhere. And audiences in colonial Hong Kong and Singapore, "free China" Taiwan, and marginalized Sinophone communities everywhere could gaze back at the world's enamored reaction shot and know that the Chinese people were integral players of the global system. And MP&GI and Shaw Brothers were sure to be there collecting the tickets, every step of the way.

## Notes

1. George Lakoff and Mark Johnson, *Metaphors We Live By* (Chicago: University of Chicago Press, 1980) 57. See also Lakoff and Mark Turner, *More than Cool Reason: A Field Guide to Poetic Metaphor* (Chicago: University of Chicago Press, 1989).
2. Trevor Whittock, *Metaphor and Film* (Cambridge: Cambridge University Press, 1990) 116.
3. These Chinese phrases are different from the English metaphor "all the world's a stage," uttered by Shakespeare to equate life with performance.
4. Rick Altman, *The American Film Musical* (Bloomington: Indiana University Press, 1987) 130.
5. Andrew F. Jones, *Yellow Music: Media Culture and Colonial Modernity in the Chinese Jazz Age* (Durham, NC: Duke University Press, 2001) 93–7.
6. Sam Ho, "The Songstress, The Farmer's Daughter, The Mambo Girl and the Songstress Again," Law Kar, ed., *Mandarin Films and Popular Songs: 40's-60's* (Hong Kong: Urban Council 1993) 59.
7. Jones 99.
8. Leo Ou-fan Lee, *Shanghai Modern: The Flowering of a New Urban Culture in China, 1930–1945* (Cambridge, MA: Harvard University Press, 1999) 86–7.
9. Jones 99.
10. Magazines like *Liangyou* rarely featured male actors—certainly not to the degree that actresses like Li Lili and Butterfly Hu were displayed. Men were most often depicted in film stills while on-screen with other women. This is partly because magazines like *Liangyou* were about modernity, and therefore fashions of the "new woman" were of greater interest. See Leo Ou-fan Lee 94.
11. On "healthy and beautiful" (*jianmei*) as female star "type" in Shanghai cinema, see Sean Macdonald, "Li Lili: Acting a Lively *jiangmei* Type," *Chinese Film Stars*, Mary Farquhar and Yingjin Zhang, eds. (London: Routledge, 2010) 50–66.
12. Stephen Teo, *Hong Kong: The Extra Dimensions* (London: BFI Publishing, 1997) 37.
13. Jean Ma, *Sounding the Modern Woman: The Songstress in Chinese Cinema* (Durham, NC: Duke University Press, 2015) 11–21, quote on page 17.
14. Shu Kei, "Notes on MP&GI," *The Cathay Story*, Wong Ain-ling, ed. (Hong Kong: Hong Kong Film Archive, 2002) 88–92.

15. Stephanie Chung Po-yin, "A Southeast Asian Tycoon and His Movie Dream: Loke Wan Tho and MP&GI," *The Cathay Story*, Wong Ain-ling, ed. 43.
16. Ma 167–8.
17. A comparison of former Shanghai composer Yao Min's music style for Hsin Hwa films and for MP&GI's films demonstrates the shift from "Shanghainese Pops" to international styles. Wong Kee-chee, "The 'MP&GI Style' in Yao Min's Film Music," *The Cathay Story*, Wong Ain-ling, ed. 256–8.
18. Kinnia Yau Shuk-ting writes that *Because of Her*'s extravagant display of multicultural dance (trained by Japanese musical director Agata Yoji), along with its use of color widescreen (MP&GI's first experiment with the new format), made it revolutionary compared to previous Chinese-language musicals. Kinnia Yau Shuk-ting, *Gangri dianying guanxi: xunzhao yazhou dianying wangle zhi yuan* (Hong Kong: Cosmos Books, 2006) 137–8.
19. As Poshek Fu writes, "Unlike Zhang Shankun or Li Zuyong, the Shaw Brothers had the vision, the resources, and a systematic business plan to build a global Chinese cinema." That plan, I would argue, included producing a coherent, multimedia picture of Shaw Bros. studio as cosmopolitan. Fu, "Introduction: The Shaw Brothers Diasporic Cinema," *China Forever: The Shaw Brothers and Diasporic Cinema*, Poshek Fu, ed. (Urbana: University of Illinois Press, 2008) 8.
20. On Shaw Brothers' relationship with Japanese studios, especially regarding labor and settings, see Yau, *Gangri dianying guanxi* 139–71.
21. That Shaw Brothers developed a new magazine, *Hong Kong Movie News*, in 1966 when the Southeast Asian audience was largely cut off for political reasons, speaks to the fact that *Southern Screen* in those early years was meant, above all, to capture the diasporic market. For more, see Yung Sai-shing, "Suzao Xingxiang/Jiangou Shenfen: cong *Nanguo dianying* dao *Xianggang Yinghua*," *Shaoshi yingshi diguo: wenhua zhongguo de xiangxiang*, Liao Kin-feng, Cheuk Pak-tong, Poshek Fu, and Yung Sai-shing, eds. (Taipei: Rye Field, 2003), 243–67.
22. Chung 44.
23. Yiu Tiong Chai, "Dian Mao: MP&GI," *Cathay: 55 Years of Cinema*, Lim Kay Tong, ed. (Singapore: Landmark Books, 1991) 146.
24. "Linda Flies Back to Hong Kong," *Southern Screen* 1 (December 1957): 2–3. "Li Lihua feiqu you feilai," *Southern Screen* 1 (December 1957): 4–7. "Haolaiwu zhi xing, Yan Jun," *Southern Screen* 1 (December 1957): 14–17. "Sino-Korean Arts and Sentiments," *Southern Screen* 1 (December 1957): 22–5. "News," *Southern Screen* 1 (December 1957): 31–2. "The Dancing Idol," *Southern Screen* 1 (December 1957): 34–5. [Note: *Southern Screen* and *International Screen* articles often include both English and Chinese translations, each with their own headline. When provided in the magazines, I use the original English headlines even when I quote the Chinese version.]
25. Leo Lee Ou-fan, "The Popular and the Classical: Reminiscences on *The Wild, Wild Rose*," *The Cathay Story*, Wong Ain-ling, ed. 176–89.
26. Graeme Turner, *Understanding Celebrity* (London: Sage Publications, 2004) 9.
27. Paul McDonald, *The Star System: Hollywood's Production of Popular Identities* (London: Wallflower Press, 2000) 11–12.

28. In 1957, Lin Dai starred in four of the top ten Chinese-language films in Taipei, including the top two. She also claimed the top two spots in 1958. In 1961, Lin Dai had three films in the top ten. In fact, Lin Dai's dominance in Taipei was unprecedented, landing at least one film in the annual top ten Chinese-language films from 1956 to 1966, even past her death by suicide in July of 1964. Huang Ren, *Lianbang dianying shidai* (Taipei: Chinese Taipei Film Archive, 2001) 50–3.
29. Jennie Germann Molz, "Cosmopolitan Bodies: Fit to Travel and Travelling to Fit," *Body & Society* 12.1 (2006): 1–21.
30. Dick Hebdige, "Fax to the future," *Marxism Today* (January 1990): 20.
31. Ulrich Beck, *The Cosmopolitan Vision* (Cambridge: Polity, 2006) 41.
32. Incidentally, the English word "fit" was colloquial for the Chinese idea of "fashionable" (*"shi mao"*) for the generation born in 1950s Hong Kong. Yau Sai-man, *Kan Yan Nan Wang: Zai Xianggang zhang da* (Hong Kong: Youth Literary Book Store, 1997) 145.
33. Poshek Fu discusses a similar training scene in MP&GI's cosmopolitan fantasy *Air Hostess*. Fu, "Modernity, Diasporic Capital, and 1950's Hong Kong Mandarin Cinema," *Jump Cut* 49 (Spring 2007) <http://www.ejumpcut.org/archive/jc49.2007/Poshek/2.html> (accessed March 25, 2011).
34. "Lin Dai at Ballet," *Southern Screen* 71 (January 1964): 20–3.
35. "Spring Frolic," *Southern Screen* 11 (January 1959): 26–7.
36. *Les Belles* program, Southern Screen Press, Hong Kong Film Archive, Hong Kong, 4.
37. *Merry-Go-Round* program/song-book, International Screen Press, Hong Kong Film Archive, Hong Kong. See also, "Merry-Go-Round," *International Screen* 4 (January 1956): 14–15.
38. "Linda in the States," *Southern Screen* 4 (March 1958): 13–15.
39. Shaw Brothers' and MP&GI's practice of demonstrating the woman's capacity to learn contrasts directly with the attitude taken in classical Hollywood, where actress's talents were depicted as natural, discovered, and intuitive, rather than developed through hard work. Only male actors were praised for training at educational institutions or through apprenticeships. Virginia Wright Wexman, *Creating the Couple: Love, Marriage, and Hollywood Performance* (Princeton: Princeton University Press, 1993) 134.
40. "Pei-pei Teaches Stewardess Dancing," *Southern Screen* 86 (April 1965): 80–1.
41. "Pei Pei's New Pupil: Miss Hong Kong 1965," *Southern Screen* 91 (September 1965): 14–15. According to Cheng Pei-pei, outside organizations would often bring their representatives to Shaw Brothers to receive training. Years later, when Shaw Brothers channeled their resources to their television network TVB, the studio invited Cheng Pei-pei back to do the fitness show *Health Dance*, which would feature Cheng as the "Jane Fonda of the East." Cheng Pei-pei, Personal interview, April 30, 2010.
42. Yu Mu-yun, *Xianggang xiaojie yu Xianggang dianying: 1946–1988* (Hong Kong: Sanlian, 1989) 20–2.
43. See also: *Air Hostess* (Yi Wen, 1959), *Because of Her* (Wang Tian-lin and Yi Wen, 1963), and *The Lark* (Hsieh Chun, 1965). Non-musical films often also spotlighted musical styles from around the world, performed by the lead actress. For instance, see *Spring Song* (Yi Wen, 1959), *The Wild, Wild Rose* (Wang Tian-lin, 1960), *The Doctor*

and the Prima Donna (Yuen Yang-an, 1960), and It's Always Spring (Yi Wen, 1962). In addition, there were countless Hong Kong films that showed off actresses' abilities to dance in contemporary Western styles, such as the mambo, the cha-cha, or rock n' roll. One memorable example is Jeanette Lin Tsui swinging to Harold Arlen's "Get Happy" in Sister Long Legs (Tang Huang, 1960).

44. In *Southern Screen*, the studio underscored Lin Dai's ability to embody cosmopolitan Parisian hairstyles by describing her "Les Belles look" as "derivative of classical French style, connoting elegance, dignity, and charm. With the current European neo-classical movement, with the old becoming new, this style is fashionable again, and has spread to America and the Far East, becoming the most popular style in the world." "New Look of Stars: 1960 Hair Styles from Hong Kong," *Southern Screen* 28 (June 1960): 10–14.
45. The fashion-show-within-the-film can be traced to similar sequences in actress-driven MGM films of the 1930s. Charlotte Cornelia Herzog and Jane Marie Gaines, "'Puffed Sleeves before Tea Time': Joan Crawford, Adrian and Woman Audiences," *Stardom: Industry of Desire*, Christine Gledhill, ed. (London: Routledge, 1991) 78.
46. According to fashion historian Yeh Le-chang, this transition from practical fashion to beautiful fashion was symptomatic of shifting cultural attitudes toward clothing more generally in the 1960s—at least in Taiwan, which was the largest market for Mandarin films like those of MP&GI and Shaws. Yeh argues that this shift also corresponded to the changing attitudes toward Western fashion styles, from acceptance in the 1950s, to fever in the 1960s. Yeh attributes the change in early 1960s Taiwan to increased economic stability, as well as the emergence of beauty pageants, the opening of fashion design schools, the increasing popularity of television and the Chiung Yao film, and the rise of malls. Yeh Le-chang, *Taiwan fuzhuang shi* (Taipei: Shangding, 2001) 139–62.
47. Roland Barthes, *The Fashion System*, Matthew Ward and Richard Howard, trans. (Berkeley: University of California Press, 1990) 251.
48. Tom Gunning, "'The Whole World within Reach': Travel Images without Borders," *Virtual Voyages: Cinema and Travel*, Jeffrey Ruoff, ed. (Durham, NC: Duke University Press, 2006) 30.
49. Richard Dyer, "Entertainment and Utopia," reprinted in *Only Entertainment*, 2nd edn (London: Routledge, 2002) 25–7.
50. *Linda Lin Dai's Wedding*, Shaw Brothers, released on March 11, 1961.
51. "Lin Tsui Sends Honeymoon Greetings to Her Fans," *International Screen* 49 (November 1959): 48–9.
52. Ivy Ling Po, "In the Sayonara Land," *Southern Screen* 70 (December 1963): 26–9.
53. "Lin Dai laixin shuo: Nierjiala Pubu meili ji!" *International Screen* 28 (February 1958): 32–3.
54. "A Letter from Lucilla Yu Ming," *International Screen* 91 (May 1963): 21.
55. "Film Queen's Seoul Sojourn," *Southern Screen* 106 (December 1966): 26–9.
56. "Mifune At-home to Yu Ming," *International Screen* 82 (August 1962): 52–3.
57. "Grace Ting Ning on Europe," *Southern Screen* 68 (October 1963): 26–7.
58. "Lin Dai Back Here Soon," *Southern Screen* 6 (May 1958): 17–18.

59. "Man hua man hua," *International Screen* 74 (December 1961): 46.
60. "Lin Cui zenme bei Haolaiwu 'kanzhong'?" *International Screen* 114 (May 1965): 18–19. See also "Lin Cui jiang chang ming Haolaiwu," *International Screen* 116 (July 1965): 8–9, and "Lin Cui Chen Hou jiuyue fei Haolaiwu," *International Screen* 118 (September 1965): 12–13.
61. According to production correspondence in the George Roy Hill Papers at the Margaret Herrick Library (Beverly Hills), Lin Tsui and fellow MP&GI star Chen Hou were indeed cast to star as Chinese immigrants in *Hawaii*. Their characters appear prominently in Chapter 4 of Michener's novel, but were excised from the script, which ultimately focused on Chapter 3.
62. "Grace Chang Captivates 60 Million American TV Audiences," *International Screen* 49 (November 1959): 40–1.
63. "Angela Yu Chien Gets a Break," *Southern Screen* 74 (April 1964): 52–5.
64. "Ou Jiahui zai Meiguo xuedao le xie sheme?" *Southern Screen* 16 (June 1959): 34–7. See also "Pearl Au in New York," *Southern Screen* 10 (December 1958): 14–5, and "Pearl's Home-coming," *Southern Screen* 15 (May 1959): 22–3.
65. "Beauty Pageant," *Southern Screen* 53 (July 1962): 52–5.
66. "Love Parade," *Southern Screen* 55 (September 1962): 16–18.
67. "Lin Dai's European Tour," *Southern Screen* 56 (October 1962): 4–9.
68. "At Home with Lin Dai," *Southern Screen* 59 (January 1963): 26–9.
69. "Lin Dai's U.S. Trip," *Southern Screen* 62 (April 1963): 31.
70. Shu-mei Shih, *The Lure of the Modern: Writing Modernism in Semicolonial China, 1917-1937* (Berkeley: University of California Press, 2001) 340.
71. Shu-mei Shih, *Visuality and Identity: Sinophone Articulations across the Pacific* (Berkeley: University of California Press, 2007).
72. For a survey of some of these reasons, see Joanne Entwistle, *The Fashioned Body: Fashion, Dress and Modern Social Theory* (Cambridge: Polity Press, 2000) 61–3, 98–101.
73. Peter Braham, "Fashion: Unpacking a Cultural Production," *Production of Culture/Cultures of Production*, Paul du Gay, ed. (London: Sage, 1997), 145.
74. Linda Williams, *Hard Core: Power, Pleasure, and the "Frenzy of the Visible"* (Berkeley: University of California Press, 1999) 48–9.
75. Synchronicity and contemporaneousness are the key features of coevality, as famously described by Johannes Fabian. See Fabian, *Time and the Other: How Anthropology Makes Its Object* (New York: Columbia University Press, 1983) 31.
76. Benedict Anderson, *Imagined Communities: Reflections on the Origin and Spread of Nationalism*, rev. edn. (London: Verso, 2006) 22–36.
77. Partha Chatterjee, *The Politics of the Governed: Reflections on Popular Politics in Most of the World* (New York: Columbia University Press, 2004) 6.
78. "Film Festival Carnival," *Southern Screen* 78 (August 1964): 20–3. MP&GI recreated the world of the Asian Pacific Film Festival in the opening scene of *The Bedside Story* (Bu Wancang, 1960), where a Hong Kong actress played by Li Mei wins an award at the "Far East Film Festival" and receives applause and kisses from men and women, all in their ethnic costumes. Li Mei's character, however, is dressed as a princess in a tiara, perhaps because it turns out that the scene is only a dream sequence.

79. For one example, this time at the Indian Film Festival, see "Shaw Paves Way to World Market," *Southern Screen* 47 (January 1962): 22–5.
80. Hazel Clark, *The Cheongsam* (Oxford: Oxford University Press, 2000) 24–5.
81. Poshek Fu writes, "Run Run Shaw repeatedly declared the studio's goals in terms of cultural nationalism." Fu, "Introduction: The Shaw Brothers Diasporic Cinema," 7. Sheldon Pollock, et al. have described the ways in which cosmopolitanism slips easily into ethnocentricism. See Carol A. Breckenridge, Sheldon Pollock, Homi K. Bhabha, and Dipesh Chakrabarty, eds. *Cosmopolitanism* (Durham, NC: Duke University Press, 2002) 5.
82. All references in this paragraph to Loke Wan Tho's correspondence with overseas film companies come from the Loke Wan Tho Collection, National Archives of Singapore.
83. Two years later, Ting Hao appeared in the campus comedy *Beauty Parade* (Tang Huang, 1961), in which her character learns English, among other skills.
84. After several casting changes, Stark eventually settled on Hong Kong-born, mixed-race Nancy Kwan, a distant relative of the Loke family. For a discussion of mixed-race casting in Hong Kong, see Chapter 2.
85. Cosmopolitanism was a facet of all of Cathay's vertically integrated film business. According to Poshek Fu, Cathay's theaters celebrated the experience of modernity and cosmopolitanism, for instance, through its architecture, furniture, and air conditioning. Fu, "Modernity, Diasporic Capital, and 1950's Hong Kong Mandarin Cinema."
86. "Motion Picture Produced on International Cooperation Standard," *International Screen* 4 (January 1956): 4–5.
87. *Hong Kong-Tokyo Honeymoon* program, International Screen Press, Hong Kong Film Archive, Hong Kong.
88. "Lucilla's European Holiday," *International Screen* 81 (August 1962): 28–9.
89. This fact was at least well-known to Singapore and Malaysian audiences, who saw images of Loke Wan Tho inaugurating new airplanes with beauty queens or representing the airline in newsreels. "New Air Plane" (1963) and "Forging Closer Ties" (1963), *Berita Singapura* newsreels, Singapore Ministry of Culture—Broadcasting Division, National Archives of Singapore.
90. Early every year, *Southern Screen* would include extensive coverage of the Asian-Pacific Film Festival, including a festival preview followed by a summary of awards—which Shaw Brothers often won handily. However, as Kinnia Yau Shuk-ting has argued, Shaw Brothers was one of the main architects of the Asian-Pacific Film Festival in the mid-1950s, and therefore the spectacle of cosmopolitanism—friendly competition, parades of national dress, handshakes and photo-ops—was staged by the studio as a public relations move that guaranteed that big studios like Shaws would maintain their oligopoly in the mainstream market. Kinnia Yau Shuk-ting, "Shaws' Japanese Collaboration and Competition as Seen through the Asian Film Festival Evolution," *The Shaw Screen: A Preliminary Study*, Wong Ain-ling, ed. (Hong Kong: Hong Kong Film Archive, 2003) 279–84.
91. "Shaws March into World Market: SB Pictures for Europe and Middle East," *Southern Screen* 65 (July 1963): 2–7.

92. "LIFE Team Visits Shaws," *Southern Screen* 103 (September 1966): 2–8.
93. "Ivy Scores with U.S. Critics, Moviegoers," *Southern Screen* 86 (April 1965): 6–7.
94. Bosley Crowther, "Screen: Run Run Shaw's No. 2 Here," *The New York Times* January 16, 1965: 14.
95. For more on Shaw Bros.' failed attempts at breaking into international markets, see Poshek Fu, "Zouxiang quanqiu: Shaosi dianyingshi chutan," Liao Kin-feng, et al., eds. 121–5.
96. "Americans Like Mandarin Movies," *Southern Screen* 82 (December 1964): 2–3.
97. Rey Chow, *Primitive Passions: Visuality, Sexuality, Ethnography, and Contemporary Chinese Cinema* (New York: Columbia University Press, 1995) 180.
98. Vanessa R. Schwartz, "The Cannes Film Festival and the Marketing of Cosmopolitanism," *It's So French! Hollywood, Paris, and the Making of Cosmopolitan Film Culture* (Chicago: University of Chicago Press, 2007) 56–99.
99. Sek Kei, "Shaw Movie Town's 'China Dream' and 'Hong Kong Sentiments,'" *The Shaw Screen*, Wong Ain-ling, ed. 40–3.
100. I. C. Jarvie, *Window on Hong Kong: A Sociological Study of the Hong Kong Film Industry and its Audience* (Hong Kong: Centre of Asian Studies, University of Hong Kong, 1977) 63.
101. Peggy Chiao Hsiung-ping, "The Female Consciousness, the World of Signification and Safe Extramarital Affairs: A 40th Year Tribute to *The Love Eterne*," *The Shaw Screen*, Wong Ain-ling, ed. 83.
102. David Bordwell, *Planet Hong Kong: Popular Cinema and the Art of Entertainment* (Cambridge, MA: Harvard University Press, 2000) 66.

# Chapter 4

# All the Right Moves: Mobile Heroes and the Shaolin Temple Film

In the previous chapter, I examined cosmopolitanism as a gendered and ethnicized discourse deployed by film studios to achieve product differentiation and maintain an oligopoly in the transnational Chinese film market. Shaw Brothers and MP&GI branded their female stars as integrated into a world stage via studio-owned media such as films and movie magazines. However, while Shaws and MP&GI could, through their formidable publicity apparatuses, control the discourses of their stars, the studios could not own the concept of cosmopolitanism itself. First, Shaws and MP&GI did not invent Chinese cosmopolitanism; the concept itself is an amalgam of images and sounds inspired by artifacts from other global cultural capitals like New York, Paris, Tokyo, and Shanghai. More importantly, as an effect of various aesthetic properties, the Chinese cosmopolitanism the studios flaunted could be appropriated by other studios, media, or even fans.

In this chapter, I explore this ethnic cosmopolitan as a function of flexible mobile tropes rather than contained studio publicity. Specifically, I want to analyze the emergence in the mid-1970s of a certain cosmopolitan male type: the Shaolin hero. These are the able-bodied young men of the popular Shaolin Temple cycle in Hong Kong and Taiwanese cinema, a spin-off of the wuxia and kung fu cycles popular in the previous two decades.[1] I use the term "mobile trope" in two senses. First, it describes tropes that evoke mobility: characters traveling, objects (such as secret scrolls and martial arts manuals) exchanging hands, cultural institutions (like Shaolin kung fu) becoming unanchored from traditional centers and becoming free to roam in the periphery. Second, it describes the fact that the tropes are not tied to any one producer, studio, genre, industry, nation, or medium. Itself derived from previous heroic ideals and narrative traditions, the trope of this cosmopolitan male hero, having won over the paying audience, is then further appropriated, revised, and spun-off into and combined with other character types, both male and female, Chinese and non-Chinese.[2] That these tropes are mobile can be explained by economic factors: competing studios, sensing that certain rhetorical conventions have powerful (and profitable) symbolic or narrative effect, develop similar (or cautiously variant) versions of the tropes in their own productions. The tropes' mobility can also be explained by socio-cultural forces: tropes spread to all corners of cultural production because they find favor among audiences living under certain social environments with certain desires and concerns. Under the wrong circumstances, some narrative and symbolic models fall flat. After all, studio-manufactured male cosmopolitans like the globetrotting James Bond knock-offs produced by Shaw Brothers in the late 1960s[3] did not catch on, whereas the mobile kung fu hero of the Shaolin Temple cycle continues to resonate among audiences to this day.

I take the cosmopolitan Shaolin hero as a function of both financial and cultural forces. The character, and the various narrative and rhetorical devices that have become associated with him, is a product of the shift to independent production in the 1970s and onward, which has led to a greater decentralization of narratives and styles, and an explosion of knock-offs and parodies. The 1970s and onward are also the years of economic globalization as well as new conceptions of mobility and diasporic identity for Chinese-speaking communities in Hong Kong, Taiwan, and elsewhere. These years are seen as the coming-of-age of the first generation raised in Hong Kong and Taiwan after the wave of migration in the years immediately preceding and following the Communist victory in mainland China in 1949. This is a generation still reflexive about its status as a diaspora—especially in Hong Kong, where migration (and return) to the colony after the Chinese Civil War, followed by a baby boom, skyrocketed the Hong Kong population from about 600,000 in 1945 to more than three million by 1960.[4] (In Taiwan, the diaspora ethos is more associated with the powerful mainland minority, the *waishengren*, rather than the long-time inhabitants: the Fujianese *benshengren*, the Hakka, and the aboriginals.) Displacement can result in a sense of nostalgia (which for some scholars is the preferred interpretation of wuxia literature and the cinema of Shaw Brothers), as well as a creation of new political and ethnic identities vis-a-vis the cultural revolutions occurring in Communist China.

Perhaps more immediate a social force is the escalated integration of Hong Kong, Taiwanese, and even Singaporean labor into the global economy.[5] In Taiwan and Singapore, this integration was planned and spearheaded at the highest levels. The Kuomintang government in Taiwan led a shift from import-substitution to aggressive export-promotion in the mid-1960s. This means an intensified assimilation into global socio-economic practices, which necessitates training in cosmopolitan skills and tasks—but, more importantly, the desire and flexibility required for developing these cosmopolitan abilities.[6] Economist Peter C. Y. Chow has developed an "openness index" tracking Taiwanese integration into the world economy through import and export, and finds a steep and steady climb from 1962 to 1980, with numbers consistently higher than those of other developed nations, as well as of Japan. He argues that this openness is a result of the government's export-promotion policy.[7] Singaporeans, too, felt integrationist policies on the levels of everyday life: English-language education, vocational training, family planning (for population control).[8] Ezra F. Vogel has shown that government-induced training and disciplining of Singaporean workers into an army of subcontractable labor is the primary reason the nation attracted foreign companies such as General Electric, Hewlett Packard, NEC, and Fujitsu to set up in Singapore.[9] In the cases of both Taiwan and Singapore, the cosmopolitanization of human capital is not purely the result of market forces, but also of centralized planning by authoritarian governments. Hong Kong has traditionally been regarded as a cradle of free market principles with little governmental intervention, but studies have shown that the training of a docile labor pool for international subcontracting was a result of the colonial government's desire to artificially stabilize the British pound by exploiting Hong Kong's large trade surpluses.[10] Therefore, the colonial government had an incentive to boost Hong Kong's international trade, which involves labor training. In the postwar decades, Hong Kong entered an era of a "flexible labor market strategy" whereby unskilled laborers were trained to take on any manufacturing tasks demanded by multinational corporations, from textile to garments to electronics. Kim-Ming Lee goes as far as to argue that this labor flexibility is enabled by Hong Kong's "transient mentality"—that is, an ethos of adaptability associated with Hong Kong's status as a diasporic city made up of displaced Chinese immigrants from the mainland.[11]

The Shaolin Temple films of the mid-1970s to mid-1980s colorfully imagined a cosmopolitan Chinese male who heroically assumes the responsibilities of the displaced Chinese and effectively manages rapidly shifting political and socioeconomic circumstances. This cosmopolitanism is allegorized by his demonstration of three main traits—mobility, adaptability, and competitiveness—all of which have special meaning in a developing society undergoing "export-promotion," "openness," and "flexible labor strategy." Mobility may result from forced conditions (diaspora, exile, defeat), but becomes a principle of agency when it seeks out new possibilities elsewhere, such as in the global market. Sven Kesselring writes that in modernity, spatial movement is perceived to be "the dynamic factor, the 'vehicle' or instrument" that drives "human beings as subjects on their way to perfection."[12] Kesselring also reminds us that this idealization of mobility is related to the quest for new horizons under global capitalism.[13] Technologies of mobility in modernity are historically the train, the car, and the plane, and, in the Shaolin Temple film, these technologies are allegorized through the robust male body capable of extensive foot travel, skilled horse riding, and gravity-defying flights across vertical and horizontal spaces. The information mobility enabled by increasing access to telephones, the Internet, and cellular networks is allegorized by the underground movement of secrets via scrolls (as in Joseph Kuo Nan-hung's 1976 *The Blazing Temple*), martial arts manuals (as in Huang Feng's 1977 *The Shaolin Plot*), or even tattoos on mobile bodies (as in Wong Jing's 1994 *The New Legend of Shaolin*).[14] While such mobilities as narrative tropes have precedents in classical Chinese literature, the many Shaolin films beginning in the 1970s fetishized in unprecedented fashion the often intriguing and ingenious ways that bodies and information can move.

Mobility is also characteristic of a diasporic perspective. With a basis in the concept of dissemination, diaspora denotes the spatial movement of people who recognize a common ancestry, into areas not necessarily defined by that ancestry. Influenced by the work of Homi Bhabha, Gilles Deleuze, Félix Guattari, and others, many scholars have gone further to argue that diaspora is not simply an empirical fact, but also a state of mind and ontological condition marked by mobility. The Shaolin films allegorize diaspora through the narrative of the burning of the Shaolin Temple, a traumatic event that is followed not by cultural finality, but by the dispersion and survival of bodies and traits that are identified as distinctively "Chinese," such as Shaolin kung fu, the legendary cradle of Chinese martial arts. The films depict the development of such a diasporic perspective in the character of the displaced Shaolin hero.

Since diaspora and global capitalism involve engaging with strangers away from home, the cosmopolite also must demonstrate a certain amount of adaptability. Once again, Jennie Germann Molz's intervention that cosmopolitanism involves bodily manipulation and accommodation (becoming "fit to travel") is instructive.[15] Adaptation and cultural/bodily flexibility become ways to deal with one of the most argued-over paradoxes of cosmopolitanism: the seemingly irreconcilable conflict between a universalist affiliation and a local/personal perspective. Adaptation does not resolve these larger ethical and philosophical debates, but it does draw attention to how, for "actually existing cosmopolitans," these polar perspectives can be transcended through performance and imagination, for instance, through ritualistic training to adapt the particular (the body, the mind) for the global. Indeed, training sequences are perhaps the most distinctive and influential features of the Shaolin Temple film.[16] As I will show later, these training sequences are marked by their pragmatism: the hero trains to adapt to changing social and political pressures, most commonly the escalating oppression by the Qing government. Training sequences are typically inspirational moments of heightened emotion and aesthetic excess (quick editing, musical montage), in which characters are transformed from mediocre fighters to unstoppable physical juggernauts, and from cocky juveniles to modest warriors. Adaptability is a demonstration of the men's willingness and ability to transform physically and spiritually, often through extensive self-sacrifice involving masochistic training rituals and abstinence from heterosexual relations.

Such training has a pragmatic purpose: to be competitive. Competition, of course, is in theory the definitive component of capitalism, and the discourse of capitalism in popular culture has relied heavily on this theory to justify its existence. Global capitalism is predicated on competition between players from across local, national, or regional borders. Thus, the allure of cosmopolitanism is its promise of competition between fellow players on a level playing field, since competition against rivals suggests a competition between equals. Of course, equality is rarely perceived by competitors (be they factory workers or corporate executives), least of all by those in (post-)colonial, developing societies like Hong Kong and Taiwan in the 1970s and 1980s. The hero who can find a way to compete as an equal player, and demonstrate that ferocious competitiveness visually through muscles and viscerally through the bloody shock of violence, becomes a hero to both the struggling proletariat and the aspiring bourgeoisie. The Shaolin Temple films allegorize global competition through competition between distant rival schools and battling ethnic groups. Later films appropriating the mobile tropes bring the allegory to the present, showing how Shaolin can make Chinese men (and in some rare cases, women) participants on a world stage, triumphing in everything from international martial arts to global sports to world-class cooking.

Chineseness (represented by Shaolin martial arts) continues to be a powerful signifier in the Shaolin films, and I would argue that it is through the films' selective deployment and interpretation of a mobile, heroic Chineseness that the audience is meant to believe that these heroes can be competitive on a world stage.[17] While there is nothing necessarily "Chinese" about Hong Kong and Taiwan, or Hong Kong cinema and Taiwanese cinema, the repeated self-fashioning of Chineseness in relation to the world stage in martial arts films of the period cannot be ignored, and in fact have at least two important industrial motivations. One is the unprecedented success of Bruce Lee, who took the international box office by storm from 1971 to 1973. All four of Lee's films released in this period highlight "Chinese" martial arts as distinctive, and ultimately superior, to styles from Thailand (*The Big Boss*), Japan (*Fist of Fury*), Italy (*The Way of the Dragon*), and the United States (*Enter the Dragon*). The success of these films inspired if not a Chinese cultural nationalism among the general public, then at least an impulse by film producers to make other films about the virtues of "Chinese martial arts." Second, let us not forget that it was precisely for a competitive advantage in the international film market that martial arts films were reinvigorated in the late 1960s. Historians of Hong Kong cinema frequently cite a famous announcement by Shaw Brothers in the studio's film magazine *Southern Screen* as the manifesto for the new "action era" martial arts film with its revolutionary style and attitude toward action. However, less remarked upon is the context in which these revolutionary principles were explained within the article. The Chinese version of the article begins by proposing the place of Chinese "tradition" on the world stage: "In this era of competition, the world film stage has shown a tendency toward 'action films'—the west with its war films and thrillers, the United States with its westerns, Japan with its samurai period dramas, and the recent trend of spy action films. Our representative 'action film' should be something Chinese: the traditional wuxia story."[18] Later, the article adds: "[T]his series of new wuxia films are certain to succeed. Though it might not appear the same as them, these films dare challenge the action films of all nations! Alongside American westerns and Japanese samurai films, our new wuxia films will certainly not be inferior, and will bring pride to the films produced in our nation!"[19] The article states that it takes a distinctively Chinese traditional genre to compete on the world film stage. Shaws' celebration of Chinese traditional skills and values can be seen on the level of narrative as well. A closer examination of the films produced under this banner reveal this cultural nationalist attitude toward success: within the narratives, skills perceived as Chinese (such as martial arts) are what enable heroic acts such as defeating oppressors and restoring family honor. These skills are highlighted as precisely the object of fascination and interest through the audiovisual display of fabulous bodies and special effects, whose excessive fabulousness and specialness connote Chineseness at a symbolic, as well as visceral, level.

Vivian Sobchack argues that such meanings (including symbolic ones) are experienced through the filmgoer's body. Informed by cultural and historical conditions, the lived body forms the foundation for a moral engagement with the film and with the world. Lacking better ethnographic evidence, I turn to a filmgoing body I know well (my own), to understand how the Shaolin Temple films corporeally "charg[e] our conscious awareness with the energies and obligations that animate our 'sensibility' and 'responsibility.'"[20] Born in the United States to self-identified Chinese parents from Taiwan, I grew up watching many Chinese-language films from Hong Kong and Taiwan. I remember viewing my first martial arts costume films at a young age and finding the ancient heroes' gravity-defying leaps to be completely mystifying. Seeing these men leap without technological assistance onto rooftops or treetops, I perceived a lack in my own body, based on my experiences playing sports and moving in everyday life. Why couldn't I jump that high? What do these men, who otherwise look like me and those in my family, possess in their legs that I clearly do not? Once, while watching one such film, complete with trick photography and other special effects to capture the ancient heroes' gravity-defying leaps, I turned to my mom and asked, "Did Chinese people really know how to fly?" Perhaps unsure of how to respond, or perhaps sensing an opportunity to impart a lesson, she answered, "Yes, if they trained hard enough." It was an answer that appeased the dilemma of my own place as an overseas Chinese unsure about Chinese tradition, at the same time that it reconciled the spiritual and the worldly for both of us as members of overlapping generations and cultures that value rationality and science. Her interpretation of the film did both by valorizing a certain kind of heroic subject: the hard-working, self-sacrificing male who seeks victory by tapping into a Chinese tradition unknowable to the non-Chinese—and then succeeds spectacularly. To this day, while watching the exceptional feats of jumping, lifting, and climbing performed in Shaolin Temple training sequences like those in *The 36th Chamber of Shaolin* (Lau Kar-leung, 1978), I perceive the lack in my own body, and then find myself, as if channeling the ethics imparted by the film and by my mother, flexing my muscles as if to train them or at the very least to remind myself that I, too, have the capacity to be a hero. Very often, the films inspire me to take Chinese martial arts classes—Shaolin, naturally.

In the Shaolin Temple films, this reconciliation of the spiritual and the worldly is played out through the dilemma of the role of religion in political and social matters. In *The 36th Chamber of Shaolin*, a leader of the temple questions whether the Buddhist temple should be involved in "worldly matters" (*shishi*). The film then goes on to suggest that not only should the temple get involved in the world, it *must*, because the ethnic Chinese traditions that it represents are the best and perhaps only way to defeat the non-Chinese invaders, the Manchus. Thus, if worldly matters are the problem, then Chinese skills are the solution. If we are to extend "worldly matters" to include contemporary ones of participation on the world stage, we can see how the Shaolin Temple films idealize the role of a cosmopolitan Chineseness for communities on the verge of an escalated globalization. This appropriation of Chineseness is analogous to the strategy Shaw Brothers (which released *The 36th Chamber of Shaolin* and many other Shaolin Temple films) took to localizing their films when a distinctive Hong Kong identity became popular in the 1970s. Poshek Fu has shown how in films like *The Teahouse* (Kuai Chih-hung, 1974), notions of the local were constructed out of myths, narratives, and characters that could be called traditionally "Chinese."[21] Similarly, when filmmakers proposed characters that were engaged in worldly matters, Chineseness provided a convenient and perhaps resonant well of symbols that proved to be effective and profitable.

## Shocking Truths

Not any kind of Chineseness will do. The Shaolin Temple films champion a pragmatic Chineseness—specifically, a pragmatic use of a "Chinese" religion represented by the Shaolin Temple.[22] Pragmatism is closely tied to mobility, adaptability, and competitiveness, and thus pragmatic Shaolin monks can heroically represent Chinese integration into a global economy in the 1970s. Jean and John Comaroff discuss the role of religion and other faith-based practices in an era of speculation-based global capitalism. They argue that as economies become increasingly tied to risky transnational finance, confidence and a faith in probability become critical to keeping a spectral system afloat. Therefore, the occult (which for the Comaroffs include religion) escalates in importance, providing confidence and mastery when there is none, building wealth not from work or capital but from faith. Like zombie conjuring, witchcraft, and tarot, religion is pragmatic because it packages uncertainty and sells it as certainty with practical, often financial, rewards.[23]

The Comaroffs' suggestion that a spectral economy feeds on spectral cultural practices is a provocative one, proposing connections between broad socio-economic phenomenon and local, lived desires. That said, in discussing the occult, the Comaroffs emphasize its relationship to the unknowable. However, the word "occult" refers not only to the unknown, the invisible, and the supernatural, but also to the *knowledge* of the unknowable. In other words, those who participate in occult activities seek not only faith, but truth. The Comaroffs de-emphasize the fact that for many believers, the occult is in fact rational and often justifies itself through scientific discourse. The Shaolin Temple films, for instance, rationalize the supernatural through certain truths of bodily training—*if you train hard enough, you can fly.*

Furthermore, the Comaroffs portray believers as by-the-letter devotees. They don't consider the possibility that churchgoers and tarot patrons can view their own practices ironically and even suspiciously. For instance, the Comaroffs show how the Universal Church of the Kingdom of God in Brazil promises wealth, conveyed through posters of BMWs on altars. But they suggest that churchgoers all believe that their participation will immediately lead to riches. The Comaroffs' lack of ethnographic detail forgoes churchgoers' negotiations with the unknowable. Perhaps it is not that those posters make churchgoers believe wealth will come from nothing, but that they inspire churchgoers to understand that wealth is accrued through hard work, diligence, and purity of mind, all of which are tenants of many religions. It is not that wealth will magically appear in abundance, but rather that the spectacular magic flaunted in the BMW posters will inspire new forms of social engagement. In other words, these occult practices shock believers into action that may or may not exactly be the actions preached in the sermons. Thus, the occult serves an allegorical function in that it tells a story (about life, the apocalypse, zombies, wizards, Shaolin monks) that in turn can be processed and carried out in other social contexts. For instance, occult stories can be allegories for worldly matters such as economic competition, anti-colonial resistance, or political/personal trauma.

Indeed, it is through the seemingly paradoxical juxtaposition between the sacred and the worldly that Walter Benjamin theorized allegory's shock effects. According to Benjamin, allegory is not simply "a playful illustrative technique," where one thing represents another, as with symbols. Rather, allegory is a powerful form of expression. Specifically, it possesses the reader/viewer through the strange and shocking, frequently juxtaposing the sacred and the profane in ways that elevates the profane to the sacred. By pointing to a something else (allegory's "other"), the allegorical text makes the everyday transcendent.[24] Benjamin's examples of shock do exactly this. A baroque painting depicting the new-born Christ in a stable "between an ox and ass" lacks the sanctity of medieval and Renaissance representations of the holy scene. Yet, through shock, this provocative and even offensive depiction elevates the everyday—the mundane details of a stable, the linens used in childbirth—to a transcendence of the everyday.[25] In this case, as with Mel Gibson's *The Passion of the Christ*, the offensive image of Jesus aims to shock the viewer into a new, perhaps more impassioned, kind of faith.

Benjamin's argument emerges out of a number of specific contexts: the history of the baroque (as a movement that arose in the wake of the Renaissance), the historiography of art (particularly, in response to neo-classicism's rejection of allegory), and the culture of early twentieth-century modernity (particularly, 1920s Germany). In applying Benjamin's theory of shock and allegory to diasporic Chinese popular culture, I do not mean to ahistoricize allegory, especially given the cultural specificity of Benjamin's work. Yet, one must recognize that cinema was an integral part of the culture of shock in which Benjamin was writing, and that shock has remained central to cinema's appeal, even as it developed in history and crossed borders.

In fact, shock can be said to be one of the martial arts genre's primary assets and affective pleasures. Bodily spectacle, gratuitous violence, and grandiose gestures, rendered extravagantly through Bazinian long-takes, Eisensteinian montage, and cutting-edge special effects, make the martial arts genre a profusion of shocking visceral thrills. In the case of 1970s martial arts, especially those directed by Chang Cheh for Shaw Brothers, violence was the shock effect of choice. While Chinese action genres have always depended on violence for excitement and suspense, Chang Cheh, who made some of the most important Shaolin Temple films, gave it a jarring brutality the genre had not seen before. Swords pierce abdomens, blood splatters like water sprinklers, and limbs (and bowels) are violently pried from the body. As Sek Kei writes, violence "has never been prominent in Chinese arts, until Chang Cheh and his films brought it to the fore with unflinchingly naked displays of violence, literally in flesh and blood."[26] That Sek Kei makes sure to note that no films before Chang Cheh's were so violent—in fact this is how Chang's films were received then and are remembered now—shows the importance of shock to the way his films are perceived. As Benjamin notes, if shocks are to be allegorical, they must not lose their ability to defy expectation and propriety: "If it is to hold its own against the tendency to absorption, the allegorical must constantly unfold in new and surprising ways. . . . Allegories become dated, because it is part of their nature to shock."[27] That they are dated also means they must be interpreted within their specific historical and cultural contexts, for what is shocking now may not be shocking later, and what is shocking to one culture may not be to another.

Violence is just one aspect of the martial arts genre's ability to shock. Other crucial forms of shock that martial arts films of the era pioneered were the use of breathtaking special effects and the blasphemous depiction of religion. One of the quintessential special effects employed in martial arts films is the use of graphic matches to simulate flying. A character's take-off from the ground is "invisibly" followed by a shot of the same character arriving on a rooftop. Or, reverse-motion is used: an actor's leap off a rooftop is cinematically rolled backward as a character's astonishing flight up onto a roof. These techniques were pioneered in the Shaw Brothers studios, and were used extensively by Chang Cheh, Lau Kar-leung, and other directors. The shock of such moments is of course the shock of the human body and its surprising physical possibilities. Chinese audiences at the time knew of Shaolin's super-human abilities, because such abilities were depicted in martial arts literature and other forms of mass culture. However, cinema provides a special kind of shock: the transparent visuality of super-human skill and the blatant disregard for gravity, which cinema as a photographic medium is thought to depict "scientifically." Even if Chinese audiences believed that such super-human feats were physically possible given the right kind of martial arts training, the cinematic rendering of such feats is no less shocking for there was nothing quite like these visual sensations seen on-screen before.

Meanwhile, the Shaolin Temple cycle of the 1970s almost exclusively depicted Chinese Buddhism as a sanctuary for martial arts rather than a place of spirituality. In Chang Cheh's *Shaolin Temple* (1976), the space of the temple is organized according to function: a courtyard for martial arts training, a room for monks' discussions, a kitchen for cooking meals, and so forth. But what's shocking about this delegation of space is that spirituality seems to be completely written out of the floor plan. One mysterious room—comprised of bizarre obstacles and mazes—seems built for no other reason than to torture students of Shaolin should they try to escape. In fact, the mystery exit path becomes a trope in Shaolin films, depicted most flamboyantly in films like Joseph Kuo Nan-hung's *The 18 Bronzemen* (1975) and Fong Ho's *Raiders of the Shaolin Temple* (1982). Even the library and the kitchen exist seemingly for the sole purpose of conditioning the bodies of Shaolin's students. The only real space for meditation that we see is a mysterious garden shelter outside of the temple, but even this space, as we later find out, is a space for martial arts training. Furthermore, the depiction of Buddhism is seen as shocking because we see Buddhist monks engaged in and receiving violence. When the temple is invaded by the Qing army, the monks' guards are trampled and speared in a bloody massacre. When the temple's fall is imminent, the monks decide to commit suicide, allowing their bodies to be burned along with the temple walls, in a scene that shocks with the intensity of the similar image of Buddhist monks' self-immolation during the Vietnam War, an image no doubt familiar to viewers in 1974. Images of monks' self-immolation also appear in *The Blazing Temple* and *The Shaolin Temple* (Chang Hsin-yen, 1982).

The juxtaposition of sacred religion and unrestrained violence is reminiscent of Benjamin's example of baby Jesus among barn animals, although of course the change of historical and cultural context means that different degrees of shocks are in order. Indeed, the use of special effects to transform the human body to a super-human, mythical body is also a kind of flattening of the profane (the biologically "realistic") and the godly (the super-human). The depiction of extreme violence in martial arts films creates a similar kind of juxtaposition. Most commentators have pointed to the realism of Chang Cheh's violence; in fact, Chang himself defends his depiction of violence as simply "reflect[ing] the violence in life."[28] But one should also acknowledge that the realism of this violence (with its biologically accurate blood and guts) is enacted through super-human (non-"realistic") vigor and strength. For the viewer, the spectacle isn't simply that a man's skull is crushed in battle, as it is at the end of Chang's *Five Shaolin Masters* (1974). It's that a human being is able to, with just one swing of a staff, inflict so much physical pressure in one move that it can crush another man's skull. It is the performance of the super-human, joined with the coarsest biological realism, which forms the spectacle of violence in these films.

These shocks become allegorical when, as in Benjamin's example of the baby Jesus, the pairing of the sacred and the profane elevates the everyday to the transcendent—to another truth, which is the referent of the allegory. In *Allegory and Violence*, literary scholar Gordon Teskey, who reads the mix of the "real" and the "sacred" as surrealistic, interprets Benjamin's theory of allegory by noting:

> By reversing the aesthetic valuation of the symbol over allegory, which had dominated German aesthetics since Goethe, Benjamin argued that the almost surrealistic character of allegorical imagery in German baroque drama forced the mind, in its quest for meaning, to abandon the realm of sense and perception for that of theological truth.[29]

I would argue, however, that the Shaolin Temple films, unlike Benjamin's examples of baroque drama and painting, are not aiming for a theological truth, but a cultural truth. These films utilize shocks to elucidate the "truth" of Chinese culture. Extreme violence exposes the true power of well-trained Chinese martial arts; special effects demonstrate the exquisite ability of the true Chinese body, as well as the aesthetic triumph of the Chinese cinema; and the juxtaposition of Buddhism and violence represents the historical "truth" that the ethnic Han Chinese were cruelly defeated by the duplicitous Manchu invaders. Furthermore, in these films, such truths are deployed to galvanize a Chinese diaspora exiled from the mainland after the rise of communist China. When the Shaolin Temple films emerged in Hong Kong, the mainland was undergoing the final years of the Cultural Revolution, a brutal social movement that explicitly expelled traditional Chinese theology and customs as culturally conservative and Rightist.[30] As a result, many in Hong Kong and Taiwan viewed their own societies as the true inheritors of Chinese tradition. Films like those of the Shaolin Temple cycle did not simply reflect the diaspora's nostalgia for the homeland; they worked through the diaspora's own sense of nationalism and anti-communism by appealing to the diaspora's sense of cultural truth and authenticity. And as the mobile tropes of the Shaolin Temple film became reappropriated in new contexts in the 1990s and 2000s, the "truth" of the Chinese body found new ways to work through anxieties about the Chinese diaspora's place in the global economy.

## Cultural Reinforcement

In the Shaolin Temple films, the carrier of cultural truth is the male, Chinese body.[31] Specifically, this is culture ingrained in the body's kinetic memory: its movements, its gestures, its physical skill. Through the body, culture travels and survives, regardless of who happens to be ruling China, or in whose borders the body happens to inhabit. As Elaine Scarry has provocatively argued, culture is remembered in the body as a result of repetition and habit. "What is remembered in the body is well remembered," she reminds readers on several occasions in her book *The Body in Pain*.[32] The truism that one never forgets how to ride a bike is an example of the way that actions are etched into the body's memory. And when such remembered actions are common to a group or community, one can say that culture is embodied. As Scarry writes, "'culture' must at least in part be seen as originating in the body, attributed to the refusal of the body to disown its own early circumstances, its mute and often beautiful insistence on absorbing into its rhythms and postures the signs that it inhabits a particular space at a particular time."[33] The cultural aspect of the body, Scarry argues, is one reason that the violent destruction of the body is an imperative of war.[34] The assumption of war is that two sides with different cultures fight for the right for one culture to subsume the other after the war.

One of the foundations of the Shaolin myth, at least as it has been disseminated in Hong Kong and Taiwan, is an image of war: the burning of the Southern Shaolin Temple in the Fujian Province.[35] This myth has its roots in Southern folk tales that primarily developed out of late Qing Dynasty literature in works like *Everlasting* (*Shengchao ding sheng wannian qing*), published in Shanghai in 1893. Some of the Shaolin heroes in these novels, like Fong Sai-yuk, Hung Hei-hwun, and Wu Wai-kin, who died as disloyal rebels in the earlier *Everlasting*, were later transformed into heroes in serial novels like *Young Heroes from Shaolin* in the 1930s.[36] According to the myths perpetuated in these publications, the ethnic Manchus who rule China as the Qing Dynasty suspect that ethnic Hans (the largest ethnic group in China) are planning a rebellion and that the Shaolin Temple has become a refuge for militias plotting to overturn the Qing and restore the previous dynasty, the Ming (*fan qing fu ming*). Therefore, the Qing court dispatches the army to burn down the Shaolin Temple. However, while many Shaolin monks and rebels die, some manage to escape across southern China and even into Taiwan to continue their rebellion. Known as the Guangdong School of martial arts fiction, these stories became especially popular in southern China and, after the Chinese civil war, flourished in Hong Kong in novels, radio broadcasts, newspaper serials, comic books, and films such as the Fong Sai-yuk cycle of the 1950s, typically starring Sek Kin in the title role.[37] The Shaolin heroes (and the burning of the Shaolin temple) even play a critical part in the foundational myth of the Hong Kong triads.[38]

In this tradition, the myth of the burning of the Shaolin Temple is told from the point of view of the losers, the Shaolin monks, who maintain that their culture has not been overtaken by the oppressive Qing government, even though their tradition's ultimate symbol (the temple itself) has been burned to ashes. They survive to continue their rebellion by mobilizing tradition for pragmatic and political purposes. The Shaolin Temple may be finished, but Shaolin martial arts, remembered in the bodies of the escaped monks, lives on.[39] This provocation (that embodied Chinese traditional culture survives in the periphery to serve the periphery) is elaborated in the Shaolin Temple films through a basic narrative structure that has become ingrained in the cycle to the point of parody. In this structure, first the cultural bodies are set in motion. Once in motion, the cultural bodies are reinforced through training. When deemed ready, the cultural bodies prove that reinforcement through action. And lastly, at the conclusion of the film, that action finds a way to continue through pedagogy and inspiration.

## Setting the Cultural Body in Motion

In many of the films, the burning of the temple by the Qing government is the catalyst for the narrative, sparking the Shaolin heroes' physical displacement as well as their emotional drive for political action. *Heroes Two* (Chang Cheh, 1974), *Five Shaolin Masters*, *Executioners from Shaolin* (Lau Kar-leung, 1977), *Heroes*

(Wu Ma, 1980), and the later *The New Legend of Shaolin* all open with the image of the temple in flames, or imply it by showing signs of the temple's destruction. In other films, the burning of the temple comes later at a more climactic moment, but the purpose is the same: to set the men into action, both geographically and emotionally. Examples include *Men from the Monastery* (Chang Cheh, 1974), *The Blazing Temple*, and *Shaolin Abbot* (Ho Meng-hua, 1979). Often, the moment of destruction is presented as a scene of trauma. Since Shaolin heroes—both religious and secular—are known to be loyal to their temple and their masters, there is frequently a scene where the heroes are torn between staying and leaving: between loyalty (despite death) and escape. Such scenes, as with those in *The Blazing Temple* and *Shaolin Abbot*, are usually resolved by raising the possibility that escape does not equal abandonment, but rather that it will allow for the spread of Shaolin and its eventual survival and redemption. At this traumatic junction, the heroes are forced to be adaptable through mobility in order to stay competitive and relevant.

In most Shaolin Temple films, however, the burning of the temple is not depicted, a likely reason being that repeating such a distinctive image would make the films appear formulaic. A more flexible strategy for depicting the mobilization of Shaolin heroes for political ends is to portray the Shaolin Temple as already a part of the periphery: as a haven for dispersed rebels seeking sanctuary and training. Historians have noted that throughout much of its later history, the Shaolin Temple has indeed been perceived as a threat to the government,[40] and the films utilize the temple's reputation as an opponent of tyranny as a way to legitimize the characters' rebellion: the characters can be simultaneously traditional (through their appropriation of the most legendary of Chinese martial arts) and progressive (to fight oppression). In the film narratives, the Shaolin Temple is thus a central semantic feature of the world of mobile heroes on the fringes of society (a world that overlaps conceptually with the *jianghu* of wuxia literature), where itinerant men can develop their bodies and disseminate their martial arts knowledge. Films with this basic formula are too many to list. The narrative structure can also be found in television serials as well, such as *The Young Heroes of Shaolin* (TVB, 1981) in Hong Kong, and *Shaolin Temple* (TTV, 1984) in Taiwan.

## Pragmatic Reinforcement of the Cultural Body

Whether in the periphery of the destroyed Shaolin Temple, or in the Shaolin Temple as part of a rebellious periphery, the itinerant heroes train physically to reinforce their body's cultural memory and keep Shaolin alive. The purpose is never strictly spiritual (for instance, to achieve nirvana, to get in touch with

Chineseness, or as a hobby), but pragmatic: to have the tangible skills to seek revenge, to fight oppression, to overthrow the government. Revenge is one of the hallmarks of Sinophone literature and film; in most Shaolin Temple films, it is what drives the desire for martial arts training. A typical narrative involves avenging a killed family member or teacher. Frequently, personal vengeance is coupled with larger collective goals. For instance, to seek revenge for a brutalized friend is to stand up for the entire working class against unfair working conditions (as in Lau Kar-leung's 1980 *Return to the 36th Chamber*). Or to seek vengeance for a raped and murdered mother is to seek justice for all who have been oppressed by the Qing government (as in Chang Cheh's 1976 *The Shaolin Avengers*).[41]

To achieve these secular goals, the male protagonists undergo training in Shaolin martial arts. What is distinctive about the films of the Shaolin Temple cycle (as opposed to martial arts literature or even the Cantonese kung fu films of the 1950s) is that training becomes a fetish for the audience's eyes and ears—and, in fact, their entire bodies. It is a fetish laced with sexual desire and jealousy not usually associated with scenes of self-cultivation. A magazine article on *The Burning Temple* boasts of the film's spectacles of "muscle beauty" (*jirou mei*) and "masculine beauty" (*nanxing mei*), which serve to entice sexual interest in some and inspire muscle training in others.[42] I wrote earlier about my personal bodily reaction to training sequences, during which I perceive my own lack and become inspired—often spontaneously—to train my own body. Such a response is not surprising given the prolonged intensity of the training sequences in these films.

Lau Kar-leung's *The 36th Chamber of Shaolin* is the best-known example. Liu Yu-de (played by Gordon Liu) enters the Shaolin Temple in order to acquire the martial arts skills necessary to fight back against the ruthlessness of the Qing army. He finds that in school, he and his friends only learn about Chinese ethics, which he discovers has no pragmatic purpose against the enemy. After proving his worthiness of entrance into the Shaolin Temple, he is faced with thirty-five chambers, each training a different part of Liu's body. He begins with the thirty-fifth chamber. There, he must achieve a certain mental calm in order to train his feet to run across logs floating on water. In the thirty-fourth chamber, he works his deltoid muscles by carrying buckets of water with both hands. Attached to each arm are knives that will pierce his torso if his deltoids become lax. In the thirty-third chamber, he works his wrists by striking a giant bell with a long pole. Other chambers work his eyes, his head, and his legs. Finally, he is allowed to start training in sword and staff combat. Most chambers present a challenge that, when failed, leads to some form of intense pain: impalement by knives, burning by incense sticks, and so forth. To prove his dedication, the film has Liu initially fail in each chamber, and we in the audience wince from the pain. We then cheer on his dedication and confidence in spite of the frequent pain, and become relieved when he has perfected the task. The training sequence thus alternates between equilibrium and disequilibrium: pain leads to relief, followed by pain in the next chamber, followed by relief once that chamber is mastered. This alternating rhythm of the sequence excites us into believing in the Shaolin disciple's heroism and capacity for mastering all challenges and developing his body.

New films in the Shaolin Temple cycle distinguish themselves from previous ones by presenting novel, often more sadistic and innovative, forms of fetishistic training rituals. Many films invent human-like apparatuses on which the heroes can train. For instance, in *Executioners from Shaolin*, Shaolin refugee Hung Hei-kwun builds an elaborate copper man with hollowed veins, modeled after the pathways of a person's energy, or qi. Hung Hei-kwun drops marbles into the hollowed veins, and he trains himself to catch the marbles as they flow down the copper man's body, so as to train himself to attack his enemy's energy at the precise moment and location he is weakest. Huang Feng's 1977 *The Shaolin Plot* has a similar training sequence involving a straw man and eggs. Meanwhile, *Shaolin Avengers* recreates the famed "invincible body" training of Fong Sai-yuk, who makes impenetrable his epidermal layer by locking himself in a tub of scalding herbs. Chang Cheh's 1978 *Invincible Shaolin* puts its hero through a number of painful rituals, each to train a distinct physical skill. Fingers: push-ups with increasingly fewer fingers (and weights on his back and an egg under his hand to ensure that his fingers are upright). Strength and balance: standing on cut tree trunks. Torso muscles: withstanding the pain of a spinning device that hits him repeatedly. Legs: jumping with weights attached to his ankles. Chest and legs: lunging forward while being tied back by elastic bands. Close-range strength: breaking out of an enclosed space that becomes increasingly cramped.

Often, the rhythm of these scenes (and therefore the momentum that drives our empathy) is supplemented with sound. A common trope of the training sequence is the use of the wooden fish (a mallet and block used in Buddhist ceremonies and named for its shape) to inspire training. For instance, in *The 36th Chamber of Shaolin*, Liu must train his wrists by striking a bell to the same rhythm as the head monk striking a wooden fish. The two create sonic harmony when the bell and the wooden fish are in sync. However, as the monk speeds up and Liu cannot maintain the beat, we get dissonance. As with the disequilibrium–equilibrium structure of the sequence as a whole, the moviegoer demands harmony, which ultimately reinforces the sense of Liu's bodily self-sacrifice and therefore his heroism. A similar scene involving a wooden fish exists in *The New Shaolin Boxers* (Chang Cheh, 1976). Another use of sound to arouse our sympathy is the inclusion of the *Rocky*-like pump-up musical montage (sometimes a pop song about hard work and defeating one's enemies), as in *Disciples of Shaolin Temple* (Hua Shan, 1985) and *War of the Shaolin Temple* (Lin Dah-tsao, 1983).

The musical montage also serves to compress time, as it functions not only to uplift the audience, but also to stitch together days, months, even years of the disciple's physical training. In the Shaolin Temple films, the length of the training is, along with the physical sacrifice, the most convincing evidence of the disciple's self-sacrifice to achieve his pragmatic goal. The use of the graphic match also denotes this passage of time, while also spectacularly displaying the results of the hard work made across that period of time. For instance, in John Woo's *Hand of Death* (1976), the character Yun Fei discovers that the only way to defeat his enemy's trick moves is with the "tiger claw" technique. To perfect the tiger claw, Yun Fei trains by learning to claw an oiled bamboo. At first, he cannot. Then we cut to a graphic match of Yun Fei repeating the action, this time getting closer to grasping the oiled bamboo. Then another graphic match, and another. With each cut, we jump ahead in time, the momentum of the editing and the improvement of Yun Fei's technique leading inevitably to the restoration of an equilibrium point: he finally grips the oiled bamboo, and shatters it.

Pragmatic training builds not only the body, but also the spirit, which is depicted in another stock trope of the Shaolin training sequence: the moment of spiritual transformation. This transformation is typically one from arrogance to humility, and requires a scene of humiliation to shock the character and (often comically) engage the film audience. The hero, such as Liu Yu-de in *The 36th Chamber of Shaolin*, arrives at the temple with a pragmatic mission: to train his body to defeat the Qing army. However, he soon discovers through a scene of humiliation that his stubbornness can only lead to failure. Specifically, Liu Yu-de learns through continual physical defeat that he must give up his preconceptions about muscle strength and physical mechanics if wants to achieve the seemingly impossible: to glide quickly over logs floating on water. In other words, he must learn to be open-minded spiritually in order to adapt to unexpected circumstances. One of the Shaolin Temple films' most famous iterations of the transformation scene is the gag in which a Shaolin disciple is forced to do temple chores for many years, never learning a single move of martial arts. The disciple complains to his masters, not knowing that the physical acts of cooking, cleaning, and taking on other household chores have already molded his body into a fighting machine. For instance, in *Return to the 36th Chamber*, the mischievous disciple Chou Jen-chieh is forced to scaffold the temple chambers for their renovation. After three years of thinking he hasn't learned anything, he quits Shaolin and returns to the secular world. As soon as he gets in a fight, he discovers that his scaffolding skills come into play: he can rapidly tie together his enemies using available rope and poles. It is an a-ha moment in which Jen-chieh learns that training comes in all forms, and can be utilized in creative ways when it is needed most.

One gathers throughout this film that the temple monks knew all along what they were doing: that they looked at Jen-chieh's skills and personality and determined what would be the best course of training for him given his pragmatic goals. This deliberate design of the disciples' training regimen is characteristic of the Shaolin Temple films' emphasis on specialized training, with all the Weberian connotations that such specialization suggests for capitalist efficiency.[43] Very often, the training sequences begin with the heroes analyzing their enemies' martial arts skills. They then determine which moves from the Shaolin repertoire would best counter the enemies'. In *Shaolin Martial Arts* (Chang Chen, 1974), the heroes strategize that the only way to defeat the Manchu cronies is through a combination of Tiger and Crane fists. The training that follows is strenuous and highly specialized. Crane fist requires specific finger skills, and we witness the heroes train at every possible moment: even the use of chopsticks during a meal becomes an opportunity to strengthen the specific finger actions necessary. In *Clan of the White Lotus* (Lo Lieh, 1980), Hong Wen-ding finds that his enemy moves like a paper doll in the wind: strong moves don't knock him down, and merely push him away. Hong Wen-ding must develop more gentle moves, so he learns "women's kung fu" from his wife. She puts him through a training regimen that includes embroidery and taking care of a baby. When mentally he becomes "half woman" (as he's called in the film), he integrates this softer approach into his Shaolin skills, and uses the combination to defeat his enemy. A more regimented example of specialized training can be seen in Chang Cheh's *Five Shaolin Masters*, in which the five monks of the film's title must fight five highly skilled enemies. The five Shaolin masters decide to divide the labor by each taking on a different villain. Each villain has his own specialized move, and it is up to the Shaolin masters to determine which specialized Shaolin move can most efficiently counter the villains'. Thus, "Shaolin Rod Skill" goes against "Flying Axe," "Ten Style Fist" against "Mantis Fist," "Whipping Technique" against "Pigtail Technique," "Rolling Move" against "Chop Palm," and so forth. In a most inspiring training sequence, we see the Shaolin masters isolating these skills and honing them to perfection, sharpening the body's movements until it can perform the moves like a well-oiled machine. Training for the "rolling move" requires tumbling around on the ground in endless circles. "Shaolin rod skill" requires repeating the same circular motions with a staff, whipping leaves and branches in a forest. The motions become more precise; the bodies get more proficient and dynamic. The spectacle here is not the violence, but the intense pleasure of witnessing the training of specific skills—martial arts skills that were often the main selling point for these films. For instance, the print advertisement for

*The Best of Shaolin Kung Fu* (Chan Siu-Pang, 1976) includes a graphical lineup of the many moves that will be perfected in the film: "Bear Scramble," "Tiger Pounce," "Leopard Paw," and so on.

## Proving the Reinforcement through Action

Yet, without the payoff (a display of violence), these extravagant training sequences remain pragmatic in theory only. The culminating scene of violence proves the efficacy of specialized training, the superiority of Shaolin martial arts, and the hope for justice while mobile and on the periphery. Following traditions in the action film genre, the climactic scene of violence is a relatively long (five to fifteen minutes) one where heroes fight the villains, during which time suspense is built by showing each side alternate having the advantage. Although there are exceptions, the final showdown typically ends with the hero finishing off the villain through a mortal blow. The mortal blow is sometimes highlighted visually through slow motion, freeze frame, or in the case of some of Chang Cheh's early 1970s films, through an ominous red tint that bloodies the screen at the moment of the strike. The mortal blow is highlighted visually not only to accentuate that spectacular moment when the film can come to a close, but also to underscore the ethical/ideological underpinnings associated with the move chosen to finish off the enemy.

In the case of the Shaolin Temple film, the mortal blow is often accompanied by a quick flashback to the Shaolin disciple training that very same move, reminding the viewer that heroic victory is a result of training. Since it comes at the end of an extended fight, the flashback functions similarly to the final graphic match that punctuates the extended training sequence. Like the training scene, the fight also builds in anxiety through the use of rhythmic editing and sound effects, and through the prolongation of suspense. The final blow is a return to a sense of equilibrium, and the flashback (also a graphic match) informs us of the conditions under which equilibrium can be possible: when specialized training is made pragmatic.

In *Five Shaolin Masters*, the heroes can finally defeat their foes because they effectively administer the lunges and strikes memorized by their bodies. Hu Dedi, for instance, who we previously saw practice his "whipping technique" by training his body to lunge a chained blade through two stalks of bamboo, gets to put his training into action, piercing the blades through two men in a shocking display of super-human strength and special effects. As if to further emphasize the role of bodily memory in this moment of triumph, the film cuts mid-action to a black-and-white flashback of Hu Dedi practicing the same move (Figures 4.1a and 4.1b). Each character's final fight culminates in

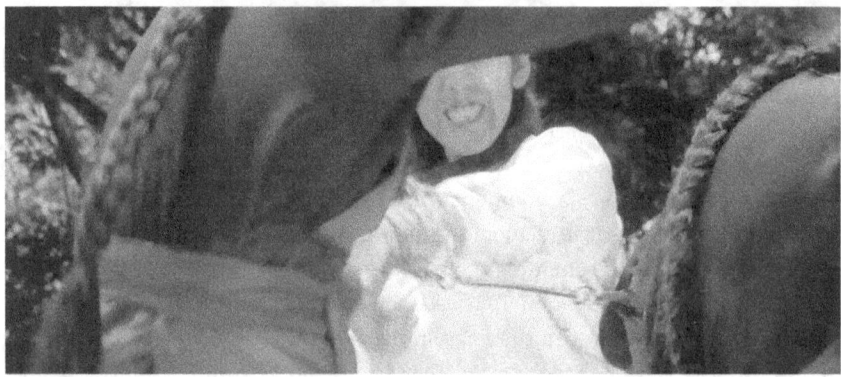

**Figures 4.1a and 4.1b** Flashback followed by graphic match during Hu Dedi's final fight in *Five Shaolin Masters*

a similar black-and-white flashback, drawing a causal relationship between the fighter's embodied cultural memory and his eventual triumph over the ethnic Other. The flashback to training is present in countless Shaolin Temple films. For instance, in the final sequence of *Hand of Death*, Yun Fei grips the villain's arm, and we get a flashback to his finally grasping the oiled bamboo and shattering it. The flashback also borrows the sound and image of shattering bamboo to make Yun Fei's mortal blow even more visceral, metaphorically suggesting that the villain's muscles and tendons are snapping. In the more recent *Tai Chi Master* (Yuen Woo-ping, 1993), we witness Jun Bao (played by Jet Li) defeating his enemy by harnessing reciprocal energies through Tai Chi martial arts, a technique he created, inspired by the manual of his old Shaolin master. During this final fight, we get a flashback to Jun Bao training with a leather ball, learning how to bounce like a ball to most efficiently thwart blows and administer the most effective hits.

## Continuing the Action through Pedagogy and Inspiration

The final fight never results in the collapse of the Qing government, as that would be a blatant historical inaccuracy obvious to a viewer with even a cursory knowledge of Chinese dynastic history. The mortal blow kills off a key general or tyrant, not the emperor. However, many films conclude with the hope of toppling the Qing Dynasty, however misguided that hope is given the well-known historical facts. Many early Shaw Brothers films end with a freeze frame, and in the Shaolin Temple films, the freeze frame captures in mid-action the Shaolin heroes off to fight the next enemy. As an allegory of post-1949 Chinese diaspora, the frozen final action is of the heroes' geographic dispersal, upholding the fight against the dominators through mobilization of the periphery. At the end of Chang Cheh's *Shaolin Temple*, the survivors of the burned-down temple disperse in multiple directions, gathering support elsewhere. *Heroes Two* ends with the four heroes setting off in different directions. "Shaolin brothers are all over the country," says one ally at the end of the film, inspiring further action (and perhaps further specialized training) by signaling to the others the need for continuity through mobility and adaptability in order to achieve their political goals.

Continuity is also ensured through another typical ending: training others. The most elaborated example is *The 36th Chamber of Shaolin*. After Liu Yu-de completes his training in the thirty-five chambers, the temple abbot invites him to hold any position in the thirty-five chambers. Liu Yu-de requests permission to open a thirty-sixth chamber, where he can teach secular students the martial arts of Shaolin so that they can learn to stand up for themselves in the real world. For making such a scandalous request, Liu Yu-de is expelled from Shaolin. Outside of the temple walls, he inspires young men in the city to become his students, and teaches them the martial arts skills he learned in Shaolin. With his new team, Yu-de fights the evil Qing general and administers the mortal blow (a head butt combination to the groin). Their victory inspires the Shaolin Temple leaders to let Yu-de open the thirty-sixth chamber. The film's final shot is a freeze frame of secular students in formation, practicing martial arts moves. Such endings reinforce the tradition of specialized training and aim to ensure that embodied cultural memory lives on beyond the temple and into the real world. It is not surprising that the era of the Shaolin Temple film also saw a renaissance in interest in martial arts training. Discourses about cultural authenticity and fighting efficiency spread in Hong Kong, Taiwan, Singapore, and elsewhere.[44] Carter Huang, star of many Shaolin Temple films, especially those of Joseph Kuo Nan-hung, opened his own martial arts school in San Antonio, Texas, news of which reads in fan magazines like the real-life fulfillment of the cultural dissemination and continuity proposed by the Shaolin Temple films.[45]

## Repurposing Shaolin

The Shaolin Temple films assert a pragmatic deployment of a mobile Chinese tradition to work through anxieties about diasporic identity, to channel energies for global economic competition, and to make sense of multiple "Chinas" in light of the Chinese Cultural Revolution on the mainland. Indeed, cinema became the "thirty-sixth chamber" for Shaolin: a venue in which values associated with Chinese tradition could be taught and made mobile, secular, pragmatic, and even political.

The films use allegory to help audiences make sense of the social and political transformations in the 1970s, since more direct references would be subject to censorship, both political and economic.[46] Gordon Teskey writes on the relationship between allegory and politics, arguing that allegories

> engage us in the practice of ritual interpretation by which [ideological] structures are reproduced in bodies and re-expressed through the voice. As a substitute for genuine political speaking, allegory elicits the ritual repetition of an ideologically significant world. Ritual is a bodily expression of hope that behind the threat that we pose to one another lies the truth of our belonging to one spiritual project.[47]

The ritual repetition of culturally meaningful, sensationally violent martial art movements thus becomes a way of speaking politically (however naively) through the body. These violent representations are also ethical interventions at political crossroads. As David Der-wei Wang writes about twentieth-century Chinese literature, "modern Chinese representation of violence can be underwritten as a violence of representation. For Chinese writers and readers alike, to represent pain and suffering is not merely to reflect external instances of violence; rather it demands to be appreciated and enlisted as a radical agency of change."[48] Allegory in particular can assume such a politically motivated voice because it is able to covertly speak in generality during specific periods of political danger. Teskey adds, "In general, allegory cares without risk. Unlike irony, which is typically subversive, allegory interprets any existing regime not as what it actually is—a political entity created through struggle—but as the natural expression of universal order."[49]

Post-1949 Taiwan was such a time of political danger. After the Republic of China fled the mainland, it violently assumed Taiwan as its new home, ruling the Taiwanese with a strict fist. Martial law lasted in Taiwan from 1948 to 1987. The 1950s and 1960s were notorious as the "white terror" period, when leftists were routinely questioned, imprisoned, and even executed for their dissenting views. Censorship was common in literature, journalism, music, and cinema, and continued into the 1980s. To speak directly of the Republic of China's loss to the communists could be grounds for regulation. The "Taiwan factor" had an enormous impact on Mandarin-dialect (including Mandarin-dubbed) films produced in Hong Kong. Because Taiwan was such an enormous market for Hong Kong cinema, and due to frequent co-productions between companies in the two industries, such political regulations became internalized by commercial Hong Kong film producers. One of the most important developments in Taiwanese cinema history is the 1973 government policy to attract foreign film investment by providing tax rebates on the importation of film negatives. A significant number of Hong Kong production companies took advantage of these tax incentives, including Chang Cheh's Chang's Film Company, which produced several Shaolin Temple films.[50] Chang was aware of Taiwan's sensitivity to political suggestion when he produced films in the 1970s, as his statements on making the historical epic *Seven Man Army* in 1975 attest.[51] In fact, as he finally revealed in his memoirs completed in 2002, Chang had never dared to talk about his early life in politics as an exile in Taiwan and Hong Kong.[52] That violent and shocking allegory became Chang's preferred outlet for externalizing his ideas on Chinese politics is not surprising given those circumstances.

In his memoirs, Chang shows restraint when discussing his political life. However, as in his films, he has plenty to say about Chinese martial arts. His remarks are a thinly veiled commentary on the twentieth-century history of migration, exile, and survival in Hong Kong and the diaspora. In these comments, Chang repeats the myth of Chinese cultural authenticity: that there was once a pure Chinese culture (in this case, a pure form of Shaolin martial arts), which was overtaken and destroyed by outside invaders (the Qing army), and was forced to move elsewhere (Southern China). This has been the central myth of diasporic Chinese cultural nationalism in Hong Kong and Taiwan following the Communist takeover and was increasingly repeated during the Cultural Revolution, when a kind of cultural "purity" was perceived to be under threat. Chang Cheh reenacts this myth in his contrast between Northern and Southern varieties of Chinese martial arts.

> In the Qing dynasty, besides the persecution of the literati, the Manchus suppressed the Han people, by banning the populace from learning or practicing the martial arts. As the political centre of the Qing dynasty was in the north, the ban was not so strictly implemented in the far-flung province of Guangdong. There were people who dared to learn and practice the martial arts in private. They could not do it openly and had to practice at night. Given so, martial arts were better preserved in the South than in the North.[53]

Thus, authentic Shaolin was on the run, embodied in the de-centered folk heroes following the burning of the Shaolin Temple. According to Chang, because of the Qing presence in the north, martial arts there became neutered of their military purpose. "Whether or not the Shaolin Temple had once burned down, the martial arts of the legends were mostly lost. The Northern style martial arts in the mainland is no longer combat effective but performing arts catered for the stage."[54] On the other hand, "Southern martial style is more combat effective than Northern martial style."[55] He comes to this conclusion by looking at the styles of fighting in each region. The Northern style, he argues, is now more operatic than militaristic. The Southern style, as he perceives it, is more practical. He especially celebrates the Wing Chun and Hung Fist styles of the South, and shows how the stances and attacks of each are more suited to practical, rather than aesthetic, purposes. It was well-known to audiences in the 1970s and 1980s that another major director of Shaolin Temple films, Lau Kar-leung, was a direct descendent of the Southern Shaolin tradition of the Hung Fist.[56]

"Combat effectiveness," as celebrated by Chang Cheh in his description of Southern martial arts, and as depicted in the Shaolin films in terms of practicality of movements, becomes associated with cultural authenticity and its survival. To survive is to rely on authentic martial arts. Conversely, authentic martial arts rely on practicality in order to survive. For an exiled Chinese populace working through its identity following the trauma of Civil War and the communist takeover, this myth of survival through adaptable efficiency is especially powerful. Although coded in the response to another trauma—the legendary fall of Shaolin—the suggestion that political retaliation and cultural survival rests on ritually training one's body in martial arts that the enemy (the Qing, the North, the communists) no longer has, delivers a subversive political punch.

In the context of postwar Chinese politics, strategic efficiency in Chang's *Five Shaolin Masters* has a special meaning. In the second half of the film, we discover that the five heroes are training their bodies to effectively defeat the Qing villains because doing so would bolster the strength of the film's true hero: Zheng Chenggong (aka Koxinga). For the Republic of China, Zheng Chenggong is the legendary hero who, in the seventeenth century, defended Taiwan against Dutch colonial powers. After the fall of the Ming Dynasty, he committed his life to using Taiwan as a base for anti-Qing rebels who vowed to overtake the Manchu invaders. Zheng Chenggong's army (seen in the final image of the film, a typical moment of Shaolin's continued training and inspiration) represents the political organization of the Han Chinese rebels exiled by the Qing invaders. That the film associates its chief hero (Zheng) with

Taiwan makes the film's allegory of post-1949 politics painfully obvious: with the traumatic loss of "home," the wandering, exiled Chinese in the diaspora (Hong Kong, Taiwan) regains its political strength by tapping into its "authentic self" (traditional martial arts), ritually training this authentic culture into the efficient male body.[57]

For whatever reason, be it political pressure or audience fatigue, such politically driven Shaolin Temple allegories did not last beyond a few years. In fact, there is a definite sense that the cycle tired itself out. As early as 1976, critics were writing about the glut of films involving the Shaolin Temple, debating the films' implications for the martial arts genre and for Chinese cinema's place on the world film stage.[58] Echoing Rick Altman's observations about genre/cycle combination in classical Hollywood,[59] Hong Kong and Taiwanese film producers attempted to profit off the Shaolin film craze while differentiating their products by experimenting with creative narrative/marketing combinations. Thus, we have *Bruce and Shaolin Kung Fu 2* (1978),[60] *Shaolin vs. Ninja* (1983), *Shaolin vs. Lama* (1983), and so forth.[61] Throughout its history, the Shaolin Temple film combined with other cycles and cultural phenomena such as youth rebellion, as with Chang Cheh's 1975 *Disciples of Shaolin* (poster tagline: "A story of youth, a film for youth"), and pop culture about high school: *Crazy Shaolin Disciples* (Yau Ka-hung, 1985), *Martial Arts of Shaolin* (Lau Kar-leung, 1986), and the TVB series *The Young Heroes of Shaolin* all depict the Shaolin Temple as something of a boarding school, complete with cliques, pranks, and romantic infatuation. Many parodies of the Shaolin Temple film emerged in film, television, and in print. Its primary tropes were further appropriated abroad. Hollywood producers took the basic Shaolin Temple premise and developed it into an Oscar-nominated franchise: *The Karate Kid* (1984, 1986, 1989, 1994, 2010). Beginning with their landmark 1993 album *Enter the Wu-Tang (36 Chambers)*, American rap collective Wu-Tang Clan narrated their upbringing on the streets of Staten Island, which they referred to as "Shaolin."[62] Thus, the "Shaolin Temple" ceased to refer solely to a physical place (in the Songshan mountains) or even a mythical one (in Southern martial arts literature and Chinese-language martial arts films). It became a frame of mind associated with extended self-cultivation and specialized training, traits deemed useful in a society that celebrates self-reliance, getting ahead, and having a career. To give just one example: the Hong Kong New Wave filmmakers' early careers in television are affectionately called their "Shaolin Temple Period."[63]

Although the political motivations of the early Shaolin Temple films became less prominent, the mobile tropes associated with the Shaolin Temple cycle persisted, perhaps suggesting that general heroic traits (such as a cosmopolitanism associated with mobility, adaptability, and competitiveness) were more resonant and more narratively robust than specific ones (such as anti-communism, diaspora politics, and cultural survival). "Combat effectiveness" made way for other kinds of effectiveness to be sharpened through training—for instance: romantic effectiveness, sexual effectiveness, and athletic effectiveness. And though the cycle parodied itself and fractured into tropes appropriated by other cycles, many of the values associated with cosmopolitanism continued. Men continued to be the embodiment of those basic values, although not always so heroically. For instance, the concept of specialized training has been appropriated for the cultivation of sexual prowess. In *36 Secrets of Courtship* (Lu Chi, 1982), young men train at the "Macho Man Training School," where they learn strategies for seduction. Specific training includes: finger skill (kneading dough to train nimble fingers), waist skill (hula-hoop training for ab and pelvic mobility), and tongue skill (licking ice cream to strengthen the tongue). However, the enemies (the women) have skills of their own, successfully taking over the chauvinistic Macho Man Training School and shutting it down, in a clever inversion of the temple-burning trope. A rather specialized form of sexual training exists in the comedy *The Sting II* (aka *The Perfect Exchange*) (Wong Jing, 1993). To seduce an evil boss's girlfriend, prison guard Chung Chor-hung (played by Tony Leung Ka-fai) decides to learn the "revolving penis" technique. This technique allows him to control his penile muscles to move in any direction on command, a skill he is confident will disarm any woman. In the training sequence, we see him tie weights to his penis, which occurs just off frame. In one such scene, he trains while leading his prisoners in an aerobics exercise, the exercise formation in the background visually resembling a Shaolin training formation, comically making a visual metaphor between sexual and martial arts training.

A less-lascivious modern-day variation on the Shaolin Temple film is Kevin Chu Yen-ping's *Shaolin Popey* (1994). In this high-school comedy, Hong Kong teenager Spinach (played by Jimmy Lin) can't match up to his campus rival, the bully Eagle. Spinach is inferior in baseball (he gets hit in the face by Eagle's base hit), he's poorer, he has no connections, and he gets bullied by Eagle and his intimidating Jeep. Most devastatingly, Spinach can't impress Eagle's girlfriend Annie, played by teen idol Vivian Hsu. On a family trip to the mainland, Spinach accidentally wanders into the vicinity of the Shaolin Temple, and starts to observe monks practicing Shaolin martial arts. Inspired by the monks (and perhaps inspired by Shaolin Temple films as well), Spinach starts to train outside of the temple walls. He carries water on his shoulders, as they do in the films. He chops wood and picks up rocks with chopsticks. With the help of a young monk from the Shaolin Temple, Spinach has weights tied to his legs, which makes carrying the water up hills even more intense. Spinach undergoes spiritual transformation via humiliation when he complains to the young monk that he's doing nothing but chores, and not learning any martial arts. In frustration, Spinach takes off his weights. The little monk chases after him and Spinach is shocked to discover that he can now leap to the top of a tree. He's inspired. He puts on more and more weights and builds up his speed. Back in Hong Kong and equipped with these new skills, he is able to defeat Eagle and win the favor of Annie.

*Shaolin Popey* is the first of several Taiwan/Hong Kong co-productions in a cycle directed by Kevin Chu Yen-ping and starring child actors Fok Siu-man and Sik Siu-lung. The former was known for his chubbiness and joviality; the latter was known for his no-nonsense demeanor and kung fu expertise. Together, the two young stars presented juxtapositions meant to comically shock the audience into laughter: Fok Siu-man would bring toilet humor into the Shaolin Temple and teach Shaolin monk Sik Siu-lung how to play his Game Boy. But Sik Siu-lung gave another shock to audiences: he was a five-year-old with mesmerizing martial arts skills. His biography became legend among movie fans. At the age of two, Sik was accepted into the Shaolin Temple, where he trained in Shaolin kung fu. At the age of four, Sik won a prize at a martial arts festival in Zhengzhou. A mere two years later, he was one of the most sought-after stars in Taiwanese and Hong Kong cinema. The legend embedded in his star persona confirmed the reputation of the Shaolin Temple as a training ground that can bring worldly rewards: accolades, fame, wealth. Sik's star persona was able to communicate this confirmation through shock: the juxtaposition of traditional martial arts typically learned through decades of training, with the image of a skinny five-year-old boy. Sik Siu-lung's ascent from the temple to the big screen represented secular success at the speed of capitalist modernity, and gave that success a child's face, instilling a work ethic consistent with a culture of cram schools and rewards-driven education symptomatic of Taiwan, Hong Kong, Singapore, and, increasingly, the People's Republic of China.

In *China Dragon* (Kevin Chu Yen-ping, 1995), Sik Siu-lung plays a character much like himself: a precocious young disciple of the Shaolin Temple who takes part in competitions. However, the stage is no longer the Chinese city of Zhengzhou, but an international one. His character arrives in Hawaii for an international martial arts competition. The allure of training is shown to have international rewards. In many recent parodies of the Shaolin Temple films and in comedies that repurpose tropes of training and adaptability, cosmopolitan skills become truly cosmopolitan in the sense that they are utilized for competition in international contests, or to develop some form of advantage in global sports. In *Shaolin Popey*, Spinach uses his Shaolin martial arts training on the pitcher's mound, where he faces off against Eagle, the batter. As his arm hammers down and his hand releases the baseball, we get the typical flashback to his training at Shaolin, swinging an axe at a tree. Spinach strikes Eagle out, and wins the girl. His victory humorously proves that Shaolin martial arts can give the thin guy an advantage over the brawnier bully. In this case, Chinese tradition (extracted from the Shaolin Temple) is deployed for an unprecedented advantage in a global sport.[64]

In *Anna in Kungfu-land* (Raymond Yip, 2003), an Asian sport is given an international platform. Anna (played by Miriam Yeung) is a half-Chinese, half-Japanese woman living in Japan. Her father is a Shaolin Temple defector, and though he had a falling out with the temple, he dreams of reuniting with it, and bringing Shaolin to Japan. Representing her father's Japanese school, Anna enters an international martial arts tournament, where she faces off against competitors from Mexico, Korea, China, and the United States. In the semifinals, Anna loses to the Shaolin squad from China. However, the Shaolin monk tells Anna that her father is Shaolin and therefore so is she. As a sign of their bond, the Shaolin team asks Anna to fight on their behalf in the finals against the American competitor, Spencer, a tall African American fighter with western boxing-like moves. The Shaolin team's evocation of shared cultural tradition (and ethnicity) inspires Anna in the final showdown. In the fight against Spencer, several of her initial strategies fail. However, we then get a black-and-white flashback to her father training. This leads to a graphic match of her in the ring echoing her father's moves, knocking down Spencer with some gravity-defying moves characteristic of Shaolin martial arts. *Anna and Kungfu-land* proposes that Shaolin can defeat all physical competitors on the international stage, regardless of size and ethnicity. The film also suggests the possibilities of a female Shaolin martial artist (the teaser for the film calls Anna "Shaolin's only female disciple"), as well as her limitations: the flashback here ties her not to her own training, but to her father's, placing her victory on the international stage within a patriarchal, as opposed to personal, tradition.

The most famous juxtaposition of Shaolin martial arts and sport is Stephen Chow's 2001 blockbuster *Shaolin Soccer*, which depicts a team of ex-Shaolin disciples relearning their martial arts skills and applying them to the sport of soccer. *Shaolin Soccer*, often didactically, states that it wants to demonstrate the applicability of Shaolin to contemporary society. In fact, Sing (the Stephen Chow character), even proclaims, "I have always been finding ways to re-package kung fu so that you ordinary people can get a better understanding of it." But the didacticism of the lead character's monologues is far less effective than the cinematic shock of digital effects, which bring the sacred (Chinese martial arts) together with the profane (soccer) in bewilderingly comical ways. Soccer players fly through the air like wuxia heroes, transforming Shaolin Iron Head into head passes, and martial arts kicks into victorious goals. *Shaolin Soccer* effectively makes us laugh in disbelief through its not-so-subtle use of "incongruity-resolution," a cognitive theory of comedy that argues that comedy is set up through a juxtaposition of seemingly irreconcilable elements, followed by a punchline that resolves these elements with unexpected logic. For instance, the joke: "Why did the cookie cry?" (incongruity) "Because his mother had been a wafer so long" (resolution).[65] Yet, because the resolution itself is not strictly logical given the setup, and rather comes off as "logically illogical," we are shocked to laughter.[66] In *Shaolin Soccer*, the incongruous elements are Shaolin martial arts and soccer; the resolution is an elaboration on the visual puns "kick" and "head," which mean different things in Shaolin and soccer, but here find a "logically illogical" harmony on the soccer field.

But this juxtaposition isn't mere action spectacle or comedic punchline. The logically illogical resolution opens up a space of contemplation in the same way that shock sets the stage for allegory. The resolution of Shaolin and soccer isn't simply the visual pun; it is also the reflective provocation: "Why should Shaolin and soccer be incongruous? Perhaps it *isn't*." In fact, *Shaolin Soccer* offers us clues that Shaolin is not only congruous with soccer, it is perhaps necessary if one is to be competitive on the world stage. The narrative conflict in *Shaolin Soccer* pits Shaolin tradition against Western science, represented here by the villainous tournament favorites (appropriately named Team Evil) that utilize performance-enhancing injections and other Western-style scientific methods to train its players. Team Evil, too, has superhuman powers, but theirs are not acquired through training, but through modern science. Both Shaolin and Team Evil portray the acquisition of success through magically rational means (or "occult" practices, as the Comaroffs would argue), but the film clearly hierarchizes Shaolin along moral lines: while both are shortcuts to success, training is seen as more authentic than injections, Chinese traditions as more effective than Western solutions. But aside from the feeling of moral superiority, the film's heroes gain practical rewards: endorsements, fame, participation in world systems of which international sport is merely one part. In Chow's films, it seems that all practical goals are in reach by some creative means, often involving Chinese tradition. In his 1994 comedy *Hail the Judge* (directed by Wong Jing), Chow's character wants simply to defeat a brothel madam at her own game: cursing. What follows is a ridiculous Shaolin-esque training sequence where he trains his mouth by lifting weights with his jaw, putting out candle flames with his tongue, and balancing chairs on his teeth. Once trained, his cursing is so powerful that it can bend metal, resurrect the dead, and, of course, take down the madam. As Stephen Chan Ching-kiu writes, in Chow's films, "the function of *wushu* is now made exceedingly pragmatic, and the question of *wuxia* spirit translated into the terms of instrumental value, with an eye always on making a big score under the conditions of everyday competition."[67]

While I disagree with Chan over temporality—as I've argued throughout this chapter, the function of Chinese martial arts has for decades been exceedingly pragmatic—Chan is right in pointing to the fact that Chow's films emphasize success in everyday competition. In fact, that there exist self-help books that teach readers how to succeed by watching Stephen Chow films makes abundantly clear that Chow's films have a moral-pragmatic dimension perceived to be useful in everyday life. The book *God of Happiness* lists "Stephen Chow's 12 secrets of success," which includes such lessons as "dreaming," "treating life as a game and a play," and "creativity."[68] Another book, *Learning Success from Stephen Chow*, reads Chow's films alongside his biography to offer tips on worldly and spiritual success.[69] These popular interpretations of Chow's work expand the everyday world of his films into the everyday engagement between competitors, often in cosmopolitan practices such as global sports or global capitalism.

I end this chapter with one additional example of the ways in which Stephen Chow's films can serve a pragmatic-moral purpose by humorously celebrating a male hero who adapts Shaolin Temple skills for competition on the world stage. In *The God of Cookery* (Lee Lik-chi and Stephen Chow, 1996), Stephen Chow plays a conman named Stephen Chow who has fooled the culinary world into thinking that he is the "god of cookery." The title is a reference to the gambling film *God of Gamblers*, which itself is a parody of gunplay films derived from wuxia generic syntax. The "God of Cookery" crown is awarded by the "France Cuisine Club," suggesting that it is up to the standard of world-class cuisine. In the cooking competition that opens the film, we see white competitors, signaling that it is an international competition. Soon, Chow's title is stripped by culinary school graduate Bull Tong, who reveals Chow to be a fake. After landing in the streets, Chow befriends a talented noodle stand cook named Sister Turkey, who falls in love with the disgraced "God of Cookery."

In the film's final sequence, Chow shows up at the God of Cookery tournament to regain his title. However, whereas before he was cruel and arrogant, now he appears wiser and matured, and even sports grey hair. We find out through flashbacks that while on a trip to the mainland, Chow accidentally dropped into the Shaolin Temple, and ended up where the true art of cooking is learned: in the Shaolin kitchen, a clever turn of the cliché of the kitchen as where the Shaolin martial arts body is trained. Flashbacks are interspersed throughout the buildup of the final showdown, as Stephen Chow and Bull

Tong face-off and prepare to cook. In the final moments of their competition, when Stephen Chow has only two minutes to prepare his dish, we see him become zen-like and begin to tenderize the meat by mobilizing his energy in a style similar to tai-chi. This then cuts to a flashback of him at the Shaolin Temple spiritually developing this specialized skill. Through this flashback, we discover that at the Shaolin Temple, Chow had a spiritual transformation and learned humility. He learned to stop exploiting Sister Turkey's cooking skills and start to accept her love for him. Chow developed the Shaolin cooking skill by looking into his heart and reflecting on the passion that Sister Turkey represented to him. While his competitors cook up fancy delicacies, he turns out a simple BBQ rice dish, the same one Sister Turkey once cooked for him because she loved him. As in the violent Shaolin Temple films, there needs to be a payoff where we see visual proof of the training's efficacy. In *The God of Cookery*, the payoff comes when the judge, the "chairperson of international gourmet," played by Hong Kong celebrity Nancy Sit as herself, eats the dish and becomes delirious. The olfactory and gustatory ecstasy is represented cinematically through hallucinatorily colorful backgrounds, split-screens, and multiple angles of Nancy Sit's orgiastic expressions. In a truly surreal moment that may be a reference to Sit's character in the TVB series *A Kindred Spirit* (1995–9), she logrolls over a giant piece of meat, using her body to tactilely represent the splendor felt on her taste buds. She then faints after climaxing, a tear dropping from her eye.

After giving this "mortal blow" to the judge, Stephen Chow's character didactically delivers the moral lesson: anybody can be a god of cookery, employing traditional Chinese skills to fulfill cosmopolitan objectives. All you need is to "use your heart" (*yong xin*). This is an assertion of democratic self-reliance, mental adaptability, and hard work—morals of many training sequences in Shaolin films. But there is another "heart" at play here: a romantic one. If the Shaolin Temple film is characterized by the simplicity of its formula (a pragmatic objective requires cosmopolitan skills and specialized training), then *The God of Cookery* surprises us with an unexpected complication: love. Although Chow's initial objective was simply to win back his world-class cooking title, by the end of the film, it is also to win the girl. And if the means to this end was initially to train in Shaolin, by the end we realize that it must also involve coming to terms with his romantic desires, something that earlier Shaolin Temple films made a specific point to exclude from the heroes' lives. As with the romantic sentimentalism of 1970s Taiwanese melodrama, romance enters the complex libidinal economy of the cosmopolitan aspirant, requiring a moral engagement of acceptance or suppression, and mediating the shaky boundaries between personal, national, and global forces.

## Notes

1. Steve Neale defines a cycle as distinct from "genre" by being "made within a specific and limited life-span, and founded, for the most part, on the characteristics of individual commercial successes." Steve Neale, *Genre and Hollywood* (London: Routledge, 2000) 6.
2. For instance, many of the observations I make about the Shaolin cosmopolitan male can also be observed in the Uma Thurman character in Quentin Tarantino's *Kill Bill: Vol. 2* (2004).
3. Examples include *Black Falcon* (Takumi Furukawa, 1967), which features James Bond's "sworn brother," *Interpol* (Yang Shu-hsi, aka Ko Nakahira, 1967), which follows "Agent 009," and *Asia-pol* (Ma Chi-ho, 1967), which imagines an Asian regional secret policy agency.
4. Fan Shuh Ching, *The Population of Hong Kong* (Hong Kong: Committee for International Coordination of National Research in Demography, 1974) 2.
5. I briefly include Singapore here to acknowledge many of its shared socio-political contexts with Hong Kong and Taiwan, as well as to acknowledge the importance of the city in the production and consumption of many films we typically consider "Hong Kong films" during this era.
6. Indeed, Ezra F. Vogel attributes Taiwan's rapid success not simply to cosmopolitan skills, but to the proclivity to openness marked by hard work, modesty, and high levels of education. Ezra F. Vogel, *The Four Little Dragons: The Spread of Industrialization in East Asia* (Cambridge, MA: Harvard University Press, 1991) 36–7.
7. Peter C. Y. Chow, "From Dependency to Interdependency: Taiwan's Development Path toward a New Industrialized Country," *Taiwan in the Global Economy: From an Agrarian Economy to an Exporter of High-Tech Products*, ed. Peter C. Y. Chow (Westport: Praeger, 2002) 256–7.
8. Jon Woronoff, *Asia's "Miracle" Economies* (Armonk: Sharpe, 1986) 128–9.
9. Vogel 78.
10. Alex H. Choi, "State-Business Relations and Industrial Restructuring," *Hong Kong's History: State and Society Under Colonial Rule*, ed. Tak-Wing Ngo (London: Routledge, 1999) 148–57.
11. Kim-Ming Lee, "Flexible Manufacturing in a Colonial Economy," *Hong Kong's History: State and Society Under Colonial Rule*, ed. Tak-Wing Ngo (London: Routledge, 1999) 168–9.
12. Sven Kesselring, "The Mobile Risk Society," *Tracing Mobilities: Towards a Cosmopolitan Perspective*, eds Weertz Canzler, et al. (Aldershot: Ashgate, 2008) 83.
13. Ibid. 84–5.
14. For Petrus Liu, the frequent narrative use of the "Secret Scripture" trope in wuxia literature allegorizes the ideology of accelerated national development in East Asia. Liu, *Stateless Subjects: Chinese Martial Arts Literature and Postcolonial History* (Ithaca: Cornell East Asia Series, 2011) 92–3.
15. Jennie Germann Molz, "Cosmopolitan Bodies: Fit to Travel and Travelling to Fit," *Body & Society* 12.1 (2006): 1–21.

16. While the training sequence is an obsession of the Shaolin Temple film, the ethos of training more generally is a hallmark of most martial arts cinema. In fact, Stephen Teo reminds us that the phrase "kung fu" is Cantonese for "the level of skill and finesse of technique that one has attained." Teo, *Chinese Martial Arts Cinema: The Wuxia Tradition* (Edinburgh: Edinburgh University Press, 2009) 4.
17. Actually, the "Chineseness" deployed in many Hong Kong films and film magazines of this era may more precisely be described as the culture and myth of Southern China (for instance, certain martial arts and operatic traditions). However, whereas a number of (mostly Hong Kong) scholars have interpreted the films' use of Southern Chinese culture as a kind of Southern regional identity with Guangzhou and Hong Kong as its capitals (see, for instance, the field of Lingnan studies), I prefer to read the substitutability of Southern Chinese culture with an essentialized "Chineseness" to be a radical acknowledgment of the unfixed, inherently translated, multiply claimable nature of Chineseness itself.
18. "Shaws Launches 'Action Era,'" *Southern Screen* 92 (October 1965): 30.
19. Ibid.
20. Vivian Sobchack, *Carnal Thoughts: Embodiment and Moving Image Culture* (Berkeley: University of California Press, 2004) 3.
21. Poshek Fu, "Zhongguo bendi hua: Shaosi yu Xianggang dianying," *Zhama shidai: wenhua shenfen, xingbie, richang shenghuo shijian yu xianggang dianying 1970s*, eds. Kwai-cheung Lo and Eva Kit Wah Man (Hong Kong: Oxford University Press, 2005) 12–15.
22. Buddhism is not indigenous to China, but in martial arts films, it is depicted as a distinctive component of Chinese tradition.
23. Jean Comaroff and John L. Comaroff, "Millennial Capitalism: First Thoughts on a Second Coming," *Millennial Capitalism and the Culture of Neoliberalism*, eds Jean Comaroff and John L. Comaroff (Durham, NC: Duke University Press, 2001) 19–27.
24. Walter Benjamin, *The Origin of German Tragic Drama* (London: Verso, 2003) 175.
25. Ibid. 183.
26. Sek Kei, "Chang Cheh's Revolution in Masculine Violence," Chang Cheh, *Chang Cheh: A Memoir* (Hong Kong: Hong Kong Film Archive, 2004) 13.
27. Benjamin 183.
28. Chang Cheh, *Chang Cheh: A Memoir* 100.
29. Gordon Teskey, *Allegory and Violence* (Ithaca: Cornell University Press, 1996) 12.
30. The costume martial arts film, more precisely the *shenguai wuxia* film, was for decades seen as feudalistic by the Chinese Communist Party, and thus outlawed until after the Cultural Revolution.
31. Some Shaolin films don't include a single woman character. Examples include Chang Cheh's *Five Shaolin Masters* and John Woo's *Hand of Death* (1976). As is often noted, women play only minor roles in most of Chang Cheh's films. Stephen Teo, "Shaws' Wuxia Films: The Macho Self-Fashioning of Zhang Che/Chang Cheh," *The Shaw Screen: A Preliminary Study*, ed. Wong Ain-ling (Hong Kong: Hong Kong Film Archive, 2003) 145–59.
32. Elaine Scarry, *The Body in Pain: The Making and Unmaking of the World* (New York: Oxford University Press, 1985) 110.

33. Ibid. 109.
34. Ibid. 112.
35. According to historian Meir Shahar, the Southern Shaolin Temple may or may not have existed. Instead, its central place in the folklore of Southern Chinese popular culture (including those of Hong Kong and Taiwan) is a result of the legitimacy its myth lends to secret societies like the Tiandihui (the Heaven and Earth Society). Meir Shahar, *The Shaolin Monastery: History, Religion, and the Chinese Martial Arts* (Honolulu: University of Hawaii Press, 2008) 183–5.
36. Ng Ho, *Gu cheng ji: lun Xianggang dianying ji su wexue* (Hong Kong: Ci Wen Hua Tang, 2008) 64–9. See also John Christopher Hamm, *Paper Swordsmen: Jin Yong and the Modern Chinese Martial Arts Novel* (Honolulu: University of Hawaii Press, 2005) 34–7.
37. For a useful breakdown of the characters and motifs of the Southern legends as they spread in Hong Kong, see Ng Ho, "Chong ti Lingnan shaolin jiushi," *Wu Hao de Xianggang dianying minsu xue* (Hong Kong: Ci Wen Hua Tang, 1993) 91–113.
38. The Shaolin myth is especially prominent in the Xi Lu Legend, which describes the formation of the Tiandihui, a secret society with ties to rebellion in Taiwan and to the triads in Hong Kong. Dian H. Murray and Qin Baoqi, *The Origins of the Tiandihui: The Chinese Triads in Legend and History* (Palo Alto: University of Stanford Press, 1994).
39. Many Shaolin Temple films have similar lines of dialogue. For instance, in Chang Cheh's *Shaolin Temple*: "The Shaolin Temple is finished. But Shaolin martial arts lives on" and in the trailer for *Men from the Monastery*: "Shaolin monastery was burned. The inmates scattered. Chinese martial arts spread."
40. Shahar 182–96.
41. Kam Louie notes that the *wu* (or martial) masculine type in Chinese fiction is characterized by his working-class status and his ideals of social harmony that rest on a belief in brotherhood and sacrifice for his fellow man in the face of oppression. This specific type of *wu* male in literature, and I would argue in the Shaolin Temple films as well, is the *haohan* (or "good fellow"), who seeks not political power or social mobility, but simply justice and fraternity. See Louie, *Theorising Chinese Masculinity: Society and Gender in China* (Cambridge: Cambridge University Press, 2002) 79–80.
42. "'Huo Shao Shaolin Si' nei yanggang qisheng," *Cinemart* 82 (October 1976): 66–7.
43. Max Weber, "The Spirit of Capitalism," *The Protestant Ethic and the Spirit of Capitalism* (London: Routledge, 2002) 13–38.
44. Most obvious is in the popularity of Shaolin guidebooks. Shaolin martial arts schools released their own publications. For instance, in Singapore, The North Shaolin School was formed in 1980 and published a yearbook of its philosophies in 1981. Bei Shao Lin, *1$^{st}$ Anniversary (1981)* (1981) (accessed at the National Library of Singapore). The Singapore Seow Tin San Athletic Association also published extensive materials regarding the spread of Chinese martial arts throughout the Nanyang region. Singapore Seow Tin San Athletic Association, *Xinzhou shaozhenshan guoji tiyu hui di ershiwu zhounian yingxi jinian tekan* (Singapore: Jin Jin Printing, 1972).

45. Zi Yu, "Huang Jiada jinjun guoji yingtan," *Cinemart* 167 (November 1983): 46–7.
46. For a discussion of the role of agency and imagination in defining the cultural nation, and the difficulties of tracking that agency due to censorship and political pressures, see Chris Berry, "If China Can Say No, Can China Make Movies? Or, Do Movies Make China? Rethinking National Cinema and National Agency," *Modern Chinese Literary and Cultural Studies in the Age of Theory*, ed. Rey Chow (Durham, NC: Duke University Press, 2000) 159–80.
47. Teskey 133.
48. David Der-wei Wang, *The Monster That Is History: History, Violence, and Fictional Writing in Twentieth-Century China* (Berkeley: University of California Press, 2004) 3.
49. Teskey 133.
50. Feii Lu, *Taiwan dianying: zhengzhi, jingji, meixue (1949–1994)* (Taipei: Yuanliu, 1998) 194.
51. Chang 70–3.
52. Ibid. 40–3.
53. Ibid. 134.
54. Ibid.
55. Ibid. 138.
56. Feng Wei, "Shaolin sanshiliu fang," *True Beauty* 56 (January 1978): 68–9.
57. The Kuomintang Nationalists in China have a history of appropriating the figure of the male rebel and the *haohan* from popular culture in representing their ideals against the communists in the Civil War years. Interestingly, the communists also appropriated this masculine figure to represent their own aspirations against the KMT. David Ownby, "Approximations of Chinese Bandits: Perverse Rebels, Romantic Heroes, or Frustrated Bachelors?" eds. Susan Brownell and Jeffrey N. Wasserstrom, *Chinese Femininities/Chinese Masculinities: A Reader* (Berkeley: University of California Press, 2002) 237–40.
58. Liu Lo Lo, "Just Observe the Cinema Climate," *Cinemart* 81 (September 1976): 20–1.
59. Rick Altman, "Reusable Packaging: Generic Products and the Recycling Process," *Refiguring American Film Genres*, ed. Nick Browne (Berkeley: University of California Press, 1998) 1–41.
60. For an analysis of cycle recombination as it pertains to Bruce Lee look-alike films, see my chapter "'Bruce Lee' after Bruce Lee: A Life in Conjectures," *Chinese Film Stars*, eds. Mary Farquhar and Yingjin Zhang (London: Routledge, 2010) 165–79.
61. This process of seemingly spurious recombination is parodied in an article that tells the story of how actors Jackie Chan, Sammo Hung, and Yuen Biao decide to compromise their values for money by making a Shaolin Temple film with proposed titles like "Shaolin Battles E.T.," "Shaolin Fights James Bond," and "Shaolin: the Last Chapter," which they hope will end the cycle once and for all. Liu Lo Lo, "Liu Lao Lao chongfan shaolin si," *Cinemart* 164 (August 1983): 40.
62. As Wu-Tang member and producer of The RZA states, "Staten Island—where we grew up, were disciplined at, had our fights at—that's Shaolin." Chi Tung, "The RZA

Revisited," *Asia Pacific Arts*, UCLA Asia Institute (September 22, 2005) <http://www.asiaarts.ucla.edu/article.asp?parentid=30251> (accessed July 31, 2009).
63. Law Kar, "The 'Shaolin Temple' of the New Hong Kong Cinema," *The Study of Hong Kong Cinema in the 1970s* (Hong Kong: The Urban Council, 1984) 114.
64. Taiwanese baseball teams have a long, successful history of participation in international baseball. From 1969 to 1996, little league teams from Taiwan won the Little League World Series seventeen times. In the 1992 Olympic Games, the first year of competitive baseball at the summer Olympics, Chinese Taipei won a silver medal. For a discussion of the national and international politics of baseball in Taiwan, see Andrew D. Morris, *Colonial Project, National Game: A History of Baseball in Taiwan* (Berkeley: University of California Press, 2011).
65. Graeme Ritchie, *The Linguistic Analysis of Jokes* (London: Routledge, 2004) 54–7.
66. Geoff King, *Film Comedy* (London: Wallflower Press, 2002) 14–15.
67. Stephen Chan Ching-kiu, "The Fighting Condition in Hong Kong Cinema: Local Icons and Cultural Antidotes for the Global Popular," *Hong Kong Connections: Transnational Imagination in Action Cinema*, Meaghan Morris, et al., eds. (Durham, NC: Duke University Press, 2005): 76.
68. Zhou Zhangyu and Yu Xinyi, *Kuaile zhi shen: Zhou Xingchi* (Taipei: Mucun, 2004) 266–7.
69. Luo Jun and Zhang Yongmei, *Xiang Zhou Xingchi xue chenggong* (Taipei: Heliopolis, 2008).

# Chapter 5

# The Cosmopolitan Brand: Film Policy as Cultural Work in the International Film Market

The preceding chapters benefited from an abundance of evidence. In examining discourses of cosmopolitanism and proposing cultural, political, industrial, and demographic explanations, I could rely on dozens, and in some cases well over 100, filmic examples from which to trace patterns and identify aesthetic and narrative trends. Stars from Linda Lin Dai in the late 1950s to Daniel Wu in the early 2000s made numerous films per year. The Shaolin and Chiung Yao cycles reflected the brazen overproduction of the Hong Kong and Taiwan film industries in the 1970s. The staggering volume of film production emerging from these relatively small locales has accounted for the convincingness and detail of some of the most important book-length studies of Hong Kong and Taiwanese cinemas.[1] For instance, it is largely due to the sheer number and diversity of films from the 1980s and 1990s that Ackbar Abbas cites in his influential essays on the "déjà disparu" that his argument seems generalizable to the industry as a whole and to Hong Kong culture more broadly during the countdown years.[2] Studies of the New Wave in Hong Kong and the New Cinema in Taiwan had a large corpus of films and filmmakers to choose from and required the cinemas' prolificness to first convince readers that these are in fact film movements, and then to argue that the films in such movements have shared aesthetic, narrative, and industrial attributes.

But how does a scholar study the films of an industry that no longer exists, that barely exists, or that is still in the process of becoming? Much has been made of the dwindling annual output of films produced in Hong Kong and especially Taiwan. Once dubbed the "Hollywood of the East" and considered the third biggest film industry in the world, Hong Kong's feature-film output sharply declined in the first decade of the twenty-first century. In 2007, Hong Kong produced only fifty films, barely a fifth of the industry's output in 1993. By

2007, Hong Kong was not even one of the biggest producers in Asia—far below the numbers of perennial powerhouses India and Japan and exploding markets China and South Korea, and even eclipsed by Indonesia and Thailand. Meanwhile, Taiwan, one of the world's top ten producers in the 1960s, produced only seventeen feature films in 2005.[3] The island's most renowned working directors were producing their films overseas. Only two of Hou Hsiao-hsien's last six features and three of Tsai Ming-liang's last seven features were primarily shot in Taiwan. And despite his reputation as a representative of Taiwan, Ang Lee has only set one film in his homeland. Scholarly articles do continue to be written about contemporary Hong Kong and Taiwanese films, however. Important, provocative, and innovative scholarship continues to come out in journals like *Film Appreciation* and *Asian Cinema*, only these articles can no longer convincingly make claims about the state of an industry or trends across films. Any creative scholar can derive conclusions out of only a handful of films, and so the best recent textual analyses of contemporary Hong Kong and Taiwanese film have been those that forgo the bigger picture altogether, focusing instead on how individual films and filmmakers reflect or rework local, national, and global phenomena such as sexuality, identity, and space. For instance, a study of cosmopolitanism in Taiwanese cinema may observe how films like *Au Revoir Taipei* (Arvin Chen, 2010), *Taipei Exchanges* (Hsiao Ya-chuan, 2010), and *Starry Starry Night* (Tom Lin Shu-yu, 2011) incorporate French and American artistic sensibilities to rework the melodrama of arrival and departure for a more fickle, ironic generation.

Yet the question of the state of the industry persists. Is it possible to write about the character of a local film industry if all we have are a handful of titles and statistical tables? No doubt we must broaden the "local film industry" to include not only feature films produced by agents in Taiwan and Hong Kong, but also nontheatrical production, location services, and below-the-line work, such that analyzing the textual and contextual "Taiwan" of the Taiwan-shot but not necessarily Taiwan-set *Life of Pi* (Ang Lee, 2012), *Shield of Straw* (Takashi Miike, 2013), *Lucy* (Luc Besson, 2014), and *Silence* (Martin Scorsese, 2016) can reveal the mutable landscapes and cultural labor of transnational Taiwanese cinema. But how do we theorize this expanded conception of the film industry? Perhaps a strategy can be found by looking at how historians have tackled the problem of Taiwanese cinema before it came into being. Guo-juin Hong sums up the nascent cinema of colonial Taiwan elegantly, calling it "film history without film and national cinema without nation."[4] Hong writes of a moment when filmmaking and filmgoing were itinerant activities. Meanwhile, Taiwan was a colony caught between two nations (China and Japan), and the nation of "national cinema" was fraught with uncertainty. What Hong is getting at with his description is that Taiwanese cinema is not simply a corpus of films, but a mobilization of an idea. To evoke "Taiwanese cinema" is to make an intervention in history, nationhood, and identity. In Hong's case, it is to uncover activities that only come into view when we look beyond the master histories of colonialism (from Japan and China) and Western academia. The parallels between Taiwanese cinema in the colonial period and today make Hong's formulation especially valuable. Contemporary Taiwanese cinema is made up of fly-by-night operations. There are no studios in the traditional sense, only independent producers with a cinematic vision or an entrepreneurial spirit. As they were in the colonial period, many of these operations are transnational in that they are collaborations with personnel, financiers, talent, and audiences overseas. Lastly, contemporary Taiwanese cinema is without a nation, found in the postwar years but lost in the 1970s with the domino effect of faltering diplomatic relations. Taiwan remains in a state where "national cinema" (*guopian*) is contested from all sides, less a reality than a dream of former glories and future prosperity, intimately tied to the ideal of national self-definition. The political stakes are somewhat different in Hong Kong, but the parallels should be clear: dwindling production numbers and a vanishing window of opportunity to resurrect a local cinema in one's own name. The idea of a "Hong Kong cinema" continues to be evoked by filmmakers, critics, programmers, audiences, and academics to insist that it exists. In fact, in this moment of danger, when local filmmaking activities diminish and are assimilated into those of mainland China, the idea of "Hong Kong cinema" is evoked perhaps more than ever. As Laikwan Pang puts it, "Hong Kong people perform their need of a concrete Hong Kong precisely because there is no more of it."[5]

In this chapter, I study contemporary Hong Kong and Taiwanese cinemas by examining the provocative and colorful insistence of "Hong Kong cinema" and "Taiwanese cinema" at the moment they appear to be vanishing. Specifically, I want to look at the ways that state representatives conjure the idea of the local industry on the world stage as a means of self-branding in a competitive global market. What words are used to describe these cinemas? Which images are used as decoration or metaphor? Indeed, what I want to look at is what these cinemas look and sound like when they are still in a dream state. My approach to industrial analysis is not one purely reliant on statistical evidence, but on textuality and imagination. What I find is that these government-produced sounds and images, in their own scattered and sometimes ineffective way, imagine "Hong Kong cinema" and "Taiwanese cinema" as cosmopolitan Chinese, a strategy of self-branding developed to position the local industries between China and the world, and specifically as a bridge between the two. This strategy is part of a larger "politics of positionality" undertaken in Taiwan and Hong Kong. In Taiwan, this strategy of becoming the world's "window to China" is not only a project of the more China-friendly Kuomintang government; the independence-leaning Democratic Progressive Party, too, has proposed ways in which Taiwan could combine its knowledge of China with its cosmopolitan experience and therefore carve out a place for itself in the global economy.[6] Hong Kong has long prospered from such a position, making use of its free port status, its colonial advantages, its cultural traditions, and its ties to southern China to become the gatekeeper between China and foreign trade partners. In Hong Kong, the drive to become a "Chinese global city" has largely been motivated by state forces, most recently with the Hong Kong Trade Development Council playing an active role in the international promotion of Hong Kong goods and services, including cinema.[7] However, there is a fear that Hong Kong's advantage will soon be eclipsed with China's own growing cosmopolitanism. Notwithstanding Shu-mei Shih's provocation that diaspora has an "expiration date," it seems that Hong Kong's cosmopolitan advantage itself will expire soon, as China learns to play its own politics of positionality and mobilize its linguistic and multicultural resources, and Hong Kong will be swallowed up and made irrelevant by an increasingly cosmopolitan China.[8] Following China's entry into the World Trade Organization (WTO) and Hong Kong and China becoming "competing partners," foreign corporations aiming to do business in China found that they could sidestep the middleman (Hong Kong) altogether, and the Hong Kong state has responded by initiating branding strategies to maintain the impression of its role as a gateway to China.[9] On the ground-level, the politics of positionality is a branding game with largely short- and medium-term aspirations.

The state then continues to be a critical player in the framing of film industries and "national cinema" discourses. In recent years, film studies has discovered the importance of looking at the global film industry in terms of its institutions, laws, and regulatory systems. This very important work has investigated the processes of co-production, financing, copyright, and other phenomena of global screen traffic. Much of this work centers on the persistent role of the nation-state in facilitating or hindering these transnational flows in the name of cultural protection, free trade, or any number of other positions. Examples include Mette Hjort's study of Danish cinema, in which she argues that especially for "minor cinemas" like Denmark's, attention must be paid to the nation-state's "politics of positionality" in the global film scene.[10] Another example is Ben Goldsmith and Tom O'Regan's study of film studios, in which they argue, among other things, that nation-states participate in courting international production and co-production by cultivating what they call "location interest."[11] One of the central means by which governments intervene in the industry is through film policy. As Michael Curtin writes, "concepts such as free flow and market forces are in fact meaningless without self-conscious state interventions to fashion a terrain for commercial operations. Markets are made, not given."[12] In other words, policy creates "conditions of possibility," which Michael Keane describes as "the factors that have led, are leading, and could lead to success."[13] Keane adds that discourses of possibility are especially resonant in areas undergoing transition and modernization, and we may include Hong Kong and Taiwan among them.

Several scholars have looked at Chinese-language cinemas from the perspective of policy. Michael Curtin's study of film and television history in China, Hong Kong, Taiwan, and Singapore astutely examines how media companies convene and reformulate geographically according to a number of factors, including government policy.[14] Darrell William Davis and Emilie Yueh-yu Yeh's book *East Asian Screen Industries* looks at how policies such as national import and exhibition quotas, as well as trade agreements and governmental initiatives, have shaped the kinds of films that are produced within and across national borders in East Asia.[15] These studies have been important to the field because they provide extensive empirical and historical evidence to support theses about transnational filmmaking in Asia. After the publication of Sheldon Lu's seminal *Transnational Chinese Cinemas* in 1997, Chinese film scholars debated transnational phenomena in Chinese cinema, but mostly limited their objects of analysis to the films themselves, making arguments about new hybrid formations of ethnicity, gender, sexuality, and genre as evidenced by narrative and style.[16] Curtin and Davis/Yeh's books demonstrate how innovative arguments about transnational industries can be made by using other forms of evidence: practitioner interviews (as with Curtin) and trade publications (Davis/Yeh). Perhaps because of the strong market-orientation of the examples, Chris Berry has argued that Curtin and Davis/Yeh's books reduce transnational filmmaking to that which is crassly profit-seeking.[17] The examples of transnational phenomena found in these books are neoliberal ones, with states acting as gatekeepers while producers navigate past borders to seek the cheapest production options and the largest paying audience. For Berry, these accounts ignore transnational practices that may operate outside, or even against, globalization, such as the filmmaking of director Jia Zhang-ke, whose films utilize cross-border resources of financing and distribution in order to reflect critically on what globalization means in contemporary China.[18] I would add that another motivation of transnational filmmaking beyond profit-maximization is national positioning. Driven by desires for recognition, cultural preservation, and security, state governments directly participate in designing and administering co-production parameters, location interest, piracy, and film training/financing, and so, as Laikwan Pang has proposed, scholars should study cultural industry policy with the same critical scrutiny they would to the national and transnational.[19]

Like most other studies on the subject, Davis and Yeh's book focuses on policy that has created new kinds of films, obscuring policy that stalls, as is so often the case with Taiwan. Doting on failure may not be of interest to a book on the profit-seeking motivations of transnational players—except to the extent that it can be a guide for what *not* to do—but I would argue that if we are to understand how policy acts as an industry- or nation-building tool, and if we are to understand how policy is also an expression of cultural formations, then it is just as important to pay attention to policy that ultimately leads nowhere. By looking solely at success, we risk treating policy as an automatic operation: a state initiative, trade agreement, or law immediately leads to changes in the industry. However, policy doesn't work this way, as if it is a "visible hand" that can sway a market. Hearts and minds—of producers, financiers, co-producers, exhibitors, audiences—need to be won if non-governmental parties are expected to play by governmental rules. In practice, policy is mucky and treated with suspicion, and requires negotiation of cultural desires and incentives to be made successful. A similar perspective on policy is found in Laikwan Pang's take on post-1997 Hong Kong cinema. Pang argues that, through government and non-governmental initiatives like the Closer Economic Partnership Arrangement (CEPA), the Focus: First Cuts series, and the Hong Kong—Asian Film Financing Forum (HAF), Hong Kong has undergone a process of re-branding to sustain its place in the regional and global film marketplace.[20] Yet, for all the talk of branding, there is no analysis of advertising—only textual analyses of films and analyses of statistical trends such as box office and annual output. How does a state brand itself? When Pang points out what the Hong Kong SAR is trying to do, her evidence is what gets made, not what the government is actually doing on the ground, which, as the editors of the anthology *Branding Cities* note, is both a "mundane and extraordinarily ambitious" endeavor.[21] Pang's focus on what ultimately gets produced may be attributed to the fact that, for good reason, Pang wants to assert the persistence of local Hong Kong content, which many are already eulogizing after the implementation of CEPA.[22] In other words, most industry studies consider co-production and regional/international interaction to solely be empirical events with measurable outcomes, rather than textual ones produced through rhetoric and attempts at legitimacy. These studies are extremely important because they track those empirical changes and give them context, but I would like to draw attention to the rhetoric—often a kind of strategic self-branding—that makes policy work, or that leads to its failure, but that in any case expresses how governments envision "possibility" at a moment of transition.

These envisionings are everywhere in contact zones between Hong Kong/Taiwan and the world. I have come to acknowledge, and even appreciate, the tireless effervescence of self-branding by observing years of policy failure in Taiwan. Year in and year out, the state—represented by the Government Information Office, the Taipei Film Commission, and the Taiwan Ministry of Culture—has devised ever more creative strategies for flaunting the cosmopolitanism of Taiwan and the Taiwanese film industry. These attempts at self-definition and self-branding speak to the ways in which national identity is not simply a kind of internal reflection on local traditions and identities, but is also an external process of cultural negotiation with the outside world. Anthropologist Anna Tsing argues that this negotiation—what she calls "friction"—is marked by a clash between parties with different interests and sometimes incommensurable visions of universal cooperation. In spaces of interconnection, such as international trade fairs in the case of the global film industry, parties pose claims of being able to work together, and through an "awkward, unequal, unstable, and creative" set of interactions and "sticky engagements," deals are proposed and cultures are co-produced.[23] As Tsing writes, "In transnational collaborations, overlapping but discrepant forms of cosmopolitanism may inform contributors, allowing them to converse—but across difference."[24] In Hong Kong and Taiwan, film policy designed to encourage transnational co-production constantly evokes a particularlized cosmopolitanism, aimed at potential foreign co-producers with their own ideals of cosmopolitan collaboration and capitalism. Through images, sounds, and narrative, differences "stick" and ultimately (or ideally) yield cooperation. In contact zones like the trade fair, film policy must materialize into a kind of cultural practice with its own texts and contexts, producers and readers. And what better way to study culture than to employ the methods of textual analysis and ethnography?

In *Production Culture*, John Caldwell argues that social and cultural practices are folded into industrial ones, and therefore to better understand the film industry, we need to study it as a living culture with its own rules of engagement, its own rituals, its own theories about itself, and its own publications.[25] And to study the industry means looking at industrial self-reflexivity: for instance, the way the industry talks about itself in trade journals, the way it embeds its own assumptions in training and technology, and the way it advertises its products to others. Conducting this kind of study requires scholars to not only look beyond studying film and TV texts, and in fact even looking beyond familiar contextual materials like fan and promotional discourse, and toward what he calls embedded texts and rituals. Embedded texts and rituals can be fully embedded within an industry and not open to the public, such as how-to manuals, pitch sessions, or association newsletters. Or they can be semi-embedded texts and rituals semi-open to the public, such as press kits and trade shows. Caldwell argues that these industrial texts and rituals allow us to understand the logic through which the industry speaks to itself and legitimizes its own practices.

In the case of Hong Kong and Taiwanese cinema, "the industry" includes many of the same players and institutions that Caldwell studies in the Hollywood case. After all, Hong Kong and Taiwan are willing participants in the same global screen industry heavily influenced by Hollywood distribution companies, as well as production consortiums like the Los Angeles-based Independent Film and Television Alliance, which puts on the annual American Film Market (AFM). Therefore, many of the objects of analysis that Caldwell identifies—embedded and semi-embedded texts and rituals—are central, analyzable texts that reflect the culture of production of Hong Kong and Taiwanese cinema on the world stage. Studying the Hong Kong and Taiwan situations is eased by their relatively few number of active players on the world stage, as well as the fact that both industries are often represented internationally by state advocacy groups: the Hong Kong Trade Development Council and Hong Kong Film Development Council in Hong Kong, and the Government Information Office (and its later incarnations) and the Taipei Film Commission in Taiwan. These state organizations produce and actively disseminate much of the embedded and semi-embedded discourse on their respective cinemas in regional and international trade events. How do these advocacy groups brand their respective cinemas? How do they legitimize the existence of "Taiwan cinema" or "Hong Kong cinema"? What words and images do they use in their publications and industrial rituals? How do they activate cultural stereotypes and histories of colonialism and neoliberalism in their branding?

The primary site for the ritual performance of this industrial self-reflexivity and the dissemination of self-reflexive semi-embedded texts is the international trade show, known in the industry as the "film market." Sales agents, buyers, and producers around the world generally agree that the three most important film markets are the Marche du Film held in Cannes in conjunction with the city's annual film festival, the European Film Market held alongside the Berlin Film Festival, and the American Film Market, held every November in Santa Monica, near Los Angeles. Hong Kong and Taiwan representatives have maintained a consistent presence at all three trade events, but I will focus on their efforts at the American Film Market, as well as two other markets important for Hong Kong and Taiwanese cinema: Hong Kong FILMART and the Asian Film Market in Busan, Korea.

Film markets are in theory trade shows for any aspect of film production, distribution, and exhibition. It is here, for instance, that a producer can become acquainted with companies that assist in underwater cinematography or where they can shop for new technologies in digital asset delivery. But, ultimately, film markets exist to facilitate the buying and selling of film properties, before, during, and after films are produced. Another important aspect of film markets is that they are a showcase for locations and services. This is where national and state governments play the most active role, highlighting locations, studios, and post-production facilities within their borders, as well as what financial incentives prospective producers can expect there. Lastly, film markets are where insiders learn about what is going on in the rest of the industry, via seminars, parties, and special issues of trade journals.

We can separate these various functions of film markets into two main ritual practices: pitching and industrial self-theorization. Pitching includes the pitching of individual films, the pitching of collections of films, and the pitching of locations and services. Pitching culture is shaped by the interests of the kinds of participants involved, the medium of marketing, and the social and physical environments of the exhibition booth, the screening room, and the industry party.

**Table 5.1** Pitching practices at film markets

| Product ("what") | Pitching agent ("who") | Marketing medium ("how") | Festival venue ("where") |
| --- | --- | --- | --- |
| Individual film | Producers, studios/distributors, sales agents | Film screenings, DVD/online screeners, trailers, rough cuts, trade journal ads, flyers | Exhibition booths, screening rooms |
| Film packages | Sales agents, studios/distributors, national/state governments | Film screenings, DVD/online screeners, trailer reels, rough cuts, trade journal ads, flyers | Exhibition booths, screening rooms, industry parties |
| Financing services | National/State governments, financial service companies | Flyers, trade journal ads | Exhibition booths, industry parties |
| (Post)production services | Production service companies, national/state governments | Flyers, trade journal ads, film reels | Exhibition booths, industry parties |
| Location services | National/State governments, production service companies | Flyers, trade journal ads, film reels | Exhibition booths, industry parties |

We can also break down the different kinds of industrial self-theorization that occur at film markets. The first is through trade journals. At the American Film Market and other markets, *Variety*, *Screen Daily*, and the *Hollywood Reporter* publish daily special reports exclusive to market participants. These special issues inform attendees of what to expect at the market, what is the status of the industry at a particular juncture, what deals are in the works, and which market attendees have been successful in buying and selling properties. The journals become a daily notebook for the market, and are also a way for the market to analyze each day's activities, seeking to understand and even theorize how, for instance, the financial crisis is affecting film sales or what are the potential effects of such-and-such's ascension as new studio boss. These daily analyses frequently set the tone for the way industry players go about their days' work. A second kind of self-theorization occurs at seminars, programmed by the market, or by special interest groups, national governments, guilds, and service providers. These seminars establish authority in the industry by defining who the experts are based on who is invited to speak on a panel. They also help various agencies gain legitimacy via expert testimony, as I will later discuss in relation to Hong Kong.

## Taiwan: A Cinema as Tall as Taipei 101

From 1999 to 2008, Taiwan was represented by the Government Information Office (GIO) at the American Film Market.[26] The GIO rented out exhibition space, providing flyers and brochures to potential buyers and co-producers, and they did this at other markets as well. We must read the GIO's international presence in conjunction with its efforts at film promotion via film policy. As I argued earlier, policy is not simply an apparatus that leads to more films, but, regardless if it succeeds or fails, is the mobilization of an idea. By studying pitching practices, we can make generalizations about strategies to create a national cinema: a national cinema as imagined by state organizations out of national cinema resources such as services, locations, talent, and culture. My argument is that the main strategy undertaken by the Taiwanese state is a specific kind of cosmopolitanism defined by an insistence on participating on the world stage. This cosmopolitanism shows Taiwanese cinema and culture as technologically and aesthetically cutting-edge and integrated with the rest of the world.

Since cosmopolitanism is a style and not just a philosophy, it can be evoked graphically in semi-embedded texts at film markets. Looking at covers of brochures provided at the Taiwan cinema booth at the American Film Market, and an advertisement placed in the trades at Hong Kong FILMART, we find repeated references to the gargantuan Taipei 101 tower, until 2010 the tallest building in the world and an emblem of what geographer Larry Ford calls Asia's "skyscraper competition"²⁷ (Figures 5.1a, b, c, d). Except as an occasional location, Taipei 101 has nothing to do with Taiwanese cinema, but both state agencies (the GIO and the Taipei Film Commission) found it advantageous to borrow the building's international cache—its "best in the world" status—to showcase Taiwanese cinema's technological and perhaps spiritual or market integration with the world

**Figure 5.1a**  *Taipei Cinema Location Guide* (Taipei Film Commission, 2008)

**Figure 5.1b** *Taiwan's Innovativeness in Film* (Government Information Office, 2007)

**Figure 5.1c** Taipei Film Commission and Ile de France Film Commission advertisement, *The Hollywood Reporter* FILMART daily edition (March 21, 2011)

**Figure 5.1d**  *Taiwan Cinema* (Government Information Office, 2006)

system; the building's stature proclaims that Taiwan "is open for business."[28] The brochure *Taiwan's Innovativeness in Film* also includes an image of Taiwan's bullet train, one of the few in the world, and which, on the face of it, has nothing directly to do with Taiwanese cinema. A 2011 advertisement placed in the *Hollywood Reporter*'s FILMART daily edition pairs Taipei 101 with the Eiffel Tower, both superimposed over a film-strip "infinity" symbol, paying tribute to two cities' and cinemas' eternal love affair (and perhaps *When Harry Met Sally* by way of *Sleepless in Seattle*) set in Hong Kong. Here, Taipei, Paris, and Hong Kong intertwine at infinity, three global cities on the same cosmopolitan wavelength. That these buildings relate to the Taiwanese film industry can only be ascertained by the Taipei Film Commission logo and URL at the bottom of the advertisement, but the iconography alone is enough to brand Taipei and Taiwanese cinema as equivalent to (or at least coexistent with) a Paris or a Hong Kong. With the brochure *Taiwan Cinema*, published by the GIO in 2006, we see a more direct metaphor between cinema and Taiwan's architectural behemoth. On the cover, stills from recent Taiwanese films are placed on top of one another, and they cast a shadow reminiscent of Taipei 101, suggesting that Taiwanese films are literally the building blocks of the kind of world-class technological prowess exemplified by the Taipei 101 tower.

Taipei 101 also appears as the first image in "US$1,000,000 Subsidy for Filmmakers in Taipei City!," a 2009 promotional video produced by the Taipei Film Commission, the kind of video that may be playing on loop in Taiwan's exhibition booth at a film market. It was also made available in a CD-ROM entitled *Taipei Cinema Location Guide* distributed at film markets, and is also available for viewing on the Taipei Film Commission's official YouTube channel.[29] In this one-minute video, produced to encourage potential international co-producers to take advantage of a million-dollar subsidy, Taipei is depicted as a bustling metropolis (Figure 5.2). Aside from flaunting the tallest building in the world, the video shows off Taipei as a city of speed. The clip begins with the nervous ticking of a clock, and the clip unfolds in mostly fast-motion. There is a car chase, a heist, and a quick getaway. Furthermore, in this quick succession of images we see storyboards and digital effects, showing off Taiwan's fluency in the language of international film and filmmaking. The clip, with its crisp colors and Tony Scott-type editing, is itself a testament to a film industry up to speed with world filmmaking standards. But this is not an intimidating kind of high-speed modernity. Rather, the video depicts Taipei as cosmopolitan but also familiar and inviting—familiar in that it fits within familiar tropes of the urban heist film, and inviting to the extent that it literally proclaims that Taiwan's financial institutions are available for looting. By the end of the video, the financial institution, in this case the bank, is revealed to be a metaphor for the government. Why bother robbing a bank, it asks, when one can simply take one million US dollars from the state? Police cars are heard in the distance—the siren there merely as a stylistic marker of urban, crime-thriller pizzazz—but never seen, thus never posing a threat. The high-tech, cosmopolitan veneer is here meant to seduce the viewer into recognizing Taipei's coevality with the rest of the world, as well as to seduce potential co-producers into wanting to carve out a piece of the city for itself. The use of the heist genre thus serves two purposes. One is to suggest that if you're on the lookout for a generic global city in which to set your urban thriller, then Taipei is the city for you.[30] And, second, is to suggest that in doing so, you can be the hero in your own heist movie. Come to Taipei and you'll be getting away with something.

**Figure 5.2** Stills from "US$1,000,000 Subsidy for Filmmakers in Taipei City!": **5.2a** First shot, Taipei 101 tower; **5.2b** The ticking of a clock, an emblem of speed and of capitalist modernity

**Figure 5.2c**  A bank heist, rendered through storyboards; **5.2d** The takeaway message: why bother robbing a bank?

Throughout these and other promotional materials, we see examples of Taiwanese policy makers, bureaucrats, and agencies making a case for Taiwan by showcasing the world standards of its above-the-line labor. Looking inside the brochures, we constantly find references to Taiwanese cinema's wins in international film festivals like Cannes, Venice, and Berlin, with repeated name-dropping of festival auteurs Hou Hsiao-hsien, Edward Yang, and Tsai Ming-liang. A flyer from the Taipei Film Commission adds that non-Taiwan-based international masters are all familiar with Taipei, including Wong Kar-wai, Tim Yip, Christopher Doyle, and of course Ang Lee. The implication is that Taiwanese cinema—including its creative workers—are up to par with international standards, and that international-grade filmmakers feel comfortable with the creative workers and locations in Taiwan.

The materials provided at film markets also emphasize Taiwan's multiculturalism. Interestingly, many of these materials remind readers of Taiwan's colonial legacies. Yong-ping Lee, Deputy Commissioner of the Taipei Department of Cultural Affairs, states this directly in the *Taipei Cinema Location Guide*:

> Taipei has naturally become a city of many-layered cultural memories, accumulated over a turbulent past that saw the Qing Dynasty, the Japanese colonial rulers, the Cold War and Martial Law eras all leaving their mark on the island's colorful history.[31]

Having been ruled by the Qing dynasty in China, the Japanese, and less directly the Americans, Taiwan is a mish-mash of cultures, as these brochures like to frequently proclaim. The implication, of course, is that you too can come and do what you want with our locations and laborers. This openness to cultural intervention is summarized by the emphasis on the cultural flexibility of Taiwan's film workers. A quote from a Taipei Film Commission brochure reads,

> Unlike in many countries, you will find Taiwanese work forces very open to different cultures and much more communicative and easy-going. In Taipei you will meet local crews that are very professional, flexible and diligent. You can count on their versatility and benefit from the low cost of services.[32]

In other words, the city government evokes cosmopolitan flexibility and friendship to ensure foreign co-producers of the compliance of the Taipei workforce. If 1960s and 1970s Taiwan famously set up export processing zones with special economic exceptions (such as unenforced labor laws and relaxed import taxes) for foreign investors to take advantage of cheap, flexible, and educatable Taiwanese laborers, the Taipei Film Commission sees the entire city as a special zone of potential international cooperation under a backdrop comprised of cosmopolitan skyscrapers and multicultural post-colonial urban spaces.[33] To ensure full cooperation of the entire city, the Taipei Film Commission even rented billboard space in Taipei's subway stations instructing local residents how to be courteous and accommodating to foreign film crews shooting in Taipei. (The image accompanying the message was of the crew from *Miss Kicki*, a 2009 Swedish co-production.) As some have argued, the state's cosmopolitan brand, with its promotion of tolerance and friendship toward strangers, is above all intended to "support a set of employment possibilities."[34]

Lastly, Taiwan's state-produced promotional materials highlight Taipei within the pantheon of cosmopolitan Chinese global cities. This is stated outright by Deputy Commissioner Yong-ping Lee when she writes in a Taipei Film Commission publication, "Of all the major cities of the global Chinese community, Taipei is easily the most cosmopolitan and multicultural, harboring an unrivaled range of distinct styles and boundless creative energies."[35] Another Taipei Film Commission brochure compares Taipei to Beijing and Shanghai, arguing that Taipei is just like those cosmopolitan cities, but then adds, only the standard of living is lower in Taipei.[36] What we witness here is a concerted effort to show how Taiwan is similar to but different from mainland China. Similar in that everything you want from China you can get from Taiwan; different in that it will be cheaper and more culturally accommodating. Here, competition between "two Chinas" registers not in a battle for cultural authenticity, but in branding strategies of cosmopolitanism within the larger global film industry.

## Hong Kong: A Cinema that Speaks your Language

The Hong Kong government's efforts for film promotion are similar to Taiwan's in that its cosmopolitanism is triggered by the growing stature of mainland China. Laikwan Pang writes that Hong Kong cinema's early success was due to the relative "irrelevance" of mainland Chinese cinema, and inversely that the felt downturn after 1997 is correlated with the rise of Hong Kong's northern neighbors. "Indeed," she argues, "the film industry's difficulties since the 1990s can be characterized by Hong Kong cinema's painstaking attempts to come to terms with China."[37] Coming to terms with China is not an abstract process or simply a mental re-orientation. Elsewhere, Pang writes of Hong Kong's recent need to "dance" around China and the rest of the world.[38] What are Hong Kong's dance steps on the grounds of international commerce? How does Hong Kong "take the lead" in this dance?

Represented by the Hong Kong Trade Development Council, Hong Kong has been a regular fixture at the American Film Market since 1999, two years after the handover to mainland China. Whereas the Taiwan booths emphasize filming locations, post-production services, and film sales, Hong Kong's film market efforts promote potential co-productions, as well as Hong Kong FILMART, Hong Kong's own film market for international partners interested in doing business in Asia. Just as Taiwan had been producing fewer and fewer films, the Hong Kong Trade Development Council recognizes the city's decline in annual output. Therefore, at the American Film Market, Hong Kong emphasizes not the films it makes, but the financial, creative, and managerial services it can provide for foreign producers. And as with Taiwan, an underlying theme in Hong Kong's materials is its cosmopolitanism. Specifically, Hong Kong can provide foreign producers with access to mainland China via policies like CEPA, but also through Hong Kong's multiculturalism, its versatility, and its relative cultural openness compared to China.

Here I want to focus not on brochures provided by the HKTDC, but on the seminar it programmed annually at the American Film Market from 2007 to 2013. The theme of all seven seminars is Hong Kong as the world's gateway into China, and it is open to all AFM attendees for a fee. The seminar instructs foreign producers to co-produce with Hong Kong in order to exploit CEPA and sidestep China's stringent import quotas.[39] The idea being sold is that since CEPA allows Hong Kong films to count as a domestic Chinese film through official co-production, then a foreign co-production with Hong Kong (as well as China) would also count as a domestic film in China. The AFM seminar is thus designed to promote this co-production strategy, and perhaps more importantly, to stress, via expert testimony, the importance of Hong Kong cinema in the facilitation of foreign entry into China, as well as the central role of Hong Kong cinema in developing the mainland Chinese exhibition sector. Despite the attractive sell of this triangular co-production ploy, and the fact that the HKTDC seminar draws huge crowds at AFM each year, the strategy has not taken off among producers around the world. Nevertheless, the HKTDC continues to engage in this ritual practice of self-theorization because regardless of its immediate outcomes, the seminar gives Hong Kong a clear and authoritative position in the global film industry as China's cosmopolitan cousin. Through the "casting" of the seminar, the HKTDC is able to establish authority for itself and varnish the cosmopolitan credentials of Hong Kong's cinematic services.

The HKTDC's seminar typically consists of a moderator (a white trade journalist) and three panelists: a Hong Kong representative, a mainland representative, and a foreign representative. (The 2009 seminar only had two panelists, but their testimonies still represented the Hong Kong, mainland, and foreign perspectives.) The panelists the HKTDC invites to speak on behalf of Hong Kong are all bilingual and have global visibility. The first year's seminar included famed Hong Kong producer Nansun Shi and the second, third, and seventh years included Hong Kong distributor Jeffrey Chan. These experts speak of the city's financial and human resources, its historical experience working with China and foreign producers, and its relative openness compared to China. The

**Table 5.2** Panelists for the Hong Kong Trade Development Council's "Hong Kong as Gateway to China" seminars held at the American Film Market

| Year | Hong Kong representative | China representative | Foreign testimonial |
|---|---|---|---|
| 2007 | Nansun Shi | Yu Dong | Peggy Chiao (Taiwan) |
| 2008 | Jeffrey Chan | Zhou Tiedong | Douglas Glen (US) |
| 2009 | Chiong Kit Phoon, Jeffrey Chan | Jeffrey Chan | Chiong Kit Phoon (US/Hong Kong) |
| 2010 | Chen On Chu, Charlie Wong | Zhou Tiedong | Meng King (US) |
| 2011 | Yvonne Chuang | Zhou Tiedong | Wei Han (US) |
| 2012 | Yvonne Chuang | Zhou Tiedong | Janet Yang (US), Tracey Trench (US) |
| 2013 | Jeffrey Chan | Zhou Tiedong | Maria Lo Orzel (US) |

seminars also include a representative from China to attest to Hong Kong's role in building the mainland film market. The first year invited Yu Dong, then of Beijing Polybona Film Distribution, and the 2008 and 2010–13 editions brought Zhou Tiedong, then-president of China Film Promotion International. The mainland representatives, in English more accented than their Hong Kong counterparts, discuss the exploding exhibition sector in China, inviting foreign producers to take advantage of CEPA to capture the Chinese film market. They also discuss the continued importance of Hong Kong co-productions in the development of mainland cinema, and they encourage potential co-producers to join into three-way partnerships to take advantage of the resources of both Hong Kong and China.

Finally, these seminars typically include a third panelist: a producer from outside Hong Kong or China who can testify to their positive experiences working in Hong Kong and China. The first year included Taiwan-based producer/policy maker Peggy Chiao, who worked on *The Drummer* (Kenneth Bi, 2007) and other co-productions.[40] The second year featured Douglas Glen, CEO of Imagi International, which produced the successful animated film *TMNT* (Kevin Munroe, 2007) with creative personnel from Hong Kong. The 2010 seminar included Meng King, an L.A.-based managing partner of Asia Film Group, which helps American producers finance films in Asia. The "casting" of the seminar—with the mainland representative with seemingly poor English, the foreign (usually American) representative with native English, and the Hong Kong representative with strong but accented English—captures the HKTDC's strategy of branding Hong Kong as China's cosmopolitan cousin. Hong Kong can navigate between both east and west. It is both cultural and linguistic translator between the two. This emphasis on Hong Kong's English ability is part of the government's larger post-1997 project to position Hong Kong as an international city that can broker cross-border commerce.[41] Linguistic flexibility has long been a calling card of Hong Kong cinema, with its production of Teochew, Amoy, Cantonese, and Mandarin films to cater to overseas audiences in the 1950s and 1960s, and its increasing Mandarin orientation post-CEPA to cater to the mainland market. "We speak your language" in the global marketplace means a fluency in English, and Hong Kong, given its colonial history and the continued stereotypes against mainland China around the world, is especially poised to take advantage of this perceived ability.[42]

All three of the parties on the seminar panel differentiate Hong Kong from China, and from other cities in the world, by focusing on the following advantages of Hong Kong: 1) a long tradition of world-class film production, 2) integration into global networks of finance and distribution, 3) linguistic advantage in that its workers speak both English and Chinese, 4) a knowledge of both international and mainland laws and policies, 5) a knowledge of both international and mainland film institutions and practices, 6) financial transparency, especially compared to the mainland, 7) openness to foreign business, as opposed to China's perceived xenophobia and suspicion, 8) efficiency and docility of labor, stemming from Hong Kong's past as a manufacturing economy, 9) a star system more robust than those in other Chinese industries, and 10) Hong Kong's multicultural sensibilities having long been a consumer of international goods, especially those from the West and from Japan. Most of these advantages are discussed as remnants of Hong Kong's legacy as a British colony, as a source of cheap labor, and as a free-trade port. This drawing from Hong Kong's previous colonial history distinguishes Hong Kong from its colonial present, arguing that Hong Kong still operates with the advantages of British colonialism even though it now belongs to China. However, that it now belongs to China is an added incentive, because Hong Kong, via CEPA as well as perceived cultural Chinese affinities, has a special advantage in penetrating the much-desired Chinese market. As stated by trade journalist Patrick Frater, who moderated the HKTDC seminars in 2007 and 2008, Hong Kong is "kind of China, but not China," or in the words of panelist Jeffrey Chan, "Hong Kong is a part of China that's not China." Hong Kong's both-but-neither status between two colonizers

Cultural Work in the International Film Market   201

gives the film industry an added value that goes beyond the usual role of an economic middleman. Rather than simply playing the part of an intermediary, Hong Kong cinema, due to its extensive knowledge and experience working in China and the rest of the world—in other words, its status as both Chinese and cosmopolitan—is rather a "complete business partner for the customer, coordinating and putting together, 'packaging and integrating,' a range of activities often beyond the capabilities of the customer."[43] Through the selection of panelists, the "script" that each panelist performs, and the mere fact that the HKTDC hosts a well-publicized and well-attended AFM seminar (no other Asian institutions do so at AFM) and reception, Hong Kong and Hong Kong cinema appear in control of all transnational traffic in the Asian region and demonstrate their ability to reach out and speak the language of the international marketplace.

As should be apparent, there is an air of superiority flaunted by the HKTDC, and an attempt to play to foreign stereotypes of mainland China as being inflexible, inscrutable, and insular—in other words, against the cosmopolitan principles of openness and hospitality. I have shown how this effect is produced on the level of language, with the mainland representative cast as linguistically less comprehensible (and thus harder to directly work with) than his Hong Kong counterpart, despite the fact that university students in mainland China have surpassed Hong Kong students in English proficiency, according to polls of international companies hiring in Asia. Thus, what is more immediately important in the contact zone of the trade fair is style and attitude. English proficiency in the seminar creates an impression of confidence and belonging—that they've been doing this for decades, as opposed to the mainland Chinese who are just joining the co-production game.

A more flamboyant display of style can be seen in the Hong Kong Film Development Council's day-long event "Hong Kong Film New Action," held at the 2009 edition of the major Asian trade fair FILMART, coordinated by the HKTDC. The event consisted of panels, special guests (such as Nansun Shi, Oliver Stone, John Woo, and Feng Xiaogang), and a lengthy introduction to Hong Kong's new generation of directors, which the Film Development Council dubbed the "New Action" of Hong Kong cinema.[44] The roll call of new directors, complete with video clips and in-person appearances, was a glitzy affair akin to a fashion show, and attendees of the event (mostly market-goers from outside of Hong Kong) were provided bilingual (Chinese and English) print materials, including an eighty-two-page hardbound book called *Hong Kong Film: New Action*, which features a pull-out photo spread of the thirty-one "New Action" directors (Figure 5.3). (The horizontal image was also published in other Film Development Council materials at the forum.) The photo-spread, with studio lighting and model poses, depicts Hong Kong cinema as youthful,

**Figure 5.3**  The Hong Kong Film Development Council's "New Action" director's photo-spread (*Hong Kong: New Action* book, 2009)

hip, and full of color. The directors are dressed in a mix of American hipster urban (throwback sneakers, chic jeans, and khakis) and Japanese flair (fashionable hairstyles and graphic tees), striking the kind of "cool" that Koichi Iwabuchi has observed state governments adopting as a branding strategy in soft politics.[45] By donning the fashions of the world, the director (not a profession known for being fashionable) stylistically proves his or her cosmopolitan credibility, and Hong Kong cinema more generally accumulates cosmopolitan capital. The brochures aren't so crass as to contrast the hip new Hong Kong directors against their counterparts on the mainland, but the brand is stamped clearly as Hong Kong-specific, and a sensibility one could borrow through co-production with Hong Kong. In addition to the fashion spread, the eighty-two-page book spotlights many of the directors' international pedigrees, namely their international film festival wins and their overseas diplomas in filmmaking: Kenneth Bi from Brock University in Canada, Vincent Chui and Dennis Law from Loyola Marymount University in the United States, Sam Leong from the Academy of Moving Images in Japan, Barbara Wong from New York University in the United States, Yu Likwai from the Institut National Supérior des Arts de Spectacle et des Techniques de Diffusion in Belgium, and so forth. Through text and image, the "new" Hong Kong cinema is imagined as up-and-coming and ready for the world.

Thus far, I have focused on state interventions in the re-branding of Taiwan and Hong Kong cinemas as cosmopolitan. While private organizations are free to define Taiwan and Hong Kong cinemas however they wish, many find it advantageous to brand themselves in manners consistent with those of the state. For instance, Hong Kong-based production services house Salon Films, which has been co-producing with foreign producers at least since *The World of Suzie Wong* in 1957, has rebranded its services as China's cosmopolitan cousin—the technologically superior enabler of co-production in China. For several years, Salon Films' promotional gimmick at Hong Kong FILMART has been to contrast Salon

Cultural Work in the International Film Market    203

Hong Kong's technological might with China's exotic traditional locations. In an advertisement placed in the trades at Hong Kong FILMART in 2009, Salon Films claims: "We make it happen" (Figure 5.4a). "We" being the camera, the active, tech-savvy agent. "It" being Chinese stories, locations, sets, symbolized by this ancient palace placed below the camera. The advertisement draws attention to

**Figure 5.4a**  Salon Films advertisement, *Hollywood Reporter* FILMART daily edition (March 24, 2009)

**Figure 5.4b**  Salon Films exhibition space, Hong Kong FILMART (2009)

Salon's "strategic alliance with the Hengdian Group" and its formidable film studio, just as the HKTDC pitched Hong Kong's alliance with China via CEPA. The masculinist pose of the Hong Kong company's camera in the image and text corresponds to a recent shift in manufacturing in Hong Kong: a shift from an emphasis on "Made in Hong Kong" to "Made by Hong Kong," as some social scientists have called it.[46] If Hong Kong was once known as a major manufacturing center, it has in recent decades repositioned as a service economy, actively coordinating and leading production, usually in the factories of southern China. If factory work is often feminized, we see how Salon Films visually erects itself in the male position, the camera eye both director and foreman of production. At the film market, Salon took this grandiose posture beyond the pages of *Variety* and *The Hollywood Reporter* and onto the trade fair grounds. In 2009 and 2010, Salon rented exhibition space at FILMART that recreates their advertisement in three-dimensional space, with a giant crane hoisting a camera above a portrait of the ancient Chinese palace, as well as above the heads of passerby (Figure 5.4b).

The inclusion of the letters "HK" at the bottom of the print advertisement to identify Salon as from Hong Kong is strategic. It allows Salon Films to borrow the cosmopolitan luster that the Hong Kong Trade Development Council has attempted to bring to Hong Kong cinema. In other words, "Hong Kong cinema" is a citation that various agents appropriate, re-branding it and strategically assuming and revising many of the connotations it has come to acquire. The same goes with Taiwanese cinema, which in recent years has seemed more like a dream than a reality. And it is precisely how that dream is shaped by forces such as the state via texts, images, and narratives in contact zones like film markets that enables national cinemas to capture the attention of the international film industry and legitimize their existence. As I have shown, those dreams often play to neocolonial desires via docile labor, cultural flexibility, and neoliberal advantages. These neocolonial desires come packaged in cosmopolitan shine: a seductive, worldly posture that is familiar and inviting, especially in contrast to the stereotypically inscrutable mainland Chinese film industry decked out in Maoist drab. For underdog nations like Taiwan and free ports like Hong Kong, cosmopolitanism is a kind of self-fashioning motivated by the urgency to survive in a cut-throat economy and a mediascape in which the idea of the "global Chinese" is being transformed in unpredictable ways. With China rising, but still looked at with suspicion on the world stage, cosmopolitanism as a "dynamic or orientation rather than a concrete identity or a stable culture" is creatively and strategically deployed as a last-ditch comparative advantage of post-colonies like Taiwan and Hong Kong.[47] This survival strategy is not immediately clear from an analysis of the films produced in these industries. After all, there are so few films being produced now that it is nearly impossible to generalize based on them. However, with a decrease in production, there is an increase in the amount of reflexive industry texts in the film market and elsewhere that actively attempt to define Taiwan and Hong Kong cinema, to gain these industries international recognition and legitimacy, to remind the rest of the world that "we're still here, we're just like you, and we can work together."

## Notes

1. Among others, see David Bordwell, *Planet Hong Kong: Popular Cinema and the Art of Entertainment* (Cambridge, MA: Harvard University Press, 2000); Stephen Teo, *Chinese Martial Arts Cinema: The Wuxia Tradition* (Edinburgh: Edinburgh University Press, 2009).
2. Ackbar Abbas, "The New Hong Kong Cinema and the *Déjà Disparu*," "Wong Kar-wai: Hong Kong Filmmaker," *Hong Kong: Culture and the Politics of Disappearance* (Minneapolis: University of Minnesota Press, 1997) 16–62.
3. The statistics cited here are from European Audiovisual Observatory, *Focus: World Film Market Trends* (2009). While we should heed Chris Berry's warnings against taking at face-value any production statistics that take Taiwan and Hong Kong as discrete and non-overlapping industries, the numbers, however hazy, do indicate a staggering decline. Chris Berry, "What is Transnational Cinema? Thinking from the Chinese Situation," *Transnational Cinemas* 1.2 (November 2010): 115–19.

4. Guo-juin Hong, "Colonial Archives, Postcolonial Archaeology: Pre-1945 Taiwan and the Hybrid Texts of Cinema before Nation," *Taiwan Cinema: A Contested Nation on Screen* (New York: Palgrave Macmillan, 2011) 13–31; quote on page 15.
5. Laikwan Pang, "Postcolonial Hong Kong Cinema: Utilitarianism and (Trans)local," *Postcolonial Studies* 10.4 (2007): 413.
6. William A. Callahan, *Contingent States: Greater China and Transnational Relations* (Minneapolis: University of Minnesota Press, 2004) 199–200.
7. Stephen Chiu and Tai-Lok Lui, *Hong Kong: Becoming a Chinese Global City* (London: Routledge, 2009).
8. Shu-mei Shih, *Visuality and Identity: Sinophone Articulations across the Pacific* (Berkeley: University of California Press, 2007) 185.
9. Chiu and Lui 144–5.
10. Mette Hjort, *Small Nation, Global Cinema: The New Danish Cinema* (Minneapolis: University of Minnesota Press, 2005).
11. Ben Goldsmith and Tom O'Regan, *The Film Studio: Film Production in the Global Economy* (Lanham: Rowman and Littlefield, 2005); quote on page 2.
12. Michael Curtin, *Playing to the World's Biggest Audience: The Globalization of Chinese Film and TV* (Berkeley: University of California Press, 2007) 22.
13. Michael Keane, "Once Were Peripheral: Creating Media Capacity in East Asia," *Media, Culture & Society* 28.6 (November 2006): 839.
14. Curtin.
15. Darrell William Davis and Emilie Yueh-yu Yeh, *East Asian Screen Industries* (London: BFI Publishing, 2008).
16. Sheldon Hsiao-peng Lu, ed., *Transnational Chinese Cinemas: Identity, Nationhood, Gender* (Honolulu: University of Hawaii Press, 1997).
17. Berry 122–3.
18. Ibid. 123–4.
19. Laikwan Pang, "From BitTorrent Piracy to Creative Industries: Hong Kong Cinema Emptied Out," *Futures of Chinese Cinema: Technologies and Temporalities in Chinese Screen Cultures*, eds. Olivia Khoo and Sean Metzger (Bristol: Intellect, 2009) 140
20. Pang, "Postcolonial Hong Kong Cinema."
21. Stephanie Hemelryk Donald, et al., "Introduction: Processes of Cosmopolitanism and Parochialism," *Branding Cities: Cosmopolitanism, Parochialism, and Social Change*, eds Stephanie Hemelryk Donald, et al. (London: Routledge, 2009) 7.
22. See, for instance, Chu Yiu-wai, "One Country Two Cultures? Post-1997 Hong Kong Cinema and Co-productions," *Hong Kong Culture: Word and Image*, ed. Kam Louie (Hong Kong: Hong Kong University Press, 2010) 131–45.
23. Anna Lowenhaupt Tsing, *Friction: An Ethnography of Global Connection* (Princeton: Princeton University Press, 2005) 4–6.
24. Ibid. 13.
25. John Thornton Caldwell, *Production Culture: Industrial Reflexivity and Critical Practice in Film and Television* (Durham, NC: Duke University Press, 2008).
26. Taiwan did not attend AFM in 2009 and 2010. However, under the name of the Taipei Film Commission, Taiwanese cinema advocates did rent exhibition space at

the European Film Market in Berlin in 2011. The GIO dissolved in 2012, after which Taiwan was represented by the Ministry of Culture and the Taipei Film Commission in international film markets.

27. Larry R. Ford, "Skyscraper Competition in Asia: New City Images and New City Form," *Imaging the City: Continuing Struggles and New Directions*, eds. Lawrence J. Vale and Sam Bass Warner, Jr. (New Brunswick, NJ: Center for Urban Policy Research, 2001) 119–44.
28. Ford writes that Singapore's skyline announces that the nation "is open for business." Ford 128.
29. "Robbery," *Taipei Cinema Location Guide*, Taipei: Taipei Film Commission, 2009, CD-ROM. "US$1,000,000 Subsidy for Filmmakers in Taipei City!" February 3, 2009, taipeifilmcommission channel, YouTube.com, <http://www.youtube.com/watch?v=Oar1Jv8Db-4> (accessed February 22, 2011).
30. The depiction of Taipei in the TFC's audio-visual pitch is thus consistent with a trend in many recent Taipei city films of depicting the city in terms of its genericity and its ever-presence, as opposed to earlier city films that represented Taipei in its disappearing specificity. See Yomi Braester, "The Impossible Task of Taipei Films," *Cinema Taiwan: Politics, Popularity and State of the Arts*, eds. Darrell William Davis and Ru-shou Robert Chen (London: Routledge, 2007) 51–9.
31. *Taipei Cinema Location Guide* (Taipei: Taipei Film Commission, 2008) 5.
32. *Taipei Film Commission*, brochure, distributed at the 2009 Asian Film Market in Busan, South Korea.
33. On export processing zones, see George Fitting, "Export Processing Zones in Taiwan and the People's Republic of China," *Asian Survey* 22.8 (August 1982): 732–44.
34. Donald, et al. 6.
35. *Taipei Cinema Location Guide* 5.
36. *Taipei Film Commission*, brochure.
37. Laikwan Pang, "Hong Kong Cinema as a Dialect Cinema?" *Cinema Journal* 49.3 (Spring 2010): 140.
38. Pang, "Postcolonial Hong Kong Cinema" 414.
39. At the time of these AFM seminars, China only imported twenty films per year for theatrical release, a statistic repeated ominously throughout the HKTDC events, as well as the fact that Hong Kong-China co-productions are not considered foreign films.
40. On Peggy Chiao's contributions to the internationalization of Taiwanese film production and spectatorship, and her efforts to bring Taiwanese film to the world market and critical/scholarly community, see Chia-chi Wu, "Festivals, Criticism and the International Reputation of Taiwan New Cinema," *Cinema Taiwan: Politics, Popularity and State of the Arts*, eds. Darrell William Davis and Ru-shou Robert Chen (London: Routledge, 2007) 77–8.
41. Kingsley Bolton, *Chinese Englishes: A Sociolinguistic History* (Cambridge: Cambridge University Press, 2003) 200. Knowledge of international languages is so crucial to the politics of positioning in the global film market that even representatives of Taiwan, where foreign languages are not studied as extensively as in a recent British

colony like Hong Kong, must showcase its language ability. Jennifer Jao, director of the Taipei Film Commission, claims that in filling the ranks of the newly established film commission, the first requirement for hiring was foreign language skills; she quickly found workers who could assist Japanese, German, English, and French-speaking crews, and then contracted speakers of other languages on a case-by-case basis. Jennifer Jao, personal interview, October 6, 2008.

42. Even for the regional market, Hong Kong has utilized English in its attempts to be the film capital of Asia. The Asian Film Awards, supported by the Hong Kong Trade Development Council, takes place in Hong Kong every year in conjunction with FILMART and the Hong Kong International Film Festival. While not necessarily the lingua franca of Asia, English is used during the Asian Film Awards ceremony, and Hong Kong can draw from its pool of "ABC" celebrities to host the show, such as Terence Yin, Lisa S, and Angela Chow. On the place of overseas Chinese in the Hong Kong film industry, see Chapter 2.
43. Michael J. Enright, Edith E. Scott, and David Dodwell, *The Hong Kong Advantage* (Oxford: Oxford University Press, 1997) 55.
44. For a brief discussion of the Hong Kong Film New Action Forum, see David Bordwell, "Jackhammers, Parties, and Markets," *Observations of Film Art* (March 28, 2009) <http://www.davidbordwell.net/blog/?p=4017> (accessed February 25, 2011).
45. Koichi Iwabuchi, "Contra-flows or the Cultural Logic of Uneven Globalization? Japanese Media in the Global Agora," *Media on the Move: Global Flows and Contra-flow*, ed. Daya Kishan Thussu (London: Routledge, 2007) 79–80.
46. Suzanne Berger and Richard K. Lester, eds, *Made by Hong Kong* (Oxford: Oxford University Press, 1997).
47. As Gerard Delanty writes, "The cosmopolitan imagination entails a view of society as an ongoing process of self-constitution through the continuous opening up of new perspectives in light of the encounter with the Other." Delanty, *The Cosmopolitan Imagination: The Renewal of Critical Social Theory* (Cambridge: Cambridge University Press, 2009) 13.

# Conclusion

In 2001, Ang Lee went onstage at the Shrine Auditorium in Los Angeles to collect the Best Foreign Language Film Oscar for *Crouching Tiger Hidden Dragon*, Taiwan's submission to the annual competition. It was a landmark accomplishment for the transnational Chinese film industry, which, as I noted in Chapter 3, had been dreaming of Oscar success for decades. In 2006, Lee returned to the Oscar limelight, winning Best Director for *Brokeback Mountain*. In his 2006 acceptance speech, Lee thanked "everybody in Taiwan, Hong Kong, China" and closed with gracious words of thanks in Mandarin. Lee had already collected top prizes at the prestigious Venice and Berlin film festivals, but the Best Director Oscar had special resonance for Taiwan, which had never before seen one of its native sons heralded on the world stage on a scale as large as this. More than 38 million watched the broadcast in the United States alone, and surely many Taiwanese households had their TVs tuned to the Oscars to see Lee receive an award that had previously been given to some of the luminaries of world cinema. Unlike his 2001 win, which was awarded in a special category reserved for the foreign, Lee's 2006 Oscar was for, in theory anyway, the best directing accomplishment in the world by anybody, regardless of nation or language. Furthermore, it was for *Brokeback Mountain*, a film that, on account of its western settings and gay themes, felt as far away as possible from the conservative Taiwan that Lee grew up in, and a testament to Lee's ability to don the costumes of any nation and empathize with the sensibilities of any race or experience. Lee had, with the whole world watching and Hollywood applauding, been accepted as a great director of the world, regardless of background. And in that moment and on that stage, he dared utter the name "Taiwan," so rarely heard in official diplomatic channels internationally, and dared speak in Mandarin. Lee did it again in 2013, when he won a second Best Director Oscar for *Life of Pi*, a multi-lingual fantasy set between continents and cultures. "I can't make this movie without the help of Taiwan," he said onstage, positioning Taiwan as an engine of a cosmopolitan cinema. At these moments of triumph, he reminded the world and his countrymen of his ethnic and national background. He became, in the eyes of many Taiwanese, not just Taiwanese and not just cosmopolitan, but both.

In recent years, Lee has been dubbed "the light of Taiwan" (*Taiwan zhi guang*) in the Taiwanese press, in publicity materials, and in everyday conversation.

The "light" of the title refers to the beacon of glory that Lee represents for the nation, and the title has also been used to describe others who have shone on the international stage, such as former New York Yankees pitcher Chien-ming Wang and Sundance darling-turned-Hollywood director Justin Lin. For the Taiwanese audience, however, Lee's accomplishment is on a different plane, largely because of the Oscar stage itself: the televised spectacle beamed a Taiwanese face to an imagined community of film lovers around the world. In terms of sheer scale and emotional valence, Lee's Oscar win is perhaps only matched by the 2004 Olympic gold medals in taekwondo won by Chen Shih-hsin and Chu Mu-yen, two other "lights of Taiwan." Chen and Chu's gold medals, the first two for Taiwan, as well as Lee Lai-shan's 1996 gold for Hong Kong, were bittersweet moments of pride that proclaimed Taiwan's and Hong Kong's competitiveness and coevality on the world stage, at the same time that they revealed the "minor" status of Taiwan and Hong Kong internationally. To appease mainland China, Taiwan cannot compete internationally in its own name, and must be dubbed "Chinese Taipei." And in the case of all three golds, there was the crushing realization of inferiority when the "national anthem" was played during the medal ceremonies. The Republic of China (the name of the government ruling Taiwan) has a national anthem, but "Chinese Taipei" does not, and so Taiwanese TV viewers watched and wept as their "lights of Taiwan" received gold to the denationalized "Flag Anthem." When Lee Lai-shan won gold in 1996, the British national anthem was played, a reminder of Hong Kong's colonial status, then in its final year, as well as a bittersweet reminder that even colonial subordination was soon to be subsumed by the People's Republic of China the following summer. Thus, that Ang Lee could proclaim "Taiwan" in his acceptance speech at the Oscars, an industry party and therefore not as susceptible to diplomatic bullying, was a coup for Taiwan and for forging new possibilities of being cosmopolitan, even if they are also hybridized, awkward, and negotiated.

Significantly, all of these "lights" came to stand for the nation/city while excelling outside of it. Ang Lee has, to date, only set one film (*Eat Drink Man Woman*, 1994) in Taiwan. Chien-ming Wang decided to skip Taiwan's Chinese Professional Baseball League and enter North America's Major League Baseball league. Justin Lin was born in Taipei, but moved to California at a very young age and has never made a film about Taiwan. The three gold medalists excelled in sports not very prominent in Taiwan or Hong Kong: taekwondo and windsurfing. These local heroes thus represent the ways in which local identities (nation, city) can be formulated and defined externally, so long as they are imagined as hybridized cosmopolitans who can hail local affiliations while being citizens of the world.

This paradox, of course, is not lost on all, and in fact has been the subject of considerable debate. At about the time of the release of *Lust, Caution* in Taiwan, online message boards were aflutter with Ang Lee conversation: on whether he is more or less a "light of Taiwan" than Chien-ming Wang, on whether he is an artist or a hack, on whether he had sold out by producing artsy "pornography," and so forth. The occasion of the film, which had won the Venice Film Festival and was the follow-up to Lee's Oscar-winning *Brokeback Mountain*, also inspired netizens in Taiwan to wonder if winning international awards for international films was more or less worthy than making films about Taiwan that do well domestically. A fan posting on a Yahoo! message forum entitled "To all the Ang Lee critics" read:

> How many times has Ang Lee mentioned "Taiwan" in the international media? And has Ang Lee ever held an American passport? [He hasn't.] Ang Lee's films have transcended East and West, telling stories that resonate widely. His abilities were nourished in this land of Taiwan; this is something we should all be proud of. Perhaps he's currently just looking for topics that interest him, and Taiwanese topics aren't what he wants to film. Just because he films topics that he has confidence in, doesn't mean we should criticize him.[1]

Another post voiced similar passions:

> Have you ever wondered why Ang Lee always says "I'm a Taiwanese person" whenever he travels abroad? It's because he loves Taiwan, and uses his personal abilities to make it known internationally. Perhaps he didn't film [*Lust, Caution*] to express his love for Taiwan, and that it's simply just another one of his marvelous films. But he's used this film to say to the world, "Taiwan has great talents that can shine on the world stage."[2]

These two posts confirm that fans are receptive to the possibility that Ang Lee can be a national hero despite not living or working in Taiwan, because his personal accomplishments on the international stage are also national accomplishments. However, in another discussion forum, entitled "Thanks to Ang Lee for all he's done for Taiwanese cinema," one user commented:

> All I can say is Ang Lee is the light of Taiwan, but I don't believe Taiwanese cinema has progressed because of Ang Lee. Just because it has an international-grade director doesn't mean all of the Taiwanese film industry has been elevated. Furthermore, Ang Lee didn't develop his skills in Taiwan, he was only born there . . . If Ang Lee films something with Taiwanese actors and talents, then he'll be helping to develop Taiwanese cinema. But whenever he gets the chance, the actors are from Hong Kong.[3]

This user takes more seriously the empirical, as opposed to merely symbolic, impact of Ang Lee's global stature, and concludes that he has in fact done very little for Taiwan. This is the subject of another heated debate on a forum comparing the directorial accomplishments of Ang Lee to local musician-turned-director Jay Chou, whose debut feature *Secret* (2007) was a huge hit in Taiwan. Chou fans scoffed at Lee's international wins and argued that box-office clout and local representation are true measurements of success, while Lee's backers insisted on the credibility of international standards, represented by festival awards and overseas education. (Lee received an MFA from New York University, a well-known fact in Taiwan.) In defense of Ang Lee's cosmopolitan artistry, one posting used a sports analogy: "Comparing Jay and Ang Lee is like comparing elementary school basketball to the NBA [National Basketball Association]."[4]

These postings reveal that, although Taiwanese cinema has been in decline, the idea of Taiwanese national cinema (*guopian*) is alive and the root of much passion and emotional investment. Just as state governments systematically sought to rebrand the idea of Taiwanese cinema, as explained in Chapter 5, fans chimed in as well, determining their own criteria for what counts as "Taiwanese" and even what counts as "cinema" for an industry producing fewer and fewer films. But beyond this, and beyond merely revealing that Taiwan's enthusiasm for Ang Lee is not as uniform as it may sometimes seem, these postings suggest that the idea of cosmopolitan celebrity, and cosmopolitanism more generally, in Taiwan continues to be ideologically fraught. The forums use Ang Lee to debate the social importance of overseas education, hard work, artistry, community, representation, patriotism, and individuality as they intersect with the idea of becoming a global citizen.

In this book, I argued that these concerns are not new in Taiwan and Hong Kong, and in fact, the question of how to become a cosmopolitan Chinese (or Taiwanese or Hong Kong) person has been one of the central concerns, and sources of entertainment, in mainstream Hong Kong and Taiwanese cinema of the past half-century. I have read cosmopolitanism "under the sign of its own anxieties," as Simon Gikandi has proposed,[5] considering questions such as: is cosmopolitanism possible? And, if so, do we want it? Under what terms can we accept it? Who does cosmopolitanism serve? The answers to these questions depend on the historical and social context during which the discourse of the cosmopolitan is evoked. But what I have found is that across the decades, anxieties over cosmopolitanism have been negotiated and sometimes resolved through the affective pleasures of cinema: its spectacles of fashion, music, and stars, as well as the saturated emotions that imbue these spectacles in on-screen and off-screen narratives. For societies imagining how they may be integrated into a larger global community, cinema provides audiovisual proof: bodies undergoing training so that they can be competitive on the world stage (as with the musical actresses and the Shaolin heroes), voices that can fluently speak the languages of the world (as with the ABC star or the Hong Kong film market representative).

The spectacle of a hybrid cosmopolitan can be sublime and strange. The speed and confidence of the Hong Kong actress singing and dancing the world's music seemed in excess of the cramped corners and immobility of everyday Hong Kong. The inflated muscles of martial arts heroes and young overseas Chinese were a shocking wonder to behold, because they inverted stereotypes of masculine bodies and provocatively suggested new possibilities of the Chinese physique and Chinese competitiveness. Film and music took audiences to the edges of the world, in tales of overseas students frolicking along the San Francisco cliffs or in the European snow, snapshots of actresses posing with Hollywood celebrities, and hip-hop stars breakdancing across continents. Cinema put the qipao next to the flamenco dress, the Chinese body in step with the African American body, and Taipei 101 alongside the Eiffel Tower. Cinema imagined the cosmopolitan figure through uncanny resemblances and strange mutations, using spectacle to entice audiences into confronting the possibilities of their bodies, their loyalties, and their relationships to strangers.

Through these spectacles, the films work through the emotional jagged edges of leaving home and returning, enduring what Ulrich Beck and Elisabeth Beck-Gernsheim term "distant love," and being the object of the global gaze.[6] These films and their intertextual discourses tread the tricky line between celebrating worldly affiliations, identities, and accomplishments, and not abandoning residual patriotic or cultural nationalist loyalties. Being-looked-at, as a long tradition of film studies has shown, is a source of both anxiety and agency, and studios and publicists in Hong Kong and Taiwan have learned how to exploit the joy of being-looked-at to elicit sensations of pride in the film industry. When "ABC" stars Nicholas Tse and Stephen Fung made the cover of American trade magazine *Screen International*, Hong Kong newspaper *Apple Daily* celebrated it.[7] When *Life Magazine* put Shaw star Jenny Hu on their cover, the studio publicized the achievement of their actress (and thus the studio) for months. But being-looked-at could also mean subordination to the racialized and patriarchal logic of international commerce and tourism, as in the case of the female flight attendants described in the introduction, or the traveling actresses in Chapter 3. Cinema, through editing, music, fashion, and narrative, found a way to transform sacrifice into triumph, and object into subject. Such is the power of the ethos of endurance. When women train their bodies to be flexible culturally, or when men train their bodies to become mobile, pragmatic, and competitive, there is the thrill of accomplishment: that with pain comes the gain of access to new horizons of social, economic, and cultural experience. And a "mood of endurance" pervades much of the melodrama of arrival and departure. Becoming cosmopolitan isn't easy, as Hong Kong and Taiwanese audiences discovered. But withstanding pain and holding back tears make the prospect of becoming cosmopolitan that much more exhilarating and inspiring. Ang Lee's path to world-status, repeated in the Yahoo! message boards on the occasion of *Lust, Caution*, is one of the most-told stories of endurance in Taiwan: challenging gender roles, risking family reputation and marital trust, and sacrificing the comforts of home, Ang Lee spent the 1980s toiling away, unemployed, in New York City, paying his dues in school and at home, working on screenplay after screenplay as an émigré while his biologist wife paid the bills. Only after years of hard work did he catch a break, and a decade later, he brought an Oscar back to Taiwan. The legend of his rise is worth comparison to any melodrama of arrival and departure, or any tale of tenacious training. While it still conjures feelings of ambiguity, the Ang Lee legend has become a story that locals tell themselves to make sense of what it means to be a competitor on the world stage, just as Linda Lin Dai musicals had done fifty years before and the *"shangshan"* fable of the Shaolin Temple continues to do today.

This book proposes a model for thinking about the role of cinema for what Mette Hjort and Duncan Petrie call "small nations" on the periphery of global image-making.[8] Cinema is an active, multipronged, and popular means of participating in international soft politics, and of imagining new possibilities of worldly encounter and global identity. As a cultural commodity that is often tuned to humanist sensibilities, cinema is especially effective for non-nations like Palestine, Quebec, Tibet, Hong Kong, and Taiwan to participate in a politics of positionality unavailable through diplomatic channels. In film festivals, award ceremonies, art houses, multiplexes, and trade shows, cinema becomes a facilitator of cross-cultural contact and cosmopolitan self-fashioning.

But what about China, a "large nation" if there ever was one, but a nation in search of its own international identity? This book bracketed off mainland China, largely to highlight the traffic of film, labor, and finance across postwar Hong Kong and Taiwan, as well as the unique formations of cosmopolitanism that emerged as a result—cultural formations that are historically elided in the China-centrism in much of Chinese studies. It's worth mentioning, too, that mainland China has imagined the cosmopolitan in very different ways within the period of my study. From 1949 to the 1980s, the "world stage" for China has been a utopian Communist one, an "internationale" aligned with the Soviet Union, Eastern Europe, North Korea, and other socialist nations. As a result, the "cosmopolitan city" in China has taken its own path from international to global,[9] and transnational encounters in cinema mixed Soviet technologies with Chinese rural particularities.[10] But there are ways in which China's cosmopolitanism has dovetailed with Hong Kong's and Taiwan's. Just as Hong Kong and Taiwanese popular culture in the 1950s and 1960s drew from the cosmopolitanism of 1930s Shanghai, mainland China's debates on popular culture and international participation in the post-Mao years reignited many of the debates and aspirations of the early Republican decades. For instance, Julia Lovell has studied China's "Nobel Prize complex"—a paradox of wanting to define one's own literature but wanting affirmation from the international committee—which raged in both the early twentieth century and in the post-1979 era.[11] The past thirty years have seen mainland China undergo many of the dilemmas of cosmopolitanism that appeared in early modern China, as well as in 1950s to 1990s Hong Kong and Taiwan. One example is the growing phenomenon of parents sending children abroad for study, which leads to debates regarding the socialist welfare state and neoliberal understandings of individualism and self-reliance.[12]

Cinema, too, has been the terrain on which cosmopolitan identities are forged. The cases of internationally renowned directors Zhang Yimou and Chen Kaige have incited much discussion in China about representation, international style, and global identity. Piracy has enabled everyday filmgoers to sidestep the quota system and cheaply consume the cinemas of the world, while tourism has enabled the well-to-do to sidestep censorship and watch uncut versions in Hong Kong and elsewhere.[13] With Chinese remakes of Hollywood films like *What Women Want* and *Dangerous Liaisons*, the rise of international film festivals in Shanghai and Beijing, and the growing visibility of multi-racial mainland stars, the stage is set for mainlanders, in all of their heterogeneity, to imagine possibilities of being cosmopolitan in ways specific to China's political and economic institutions, racial discourses, and consumption habits.

But the biggest spectacle of China's cosmopolitan self-fashioning to date has been the staging of the 2008 Beijing Olympic Games, dubbed by foreign media as China's "coming-out party." However, cultural anthropologist Susan Brownell, who was hired by the Olympic organizers as a foreign expert, observes that only about 15 percent of the efforts of the Beijing organizers were aimed at international outreach. The remaining 85 percent were intended to pitch China's internationalism and China's participation in international ritual to domestic viewers. For instance, one initiative brought the Olympics into mainland elementary schools, with students staging mock opening ceremonies and performing the fashion and styles of the world, thus acquiring "knowledge they need to be Chinese in the world."[14] This exercise, reminiscent of the around-the-world musical numbers of 1950s and 1960s Hong Kong cinema, demonstrated to domestic participants the attainability of the world through training, performance, and entertainment.

The performance of the world Brownell describes is one of many examples I've encountered in which the historical experiences of Hong Kong and Taiwan seem to resonate with China in its contemporary cosmopolitanization. Most revealing about the hybridization of that cosmopolitanization is that Hong Kong and Taiwan seem to play similar roles for China that the overseas Chinese played for Hong Kong and Taiwan decades prior. Mainland China has turned to Hong Kong and Taiwan as models for how to become both cosmopolitan and Chinese. As Kwai-cheung Lo writes of Hong Kong in the mainland imaginary, "At a time when Communism no longer has a powerful ideological grip on mainland China and nationalism has risen to fill the moral vacuum, Hong Kong, as an international Chinese city, may have become an illuminating model for compatriots seeking to understand what it means to be 'Chinese' in a global age."[15] Aihwa Ong writes that overseas Chinese throughout Asia have become the "pacesetters in articulating the larger contours of an organic unity of Chinese people scattered throughout the world" and this has reconfigured the relationship between China and Hong Kong, Taiwan, and Sinophone communities in Southeast Asia.[16] For Ong, mainland China seeks coevality with the rest of the world, and Han Chinese in Hong Kong and Taiwan, imagined as part of a greater China, are the closest in temporality (the "pacesetters") to the cosmopolitan clock. The image of the clock reappears in Hai Ren's study of neoliberalism in China. Ren writes of China's attempt at "synchronization" with Hong Kong, symbolically rendered through the iconic "countdown clock" at Tiananmen Square, which looked forward to the moment when China and Hong Kong would lock together in temporality and economic destiny.[17]

Today, cinematic synchronization can be seen on the levels of content production, industrial practice, technological prowess, and labor. Cultural exchange, such as the transnational remake, becomes one way in which mainland Chinese studios can seek industrial and cultural coevality in a context of uneven regional development. The early 2000s wave of Asia-to-Hollywood remakes, as with properties like *Ringu* and *Infernal Affairs*, has shifted more recently to intra-Asian remakes, particularly of film properties from South Korea, which today represents a paragon of international blockbuster success in Asia. Kai Soh and Brian Yecies discuss mainland Chinese audience perception of Korean film properties vis-à-vis China and argue that film remakes like *20 Once Again* (2015) activate audience interest in domestic films via cross-cultural stardom and cross-border localization, and, in so doing, "enhanc[e] both the productivity and quality of China's creative and cultural industries" and "enabl[e] China to play a larger role in the global creative community."[18] Soh and Yecies discuss the importance of "performance standards" and "film direction" in the globalization of Chinese cinema through China–Korea exchange, but neglect to mention the role that Taiwan plays in China's cosmopolitan ambitions. The movie *20 Once Again*, mainland studio Beijing Century Media Culture's remake of the hit Korean comedy *Miss Granny* (Hwang Dong-hyuk, 2014), is directed by the Taiwanese Leste Chen, whose early films *The Heirloom* (2005) and *Eternal Summer* (2006) were internationally distributed. In *20 Once Again*, a grandmother finds herself in a twenty-year-old's body, and much of its comedic appeal comes from watching a young actress perform the culture and mannerisms of the older actress. The younger actress is played by mainlander Yang Zishan, who delightfully mimics her older counterpart, Taiwan cinema legend Kuei Ya-lei, star of Healthy Variety films like *Home Sweet Home*. In *20 Once Again*, Kuei Ya-lei's 1970s Taiwan stardom is also evoked by the younger actress's song-and-dance performances of Taiwanese pop star Teresa Teng. As we've seen from the 1960s Hong Kong musicals and the 1970s Taiwanese romances, performance of the overseas version of the self, whether the jet-set traveler, the struggling student, or the vanished specter, enhances the cosmopolitan credibility of domestic stars, studios, and industries. That credibility helped make *20 Once Again* a box-office success and, in turn, inspire *Beautiful Accident* (2017), a mainland remake of another Korean body-switch comedy *Wonderful Nightmare* (Kang Hyo-jin, 2015). Perhaps not surprisingly, a Taiwan-based filmmaker, Ho Wi-ding, was hired to direct, while Taiwanese superstar Kwai Lun-mei was cast in the lead role to channel the perceived world-class comedy filmmaking of South Korea. China's mimicry of Korean cosmopolitanism thus depends on Taiwanese bodies, performance, direction, and pop culture referents, with perceived Han Chinese cultural proximity mediating China's own embrace of the cosmopolitan.

Stardom, through discourses of fashion and global "cool," represents an ideal of being up to date with the rest of the world. Stars can embody the cutting-edge of style and temperament, their faces and bodies representing the cutting-edge of desirability. Stars can also be seen as ideal types that audiences strive to be, but are not yet, and therefore occupy a temporality just ahead of normal. As such they are often exotic, uncanny beings, like the mixed-race Maggie Q and the muscular L. A. Boyz in Hong Kong and Taiwan. In post-1978 China, stars from Taiwan and Hong Kong have continuously been the most popular singers and actors, and, in fact, China, having been sheltered from the bourgeois concept of stardom for decades, modeled its notion of celebrity based on that in Hong Kong and Taiwan.[19] Just as Chinese Americans and Canadians Daniel Wu, Edison Chen, Nicholas Tse, and Stephen Fung represented a new "cool" in Hong Kong films like *Young & Dangerous: The Prequel* and *Gen-X Cops*, Hong Kong and Taiwan actors like Tony Leung Chiu-wai and Shu Qi exude an uncommon worldly confidence, even swagger, when cast in mainland films like *Red Cliff* (John Woo, 2008) and *Journey to the West: Conquering the Demons* (Stephen Chow, 2013). "They're just different," one could say, and they bear that difference on the level of fashion, physique, and accent. I would go as far as to say that, in the absence of second-generation mainland Chinese Americans "returning" to become actors and musicians in Beijing and Shanghai, stars from Hong Kong and Taiwan are the "ABC stars" of the mainland Chinese entertainment industry, and spectacularly represent for mainland audiences possibilities of being Chinese but also of being tapped into cosmopolitan circuits of style and artistry.[20]

Perhaps no mainland film flaunted that cosmopolitan style as brazenly or notoriously as *Tiny Times* (2013), directed by Guo Jingming from his own online novel. Decried at home and internationally was the film's rampant materialism, exhibited through barely hidden product placement and the four lead characters' narcissistic obsessions with designer labels, whether as consumers or as laborers in the international marketplace for high fashion. The hugely successful film, which spawned three sequels, was nevertheless celebrated by fans for tapping into the worldly aspirations of young urban women in China, depicting dreams of upward and outward mobility and imagining local fluency in the language of international brands and global industry practice. It is a verbal fluency (characters joke about proper international pronunciation), but also a fashion one, too: being able to pronounce international brands but also to wear and design them correctly. Even off the catwalk, male and female characters in *Tiny Times* are often framed, composed, and dressed as if in a fashion ad, every moment in real life subject to the gaze of the panoptic desiring consumer. In a larger framework, this is also the gaze of an industry possessing and utilizing cosmopolitan bodies as corporeal proof: the natural ability to give shape to dresses and tuxedos, to fill out world brands with Chinese bodies, and then to in turn take ownership of the world through the muscles beneath or the confident strut that brings Chinese cosmopolitanism to life. In *Tiny Times*, those bodies are once again from Taiwan. Of the seven top-billed cast members, five were best-known as hailing from the Taiwanese film, TV, fashion, or music industries: Kuo Tsai-chieh, Ko Chen-tung, Rhydian Vaughan, Bea Hayden, and Evonne Hsieh. In an unusual move, the film credits the cast and crew in the opening titles not only by name, but also by their non-mainland origins. Thus, Kuo Tsai-chieh is introduced onscreen as Lily, played by "Kuo Tsai Chieh (China Taiwan)" (Figure C.1). Whereas the label "China Taiwan" is usually used internationally as a clumsy political necessity, here it is unprovoked, seemingly superficial, in a film for the mainland

**Figure C.1** Crediting "China Taiwan" in *Tiny Times*

audience under the banner of what Emilie Yueh-yu Yeh and Darrell Davis term "new localism."[21] Given this domestic context, why draw attention to the political awkwardness between the "two Chinas" except to acknowledge a difference that adds value and credibility? The "Taiwan" of "China Taiwan" names that difference while the "China," neither a strict noun or adjective, folds "Taiwan" in as a possessive. In the pageant of worldly desires, "China Taiwan," like the clumsy diasporization implied by "American-born Chinese", gives flesh to the possibility of possessing the world by taking possession of similar-but-different, local-but-global ethnic bodies overseas.

As counterpoint to the numbing global consumerism of *Tiny Times*, I end this book with a scene that suggests an alternative vision of mainland Chinese cosmopolitanism, one that's less heroic in its accumulation of global capital and its annexation of the diaspora. It's a scene from *Platform*, the acclaimed 2000 film by mainland director Jia Zhang-ke. In the early 2000s, directors like Jia, Gu Changwei, and others began to reflect on coming-of-age in China in the Deng Xiaoping era, decades of rapid transformation following the opening of the Chinese economy and a rapid integration into the world political and consumer systems. These films captured the confusion of a generation coming to terms with turbulent new ideas of home and individuality. The films of Jia Zhang-ke have been celebrated for employing "on-the-spot" realism—a gritty, fly-on-the-wall style—in narrating the lives of ordinary people in his hometown of Fenyang and beyond. But what Jia unearthed in his excavation of the local is a deep fascination with and yearning for the world abroad: the translocal, the transnational, the planetary. Characters in *Xiao Wu* (1998) and *Unknown Pleasures* (2002) are cold and awkward except when singing Taiwanese pop songs in karaoke. In *Useless* (2007), Jia captures the daily rituals of mainlanders who help produce international haute couture culture, from the factory workers who manufacture it, to the fashion designers who conceive it, and the nouveau riche who lust for it. *The World* (2004) depicts young people working at an Epcot Center-like theme park, where they dream of getting away from their humdrum, even oppressive, existences, but become inadvertent participants in the nation's façade of international mobility. Their only escape from their false performance of the world is—in a tragic take on the dream of romantic space explored in Chapter 1—through ecstatic animated fantasies or through suicide.

*Platform* is Jia's historical epic portrait of music performers who transition from the socialist anthems of the post-Cultural Revolution years to the "rock and breakdance" of the years just before the Tiananmen massacre. In unadorned long takes, Jia captures a generation of youth discovering bell bottoms, perms, and slam dancing emanating from the West but filtered through Hong Kong, Taiwan, Shanghai, and Guangzhou. As they become disillusioned by the remnants of China's past—visualized by the daunting ruin-like structures that the characters venture through in the film—this generation discovers the idea of the individual, for so long suppressed by an ideology of the collective in Communist China. But the individual in *Platform* is paradoxically a function of the "world out there" and a belonging to community beyond local and national walls. The desire of the individual is expressed through foreign fashions, and above all, through foreign popular music and dance.[22]

In one scene toward the end of the film, we discover that former dancer Ruijuan is now working in an office. In Jia's signature elliptical way, the film does not explain how Ruijuan arrived here, just as her sudden breakup with her longtime boyfriend was not explained in an earlier scene. Jia tends to keep narrative causation out of his films, preferring an observational mode that allows audiences to deduce causality based on their own emotional and practical experiences.[23] Ruijuan's office scene, too, lacks narrative drive in any traditional sense. The scene is dimly lit, and Jia keeps his camera still and at a distance to emphasize the cold desolation of the office environs. Ruijuan waters a plant and fumbles through papers at her desk, while Taiwanese pop singer Su Rui's "Is it True?" comes on the radio. As if possessed by this foreign song, Ruijuan starts to sway back and forth. Soon she puts down the papers and starts to dance, her small rhythmic movements becoming grand glides and pirouettes while the lyrics lament the dead-end she's found herself in. In European ballet moves via socialist opera, set to the sentimental beat of a Taiwanese pop ballad, Ruijuan's body finds expression for her personal and romantic longing. In the dead of night, between filing cabinets and beige walls, her worldly desires spontaneously take shape in the throes of cosmopolitan song and dance.

# Notes

1. hasnoopy, "*Piping Li An de ren kan kan*" forum posting, *Yahoo! Movies Taiwan*, September 10, 2007, tw.mb.yahoo.com (accessed November 8, 2007).
2. ddffgh, "*Piping Li An de ren kan kan*" forum posting, *Yahoo! Movies Taiwan*, September 11, 2007, tw.mb.yahoo.com (accessed November 8, 2007).
3. flying, "*Ganxie Li An wei Taiwan dianying zuo de yiqie*" forum posting, *Yahoo! Movies Taiwan*, September 12, 2007, tw.mb.yahoo.com (accessed November 8, 2007).
4. thekid, "*You Zhongdong de dianying zai Li An Se Jie jiu bie xiang na xia renyi Jin Ma Jiang*" forum posting, *Yahoo! Movies Taiwan*, October 12, 2007, tw.mb.yahoo.com (accessed November 14, 2007).
5. Simon Gikandi, "Between Roots and Routes: Cosmopolitanism and the Claims of Locality," *Rerouting the Postcolonial: New Directions for the New Millennium*, Janet Wilson, et al., eds. (London: Routledge, 2010) 22–35, quote on page 26.
6. Ulrich Beck and Elisabeth Beck-Gernsheim, *Distant Love* (Cambridge: Polity, 2014).
7. "Feng Delun, Xie Tingfeng," *Apple Daily* (March 30, 1999): C7.
8. Mette Hjort and Duncan Petrie, eds, *The Cinema of Small Nations* (Edinburgh: Edinburgh University Press, 2007).
9. Terhi Rantanen, "Flows and Contra-flows in Transitional Societies," *Media on the Move: Global Flow and Contra-flow*, Daya Kishan Thussu, ed. (London: Routledge, 2007) 168–77.
10. Tina Mai Chen, "Socialist Geographies, Internationalist Temporalities and Travelling Film Technologies: Sino-Soviet Film Exchange in the 1950s and 1960s," *Futures of Chinese Cinema: Technologies and Temporalities in Chinese Screen Cultures*, Olivia Khoo and Sean Metzger, eds. (Bristol: Intellect, 2009) 73–93.
11. Julia Lovell, *The Politics of Cultural Capital: China's Quest for a Nobel Prize in Literature* (Honolulu: University of Hawaii Press, 2006).
12. T. E. Woronov, "Chinese Children, American Education: Globalizing Child Rearing in Contemporary China," *Generations and Globalization: Youth, Age, and Family in the New World Economy*, Jennifer Cole and Deborah Durham, eds. (Bloomington: Indiana University Press, 2007) 29–51. On the role of the state in the creation of "global citizens," see Susan Greenhalgh, *Cultivating Global Citizens: Population in the Rise of China* (Cambridge, MA: Harvard University Press, 2010).
13. Howard W. French, "Cinephiles, Pack Your Bags. An Uncut Version Awaits," *The New York Times* (December 19, 2007) <http://www.nytimes.com/2007/12/19/world/asia/19shanghai.html> (accessed April 12, 2011). See also Patrick Frater, "Ecstasy Enjoys Explosive Launch in HK, Taiwan," *Film Business Asia* (April 14, 2011) <http://www.filmbiz.asia/news/ecstasy-enjoys-explosive-launch-in-hk-taiwan> (accessed April 14, 2011).
14. Susan Brownell, "China's National Image in the Beijing Olympics and Shanghai Expo," UCLA, Los Angeles, January 27, 2011, roundtable remarks.
15. Kwai-cheung Lo, *Chinese Face/Off: The Transnational Popular Culture of Hong Kong* (Champaign: University of Illinois Press, 2005) 11.

16. Aihwa Ong, *Flexible Citizenship: The Cultural Logics of Transnationality* (Durham, NC: Duke University Press, 1999) 52.
17. Hai Ren, *Neoliberalism and Culture in China and Hong Kong: The Countdown of Time* (London: Routledge, 2010).
18. Kai Soh and Brian Yecies, "Korean-Chinese Film Remakes in a New Age of Cultural Globalisation: Miss Granny (2014) and *20 Once Again* (2015) along the Digital Road," *Global Media and China* 2.1 (March 2017) 84.
19. Elaine Jeffreys and Louise Edwards, "Celebrity/China," *Celebrity in China*, Louise Edwards and Elaine Jeffreys, eds. (Hong Kong: Hong Kong University Press, 2010) 2–3.
20. Chinese Americans are gradually exploiting China's untapped craving for sounds and images of Chinese cosmopolitanism. Former "ABC" star David Wu is now the ubiquitous "Wu man" in China, where he teaches English slang through his language program Talk da Talk. The bourgeoning English-language media sector in China has also provided opportunities for fast-talking, free-wheeling Chinese Americans like Chi Tung, former TV host for the Shanghai Media Group. For a blow-by-blow chronicle of Chinese Australians becoming pop idols in Beijing, see Royce Akers, "My Brother was in a Chinese Boy Band," *Vice Magazine* (April 2010) <http://www.viceland.com/int/v17n4/htdocs/my-brother-was-in-chinese-boy-band-395.php> (accessed April 21, 2010).
21. Emilie Yueh-yu Yeh ties "new localism" to *Tiny Times* in "Home is Where Hollywood Isn't: Recasting East Asian Film Industries," *Media Industries* 1.2 (2014) <http://dx.doi.org/10.3998/mij.15031809.0001.212> (accessed July 3, 2017).
22. Numerous commentators have noted the importance of popular music in expressing desire in Jia's films. For instance, see Kin-Yan Szeto, "A Maoist Heart: Love, Politics and China's Neoliberal Transition in the Films of Jia Zhangke," *Visual Anthropology* 22.2–3 (2009): 95–107.
23. Michael Berry, *Xiao Wu, Platform, Unknown Pleasures: Jia Zhangke's "Hometown Trilogy"* (London: BFI Publishing, 2009) 55–6.

# Works Cited

## Books and Articles

Abbas, Ackbar. *Hong Kong: Culture and the Politics of Disappearance*. Minneapolis: University of Minnesota Press, 1997.

—. "The New Hong Kong Cinema and the *Déjà Disparu*," "Wong Kar-wai: Hong Kong Filmmaker." *Hong Kong: Culture and the Politics of Disappearance*. Minneapolis: University of Minnesota Press, 1997. pp. 16–62.

Alim, H. Samy. "Straight Outta Compton, Straight *aus München*: Global Linguistic Flows, Identities, and the Politics of Language in a Global Hip Hop Nation." *Global Linguistic Flows: Hip Hop Cultures, Youth Identities, and the Politics of Language*. Eds. H. Samy Alim, Awad Ibrahim, and Alastair Pennycook. London: Routledge, 2009. pp. 1–24.

Altman, Rick. *The American Film Musical*. Bloomington: Indiana University Press, 1987.

—. "Reusable Packaging: Generic Products and the Recycling Process." *Refiguring American Film Genres*. Ed. Nick Browne. Berkeley: University of California Press, 1998. pp. 1–41.

Anderson, Benedict. *Imagined Communities: Reflections on the Origin and Spread of Nationalism*. Rev. edn. London: Verso, 2006.

Ang, Ien. *On Not Speaking Chinese: Living between Asia and the West*. London: Routledge, 2001.

Appadurai, Arjun. *Modernity at Large: Cultural Dimensions of Globalization*. Minneapolis: University of Minnesota Press, 2006.

Appiah, Kwame Anthony. "Against National Culture." *Text and Nation: Cross-Disciplinary Essays on Cultural and National Identities*. Eds. Laura García-Moreno and Peter C. Pfeiffer. Columbia: Camden House, 1996. pp. 175–90.

—. *Cosmopolitanism: Ethics in a World of Strangers*. New York: Norton, 2006.

Barthes, Roland. *The Fashion System*. Trans. Matthew Ward and Richard Howard. Berkeley: University of California Press, 1990.

Basu, Dipannita and Sidney J. Lemelle. *The Vinyl Ain't Final: Hip Hop and the Globalization of Black Popular Culture*. London: Pluto Press, 2006.

Beck, Ulrich. *The Cosmopolitan Vision*. Trans. Ciaran Cronin. Cambridge: Polity, 2006.

Beck, Ulrich and Elisabeth Beck-Gernsheim. *Distant Love*. Cambridge: Polity, 2014.

Beltrán, Mary C. "The New Hollywood Racelessness: Only the Fast, Furious, (and Multiracial) Will Survive." *Cinema Journal* 44.2 (Winter 2005): 50–67.

Benjamin, Walter. *The Origin of German Tragic Drama*. London: Verso, 2003.

Berger, Suzanne and Richard K. Lester, eds. *Made by Hong Kong*. Oxford: Oxford University Press, 1997.

Berry, Chris. "If China Can Say No, Can China Make Movies? Or, Do Movies Make China? Rethinking National Cinema and National Agency," *Modern Chinese Literary and Cultural Studies in the Age of Theory*. Ed. Rey Chow. Durham, NC: Duke University Press, 2000. pp. 159–80.

—. "*Wedding Banquet*: A Family (Melodrama) Affair." *Chinese Films in Focus: 25 New Takes*. Ed. Chris Berry. London: BFI Publishing, 2003. pp. 183–90.

—. "'What"s Big about the Big Film?' 'De-Westernizing' the Blockbuster in Korea and China." *Movie Blockbusters*. Ed. Julian Stringer. London: Routledge, 2003. pp. 217–29.

—. "What is Transnational Cinema? Thinking from the Chinese Situation." *Transnational Cinemas* 1.2 (November 2010): 111–27.

Berry, Chris and Mary Farquhar. *China on Screen: Cinema and Nation*. New York: Columbia University Press, 2006.

Berry, Michael. *Xiao Wu, Platform, Unknown Pleasures: Jia Zhangke's "Hometown Trilogy."* London: BFI Publishing, 2009.

Bhabha, Homi K. "Unsatisfied: Notes on Vernacular Cosmopolitanism." *Text and Nation: Cross-Disciplinary Essays on Cultural and National Identities*. Eds. Laura García-Moreno and Peter C. Pfeiffer. Columbia: Camden House, 1996. pp. 191–207.

Bolton, Kingsley. "Hong Kong English: Autonomy and Creativity." *Hong Kong English: Autonomy and Creativity*. Ed. Kingsley Bolton. Hong Kong: Hong Kong University Press, 2002. pp. 1–25.

—. *Chinese Englishes: A Sociolinguistic History*. Cambridge: Cambridge University Press, 2003.

Bordwell, David. *Planet Hong Kong: Popular Cinema and the Art of Entertainment*. Cambridge, MA: Harvard University Press, 2000.

—. *Figures Traced in Light: On Cinematic Staging*. Berkeley: University of California Press, 2005.

—. "Jackhammers, Parties, and Markets." *Observations of Film Art*, March 28, 2009. <http://www.davidbordwell.net/blog/?p=4017> (accessed February 25, 2011).

Braester, Yomi. "The Impossible Task of Taipei Films." *Cinema Taiwan: Politics, Popularity and State of the Arts*. Eds. Darrell William Davis and Ru-shou Robert Chen. London: Routledge, 2007. pp. 51–9.

Braham, Peter. "Fashion: Unpacking a Cultural Production." *Production of Culture/ Cultures of Production*. Ed. Paul du Gay. London: Sage, 1997. pp. 119–76.

Braudy, Leo. "The Genre of Nature." *Refiguring American Film Genres: History and Theory*. Ed. Nick Browne. Berkeley: University of California Press, 1998. pp. 278–309.

Breckenridge, Carol A., Sheldon Pollock, Homi K. Bhabha, and Dipesh Chakrabarty, eds. *Cosmopolitanism*. Durham, NC: Duke University Press, 2002.

Brereton, Pat. *Hollywood Utopia: Ecology in Contemporary American Cinema*. Bristol: Intellect Books, 2005.

Caldwell, John Thornton. *Production Culture: Industrial Reflexivity and Critical Practice in Film and Television*. Durham, NC: Duke University Press, 2008.

Callahan, William A. *Contingent States: Greater China and Transnational Relations*. Minneapolis: University of Minnesota Press, 2004.

Carroll, Noël. "Ethnicity, Race, and Monstrosity: The Rhetorics of Horror and Humor." *Beauty Matters*. Ed. Peg Zeglin Brand. Bloomington: Indiana University Press, 2000. pp. 37–56.

Chambers, Iain. *Border Dialogues: Journeys in Postmodernity*. London: Routledge, 1990.

Chan Kwok-bun. *Chinese Identities, Ethnicity and Cosmopolitanism*. London: Routledge, 2005.

Chan, Stephen Ching-kiu. "The Fighting Condition in Hong Kong Cinema: Local Icons and Cultural Antidotes for the Global Popular." *Hong Kong Connections: Transnational Imagination in Action Cinema*. Ed. Meaghan Morris, et al. Durham, NC: Duke University Press, 2005. pp. 63–79.

Chang Cheh. *Chang Cheh: A Memoir*. Hong Kong: Hong Kong Film Archive, 2004.

Chang Tao-fan. *Liu xuesheng zhi lian*. Taipei: Tao-fan Wenyi, 1978.

Chang, Wellington. *Meiguo ge daxue ji xueyuan yu liumei jiangxuejin shenqing shuxin*. Taipei: Meidao Meiyu, 1971.

Chatterjee, Partha. *The Politics of the Governed: Reflections on Popular Politics in Most of the World*. New York: Columbia University Press, 2004.

Chen, Tina Mai. "Socialist Geographies, Internationalist Temporalities and Travelling Film Technologies: Sino-Soviet Film Exchange in the 1950s and 1960s." *Futures of Chinese Cinema: Technologies and Temporalities in Chinese Screen Cultures*. Eds. Olivia Khoo and Sean Metzger. Bristol: Intellect, 2009. pp. 73–93.

Chen Tzong-hsien. "Wo guo fudao liuxuesheng huiguo fuwu zhi yanjiu." MA Thesis. National Chengchi University, 1977.

Cheung, Esther M. K. "*Durian Durian*: Defamiliarisation of the 'Real.'" *Chinese Films in Focus II*. Ed. Chris Berry. London: BFI Publishing, 2008. pp. 90–7.

—. *Fruit Chan's Made in Hong Kong*. Hong Kong: Hong Kong University Press, 2009.

Chi Lung-zin. "Qiong Yao xiaoshuo (1963–1979) zhong de xingbie yu lishi." *Liuxing Tianxia: dangdai Taiwan tongsu wenxue lun*. Eds. Yao-Te Lin and Meng Fang. Taipei: Times Publishing, 1992. pp. 59–86.

Chion, Michel. *The Voice in Cinema*. Trans. Claudia Gorbman. New York: Columbia University Press, 1999.

Chiu, Stephen and Tai-Lok Lui. *Hong Kong: Becoming a Chinese Global City*. London: Routledge, 2009.

Chiung Yao. "Afterword." *Ren zai tianya*. Hong Kong: Crown, 1992. pp. 234–9.

Choi, Alex H. "State–Business Relations and Industrial Restructuring." *Hong Kong's History: State and Society under Colonial Rule*. Ed. Tak-Wing Ngo. London: Routledge, 1999. pp. 141–61.

Chow, Peter C. Y. "From Dependency to Interdependency: Taiwan's Development Path toward a New Industrialized Country." *Taiwan in the Global Economy: From an Agrarian Economy to an Exporter of High-Tech Products*. Ed. Peter C. Y. Chow. Westport: Praeger, 2002. pp. 241–78.

Chow, Rey. *Primitive Passions: Visuality, Sexuality, Ethnography, and Contemporary Chinese Cinema*. New York: Columbia University Press, 1995.
—. *Sentimental Fabulations, Contemporary Chinese Films*. New York: Columbia University Press, 2007.
Chu Yiu-wai. "One Country Two Cultures? Post-1997 Hong Kong Cinema and Co-productions." *Hong Kong Culture: Word and Image*. Ed. Kam Louie. Hong Kong: Hong Kong University Press, 2010. pp. 131–45.
Chun, Gloria Heyung. "Shifting Ethnic Identity and Consciousness: U.S.-born Chinese American Youth in the 1930s and 1950s." *Asian American Youth: Culture, Identity, and Ethnicity*. Eds. Jennifer Lee and Min Zhou. London: Routledge, 2004. pp. 113–28.
Chung, Yuehtsen Juliette. *Struggle for National Survival: Eugenics in Sino-Japanese Contexts, 1896–1945*. New York: Routledge, 2002.
Clark, Hazel. *The Cheongsam*. Oxford: Oxford University Press, 2000.
Cohen, Mitchell. "Rooted Cosmopolitanism." *Dissent* 39.4 (Fall 1992): 483–7.
Comaroff, Jean and John L. Comaroff. "Millennial Capitalism: First Thoughts on a Second Coming." *Millennial Capitalism and the Culture of Neoliberalism*. Eds. Jean Comaroff and John L. Comaroff. Durham, NC: Duke University Press, 2001. pp. 1–56.
—. "Reflections on Youth, from the Past to the Postcolony." *Frontiers of Capital: Ethnographic Reflections on the New Economy*. Eds. Melissa S. Fisher and Greg Downey. Durham, NC: Duke University Press, 2006. pp. 267–81.
Curtin, Michael. *Playing to the World's Biggest Audience: The Globalization of Chinese Film and TV*. Berkeley: University of California Press, 2007.
Davis, Darrell William and Emilie Yueh-yu Yeh. *East Asian Screen Industries*. London: BFI Publishing, 2008.
de Block, Liesbeth and David Buckingham. *Global Children, Global Media: Migration, Media and Childhood*. New York: Palgrave, 2007.
Delanty, Gerard. *The Cosmopolitan Imagination: The Renewal of Critical Social Theory*. Cambridge: Cambridge University Press, 2009.
Deleuze, Gilles and Félix Guattari. *A Thousand Plateaus: Capitalism and Schizophrenia*. Trans. Brian Massumi. London: Athlone Press, 1988.
—. *What is Philosophy?* Trans. Hugh Tomlinson and Graham Burchell. New York: Columbia University Press, 1994.
Derrida, Jacques. *Specters of Marx: The State of the Debt, the Work of Mourning, & the New International*. Trans. Peggy Kamuf. New York: Routledge, 1994.
Der-wei Wang, David. "Jia Baoyu ye shi liuxuesheng: wan qing de liuxuesheng xiaoshuo." *Xiaoshuo Zhongguo: wan qing dao dangdai de zhongwen xiaoshuo*. Taipei: Rye Field, 1993. pp. 229–36.
Dikötter, Frank. *Imperfect Conceptions: Medical Knowledge, Birth Defects and Eugenics in China*. London: Hurst, 1998.
Donald, Stephanie Hemelryk, Eleonore Kofman, and Catherine Kevin. "Introduction: Processes of Cosmopolitanism and Parochialism." *Branding Cities: Cosmopolitanism,*

*Parochialism, and Social Change*. Eds. Stephanie Hemelryk Donald, Eleonore Kofman, and Catherine Kevin. London: Routledge, 2009. 1–13.

Donnelly, K. J. *The Spectre of Sound: Music in Film and Television*. London: BFI Publishing, 2005.

Dyer, Richard. "The Light of the World." *White: Essays of Race and Culture*. London: Routledge 1997. pp. 82–144.

—. "Entertainment and Utopia." *Only Entertainment*. 2nd edn. London: Routledge, 2002. pp. 19–35.

Elliott, Anthony and Charles Lemert. *The New Individualism: The Emotional Costs of Globalization*. London: Routledge, 2006.

Enright, Michael J., Edith E. Scott, and David Dodwell. *The Hong Kong Advantage*. Oxford: Oxford University Press, 1997.

Entwistle, Joanne. *The Fashioned Body: Fashion, Dress and Modern Social Theory*. Cambridge: Polity Press, 2000.

Fabian, Johannes. *Time and the Other: How Anthropology Makes Its Object*. New York: Columbia University Press, 1983.

Fan, Ming-ju. *Zhong li xun ta: Taiwan nüxing xiaoshuo zonglun*. Taipei: Rye Field, 2008.

Fan Shuh Ching. *The Population of Hong Kong*. Hong Kong: Committee for International Coordination of National Research in Demography, 1974.

Fisher, Steven Frederick. "Eurasians in Hong Kong: A Sociological Study of a Marginal Group." M.Phil. Thesis. University of Hong Kong, 1975.

Fitting, George. "Export Processing Zones in Taiwan and the People's Republic of China." *Asian Survey* 22.8 (August 1982): 732–44.

Ford, Larry R. "Skyscraper Competition in Asia: New City Images and New City Form." *Imaging the City: Continuing Struggles and New Directions*. Eds. Lawrence J. Vale and Sam Bass Warner, Jr. New Brunswick, NJ: Center for Urban Policy Research, 2001. pp. 119–44.

Forman, Murray. *The 'Hood Comes First: Race, Space, and Place in Rap and Hip-Hop*. Middletown: Wesleyan University Press, 2002.

Forte, Maximilian C., ed. *Indigenous Cosmopolitans: Transnational and Transcultural Indigeneity in the Twenty-First Century*. New York: Lang, 2010.

Foucault, Michel. "What is an Author?" *Language, Counter-Memory, Practice: Selected Essays and Interviews*. Ed. Donald F. Bouchard. Ithaca: Cornell University Press, 1977. pp. 113–38.

Fu, Poshek. "Zouxiang quanqiu: Shaosi dianyingshi chutan." *Shaoshi yingshi diguo: wenhua zhongguo de xiangxiang*. Eds. Liao Kin-feng, Cheuk Pak-tong, Poshek Fu, and Yung Sai-shing. Taipei: Rye Field, 2003. pp. 115–27.

—. "Zhongguo bendi hua: Shaosi yu Xianggang dianying." *Zhama shidai: wenhua shenfen, xingbie, richang shenghuo shijian yu xianggang dianying 1970s*. Eds. Kwai-cheung Lo and Eva Kit Wah Man. Hong Kong: Oxford University Press, 2005. pp. 9–15.

—. "Modernity, Diasporic Capital, and 1950's Hong Kong Mandarin Cinema." *Jump Cut* 49 (Spring 2007) <http://www.ejumpcut.org/archive/jc49.2007/Poshek/2.html> (accessed March 25, 2011).

—. "Introduction: The Shaw Brothers Diasporic Cinema." *China Forever: The Shaw Brothers and Diasporic Cinema*. Ed. Poshek Fu. Urbana: University of Illinois Press, 2008. pp. 1–25.

Funnell, Lisa. "Repatriation of Overseas Chinese Stars in Post-1997 Hong Kong Cinema: Daniel Wu, a Case Study." *Transnational Cinemas* 2.2 (2012): 163–78.

Gateward, Frances. "Wong Fei-Hung in Da House: Hong Kong Martial-Arts Films and Hip-Hop Culture." *Chinese Connections: Critical Perspectives on Film, Identity, and Diaspora*. Eds. Tan See-Kam, Peter X Feng, and Gina Marchetti. Philadelphia: Temple University Press, 2009. pp. 51–67.

George, Susanna. "Media and Globalisation: A View from the Margins." *Feminist Media Studies* 4.1 (March 2004): 85–92.

Geraghty, Christine. "Re-examining Stardom: Questions of Texts, Bodies and Performance." *Reinventing Film Studies*. Eds. Christine Gledhill and Linda Williams. London: Arnold, 2000. pp. 183–201.

Gikandi, Simon. "Between Roots and Routes: Cosmopolitanism and the Claims of Locality." *Rerouting the Postcolonial: New Directions for the New Millennium*, Eds. Janet Wilson, et al. London: Routledge, 2010. pp. 22–35.

Gilman, Sander L. *Making the Body Beautiful: A Cultural History of Aesthetic Surgery*. Princeton: Princeton University Press, 1999.

Goldsmith, Ben and Tom O'Regan. *The Film Studio: Film Production in the Global Economy*. Lanham: Rowman and Littlefield, 2005.

Greene, J. Megan. *The Origins of the Developmental State in Taiwan: Science Policy and the Quest for Modernization*. Cambridge, MA: Harvard University Press, 2008.

Greenhalgh, Susan. *Cultivating Global Citizens: Population in the Rise of China*. Cambridge, MA: Harvard University Press, 2010.

Grewal, Inderpal. *Transnational America: Feminisms, Diasporas, Neoliberalisms*. Durham, NC: Duke University Press, 2005.

Gunning, Tom. "'The Whole World within Reach': Travel Images without Borders." *Virtual Voyages: Cinema and Travel*. Ed. Jeffrey Ruoff. Durham, NC: Duke University Press, 2006. pp. 25–41.

Hall, Stuart. "The Spectacle of the 'Other.'" *Representation: Cultural Representations and Signifying Practices*. Ed. Stuart Hall. London: Sage, 1997. pp. 223–90.

Hamm, John Christopher. *Paper Swordsmen: Jin Yong and the Modern Chinese Martial Arts Novel*. Honolulu: University of Hawaii Press, 2005.

Hansen, Miriam Bratu. "The Mass Production of the Senses: Classical Cinema as Vernacular Modernism." *Modernism/Modernity* 6.2 (April 1999): 59–77.

Harrison, Anthony Kwame. "Multiracial Youth Scenes and the Dynamics of Power: New Approaches to Racialization within the Bay Area Hip Hop Underground." *Twentieth-century Color Lines: Multiracial Change in Contemporary America*. Eds. Andrew Grant Thomas and Gary Orfield. Philadelphia: Temple University Press, 2009. pp. 201–19.

Hebdige, Dick. "Fax to the future." *Marxism Today* (January 1990): 20.

Herzog, Charlotte Cornelia and Jane Marie Gaines. "'Puffed Sleeves before Tea Time': Joan Crawford, Adrian and Woman Audiences." *Stardom: Industry of Desire*. Ed. Christine Gledhill. London: Routledge, 1991. pp. 74–91.

Hjort, Mette. *Small Nation, Global Cinema: The New Danish Cinema*. Minneapolis: University of Minnesota Press, 2005.
Hjort, Mette and Duncan Petrie, eds., *The Cinema of Small Nations*. Edinburgh: Edinburgh University Press, 2007.
Ho, Sam. "The Songstress, The Farmer's Daughter, The Mambo Girl and the Songstress Again." *Mandarin Films and Popular Songs: 40's–60's*. Ed. Law Kar. Hong Kong: Urban Council, 1993. pp. 59–78.
Hong, Guo-juin. "Historiography of Absence: Taiwan Cinema before New Cinema 1982." *Journal of Chinese Cinemas* 4.1 (March 2010): 5–14.
—. *Taiwan Cinema: A Contested Nation on Screen*, New York: Palgrave Macmillan, 2011.
Hou, Chi-ming and Ching-hsi Chang. "Education and Economic Growth in Taiwan: The Mechanism of Adjustment." *Experiences and Lessons of Economic Development in Taiwan*. Eds. Kwoh-ting Li and Tzong-shian Yu. Taipei: Academia Sinica, 1982. pp. 469–521.
Hsieh, Janet. *Dai 100 zhi yashua qu lüxing*. Taipei: Gao Bao, 2010.
Hsiung-ping, Peggy Chiao. "The Female Consciousness, the World of Signification and Safe Extramarital Affairs: A 40$^{th}$ Year Tribute to *The Love Eterne*." *The Shaw Screen: A Preliminary Study*. Ed. Wong Ain-ling. Hong Kong: Hong Kong Film Archive, 2003. pp. 75–85.
Hu, Brian. "The KTV Aesthetic: Popular Music Culture and Contemporary Hong Kong Cinema." *Screen* 47.4 (Winter 2006) 407–24.
—. "'Bruce Lee' after Bruce Lee: A Life in Conjectures," *Chinese Film Stars*. Eds. Mary Farquhar and Yingjin Zhang. London: Routledge, 2010. pp. 165–79.
Huang Jian-ye, ed. *Kua shiji Taiwan dianying shilu: 1898–2000 (zhong)*. Taipei: Council for Cultural Affairs, 2005.
Huang Ren. *Dianying alang: Bai Jingrui*. Taipei: Asia-Pacific Press, 2001.
—. *Lianbang dianying shidai*. Taipei: Chinese Taipei Film Archive, 2001.
—. "Lianbang tuidong zhengfu dianying zhengce." *Lianbang dianying shidai*. Ed. Huang Ren. Taipei: Chinese Taipei Film Archive, 2001. pp. 34–41.
Illouz, Eva. *Consuming the Romantic Utopia: Love and the Cultural Contradictions of Capitalism*. Berkeley: University of California Press, 1997.
Iwabuchi, Koichi. "Contra-flows or the Cultural Logic of Uneven Globalization? Japanese Media in the Global Agora." *Media on the Move: Global Flows and Contra-flow*. Ed. Daya Kishan Thussu. London: Routledge, 2007. pp. 67–83.
Jameson, Frederic. *Signatures of the Visible*. London: Routledge, 1990.
Jarvie, I. C. *Window on Hong Kong: A Sociological Study of the Hong Kong Film Industry and its Audience*. Hong Kong: Centre of Asian Studies, University of Hong Kong, 1977.
Jeffreys, Elaine and Louise Edwards. "Celebrity/China." *Celebrity in China*. Eds. Louise Edwards and Elaine Jeffreys. Hong Kong: Hong Kong University Press, 2010. pp. 1–20.
Johansson, Perry. "White Skin, Large Breasts: Chinese Beauty Product Advertising as Cultural Discourse." *China Information* 8.2–3 (Autumn–Winter 1998): 59–84.
Jones, Andrew F. *Yellow Music: Media Culture and Colonial Modernity in the Chinese Jazz Age*. Durham, NC: Duke University Press, 2001.
Jurriëns, Edwin and Jeroen de Kloet. *Cosmopatriots: On Distant Belongings and Close Encounters*. Amsterdam: Rodopi, 2007.

Kan Chu-cheng. *Meijian liuxue shenqing yu shuxin*. Taipei: Zhongxi Liuxue, 1982.

Keane, Michael. "Once Were Peripheral: Creating Media Capacity in East Asia." *Media, Culture & Society* 28.6 (November 2006): 835–55.

Kesselring, Sven. "The Mobile Risk Society." *Tracing Mobilities: Towards a Cosmopolitan Perspective*. Eds. Weertz Canzler, et al. Aldershot: Ashgate, 2008. pp. 77–102.

Khullar, Sonal. *Worldly Affiliations: Artistic Practice, National Identity, and Modernism in India, 1930–1990*. Berkeley: University of California Press, 2015.

King, Geoff. *Film Comedy*. London: Wallflower Press, 2002.

Kolodziejczyk, Dorota. "Cosmopolitan Provincialism in a Comparative Perspective." *Rerouting the Postcolonial: New Directions for the New Millennium*. Eds. Janet Wilson, et al. London: Routledge, 2010. pp. 151–62.

Kung Hung. *Ying chen hui yi lu*. Taipei: Crown, 2005.

Lakoff, George and Mark Johnson. *Metaphors We Live By*. Chicago: University of Chicago Press, 1980.

Lakoff, George and Mark Turner. *More than Cool Reason: A Field Guide to Poetic Metaphor*. Chicago: University of Chicago Press, 1989.

Law Kar. "The 'Shaolin Temple' of the New Hong Kong Cinema." *The Study of Hong Kong Cinema in the 1970s*. Hong Kong: The Urban Council, 1984. pp. 110–14.

Lee, Kim-Ming. "Flexible Manufacturing in a Colonial Economy." *Hong Kong's History: State and Society Under Colonial Rule*. Ed. Tak-Wing Ngo. London: Routledge, 1999. pp. 162–79.

Lee, Leo Ou-fan. *The Romantic Generation of Modern Chinese Writers*. Cambridge, MA: Harvard University Press, 1973.

—. "'Modernism' and 'Romanticism' in Taiwan Literature." *Chinese Fiction from Taiwan: Critical Perspectives*. Ed. Jeannette L. Faurot. Bloomington: Indiana University Press, 1980. pp. 6–30.

—. "On the Margins of the Chinese Discourse: Some Personal thoughts on the Cultural Meaning of the Periphery." *The Living Tree: The Changing Meaning of Being Chinese Today*. Ed. Tu Wei-ming. Stanford: Stanford University Press, 1994. pp. 221–38.

—. *Shanghai Modern: The Flowering of a New Urban Culture in China, 1930–1945*. Cambridge, MA: Harvard University Press, 1999.

—. "The Popular and the Classical: Reminiscences on *The Wild, Wild Rose*." *The Cathay Story*. Ed. Wong Ain-ling. Hong Kong: Hong Kong Film Archive, 2002. pp. 176–89.

Lee Tain-dow. *Taiwan dianying, shehui yu lishi*. Taipei: Yatai, 1997.

Lee, Vicky. *Being Eurasian: Memories across Racial Divides*. Hong Kong: Hong Kong University Press, 2004.

Leong, Solomon. "Who's the Fairest of them All? Television Ads for Skin-Whitening Cosmetics in Hong Kong." *Asian Ethnicity* 7.2 (June 2006): 167–81.

Levitt, Peggy. *Artifacts and Allegiances: How Museums Put the Nation and the World on Display*. Berkeley: University of California Press, 2015.

Lin, Angel. "'Respect for Da Chopstick Hip Hop': The Politics, Poetics, and Pedagogy of Cantonese Verbal Art in Hong Kong." *Global Linguistic Flows: Hip Hop Cultures, Youth Identities, and the Politics of Language*. Eds. H. Samy Alim, Awad Ibrahim, and Alastair Pennycook. London: Routledge, 2009. pp. 159–78.

Lin Fang-mei. *Jie du Qiongyao aiqing wangguo*. Taipei: Commercial Press, 2006.

Lin, Wenchi. "More than Escapist Romantic Fantasies: Revisiting Qiong Yao Films of the 1970s." *Journal of Chinese Cinemas* 4.1 (March 2010): 45–50.

Liou Wei-gong. "Lin Zhiling shi chenggong de meixue jingji shangpin." *Liu xing li: Taiwan shishang wenhua ji*. Ed. Albert Chen. Taipei: Unitas Publishing, 2007. pp. 30–4.

Liu Chi. *Liuxue sanji*. Taipei: Water Buffalo, 1967.

Liu Hsien-cheng. *Taiwan dianying, shehui yu guojia*. Taipei: Yatai, 1997.

Liu, Petrus. *Stateless Subjects: Chinese Martial Arts Literature and Postcolonial History*. Ithaca: Cornell East Asia Series, 2011.

*Liuxue zhi lu*. Taipei: Zhongxi Liuxue, 1973.

Lo, Kwai-Cheung. *Chinese Face/Off: The Transnational Popular Culture of Hong Kong*. Champaign: University of Illinois Press, 2005.

Lord, R. and B. K. T'sou. "Chinese and the Cultural Eunuch Syndrome." *The Language Bomb*. Hong Kong: Longman, 1985. pp. 15–19.

Louie, Kam. *Theorising Chinese Masculinity: Society and Gender in China*. Cambridge: Cambridge University Press, 2002.

Lovell, Julia. *The Politics of Cultural Capital: China's Quest for a Nobel Prize in Literature*. Honolulu: University of Hawaii Press, 2006.

Lu, Fei-I. *Taiwan dianying: zhengzhi, jingji, meixue (1949–1994)*. Taipei: Yuanliu, 1998.

Lu, Sheldon Hsiao-peng, ed. *Transnational Chinese Cinemas: Identity, Nationhood, Gender*. Honolulu: University of Hawaii Press, 1997.

Luo Jun and Zhang Yongmei. *Xiang Zhou Xingchi xue chenggong*. Taipei: Heliopolis, 2008.

Ma Hsing-yeh. *Wo de liuxue shenghuo*. Taipei: China Daily News, 1981.

Ma, Jean. *Sounding the Modern Woman: The Songstress in Chinese Cinema*. Durham, NC: Duke University Press, 2015.

Ma, Lawrence J. C. and Carolyn Carter, eds. *The Chinese Diaspora: Space, Place, Mobility, and Identity*. Lanham: Rowman & Littlefield, 2003.

Ma Shih-fang. "Olive Tree." *Taiwan liuxing yinyue 200 zui jia zhuanji*. Eds. Cora Tao, Ma Shih-fang, and Yeh Yun-ping. Taipei: China Times Publishing. pp. 124–5.

McDonald, Paul. *The Star System: Hollywood's Production of Popular Identities*. London: Wallflower Press, 2000.

Macdonald, Sean. "Li Lili: Acting a Lively *jiangmei* Type." *Chinese Film Stars*. Eds. Mary Farquhar and Yingjin Zhang. London: Routledge, 2010. pp. 50–66.

Man, Eva Kit Wah. "Female Bodily Aesthetics, Politics, and Feminine Ideals of Beauty in China." *Beauty Matters*. Ed. Peg Zeglin Brand. Bloomington: Indiana University Press, 2000. pp. 169–96.

Molz, Jennie Germann. "Cosmopolitan Bodies: Fit to Travel and Travelling to Fit." *Body & Society* 12.1 (2006): 1–21.

Morris, Andrew D. *Colonial Project, National Game: A History of Baseball in Taiwan*. Berkeley: University of California Press, 2011.

Murray, Dian H. and Qin Baoqi. *The Origins of the Tiandihui: The Chinese Triads in Legend and History*. Palo Alto: University of Stanford Press, 1994.

Naficy, Hamid. *An Accented Cinema: Exilic and Diasporic Filmmaking*. Princeton: Princeton University Press, 2001.

Nakashima, Cynthia L. "Servants of Culture: The Symbolic Role of Mixed-Race Asians in American Discourse." *The Sum of Our Parts: Mixed Heritage Asian Americans*. Eds. Teresa Williams-León and Cynthia L. Nakashima. Philadelphia: Temple University Press, 2001. pp. 35–47.

Neale, Steve. *Genre and Hollywood*. London: Routledge, 2000.

Ng Ho. "Chong ti Lingnan shaolin jiushi." *Wu Hao de Xianggang dianying minsu xue*. Hong Kong: Ci Wen Hua Tang, 1993. pp. 91–113.

—. *Gu cheng ji: lun Xianggang dianying ji su wexue*. Hong Kong: Ci Wen Hua Tang, 2008.

Nguyen-vo, Thu-huong. "History Interrupted: Life and Material Death in South Vietnamese and Diasporic Works of Fiction." *Journal of Vietnamese Studies* 3.1 (Winter 2008): 1–35.

Nishime, Leilani. "The Mulatto Cyborg: Imagining a Multiracial Future." *Cinema Journal* 44. 2 (Winter 2005): 34–49.

—. "*The Matrix* Trilogy, Keanu Reeves, and Multiraciality at the End of Time." *Mixed Race Hollywood*. Eds. Mary Beltrán and Camilla Fojas. New York: NYU Press, 2008. pp. 290–312.

Ong, Aihwa. *Flexible Citizenship: The Cultural Logics of Transnationality*. Durham, NC: Duke University Press, 1999.

—. "Splintering Cosmopolitanism: Asian Immigrants and Zones of Autonomy in the American West." *Sovereign Bodies: Citizens, Migrants, and the State*, Eds. Thomas Blom Hansen and Finn Stepputat. Princeton: Princeton University Press, 2005. pp. 257–75.

—. *Neoliberalism as Exception: Mutations in Citizenship and Sovereignty*. Durham, NC: Duke University Press, 2006.

Ongiri, Amy Abugo. "'He Wanted to be Just Like Bruce Lee': African Americans, Kung Fu Theater and Cultural Exchange at the Margins." *Journal of Asian American Studies* 5.1 (February 2002): 31–40.

Ownby, David. "Approximations of Chinese Bandits: Perverse Rebels, Romantic Heroes, or Frustrated Bachelors?" Eds. Susan Brownell and Jeffrey N. Wasserstrom. *Chinese Femininities/Chinese Masculinities: A Reader*. Berkeley: University of California Press, 2002. pp. 226–50.

Pang, Laikwan. "Postcolonial Hong Kong Cinema: Utilitarianism and (Trans)local." *Postcolonial Studies* 10.4 (2007): 413–30.

—. "From Bittorent Piracy to Creative Industries: Hong Kong Cinema Emptied Out." *Futures of Chinese Cinema: Technologies and Temporalities in Chinese Screen Cultures*. Eds. Olivia Khoo and Sean Metzger. Bristol: Intellect, 2009. pp. 131–46.

—. "Hong Kong Cinema as a Dialect Cinema?" *Cinema Journal* 49.3 (Spring 2010): 140–3.

Park, Jane. "Virtual Race: The Racially Ambiguous Action Hero in *The Matrix* and *Pitch Black*." *Mixed Race Hollywood*. Eds. Mary Beltrán and Camilla Fojas. New York: NYU Press, 2008. pp. 182–202.

Po-yin, Stephanie Chung. "A Southeast Asian Tycoon and His Movie Dream: Loke Wan Tho and MP&GI." *The Cathay Story*. Ed. Wong Ain-ling. Hong Kong: Hong Kong Film Archive, 2002. pp. 36–51.

Pu, Yu-Rong. "Comparisons of Cosmetic Advertisements: Strategies for Cultural Adaptations in Women's Magazines in Taiwan." MA Thesis. University of Florida, 2003.
Rafael, Vicente L. *White Love and Other Events in Filipino History*. Durham, NC: Duke University Press, 2000.
Rantanen, Terhi. "Flows and Contra-flows in Transitional Societies." *Media on the Move: Global Flow and Contra-flow*. Ed. Daya Kishan Thussu. London: Routledge, 2007. pp. 163–78.
Ren, Hai. *Neoliberalism and Culture in China and Hong Kong: The Countdown of Time*. London: Routledge, 2010.
Reyes, Angela. "Appropriation of African American Slang by Asian American Youth." *Journal of Sociolingustics* 9.4 (November 2005): 509–32.
Ritchie, Graeme. *The Linguistic Analysis of Jokes*. London: Routledge, 2004.
Rondilla, Joanne L. "Making a Better Me? Pure. White. Flawless." *Is Lighter Better? Skintone Discrimination among Asian Americans*. Eds. Joanne L. Bondilla and Paul Spickard. Lanham: Rowman & Littlefield, 2007. pp. 79–104.
Rushton, Richard. "What Can a Face Do? On Deleuze and Faces." *Cultural Critique* 51 (Spring 2002): 219–37.
Scarry, Elaine. *The Body in Pain: The Making and Unmaking of the World*. New York: Oxford University Press, 1985.
Schneider, Laurence. *Ku Chieh-kang and China's New History*. Berkeley: University of California Press, 1971.
Schwartz, Vanessa R. *It's So French! Hollywood, Paris, and the Making of Cosmopolitan Film Culture*. Chicago: University of Chicago Press, 2007.
Sek Kei. "Chang Cheh's Revolution in Masculine Violence." *Chang Cheh: A Memoir*. Ed. Chang Cheh. Hong Kong: Hong Kong Film Archive, 2004. pp. 11–19.
—. "Shaw Movie Town's 'China Dream' and 'Hong Kong Sentiments.'" *The Shaw Screen: A Preliminary Study*. Ed. Wong Ain-ling. Hong Kong: Hong Kong Film Archive, 2003. pp. 37–47.
Shahar, Meir. *The Shaolin Monastery: History, Religion, and the Chinese Martial Arts*. Honolulu: University of Hawaii Press, 2008.
Shih, Shu-mei. *The Lure of the Modern: Writing Modernism in Semicolonial China, 1917–1937*. Berkeley: University of California Press, 2001.
—. *Visuality and Identity: Sinophone Articulations across the Pacific*. Berkeley: University of California Press, 2007.
—. "Introduction: What Is Sinophone Studies?" *Sinophone Studies: A Critical Reader*. New York: Columbia University Press, 2013. pp. 1–16.
—. "Foreword: The Sinophone Redistribution of the Audible." *Sinophone Cinemas*. Eds. Audrey Yue and Olivia Khoo. London: Palgrave Macmillan, 2014. pp. 3–12.
Shu Cheng Guang. *Au, Niu, Jia, Nanfei liuxue shenqing*. Taipei: Xiaoyuan, 1978.
Shu Kei. "Notes on MP&GI." *The Cathay Story*. Ed. Wong Ain-ling. Hong Kong: Hong Kong Film Archive, 2002. pp. 86–107.
Slate, Nico. *Colored Cosmopolitanism: The Shared Struggle for Freedom in the United States and India*. Cambridge, MA: Harvard University Press, 2012.

Sobchack, Vivian. *Carnal Thoughts: Embodiment and Moving Image Culture*. Berkeley: University of California Press, 2004.

Soh, Kai and Brian Yecies, "Korean-Chinese Film Remakes in a New Age of Cultural Globalisation: Miss Granny (2014) and *20 Once Again* (2015) along the Digital Road." *Global Media and China* 2.1 (March 2017): 74–89.

Sun Chen. "Investment in Education and Human Resource Development in Postwar Taiwan." *Cultural Change in Postwar Taiwan*. Eds. Stevan Harrell and Huang Chün-chieh. Taipei: SMC Publishing, 1994. pp. 91–110.

Szerszynski, Bronislaw and John Urry. "Visuality, Mobility and the Cosmopolitan: Inhabiting the World from Afar." *The British Journal of Sociology* 57.1 (March 2006): 113–31.

Szeto, Kin-Yan. "A Maoist Heart: Love, Politics and China's Neoliberal Transition in the Films of Jia Zhangke." *Visual Anthropology* 22.2–3 (2009): 95–107.

Tagg, Philip and Bob Clarida. *Everyday Tonality: Towards a Tonal Theory of What Most People Hear*. New York: Mass Media Music Scholar's Press, 2009.

—. "Method and Procedure." *Ten Little Title Tunes*. New York: Mass Media Music Scholar's Press, 2003. pp. 93–154.

*Taipei Cinema Location Guide*. Taipei: Taipei Film Commission, 2008.

Tan Chee-Beng. *Chinese Overseas: Comparative Cultural Issues*. Hong Kong: Hong Kong University Press, 2004.

Tao Longsheng. *Liuxuesheng yu zhongguo shehui*. Taiwan Student Bookstore, 1978.

Teng, Emma Jinhua. "Eurasian Hybridity in Chinese Utopian Visions: From 'One World' to 'A Society Based on Beauty' and Beyond." *Positions* 14.1 (Spring 2006): 131–63.

Teo, Stephen. *Hong Kong: The Extra Dimensions*. London: BFI Publishing, 1997.

—. "'Shaws' *Wuxia* Films: The Macho Self-Fashioning of Zhang Che/Chang Cheh." *The Shaw Screen: A Preliminary Study*. Ed. Wong Ain-ling. Hong Kong: Hong Kong Film Archive, 2003. pp. 145–59.

—. *Chinese Martial Arts Cinema: The Wuxia Tradition*. Edinburgh: Edinburgh University Press, 2009.

Teskey, Gordon. *Allegory and Violence*. Ithaca: Cornell University Press, 1996.

Todorov, Tzvetan. *The Poetics of Prose*. Ithaca: Cornell University Press, 1977.

Tsai Kuo-jung. *Zhongguo jindai wenyi dianying yanjiu*. Taipei: Taipei Film Archive, 1985.

Tsing, Anna Lowenhaupt. *Friction: An Ethnography of Global Connection*. Princeton: Princeton University Press, 2005.

Turner, Graeme. *Understanding Celebrity*. London: Sage Publications, 2004.

Tzeng Huoy-jia. *Cong liuxing gequ kan Taiwan shehui*. Taipei: Laureate, 1998.

Udden, James. *No Man is an Island: The Cinema of Hou Hsiao-hsien*. Hong Kong: Hong Kong University Press, 2009.

Vogel, Ezra F. *The Four Little Dragons: The Spread of Industrialization in East Asia*. Cambridge, MA: Harvard University Press, 1991.

Wang, David Der-wei. "Jia Baoyu ye shi liuxuesheng: wan qing de liuxuesheng xiaoshuo." *Xiaoshuo Zhongguo: wan qing dao dangdai de zhongwen xiaoshuo*. Taipei: Rye Field, 1993. pp. 229–36.

—. *The Monster That Is History: History, Violence, and Fictional Writing in Twentieth-Century China*. Berkeley: University of California Press, 2004.
Wang, Grace. *Soundtracks of Asian America: Navigating Race through Musical Performance*. Durham, NC: Duke University Press, 2015.
Wang, L. Ling-chi. "The Structure of Dual Domination: Toward a Paradigm for the Study of the Chinese Diaspora in the United States." *Amerasia Journal* 21.1-2 (1995): 149-69.
Weber, Max. "The Spirit of Capitalism." *The Protestant Ethic and the Spirit of Capitalism*. London: Routledge, 2002. pp. 13-38.
Wexman, Virginia Wright. *Creating the Couple: Love, Marriage, and Hollywood Performance*. Princeton: Princeton University Press, 1993.
White, Bruce. "The Local Roots of Global Citizenship: Generational Change in a Kyushu Hamlet." *Japan's Changing Generations: Are Young People Creating a New Society?*. Eds. Gordon Mathews and Bruce White. London: Routledge, 2004. pp. 47-63.
Whittock, Trevor. *Metaphor and Film*. Cambridge: Cambridge University Press, 1990.
Wicks, James. "Projecting a State That Does Not Exist: Bai Jingrui's *Jia zai Taibei/Home Sweet Home*." *Journal of Chinese Cinemas* 4.1 (March 2010): 15-26.
Wilkins, Fanon Che. "Shaw Brothers Cinema and the Hip-Hop Imagination." *China Forever: The Shaw Brothers and Diasporic Cinema*. Ed. Poshek Fu. Urbana: University of Illinois Press, 2008. pp. 224-45
Williams, Linda. "Melodrama Revised." *Refiguring American Film Genres: History and Theory*. Ed. Nick Browne. Berkeley: University of California Press, 1998. pp. 42-88.
—. *Hard Core: Power, Pleasure, and the "Frenzy of the Visible."* Berkeley: University of California Press, 1999.
Williams, Raymond. *Marxism and Literature*. Oxford: Oxford University Press, 1977.
Wollaeger, Mark. *Modernism, Media, and Propaganda: British Narrative from 1900 to 1945*. Princeton: Princeton University Press, 2006.
Wong, Bernard P. "Hong Kong Immigrants in San Francisco." *Reluctant Exiles? Migration from Hong Kong and the Overseas Chinese*. Ed. Ronald Skeldon. Hong Kong: Hong Kong University Press, 1994. pp. 235-55.
Wong Kee-chee. "The 'MP&GI Style' in Yao Min's Film Music." *The Cathay Story*. Ed. Wong Ain-ling. Hong Kong: Hong Kong Film Archive, 2002. pp. 256-9.
Wong, Sau-ling C. "When Asian American Literature Leaves 'Home': On Internationalizing Asian American Literary Studies." *Crossing Oceans: Reconfiguring American Literary Studies in the Pacific Rim*. Eds. Noelle Brada-Williams and Karen Chow. Hong Kong: Hong Kong University Press, 2004. pp. 29-40.
Woronoff, Jon. *Asia's "Miracle" Economies*. Armonk: Sharpe, 1986.
Woronov, T. E. "Chinese Children, American Education: Globalizing Child Rearing in Contemporary China." *Generations and Globalization: Youth, Age, and Family in the New World Economy*. Eds. Jennifer Cole and Deborah Durham. Bloomington: Indiana University Press, 2007. pp. 29-51.
Wu, Chia-chi. "Festivals, Criticism and the International Reputation of Taiwan New Cinema." *Cinema Taiwan: Politics, Popularity and State of the Arts*. Eds. Darrell William Davis and Ru-shou Robert Chen. London: Routledge, 2007. pp. 75-92.
Xiang Jiang Yan Ren. *Shi da mingxing qing ai shengya*. Hong Kong: Huan Qiu, 2007.

Yang, Chi-Fu Jeffrey, et al. "Male Body Image in Taiwan Versus the West: *Yanggang Zhiqi* Meets the Adonis Complex." *American Journal of Psychiatry* 162 (2005): 263–9.

Yau, Kinnia Shuk-ting. "Shaws' Japanese Collaboration and Competition as Seen through the Asian Film Festival Evolution." *The Shaw Screen: A Preliminary Study*. Ed. Wong Ain-ling. Hong Kong: Hong Kong Film Archive, 2003. pp. 279–91.

—. *Gangri dianying guanxi: xunzhao yazhou dianying wangle zhi yuan*. Hong Kong: Cosmos Books, 2006.

Yau Sai-man. *Kan Yan Nan Wang: Zai Xianggang zhang da*. Hong Kong: Youth Literary Book Store, 1997.

Yeh, Emilie Yueh-yu. "A National Score: Popular Music and Taiwanese Cinema." Diss. University of Southern California, 1995.

—. "College Folk and National Identity: *Land of the Brave* (1981)," "A National Score: Popular Music and Taiwanese Cinema." Dissertation. University of Southern California, 1995.

—. "The Road Home: Stylistic Renovations of Chinese Mandarin Classics." *Cinema Taiwan: Politics, Popularity and State of the Arts*. Eds. Darrell William Davis and Ru-shou Robert Chen. London: Routledge, 2007. pp. 203–16.

—. "Home is Where Hollywood Isn't: Recasting East Asian Film Industries." *Media Industries* 1.2 (2014) <http://dx.doi.org/10.3998/mij.15031809.0001.212> (accessed July 3, 2017).

Yeh, Emilie Yueh-yu and Darrell William Davis. "Japan Hongscreen: Pan-Asian Cinemas and Flexible Accumulation." *Historical Journal of Film, Radio and Television* 22.1 (2002): 61–82.

—. *Taiwan Film Directors: A Treasure Island*. New York: Columbia University Press, 2005.

Yeh Le-chang. *Taiwan fuzhuang shi*. Taipei: Shangding, 2001.

Yiu Tiong Chai. "Dian Mao: MP&GI." *Cathay: 55 Years of Cinema*. Ed. Lim Kay Tong. Singapore: Landmark Books, 1991. pp. 143–67.

Yu Mu-yun. *Xianggang xiaojie yu Xianggang dianying: 1946–1988*. Hong Kong: Sanlian, 1989.

Yue, Audrey and Olivia Khoo. "Framing Sinophone Cinemas." *Sinophone Cinemas*. Eds. Audrey Yue and Olivia Khoo. London: Palgrave Macmillan, 2014. pp. 3–12.

Yung Sai-shing. "Suzao Xingxiang/Jiangou Shenfen: cong *Nanguo dianying* dao *Xianggang Yinghua*." *Shaoshi yingshi diguo: wenhua zhongguo de xiangxiang*. Eds. Liao Kin-feng, Cheuk Pak-tong, Poshek Fu, and Yung Sai-shing. Taipei: Rye Field, 2003. pp. 243–67.

Zhang Longxi. *Unexpected Affinities: Reading across Cultures*. Toronto: University of Toronto Press, 2007.

Zhang, Yingjin. *Cinema, Space, and Polylocality in a Globalizing China*. Honolulu: University of Hawaii Press, 2010.

Zhang, Yingjin and Mary Farquhar. "Introduction: Chinese Film Stars." *Chinese Film Stars*. Eds. Mary Farquhar and Yingjin Zhang. London: Routledge, 2010. pp. 1–16.

Zhang, Zhen. *An Amorous History of the Silver Screen: Shanghai Cinema, 1896–1937*. Chicago: University of Chicago Press, 2005.

Zhou, Min. "Coming of Age at the Turn of the Twenty-First Century: A Demographic Profile of Asian American Youth." *Asian American Youth: Culture, Identity, and Ethnicity*. Eds. Jennifer Lee and Min Zhou. London: Routledge, 2004. pp. 33–50.

Zhou Zhangyu and Yu Xinyi. *Kuaile zhi shen: Zhou Xingchi*. Taipei: Mucun, 2004.

## Presentations

Brownell, Susan. "China's National Image in the Beijing Olympics and Shanghai Expo." UCLA, Los Angeles. January 27, 2011. Roundtable remarks.

Kochhar-Lindgren, Gray. "Static: Ghostwriting, Hong Kong, and Globalization." University of Hong Kong. November 10, 2009. Lecture.

## Newspaper and Magazine Articles

Akers, Royce. "My Brother was in a Chinese Boy Band." *Vice Magazine* April 2010 <http://www.viceland.com/int/v17n4/htdocs/my-brother-was-in-chinese-boy-band-395.php> (accessed April 21, 2010).

"Americans Like Mandarin Movies." *Southern Screen* 82 (December 1964): 2–3.

"Angela Yu Chien Gets a Break." *Southern Screen* 74 (April 1964): 52–5.

"At Home with Lin Dai." *Southern Screen* 59 (January 1963): 26–9.

"Babes—nüsheng ai nansheng" (review). *The Box Office* 260 (August 28, 1996): 55.

"Bai Jingrui, Huang Zhuohan song le yi kou qi: Qin Xianglin tongyi yanchu Yi Lian You Meng." *Cinemart* 60 (December 1974): 61.

Bao Bao. "Q nü lian jie zhong zhi Xing Liyuan yao pai guanggao". *Hong Kong Daily News* March 16, 1999: C01.

"Beauty Pageant." *Southern Screen* 53 (July 1962): 52–5.

Beech, Hannah. "Eurasian Invasion." *Time.com* April 23, 2001 <http://www.time.com/time/magazine/article/0,9171,106427,00.html> (accessed December 13, 2010).

Bei Shao Lin. *1$^{st}$ Anniversary (1981)*. 1981. (accessed at the National Library of Singapore).

Cai Yuchun. "Janet, dai zhe haoqi qu lüxing." *Harper's Bazaar Taiwan*. Rpt. in *Yahoo! Fashion Taiwan*, June 14, 2008 <http://tw.fashion.yahoo.com/article/url/d/a/080714/23/dk4.html> (accessed December 22, 2010).

"Chan Si-si: A Veteran Starlet of the Great Wall." *Union Pictorial* 51 (February 1960): 11–13.

Chen Jiaxin. "Xie Tingfeng tiaojiang san wu mai bao xian." *Sing Tao Daily* January 6, 1999: Entertainment A27.

Chen Meixiang. "Maggie Q *Wu Yanzu fu jiu qing*." *Apple Daily* June 4, 2002: C04.

Chen Qiumei. "You yi ke fangren de haizi xin: Wu Dawei." *Nong Nong* 100 (November 1992): 88.

Crowther, Bosley. "Screen: Run Run Shaw's No. 2 Here." *The New York Times* January 16, 1965: 14.

"The Dancing Idol." *Southern Screen* 1 (December 1957): 34–5.

Dunn, Ashley. "Rapping to a Bicultural Beat: Dancing Trio from Irvine—the L.A. Boyz—Scores a Hit in Taiwan." *Los Angeles Times* April 5, 1993 <http://articles.latimes.com/1993-04-05/entertainment/ca-19527_1_dancing-trio> (accessed January 26, 2011).

"Feng Delun, Xie Tingfeng." *Apple Daily* March 30, 1999: C7.

Feng Wei. "Shaolin sanshiliu fang." *True Beauty* 56 (January 1978): 68–9.

Feng Yixian. "Janet bingtai jianfei 22 gongjin, baoshi de youyuzheng." *Next Magazine* 499. Rpt. in <http://85st.5dforum.com/viewthread.php?action=printable&tid=2348> (accessed December 22, 2010).

"Film Festival Carnival." *Southern Screen* 78 (August 1964): 20–3.

"Film Queen's Seoul Sojourn." *Southern Screen* 106 (December 1966): 26–9.

Frater, Patrick. "Ecstasy Enjoys Explosive Launch in HK, Taiwan." *Film Business Asia* April 14, 2011 <http://www.filmbiz.asia/news/ecstasy-enjoys-explosive-launch-in-hk-taiwan> (accessed April 14, 2011).

French, Howard W., "Cinephiles, Pack Your Bags. An Uncut Version Awaits." *The New York Times* December 19, 2007 <http://www.nytimes.com/2007/12/19/world/asia/19shanghai.html> (accessed April 12, 2011).

"Grace Chang Captivates 60 Million American TV Audiences." *International Screen* 49 (November 1959): 40–1.

"Grace Ting Ning on Europe." *Southern Screen* 68 (October 1963): 26–7.

Gu Liyang. "Gen-X Cops" (review). *Next Magazine* December 21, 2000: 242.

"Guai mui zai se fai ceon." *Sing Tao Daily* February 3, 2003: Z2.

"Haolaiwu zhi xing, Yan Jun." *Southern Screen* 1 (December 1957): 14–17.

He Peiru. "The Real Woman in the Real World." *FHM International Chinese Edition* 120 (June 2010): 95.

Hu, Brian. "Column: Pop Goes the C-Words." *Asia Pacific Arts*. UCLA Asia Institute, April 13, 2006 <http://www.asiaarts.ucla.edu/article.asp?parentid=42893> (accessed December 27, 2010).

"Hu Yanni: mei zai qizhi li." *Cinemart* 5 (May 1970): 35.

"Huigui Zhongying yi nian lai." *Milky Way Pictorial* 142 (January 1970): 6.

"'Huo Shao Shaolin Si' nei yanggang qisheng." *Cinemart* 82 (October 1976): 66–7.

"An Interview with Prof. Pai Ching Jui." *Milky Way Pictorial* 142 (January 1960): 18.

"Ivy Scores with U.S. Critics, Moviegoers." *Southern Screen* 86 (April 1965): 6–7.

Jabbar. "Kuaile shi shenme? Cong Tsai Kangyong chu gui tan qi." *United Daily News Blog* December 6, 2008 <http://blog.udn.com/cooljabbar/2449731> (accessed December 22, 2010).

"Jenny Hu to Produce Her Own Films." *Cinemart* 1 (January 1970): 42–3.

"Jie xi qiang Jin Zhong, Janet bi tui Gao Huijun, Tian Li." *Next Magazine* 359. Rpt. in *Otaru Blog* (May 3, 2008) <http://hi.baidu.com/otaru/blog/item/520b22faf65e3b8c9e5146c0.html> (accessed December 22, 2010).

Lanuque, Arnaud. "Interview Bey Logan." *Hong Kong Cinemagic* December 18, 2004 <http://www.hkcinemagic.com/en/page.asp?aid=71&page=1> (accessed December 27, 2010).

"A Letter from Lucilla Yu Ming." *International Screen* 91 (May 1963): 21.
"Li Lihua feiqu you feilai." *Southern Screen* 1 (December 1957): 4–7.
"LIFE Team Visits Shaws." *Southern Screen* 103 (September 1966): 2–8.
"Lin Cui Chen Hou jiuyue fei Haolaiwu." *International Screen* 118 (September 1965): 12–13.
"Lin Cui jiang chang ming Haolaiwu." *International Screen* 116 (July 1965): 8–9.
"Lin Cui zenme bei Haolaiwu 'kanzhong'?" *International Screen* 114 (May 1965): 18–19.
"Lin Dai at Ballet." *Southern Screen* 71 (January 1964): 20–3.
"Lin Dai Back Here Soon." *Southern Screen* 6 (May 1958): 17–18.
"Lin Dai laixin shuo: Nierjiala Pubu meili ji!" *International Screen* 28 (February 1958): 32–3.
"Lin Dai's European Tour." *Southern Screen* 56 (October 1962): 4–9.
"Lin Dai's U.S. Trip." *Southern Screen* 62 (April 1963): 31.
Lin Guihong. "Huo gun chi duo le niupai hambao, tili tebie." *Commons Daily* March 9, 2003. *WiseNews* database, February 1, 2010.
"Lin Qingxia li wai he yi: di ku dou zhe Esprit." *Tin Tin Daily News* March 16, 1999: B02.
"Lin Qingxia wei laogong zuo sheng zhao pai." *Hong Kong Commercial Daily* March 16, 1999: C08.
"Lin Tsui Sends Honeymoon Greetings to Her Fans." *International Screen* 49 (November 1959): 48–9.
Lin Wanyin. "Janet baobei mei ji zhuchiren, kang yan yang jiu kao zhe 3 ping." *United Daily News Happy Life Weekly* <http://mag.udn.com/mag/happylife/printpage.jsp?f_ART_ID=202459> (accessed December 22, 2010).
"Linda Flies Back to Hong Kong." *Southern Screen* 1 (December 1957): 2–3.
"Linda in the States." *Southern Screen* 4 (March 1958): 13–15.
Ling Po, Ivy. "In the Sayonara Land." *Southern Screen* 70 (December 1963): 26–9.
Liu Lo Lo. "Just Observe the Cinema Climate." *Cinemart* 81 (September 1976): 20–1.
—. "Liu Lao Lao chongfan shaolin si." *Cinemart* 164 (August 1983): 40.
Liu Youpan. "94 nian yi yue ding qi sai." *The Box Office* 195 (February 1994): 33.
"Love Parade." *Southern Screen* 55 (September 1962): 16–18.
"Lucilla's European Holiday." *International Screen* 81 (August 1962): 28–9.
"Man hua man hua." *International Screen* 74 (December 1961): 46.
"Merry-Go-Round." *International Screen* 4 (January 1956): 14–15.
"Mifune At-home to Yu Ming." *International Screen* 82 (August 1962): 52–3.
"Motion Picture Produced on International Cooperation Standard." *International Screen* 4 (January 1956): 4–5.
"New Look of Stars: 1960 Hair Styles from Hong Kong." *Southern Screen* 28 (June 1960): 10–14.
"News." *Southern Screen* 1 (December 1957): 31–2.
"Ou Jiahui zai Meiguo xuedao le xie sheme?" *Southern Screen* 16 (June 1959): 34–7.
"Pearl Au in New York." *Southern Screen* 10 (December 1958): 14–15.
"Pearl's Home-coming." *Southern Screen* 15 (May 1959): 22–3.

"Pei-pei Teaches Stewardess Dancing." *Southern Screen* 86 (April 1965): 80–1.

"Pei Pei's New Pupil: Miss Hong Kong 1965." *Southern Screen* 91 (September 1965): 14–15.

"Photo Opportunity: Kodak, Fuji Face Off in Neutral Territory, China's Vast Market." *Wall Street Journal Europe* May 29, 1996: 1, 7.

Podvin, Thomas and David Vivier. "Interview with Gordon Chan, from the Beat Heat to A-1." *Hong Kong Cinemagic* January 13, 2005 <http://www.hkcinemagic.com/en/page.asp?aid=319&page=6> (accessed December 25, 2010).

"Puyu yi ban de xin xing Zhu Fang." *Milky Way Pictorial* 91 (October 1965): 42–3.

"Shaoshi xin xing: Hu Yanni." *Southern Screen* (August 1965): 30.

"Shaw Paves Way to World Market." *Southern Screen* 47 (January 1962): 22–5.

"Shaws Launches 'Action Era.'" *Southern Screen* 92 (October 1965): 30.

"Shaws March into World Market: SB Pictures for Europe and Middle East." *Southern Screen* 65 (July 1963): 2–7.

"Sino-Korean Arts and Sentiments." *Southern Screen* 1 (December 1957): 22–5.

"Spring Frolic." *Southern Screen* 11 (January 1959): 26–7.

Tsai, Eva. "Boyz, Babes &. . .: American Chinese Climb the Taiwan Pop Chart." *Sinorama* 218 (August 1996): 52–9.

Tung, Chi. "The RZA Revisited." *Asia Pacific Arts*. UCLA Asia Institute, September 22, 2005 <http://www.asiaarts.ucla.edu/article.asp?parentid=30251> (accessed July 31, 2009).

Tung, Jan. "M zi zou gaan zai gim jiu lou pei gu, Ng Jin Zou gam wai ngai seot hei sang." *Hong Kong Daily News* February 26, 2001: C04.

Wang Lanfen. "L.A. Boyz laopo L hao." *Min Sheng Bao* August 19, 1995: Film/TV: 11.

"Wang Lihong 'chu chang' bei xiao ABC kouyin de Putonghua jiang taici." *Sina News* November 1, 2007 <http//news.sina.com.tw/ents/sinacn/cn/2007-11-01/111835181559> (accessed December 4, 2007).

"Wong Jingwai: dou hip faat jin 'gan fu jyun mei.'" *Wen Wei Po* February 23, 2008 <http://paper.wenweipo.com/2008/02/23/HK0802230035.htm> (accessed December 27, 2010).

Wu Chongjia. "Hei pi sheng shou bai." *China Times Weekly* 1579 (May 27, 2008). Rpt. in *Janet Hsieh's Website* <http://janethsieh.site88.net/index.php?load=read&id=18> (accessed December 21, 2010).

"'X shidai' nianqingren te zheng." *Wen Wei Po* June 21, 1999: Entertainment section.

Zhou Yuxun. "Janet bu 'Zhuang' shishang ye hen mei." *Youth Daily News* December 15, 2007 <http://news.gpwb.gov.tw/newsgpwb_2009/news.php?css=3&nid=32356&rtype=8> (accessed December 22, 2010).

Zhu Liqun. "L.A. Boyz *xia yue quan sheng xunhui yanchang*." *Min Sheng Bao* January 20, 1994: Film/TV: 11.

Zhu Meifang. "Janet qiao fangshai, hei liang daiyan gua baozheng." *China Times Showbiz* May 25, 2009 <http://showbiz.chinatimes.com/2009Cti/Channel/Showbiz/showbiz-news-cnt/0,5020,110511+112009052500013,00.html> (accessed December 22, 2010).

Zi Yu. "Huang Jiada jinjun guoji yingtan." *Cinemart* 167 (November 1983): 46–7.

"Zing cing: Wong Jingwai tai lou jau san jyun." *Oriental Daily News* February 23, 2008: A8.

## Pamphlets

Babes. *Babes*. Liner notes. CD. Golden Point, 1995.
*Hong Kong-Tokyo Honeymoon*. Program, International Screen Press, Hong Kong Film Archive, Hong Kong, 1957.
*Les Belles*. Program. Southern Screen Press, Hong Kong Film Archive, Hong Kong, 1961.
*Merry-Go-Round*. Program/Song-book. International Screen Press, Hong Kong Film Archive, Hong Kong, 1956.
Singapore Seow Tin San Athletic Association, *Xinzhou shaozhenshan guoji tiyu hui di ershiwu zhounian yingxi jinian tekan*. Singapore: Jin Jin Printing, 1972.
Wang, Leehom. *Shangri-La*. Liner notes. CD. Sony Music Taiwan, 2004.

## Audio-visual Materials

"Forging Closer Ties." *Berita Singapura* newsreels. Singapore Ministry of Culture—Broadcasting Division. 1963. National Archives of Singapore, Singapore.
"Huahang guanggao Lin Zhiling airline commercial." 28 August 2009. t5e2 channel. YouTube.com <http://www.youtube.com/watch?v=wNl8EUfaqGQ> (accessed April 21, 2011).
"Interviews: Daniel Lee—Director." *Three Kingdoms: Resurrection of the Dragon*. Dir. Daniel Lee. 2008. Lionsgate, 2010. DVD.
"Linda Lin Dai's Wedding." Shaw Brothers. March 11, 1961. Digi Beta.
"New Air Plane." *Singapura* newsreels. Singapore Ministry of Culture—Broadcasting Division. 1963. National Archives of Singapore, Singapore.
"Robbery." *Taipei Cinema Location Guide*. Taipei: Taipei Film Commission, 2009. CD-ROM.
"Teji xin ji yuan." *IT dangan II* [IT File 2]. Narr. Edison Chen. RHK, December 26, 2000. Television.
"US$1,000,000 Subsidy for Filmmakers in Taipei City!" February 3, 2009. taipeifilmcommission channel. YouTube.com. <http://www.youtube.com/watch?v=Oar1Jv8Db-4> (accessed February 22, 2011).
Wang, Leehom and Jin, perf. "Heroes of Earth." *Heroes of Earth*. Sony Music Taiwan, 2005.
*Wo ai hei se hui*. Channel [V] Taiwan. July 9, 2007. Television.

## Personal Interviews

Chen, Edison. Personal interview. October 20, 2011.
Cheng Pei-pei. Personal interview. April 30, 2010.
Jao, Jennifer. Personal interview. October 6, 2008.
Logan, Bey. Personal interview. February 18, 2010.
Ng, Carl. Personal interview. February 25, 2010.
Yuan, Eugenia. Personal interview. February 12, 2010.

## Forum Posts

ddffgh. "*Piping Li An de ren kan kan*" forum posting. *Yahoo! Movies Taiwan*, September 11, 2007. tw.mb.yahoo.com (accessed November 8, 2007).

flying. "*Ganxie Li An wei Taiwan dianying zuo de yiqie*" forum posting. *Yahoo! Movies Taiwan*, September 12, 2007. tw.mb.yahoo.com (accessed November 8, 2007).

hasnoopy. "*Piping Li An de ren kan kan*" forum posting. *Yahoo! Movies Taiwan*, September 10, 2007. tw.mb.yahoo.com (accessed November 8, 2007).

thekid. "*You Zhongdong de dianying zai Li An Se Jie jiu bie xiang na xia renyi Jin Ma Jiang*" forum posting. *Yahoo! Movies Taiwan*, October 12, 2007. tw.mb.yahoo.com (accessed November 14, 2007).

# Index

*18 Bronzemen, The*, 152
*20, 30, 40* (film), 3
*20 Once Again*, 216–17
*36 Chambers of Courtship*, 168
*36th Chamber of Shaolin, The*, 15, 149, 157–9, 163

*Accidental Trio* (aka *Not Coming Home Today*), 37–8, 41
*Air Hostess*, 3, 129
airports, 19–20, 39
American-born Chinese (ABCs), 13, 14, 63–5, 66–7, 69–78, 80, 86, 89, 92–100, 208n, 213, 218
　healthiness and, 77–8, 90–1
　*see also* Chinese Americans
American Film Market (AFM), 15–16, 186, 188, 197–201
Ang, Ien, 9, 96
*Anna in Kungfu-land*, 170
Appiah, Kwame Anthony, 5, 11, 56
Asian Film Market (trade show), 186
Au, Pearl, 124

*Au Revoir Taipei*, 180
Au-yeung, Jin, 67, 97, 98
*Avenging Fist*, 71

Babes (pop group), 73, 77
Bai Jingrui *see* Pai Ching-jui
*Beautiful Accident*, 217
*Because of Her*, 113
Beck, Ulrich, 8, 9, 56, 115, 213
Benjamin, Walter, 150–1, 153
Berry, Chris, 7, 32, 74, 183
*Best of Shaolin Kung Fu, The*, 161
Bhabha, Homi, 11
*Bishonen*, 72, 78–9
*Black Falcon*, 19
*Blazing Temple, The*, 146, 153, 156
*Brokeback Mountain*, 209
*Burning Temple, The*, 157

Caldwell, John, 185–6
*Call of the Mountains*, 33–4
Cathay Organization *see* Motion Picture & General Investment Co. Ltd.

Central Motion Picture Corporation (CMPC), 21, 22, 24–5, 27, 35, 59n
Chan, Gordon, 94
Chan Si-si, Angel, 81, 84
Chang Cheh, 151, 152, 153, 165–6
Chang, Grace, 113, 114, 115, 124, 128
Chen, Edison, 14, 69, 70, 72, 93, 95–6, 99
Chen, Leste, 217
Chen Kun-hou, 36–7
Cheng Pei-pei, 73, 118–19, 138n
China
  2008 Beijing Olympic Games, 215–16
  cosmopolitanism, 214–20
  film market appearances, 198–200
China Airlines, 3–5, 20
*China Dragon*, 169
Chinese Americans, 63–7, 87, 96–8, 100n, 217–18, 222n; see also American-born Chinese (ABCs)
Chinese cinema studies
  film policy in, 183–4
  Sinophone, 10–11
  transnational, 7, 10
Chiung Yao, 23, 26–7, 49
  "Chiung Yao film," 26–8, 41–2
Chou, Jay, 212
Chow, Rey, 22, 24, 33, 42, 56, 135
Chow, Stephen, 170–3
Chu Fang, 81

Chung, Christy, 91
*Cinderella and Her Little Angels*, 120–1, 122
*City Hero*, 82, 84
*City of Glass*, 94
*City of Sadness, A*, 93
*Clan of the White Lotus*, 160
*Clones, The* (TVB serial), 66
Closer Economic Partnership Arrangement (CEPA), 184, 198, 200
*Coffin from Hong Kong*, 124
Comaroff, Jean and John, 69, 149–50
*Cop on a Mission*, 80, 94
co-productions, 85, 86, 113, 114, 127–9, 193–4, 196–202
cosmopolitanism
  air travel and, 20, 98, 129
  allegory and, 15, 145
  antiquity, 5, 109
  anxiety around, 21, 28, 50, 52, 212
  bodies of, 74, 84
  Chinese, 9, 76, 98–9, 135, 143, 149, 181–2
  colonialism and, 196, 200–1, 205
  fashion and, 120–3, 125–7, 201–2, 218
  global culture and, 6–7, 8, 120–1
  hybridized, 9–10, 209–10, 213
  imagined, 8–10, 125, 146, 205
  the Sinophone and, 10

training for, 52, 115–16, 118–19, 146
vernacular, 11–12
*Crouching Tiger Hidden Dragon*, 209
Crowther, Bosley, 132
Curtin, Michael, 182–3

Davis, Darrell William, 24, 72, 183, 219
Deleuze, Gilles and Félix Guattari, 8–9, 84
Derrida, Jacques, 51, 52
*Devotion*, 20
*Dinah Shore Chevy Show*, 124
*Disciples of Shaolin Temple*, 159
*Dragon Squad*, 85
*Dreams Come True*, 61n
*Dummy Mommy without a Baby*, 95

English language, 11, 66, 92–6, 97, 128, 199–201
African American Vernacular English (AAVE), 95, 96, 97
*Enter the Phoenix*, 95
Esprit, 85–6
*Eternal Love, The*, 31
*Eternal Obsession, The*, 82
Eurasians *see* mixed-race
*Executioners from Shaolin*, 155, 158
*Eye 2, The*, 70

faces, 80, 83, 84–6, 91
*Fantasies behind the Pearly Curtain*, 27, 49–50

*Fatal Love*, 78
film markets, 186–8; *see also* American Film Market (AFM), FILMART
film sound
  *acousmetre*, 54
  coming of, 111
  dubbing, 93, 94
  synchronous sound, 93–4, 95
  training sequences and, 158–9
  *see also* popular songs in film
FILMART, 16, 186, 188, 197, 201–4
*Final Option*, 94
*Finale in Blood*, 78
*Five Shaolin Masters*, 153, 155, 160, 161–2, 166
flight attendants, 3–5, 118–19
*Four Loves*, 27
*Fun Taiwan*, 89
Fung, Stephen, 72, 73, 78, 213

*Gen-X Cops*, 72, 73, 86
*Gen-Y Cops*, 72, 85, 86, 95, 106n
ghosts, 50–1, 67–8, 70–1
global cities, 6–7, 193–4, 197
*God of Cookery, The*, 172–3
*Greatest Civil War on Earth, The*, 3
Gunning, Tom, 121

*Hail the Judge*, 171–2
*Hand of Death*, 159, 162
Hansen, Miriam, 11
*Hawaii* (film), 124, 140n

healthy realism (*jiankang xieshi*), 13, 14, 22, 24–5, 27
healthy variety (*jiankang zhongyi*), 25, 27–8
*Heart to Hearts*, 93
*Heavenly Kings*, 97
*Her Tender Heart*, 19
*Heroes*, 155–6
*Heroes Two*, 155, 163
hip-hop, 96–100
*Home Sweet Home*, 14, 19, 30, 38–41, 44, 217
Hong, Guo-juin, 24–5, 180–1
Hong Kong
  Eurasians in, 81; see also mixed-race
  flexible labor market strategy, 145
  gateway to China, 182, 198–205
  language in, 92–3, 94
Hong Kong Film Development Council, 15, 186, 201–2
*Hong Kong-Tokyo Honeymoon*, 119, 128
Hong Kong Trade Development Council (HKTDC), 15, 182, 186, 197–202, 204
Hou Hsiao-hsien, 36–7, 180, 196
*House of Fury*, 94
Hsieh, Janet, 14, 87–92
Hu, Jenny, 73, 80, 81–3, 84, 87, 213

*Invincible Shaolin*, 158

*Jan Dara*, 91
Jia Zhang-ke, 183, 219–20

Jones, Andrew, 111, 112
*Journey to the West: Conquering the Demons*, 218

Kang Youwei, 69
*Karate Kid, The*, 167
*Kingdom and the Beauty, The*, 132
Kung Hung, 22
Kuomintang Party, 22–3, 144
Kwan, Nancy, 80, 81, 85

L. A. Boyz, 14, 64, 73, 75–8, 89, 94, 96, 99
Lakoff, George, 108
Lam Fung, 114
*Land of the Brave*, 35–6
*Lark, The*, 19
*Last Woman of Shang, The*, 125, 135
Lee, Ang, 95, 180, 196, 209–12, 214
Lee, Bruce, 147
Lee, Daniel, 87
Lee, Leo Ou-fan, 9, 27, 112
Lee Hsing, 27
Lee Tain-dow, 25, 26, 42
Lee Yong-ping, 196–7
*Les Belles*, 116–20, 122, 125, 135
Leung Chiu-wai, Tony, 218
Li Jinhui, 110–11
Li Xing *see* Lee Hsing
*Life of Pi* (film), 180, 209
Lin Chiling, 3, 5
Lin Dai, Linda, 15, 115–22, 124–6, 128–9, 132

Lin Fang-mei, 26
Lin Tsui, 122, 124
Ling Po, Ivy, 122, 132–3
Liu Chia-chang, 27, 49
*liuxuesheng see* overseas students
Lo, Kwai-Cheung, 72, 76, 216
Lok Wan Tho *see* Motion Picture & General Investment Co. Ltd.
*Long Way from Home*, 31, 34, 43–4
*Lost Romance, The*, 31
*Lovable You* (aka *Cute Girl*), 36
*Love Can Forgive and Forget*, 50, 52–3, 55
*Love Eterne, The*, 25, 132
*Love in a Cabin*, 43, 45
*Love Parade*, 119, 121–2, 125, 126–7, 135
*Love Undercover*, 94
*Lucy* (film), 180
*Lust, Caution*, 210–11

Ma, Jean, 112
*Mambo Girl*, 113
*Manhattan Midnight*, 85, 86
martial arts film, 151–2; see also Shaolin Temple film (cycle)
melodrama, 21–2, 24, 32
*Men from the Monastery*, 156
*Merry-Go-Round*, 118
*Midnight Caller*, 78
*Miss Kicki*, 197
mixed-race, 64, 70, 71, 72, 80–7
*Model from Hell*, 70

Molz, Jennie Germann, 115–16, 119, 146
*Moon River* (film), 14, 45, 46–9
Motion Picture & General Investment Co. Ltd. (MP&GI), 3, 15, 81, 109, 110, 112–15, 118, 119, 127–9, 135–6
*International Screen* magazine, 15, 113–14, 122–4, 128
Lok Wan Tho, 81, 112–13, 127–8, 129
muscles, 64, 71, 73, 75–80, 157
musicals (film genre), 15, 110–13, 115, 119, 122
*My Cape of Many Dreams*, 50–1, 52, 53–6
*My Way*, 32–3

*Naked Weapon*, 86
*New Legend of Shaolin, The*, 146, 156
*New Shaolin Boxers, The*, 158
*Nine Girls and a Ghost*, 70
Nishime, Leilani, 71

*Once More in the Evening* (aka *It's Sunset Again*), 44
Ong, Aihwa, 13, 51, 216
overseas students (*liuxuesheng*), 9, 20, 26, 28–30, 51
characters in films, 14, 21–2, 31–41, 43–5, 49–51, 52–3
literature of, 13, 20, 28, 30–1, 33, 35
*Oyster Girl*, 25

Pai Ching-jui, 27, 37–40, 44–5, 49, 58n
Pang, Laikwan, 181, 183–4, 197
*Peony Pavilion* (2001 film), 79–80
*Platform*, 219–20
popular songs in film, 36, 45–8, 111, 219–20
  "Cloak of Dreams," 54–6
  "Fantasies behind the Pearly Curtain," 49–50
  "Not Coming Home Today," 38
Preminger, Otto, 124
propaganda, 21–3, 24–5, 27
*Purple Storm*, 71, 72, 86

Q, Maggie, 14, 69–70, 80, 84–7, 91, 95
Qiong Yao *see* Chiung Yao

Rafael, Vicente L., 51
*Raiders of the Shaolin Temple*, 152
*Red Cliff*, 218
remakes, 215, 216–17
*Return to the 36th Chamber*, 157, 159–60
*Run Lover Run*, 41
*Rush Hour 2*, 85

Salon Films, 202–4
*Samsara*, 91
Scarry, Elaine, 154
Sek Kei, 135, 151
sentimental romanticism, 24–5, 27–8, 31, 35

*Seven Man Army*, 165
*Seven Swords*, 87
*Shaolin Abbot*, 156
*Shaolin Avengers, The*, 157, 158
*Shaolin Martial Arts*, 160
*Shaolin Plot, The*, 146, 158
*Shaolin Popey*, 168–70
*Shaolin Soccer*, 15, 170–1
Shaolin Temple
  burning of, 15, 146, 154–6, 166
  literary depictions of, 154–5
*Shaolin Temple* (1976 film), 152–3, 163
*Shaolin Temple, The* (1982 film), 153
*Shaolin Temple* (1984 TTV serial), 156
Shaolin Temple film (cycle), 143–9, 166
  hybridization and parody, 167–73
  narrative conventions, 155–63
  religion and, 149, 152–4
  *see also* training sequences
Shaw Brothers, 15, 81–2, 109, 110, 112, 113–19, 122, 124, 126–7, 129–36, 144, 149
  *Southern Screen* magazine, 15, 81, 113–14, 116, 118, 122, 124–5, 127, 129–35, 147
*Shield of Straw*, 180
Shih, Shu-mei, 10, 125, 182
*Shining Spring*, 32
Shu Qi, 85, 218
Shunza, 64, 96
Sik Siu-lung, 169

*Silence* (2016 film), 180
*Silent Wife, The*, 27
Sinophone, the
  and cinema, 11
  and language, 10–11
skin tone, 87–92
Sobchack, Vivian, 148
*Songs of the Peach Blossom River*, 112
sound *see* film sound; *see also* English language
*Spring Frolic*, 117
*Spring in Autumn*, 36–7
Stark, Ray, 81, 128
*Starry Starry Night*, 180
*Sting II, The* (aka *The Perfect Exchange*), 168
*Street Angel*, 111
Sung, Shawn, 78, 96
*Sweet Dreams* (aka *A Dream of Love*), 20

Tagg, Philip, 48, 61n
*Tai Chi Master*, 162
Taipei 101 (building), 188–94
*Taipei Exchanges*, 180
Taipei Film Commission, 15, 185, 186, 189–97
Taiwan
  brain drain from, 29–30
  diplomatic setbacks, 13, 14, 26, 30, 34, 180
  English in, 93
  export-promotion policy, 144–5
  film policy, 165, 188, 193–6

Government Information Office (GIO), 15, 25, 185, 186, 188–93
  "Ten Major Construction Projects," 34, 44
  *see also* Central Motion Picture Corporation, healthy realism, healthy variety, Kuomintang Party, overseas students, Taipei 101, Taipei Film Commission
Taiwan cinema studies, 179–81
*Tale from the East, A*, 70
Tao, David, 73, 76, 96
*Teahouse, The*, 149
Teng, Teresa, 217
Teskey, Gordon, 153, 164
*Three* (film), 70
*Three Kingdoms: Resurrection of the Dragon*, 86–7
Ting Hao, 81, 123–4, 128
*Tiny Times*, 218–19
training sequences, 52, 116, 146, 149, 157–61, 168–73
*Trivial Matters*, 95, 106n
Tsai Ming-liang, 180, 196
Tse, Nicholas, 14, 72, 73, 75, 95, 213
Tsing, Anna, 185
*Twins Effect, The*, 70
*Two Ugly Men*, 40–1

Union Film (studio), 22, 25
*Unknown Pleasures*, 219
*Useless* (film), 219–20

*Victory* (film), 27

Wang, David Der-wei, 28, 164
Wang, Leehom, 71, 73, 75–6, 78, 94, 97, 98–9
*War of the Shaolin Temple*, 159
*Whatever Things* (TV show), 95
Williams, Linda, 24, 126
Wollaeger, Mark, 23
*Wonder Women*, 78
Wong, Anthony, 70, 84
Wong, Michael, 75, 78, 82–4, 86, 87, 93–4
Wong, Wilfred, 96
Wong Jing, 86
world cred, 99–100
*World of Suzie Wong, The*, 81, 128, 202
*World, The* (film), 108, 220
Wu, Daniel, 14, 69, 71, 72, 73, 86, 94, 95, 97
  muscles of, 75, 78–80
Wu, David, 70, 75, 77, 78
Wu-Tang Clan, 97, 167

*Xiao Wu*, 219
XIMP, 94

Yeh, Emilie Yueh-yu, 24, 36, 42, 46, 72, 183, 219
Yeh, Sally, 93
Yin, Terence, 72, 73, 78
Yonfan, 78–9
*Young & Dangerous: The Prequel*, 72, 73
*Young Heroes of Shaolin, The* (TVB serial), 156, 167
Yu Chien, Angela, 124
Yuan, Eugenia, 70, 73, 91

Zhang Che *see* Chang Cheh
Zhou Xuan, 111, 112

EU representative:
Easy Access System Europe
Mustamäe tee 50, 10621 Tallinn, Estonia
Gpsr.requests@easproject.com

www.ingramcontent.com/pod-product-compliance
Lightning Source LLC
Chambersburg PA
CBHW071835230426
43671CB00012B/1968